DEFOE'S TOUR AND EARLY MODERN BRITAIN

Authoritative yet accessible, this is the first-ever comprehensive account of a true landmark in eighteenth-century travel writing. Daniel Defoe's *Tour thro' the Whole Island of Great Britain* is constantly cited even now by students in practically every branch of history, and there are few topics essential to our understanding of the nation in the early modern period that do not show up in its pages. Historians since the late nineteenth century have looked to the *Tour* as one of the richest and most insightful works describing Britain in the lead-up to the Industrial Revolution, and critics and biographers of Defoe have regularly named it as among his most characteristic and central works. Indispensable for virtually any interdisciplinary approach to the nation in this period, this new study provides wide-reaching, up-to-date analysis of the content of the *Tour*, and of its methods, sources, form, and vast historical significance.

PAT ROGERS is Distinguished University Professor Emeritus, formerly Eminent Scholar, and DeBartolo Chair in the Liberal Arts at the University of South Florida. He has held full time teaching posts at the universities of Cambridge, London, Wales, and Bristol, and has published extensively on literature from the seventeenth and eighteenth centuries, as well as teaching courses up to the twentieth century. His previous works on Defoe include *The Text of Great Britain: Theme and Design in Defoe's Tour* (1998), editions of the *Tour* (1971: 1989), *Defoe: The Critical Heritage* (1972), a study of *Robinson Crusoe* (1979), and an edition of *Moll Flanders* (1993). He is a contributor to the forthcoming collections *The Oxford Handbook to Daniel Defoe* and *Defoe in Context* (Cambridge University Press).

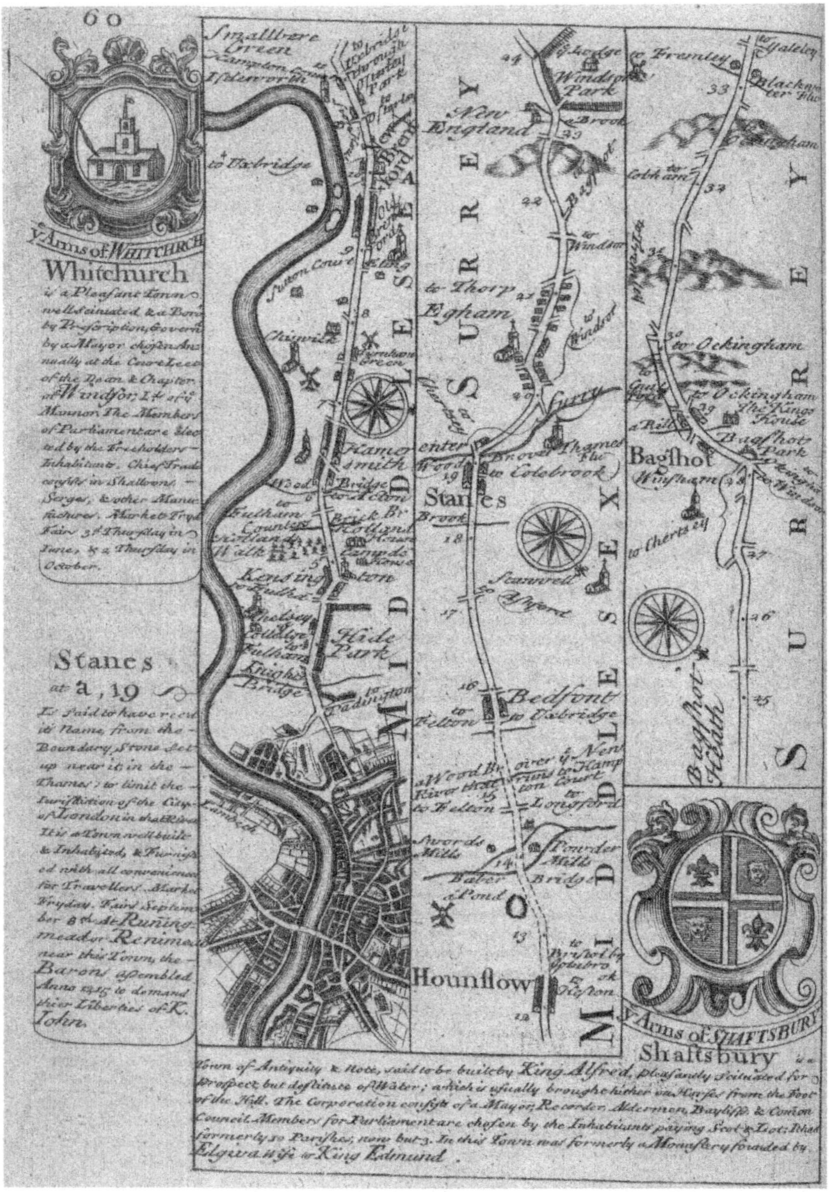

Frontispiece: A section from the road from London to Bristol, in *Britannia Depicta: or Ogilby Improv'd* (1720).

DEFOE'S TOUR AND EARLY MODERN BRITAIN

Panorama of the Nation

PAT ROGERS
University of South Florida

CAMBRIDGE
UNIVERSITY PRESS

CAMBRIDGE
UNIVERSITY PRESS

University Printing House, Cambridge CB2 8BS, United Kingdom

One Liberty Plaza, 20th Floor, New York, NY 10006, USA

477 Williamstown Road, Port Melbourne, VIC 3207, Australia

314–321, 3rd Floor, Plot 3, Splendor Forum, Jasola District Centre,
New Delhi – 110025, India

103 Penang Road, #05–06/07, Visioncrest Commercial, Singapore 238467

Cambridge University Press is part of the University of Cambridge.

It furthers the University's mission by disseminating knowledge in the pursuit of education, learning, and research at the highest international levels of excellence.

www.cambridge.org
Information on this title: www.cambridge.org/9781009098861
DOI: 10.1017/9781009106412

First published 2022

A catalogue record for this publication is available from the British Library.

ISBN 978-1-009-09886-1 Hardback

for Tim Blanning

Contents

Acknowledgements

Two anonymous readers for the publishers made invaluable comments on an earlier draft. They corrected my mistakes and indicated several other ways in which the book could be improved. I am also grateful for the support and encouragement of the editor at Cambridge University Press, Bethany Thomas, along with her colleague George Laver. And I wish to acknowledge the careful work of the copy editor, David Watson. It is impossible to state or repay the huge debt I owe to many colleagues, friends and reviewers of earlier books, in enhancing my understanding of Defoe and his work. However, the dedication does feebly acknowledge the scale of my obligations in the first two of those categories to Tim Blanning over more than half a century. Thanks are also due to Catharine Lee for her help in locating and checking materials. On a personal level, Adrienne Condon must come first in return for the innumerable ways in which she has coped with the demands that I made on her in the course of writing the book.

Some portions of this book have appeared in a different form as follows: Chapter 1, 'Defoe's *Tour* and the Identity of Great Britain', in *The Cambridge Companion to Daniel Defoe*, ed. John Richetti (Cambridge: Cambridge University Press, 2008), 102–20. Chapter 2, 'Embedding and Embodying the Nation: Textual Practices and Form in *A Tour thro' Great Britain*', in *Positioning Daniel Defoe's Non-fiction: Form, Function, Genre*, ed. Aino Mäkikalli and Andreas Muller (Newcastle upon Tyne: Cambridge Scholars Press, 2011), 61–79. Chapter 5, 'Defoe's *Tour* and the Historiography of Early Modern Britain', *Journal for Eighteenth-Century Studies*, 42 (2019): 365–79. Chapter 8, 'Daniel Defoe and the Local Proverb,' *Proverbium*, 20 (2003): 359–66. Chapter 9, 'The Topographical Sources of Defoe's *Tour*', *Review of English Studies*, 70 (2019): 702–15. Chapter 10, 'Road-testing the First Turnpikes: The Enduring Value of Daniel Defoe's Account of English Highways',

Journal of Transport History, 40 (2019): 211–31. Chapter 11, 'Daniel Defoe on Bristol: The Description of the City in *A Tour thro' Great Britain* and its Context', *Transactions of the Bristol and Gloucestershire Archaeological Society*, 136 (2018): 263–78. I am grateful for permission given by publishers and editors to reprint these items.

Illustrations

Maps

Tables

Abbreviations

Backscheider	Paula Backscheider, *Daniel Defoe: His Life.* Baltimore: Johns Hopkins University Press, 1989
Bowen	Emanuel Bowen, *Britannia Depicta: or Ogilby Improv'd.* London, 1720, reprinted Newcastle upon Tyne: Frank Graham, 1970
CET	Daniel Defoe, *The Complete English Tradesman.* 2 vols. London, 1725–7
Fiennes	*The Journeys of Celia Fiennes*, ed. Christopher Morris, London: Cresset Press, 2nd ed., 1949.
Letters	*The Letters of Daniel Defoe*, ed. G. H. Healey. Oxford: Clarendon Press, 1955
Libraries	*The Libraries of Daniel Defoe and Phillips Farewell*, ed. Helmut Heidenreich. Berlin: for the author, 1970
Macky	John Macky, *A Journey through England* [*Scotland*] *in Familiar Letters.* 3 vols. London, 1714–23
ODNB	*Oxford Dictionary of National Biography*
Plan	Daniel Defoe, *A Plan of the English Commerce.* London, 1728
Tour	*A Tour thro' the Whole Island of Great Britain*, in *Writings on Travel, Discovery and History by Daniel Defoe*, ed. John McVeagh. 3 vols. London, 2001. This is the edition quoted in the text, with volume and page numbers within parentheses.

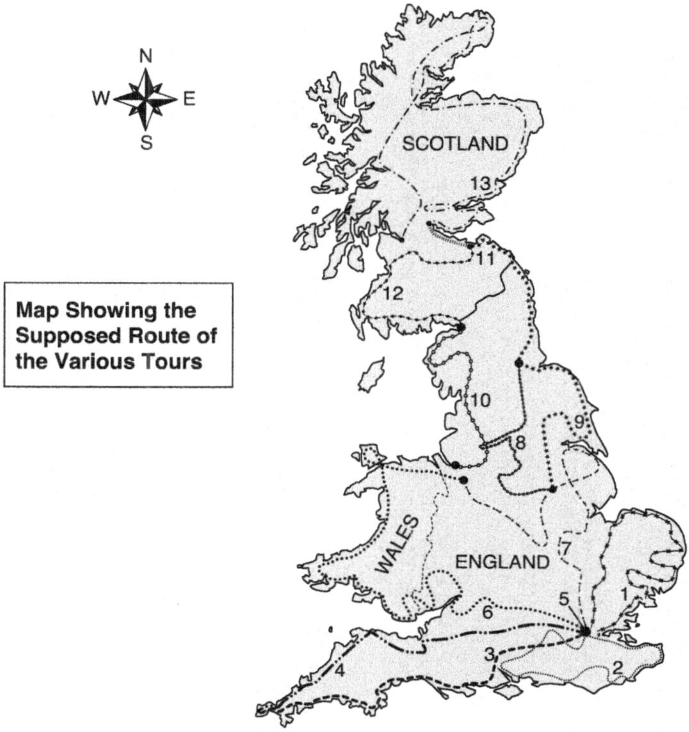

Map 1 Map illustrating the supposed routes of the *Tour*

Introduction

By general consensus, Daniel Defoe's *Tour thro' the Whole Island of Great Britain* is one of the most important books written about the nation in the eighteenth century. Few historians surveying the landscape of the age manage to get by without its aid. It is one of the small number of works from the period with enough continuing appeal to have served as a Book at Bedtime on BBC Radio 4, and its opening section formed the basis for a programme in a television series on *Great British Journeys*. In 2018 a *Guardian* article by Robert McCrum placed it no. 89 among the 100 best non-fiction books of all time (the numbering was in reverse chronological order). For several decades after its first appearance, the work was periodically refurbished in new editions, while modern times have seen it emerge in a variety of guises – as a deluxe coffee-table book, as a staple of the Everyman series, as a student text for Penguin and finally as the first scholarly version. Almost all of Defoe's many biographers treat it as one of his key productions. Yet until now there has been no comprehensive account of its aims and methods, historical significance, form and rhetorical design, or place in the development of travel writing, among other defining attributes.

An earlier book I published on this work, *The Text of Great Britain: Theme and Design in Defoe's Tour* (1998), was very different in its aims, content and scope. That work sought to analyse the history of composition, along with particular sections and contents, for example the georgic element, the borrowings in the text from Camden and the portion on the Wonders of the Peak, plus analogies with Defoe's *Captain Singleton*. It took up the historical significance of the book only in the final chapter of fourteen pages.[1] While it touched on the intellectual design of the *Tour* in the Introduction, there was no attempt to offer any full account of its form. My hope is that the present volume treats matters of more general interest to students of the period. The passage of time has enabled me to consult much new scholarship, not just on Defoe (many articles, plus sections of biographies and other monographs published since 2000), but also a wealth of writings on early modern Britain by social, economic and political historians.[2] No previous study has drawn on such materials to locate the work in its time, as the most capacious panorama of the age.

We are now approaching the tercentenary of the *Tour*, as the first of the three volumes came out in 1724, followed by the second and third in 1725 and 1726. Eight further editions came out by 1779, having expanded in the process to four volumes. The earlier ones underwent revision by the novelist and printer Samuel Richardson. However, it was not until the twentieth century that full recognition arrived of the work's extraordinary qualities. Eminent historians as distinct in outlook and interests as G. M. Trevelyan and G. D. H. Cole proclaimed the merits of the *Tour*, as it furnishes the most comprehensive first-hand survey of the nation at a crucial stage in its evolution. In the late 1920s Cole also oversaw two editions of the *Tour*, one of them included in the Everyman series and providing access to the text for a wide range of readers. At the same juncture a luxury version of the London segments (Letter 5, mostly) was published, with a strong emphasis on topographic detail. A new phase of interest in the 1970s and 1980s saw two abridged editions and a reprint by the Folio Society. This coincided with a growth of scholarly activity in books and articles, which reached most valuable expression in the appearance of the first complete annotated text, edited by John McVeagh in 2001. Since then the work has continued to attract scholarly attention in biographic and critical studies.

Capital Matters

Defoe's lifetime, from 1660 to 1731, witnessed many of the developments that would usher in the culminating phase of early modern Britain. In Letter 5, as part of a comprehensive overview of his native London, he locates in turn some of the public institutions that met the needs of a post-medieval state. Many of these, marked with an asterisk here, had come into full existence in the previous thirty-five years since the Revolution of 1688–9, while others marked with a dagger had undergone major changes in that period, including the erection of new premises. They include the Royal Exchange†, the Custom House†, the Bank of England*, the South Sea Company*, the East India Company†, the Royal African Company*, the Admiralty†, the Exchequer, the offices of the secretary of state† and master of the ordnance, the Privy Council, Parliament, Westminster Hall, insurance companies*, the Excise Office†, the numerous markets (with a facetious augmentation, the 'Bubble Market' kept at Exchange Alley), the Port of London†, fire services*, water provision†, gaols, schools, the royal palaces, theatres†, hospitals†, almshouses and much else. The infrastructure of the city is reviewed, for example the Fleet Canal, together with docks and wharves that were essential to the growth of an economy increasingly reliant on international trade. Some ancient foundations are mentioned, such as the historic gates of the city, along with Westminster Abbey – but the writer is obviously more excited by the recent completion of St Paul's Cathedral. He devotes almost 1,500 words to Wren's masterpiece, as against 660 on the Abbey, which he introduces with the words, 'a venerable old Pile of Building, it is indeed, but so old and weak, that had it not been taken in Hand some Years ago, and great Cost bestowed in upholding and repairing it, we might, by this Time, have called it a Heap, not a Pile, and not a Church, but the Ruins of a Church'. Equally uncomplimentary things are said about Westminster Hall, ending with the assertion that it 'really looks like a Barn at a Distance' (2: 110).

At the conclusion of his account, the author pauses briefly to update information he has supplied. He enumerates various works in progress, including 'the fine new Church of St. *Martin*'s in the *Fields*', still unconsecrated, together with a sprinkling of Hawksmoor's masterpieces among the Queen Anne churches (some recently completed, others still under construction). Other unfinished projects are the new Treasury buildings in Whitehall by Thomas Ripley; Guy's Hospital; two large wings for Bedlam Hospital; a large Baptist meeting-house in Spitalfields; the new South Sea House in Threadneedle Street; a street being built on the Artillery Ground, that is on the north side of Chiswell Street, along with an extension to Tindal's burial ground nearby; an iron balustrade on the dome of St Paul's; and 'A new *Bear-Garden.*, called *Figg*'s *Theater*, being a Stage for the Gladiators or Prize-Fighters' (2: 121–2). No contemporary source gives us such an urgent sense of the building mania that was enveloping London. But this is just to skim the surface of Defoe's enthusiastic overview of the dynamo that the capital had become.

Near the start of this letter, Defoe sets out what he calls 'A Brief Description of the New Buildings erected in and around the Cities of *London* and *Westminster* and the Borough of *Southwark*, since the Year 1666' (2: 74). It is not all that brief, since the detailed itemisation he makes of these changes in the landscape, great and small, occupies no less than 2,600 words. It is not any cause for astonishment that the Great Fire marks the datum line of this exercise. What we might forget is that the author was one among a diminishing number of Londoners, still active in 1725, who retained a memory of the city as it appeared before the Fire, even if it was a childhood recollection, and who had witnessed the rebuilding process. A noteworthy passage concerns the removal of some great 'Palaces of the Nobility' that have disappeared to be replaced by new developments, including the Savoy, which 'may be said to be, not a House, but a little Town' (2: 76). But the account descends from the princely heights to small streets, forgotten alleys and suburban meadows, now turned into impressive thoroughfares. Defoe finds room to mention future developments, including 'Three Projects' on the drawing board – most significantly, the scheme for 'making another bridge over the *Thames*' (2: 79), a vision that the author would never see realised. As well as this, a lengthy section is allocated to a proposal from an unknown hand which never came to fruition, that is 'A Scheme for a *Royal Palace* in the Place of *White-Hall*,' involving such long needed change such as the creation of new purpose-built accommodation for the courts of justice and various government departments (2: 103–8). For Defoe, London is the epicentre of an expanding world, in terms both of physical space and of social, political and financial affairs.

The *Tour* is not touristy in a modern way. For example, it hardly mentions the Tower of London except as a prison, the home of a menagerie and the place where the Ordnance Office is located. There is no guide to places of hospitality, and no recommendations for delighting in water sports on the busy, but insalubrious, river. Nevertheless, Defoe greets us with a 'Line of Measurement', beating the bounds over an extent of nineteen miles, four furlongs and twenty-one rods, to which he adds south of the Thames a further seventeen miles, six furlongs and eighteen rods (2: 67–73). He makes it a kind of introductory glimpse of the scale of the city, merging into a voyage of discovery, even a mystery quest:

> Here the Line turns *South*, and indents to the Corner of *Bedford Row*, and leaving some few Houses, with the Cock-Pit, and Bowling Green, goes on the Back of *Gray's Inn Wall*, to *Gray's Inn Lane*, then turns on the Outside of the Buildings, which are on the *West* Side of *Gray's Inn Lane*, going *North* to the Stones End, when turning *East*, it passes to the New River Bridge without *Liquor-pond Street*, so taking in the *Cold Bath* and the *Bear Garden*; but leaving out Sir *John Old-Castle*'s and the *Spaw*, goes on *East* by the *Ducking-Pond* to the end of *New Bridewell*, and crossing the *Fairfield*, comes into the *Islington* Road by the Distiller's House, formerly Justice *Fuller*'s. (2: 68)

The reader feels impelled to follow this seductive trail, almost as though listening to the guidance of a ghostly satellite navigation system. We are anxious not to get lost around Liquorpond Street, in case after passing the

Cold Bath we should miss the turn to the Ducking Pond and accidentally find ourselves heading out into an uncharted district on the edge of town where an isolated tavern stood, named after the former home of Sir John Oldcastle (the executed rebel who supplied some features for the character of Falstaff). Without this help, we should struggle to escape the maze.

A Changing Landscape

One of the pioneers of the Industrial Revolution, Abraham Darby I, may even have been known to Defoe in Bristol (see Chapter 11). The author was certainly acquainted with some of the individuals who took part in the launch of new corporations such as the Bank of England during the 1690s, and also in ventures at the end of the century including the ill-fated Darien project. For that matter, his own *Essay upon Projects* (1697) had launched his own career as a writer. Three decades later, *Augusta Triumphans* (1728) would come almost at the culmination of his varied canon. These two books would offer proposals for all sorts of innovations – spread across fields such as highway engineering, insurance, pensions, lotteries, banks, the pay of seamen and an academy for women, all from the *Essay*, with a foundling hospital, a university of London, a suppression of madhouses used by husbands to lock up their wives, a conservatoire for English musicians, a plan to curtail gin-drinking and a scheme to prevent street robberies, all from the later pamphlet. (We shall see in Chapter 10 that Defoe had given considerable thought to the suppression of roadside crime.) Together, this collection of forward-looking ideas might survive as a blueprint for the Enlightenment. In the *Tour* he would argue the case for a Forth–Clyde canal, sixty-five years before this came to fruition (3: 198, 209–10).

Nicholas Rogers has linked Defoe with Joseph Addison in a pair of 'cultural pacemakers', and the description is apt.[3] His role as a commentator on the era in which he lived and wrote becomes clear if we think of some of the common phrases applied to it. To confine ourselves to those used in book titles, terms abound such as 'the Financial Revolution in England', 'England in Transition', 'Britain Transformed', 'Preindustrial England', 'the Agricultural Revolution', 'the English Urban Renaissance', 'the Transformation of the Public Sphere', 'the Discovery of Britain', 'the Augustan World', 'Forging the Nation', 'the Making of the English Middle Class', 'the Impact of English Towns', 'England's Apprenticeship', 'the Monster City' and more. Defoe has something pertinent to say on each of these, usually based on first-hand experience – his first forty years, after all, passed in 'the Century of Revolution'. The developments that he witnessed, along with the nation, brought into being what E. A. Wrigley calls 'The Transformation of Traditional Society'. To a degree, he even participated in this process, during his eventful career. He started out life in the guise of Daniel Foe, born into a modest commercial family in the City, potential candidate for the ministry and unsuccessful businessman. By the time that he wrote the *Tour* he had turned himself into the famous Daniel Defoe, author of one of the great classics in world literature, client of the rich and powerful, landowner, respected citizen of a prosperous parish on the edge of the capital and tireless apologist for the ascendant mercantile classes.

From the point of view of his religious background and support of the Protestant monarchy, not to mention his periodic expression of little Englander attitudes, he may seem an unlikely figure to serve as a luminary of the tolerant age of enlightenment, along with the cosmopolitan intellectuals who stood at the head of the movement. Yet the *Tour* celebrates secular change; displays scepticism with regard to traditional myths and superstitions; commends improvements in public investments such as roads and hospitals; identifies progress in technology and manufacturing; and exalts better material conditions, while it embodies close observation of the real facts of life. In one way it resembles a potted version of the *Encyclopédie*, brought down within a domestic frame. Later on, in Chapter 5, we shall see that an expression such as 'Defoe's England' no longer functions as a toponym: instead it has become a historical marker, defining an entire cultural landscape.

Hardly a topic arises, essential to our understanding of the period, that does not show up in the *Tour*. A single example will illustrate the point. In her seminal discussion of 'Horses in Early Modern England: for Service, for Pleasure, for Power', Joan Thirsk has occasion to adduce Northern grooms and breeders on account of the care they devoted to upkeep and training.[4] The passage she cites in support of this observation runs as follows:

> [Those Fellows] take such indefatigable Pains with them, that they bring them out like Pictures of Horses, not a Hair amiss in them; they lye constantly in the Stables with them, and feed them by Weight and Measure; keep them so clean, and so fine, I mean in their Bodies, as well as their Outside, that, in short, nothing can be more nice. Here were several Horses sold for 150 Guineas a Horse; but then they were such as were famous for the Breed, and known by their Race, almost as well as the *Arabians* know the Genealogy of their Horses. (2: 197)

These thoughts are greatly amplified when the narrative reaches the heart of the horse-breeding district near Bedale in North Yorkshire (3: 89–90). We should not be surprised at the level of knowledge displayed here, since Defoe had actually been in business as a horse-trader.

If there had been travel expenses in the eighteenth century, what allowances could Defoe have claimed? (It was apt that he eventually became a surveyor of the roads for his parish.) Over the course of five decades and more, he jogged up and down the highways and byways of the land, observing almost everything that was going on in a changing landscape. This at a time when the most comfortable way of getting round the country was by coach. In the early 1700s it took almost twenty-four hours to go from London to Cambridge, thirty-six hours to reach Birmingham, fully half a week for Manchester, six days for Newcastle and ten days for Edinburgh. But more often Defoe traversed the rutted carriageways of the nation on horseback. Usually he was unaccompanied, a stranger who raised eyebrows when he mysteriously showed up, along with puzzled glances when he left just as abruptly. Sometimes the locals were far from welcoming when news had come of his impending arrival. Once a judge warned the local grand jury that seditious persons were in the neighbourhood, and advised the justices of the peace to take them into custody. A magistrate issued a warrant for Defoe's arrest, and he had to make a hasty departure.[5] His offence was to collect information on the political and commercial situation of the towns that he passed through on his journeys for Robert Harley. If the authorities had managed to close down his peregrinations, years later the *Tour* would have been a poorer thing.

Unmistakably, Defoe had a closer knowledge of Britain in its depth and breadth than most other commentators, even allowing for some inevitable gaps.[6] On his circuit of the country for Harley in 1705, he established a network of more than sixty individuals to distribute government propaganda.[7] Later he developed an even more extensive intelligence operation during his time in Edinburgh. The claim he made in 1710 appears to stand up: 'I have Sir Since I have Serv'd (as you kno') Established a Generall Correspondence, and at Some Charge Maintain'd it, by which I have a Fixt Intelligence (I May Say) all Over Brittain, But Especially in the North.'[8] In letters back to his patron, he mentions other contacts, and over the course of time he made further acquaintances in different localities.

Links with some of his informants may date back as far as the 1680s. Thus, we find him meeting with a linen draper in Norwich; visiting a leading citizen of Liverpool; conferring with an attorney in Shrewsbury; setting up a link with Timothy Wesley (brother of his schoolfellow Samuel and uncle of John Wesley); contacting several dissenting ministers in towns such as Lutterworth; getting in touch with merchants in places like Gainsborough; lodging with a JP in Brentford, who had recently been dismissed for his Whig sympathies; and seeking out an obscure Quaker working as a glover on the Welsh borders, named Icabod Bowen. On journeys north, he stayed with the postmaster at Newcastle. When he was in trouble over *The Shortest Way with the Dissenters*, he went into hiding with a poor weaver in Spitalfields. When he traversed the Lowlands of Scotland, he employed an agent name Pierce, who knew the area well. His point man in Sudbury was the butcher, later broker and land agent John Morley. It happens that Morley, through his connections with the Harley family, became well known to Alexander Pope and Matthew Prior. But in the overwhelming number of cases, such individuals were invisible to the metropolitan elite. The picture we get from most of those who comment on the state of the nation – whether politicians, pamphleteers or poets – is inscribed in a narrow frame, socially and geographically. With other travel writers, including such able practitioners as Celia Fiennes, we scarcely ever have any sustained contact with the lower orders. Defoe was the only major English writer of the age who regularly got about, to hobnob with all and sundry.

One other factor gave him an exceptional, if not unique, set of qualifications. For years he was the trusted agent of Sidney Godolphin and Robert Harley, the last two lord treasurers of Britain (if we except Lord Poulet and the Duke of Shrewsbury, who held the post in a very brief interim role). They were followed by three earls who served as first lord of the treasury, Halifax, Stanhope and Sunderland: Defoe carried out confidential work for each of them. As we shall see in Chapter 6, he was closely involved with some principal figures in Scottish politics while employed on behalf of his patrons in Edinburgh. He knew leading entrepreneurs and moneyed men, some of this while occupying positions in government service during the 1690s. His varied business career brought him contacts and contracts in various parts of the kingdom. His training at a leading dissenters academy under the distinguished teacher Charles Morton gave him a background in matters concerning religion and education that he would put to good use. Equally, his paper, the *Review*, clearly reached a wide audience around the nation. It is hard to think of anyone whose life touched so many corners of society.

The conclusion is irresistible. If we want a single guide to Britain at the start of the eighteenth century, this is the place to start. Well informed, mostly up to the minute in its coverage and ranging into so many crevices of life as it was lived up and down the country, the *Tour* has no serious rivals. It comes from an observer who had lived through the Plague and the Great Fire; taken part in the Monmouth Rebellion and joined William III's victorious army on its way to London (3: 43–9). He had witnessed events surrounding the Union with Scotland, the first Jacobite rising (as described in Chapter 6) and the South Sea Bubble (Chapter 7). He had been one of the main contributors to a growing debate on the touchy subject of the succession in pamphlets such as *An Answer to a Question that Nobody Thinks of, viz., But what if the Queen should Die?* (1713). How many other items would he need to have added to his CV before he is seen to match the job description? He did not get everything right, but none of us do.

The Contexts of the *Tour*

It is a pity in some ways that Defoe's fame has rested so heavily on *Robinson Crusoe* and *Moll Flanders*, along with his incarceration in the pillory as a result of *The Shortest Way with the Dissenters*. These, of course, hold momentous weight in any assessment of the state of literature in this period, but they tend to divert attention from the author's other achievements. He has been well described by Maxine Berg as 'prolific pamphleteer, social and economic commentator, novelist, indeed veritable pundit of his age.'[9] As Peter Earle, himself a learned scholar in social and economic history, has observed, 'The reader of Defoe is constantly amazed at the breadth and depth of his knowledge.'[10] In particular, Defoe's writings on these themes in the 1720s have often been sidelined, to the detriment of a just appraisal of his output as a whole. These contain some of his most representative and lasting work, powered by his close knowledge of trade and his passionate advocacy of 'improvement'. This is a concept central to the ideology of an age undergoing large structural changes in some of the very areas where Defoe was best equipped to comment – among them the textile trade, the location of industry, channels of distribution, transport and communications. He was far more alive to agricultural issues than used to be thought, pointing out disparate patterns of husbandry and the varied soils found in separate corners of the country.

We need only consider a selection of these books, all written around or just after the time that Defoe composed the *Tour*. They comprise *The Complete English Tradesman* (1725–7); *A General History of Discoveries and Improvements* (1725–6); *A Brief Deduction of the Original, Progress, and Immense Greatness of the British Woollen Manufacture* (1727); *A Plan of the English Commerce* (1728); *An Humble Proposal to the People of England, for the*

Encrease of their Trade, and Encouragement of their Manufactures (1729); and *A Brief State of the Inland or Home Trade of England* (1730). If mounting evidence makes it more and more probable that we should allot to Defoe a large share in *Atlas Maritimus* (1728), this attribution further strengthens the case (see Chapter 12). To gain concrete evidence in a short space that demonstrates the range of his information, it is enough to look at the list of 'The Several Manufactures of *Great-Britain*, as they are settled for the making in the several Counties, Towns, and Villages of *England*', found in the second volume of the *Tradesman*. There follows a table of the manufacturing centres of the nation, descending to places as small as Coggeshall and Rochdale. The table occupies ten pages of small print out of which four are devoted to Britain's trading partners, covering most countries in Europe as far east as Muscovy, and supplying information on the specialities of each town as well as its geographic situation. Should we wish to know it, we can find out where seamen's high-crowned caps are made (Bewdley, as the *Tour* also tells us), or the source of the zinc ore named lapis caliminaris (the Mendip Hills); or the place to get linseywoolsey goods (Kidderminster, similarly listed in the *Tour*); or the produce of the estate of the Duke of Queensberry in Nithsdale (lead, as the *Tour* confirms). Whenever possible, Defoe quotes hard figures on matters like imports and exports, citing customs records down to a hogshead, a gallon, or a ton.[11]

Detailed examination of the text of the *Tour* in successive chapters will show how often it provided a basis for this group of books. We might even say that Defoe worked out his ideas on the subjects under review when he put his considered view on Britain into the form of fictional journeys, starting in 1724. Inevitably, the seven books listed contain a good deal of repetition – the first part of the *Atlas* is little more than a rearrangement of coastal sections in the *Tour*. But collectively they provide a masterful outline of historical, geographic, financial and social factors that conditioned Britain's rise to the status of a great power and the origins of its incipient empire. Obviously the author did not have to face many of the contentious issues raised today by the imperial project.

A major theme of all these books from the 1720s is the rise of the mercantile community to a new elite status within society. In the *Tour*, a key passage announcing this topic comes in the opening Letter, where the author describes a number of seats near Chelmsford and Colchester owned by London merchants:

> I mention this, to observe how the present encrease of Wealth in the City of *London*, spreads it self into the Country, and plants Families and Fortunes,

> who in another Age will equal the Families of the antient Gentry, who perhaps were Bought out. I shall take Notice of this in a general Head, and when I have run thro' all the Counties, collect a List of the Families of Citizens and Tradesmen thus established in the several Counties, especially round *London*. (1: 60)

All the individuals and families mentioned in this segment of the text can be identified, and their relevance to the main concerns of the work can be traced.[12] Some were active as Whig MPs, others held offices in the City of London, and others stood at the head of the great trading corporations. Embedded within the *Tour* is a microhistory of this class (see also Chapter 7 on members of the group who suffered as a result of South Sea).

Timely Interventions

On several occasions Defoe managed to turn up on cue, when someone was needed to observe events that affected a significant segment of the population. For example, it is no accident that he was quickly able to make his voice heard on the threat of the Bubonic Plague after it reached Marseilles in 1720, killing slightly more than half of the population, with powerful warnings couched in both fictional and non-fictional form. He had been thinking about this subject since the outset of the plague in London in 1665, when his father may have evacuated the family to a safe distance, but he could have had first-hand accounts from his uncle Henry Foe, a saddler. Around the same time as the plague arrived, the silk weavers of Spitalfields fomented opposition to the import of fashionable calico from India, which they believed damaged their own trade. In 1719 and 1720 they organised protests in London, including attacks on the calico works, which resulted in direct confrontation with the City's trained bands, an armed militia. Defoe wrote articles in the newspapers supporting the cause of the silk weavers: he probably had long contacts with this community from his upbringing within the textile trade. As noted, when he went on the run after he became a wanted man in 1703 on account of *The Shortest Way with the Dissenters*, he hid in the home of a weaver named Nathaniel Sammon, who had helped to distribute an incendiary set of political demands, *Legion's Memorial*, two years before (Defoe was the probable author).

Many more examples could be given to illustrate his knack of being on the spot when major action took place. He witnessed political riots in England and Scotland, while working as an undercover agent for Robert Harley. Sometimes he was at the centre of the storm when a major public issue came to the surface, as when he presented the Kentish petition to Speaker Harley in 1701, perhaps flanked by 'Sixteen Gentlemen of

Quality'. His appearance in the pillory as a result of *The Shortest Way* took place outside the Royal Exchange and Cheapside, located at the symbolic heart of the financial revolution which had so transformed the country in recent years. (His third stint took place in Fleet Street, already a home of the book trade though not yet of the newspaper industry.) Few commentators on the state of the nation had seen the inside of a debtors' gaol, gone through bankruptcy, lost their business for reasons largely beyond their control, faced proceedings for outlawry, or ended up in Newgate gaol. If he had never been quite 'down and out' in eighteenth-century London, as Tim Hitchcock calls the subject of his own book on the poor, Defoe knew what it was like to be hopelessly under water in financial terms, and to have to go into hiding to escape creditors.[13] Equally few writers could have engaged in exotic trades such as the sale of civet cats for perfume, or invested in a firm that experimented with diving bells off the Cornish coast. For that matter, none had proposed a scheme to build new brick houses near the Houses of Parliament, or launched a plan to settle refugees from the German Palatinate in a quiet corner of the New Forest (1: 232–8). Hardly anybody else had the vision to discern the possibilities of a canal to join the Forth and the Clyde (3: 198, 209–10). Nobody else in this category had single-handedly run a journal of news and opinion from London and Edinburgh for nine years. It does not appear that Addison, Steele, Pope, Gay, Richardson or Fielding ever ventured further north on the mainland than Chester. Swift may have been kidnapped in his infancy by a nurse who carried him to Whitehaven – but that hardly counts.

Almost uniquely, Defoe was a Londoner who made it his business to get to know as much as he could of the provinces. He established first-hand contacts with individuals in ports like Bristol and Liverpool, coal towns like Newcastle, centres of the textile industry like Halifax, provincial capitals like Norwich, quiet nooks in the provinces like Bridgwater and Beccles. As noted, he got to talk with men and women of all conditions in almost every corner of the kingdom (see also Chapter 8). Unlike ninety-nine per cent of the English population, he spent long periods living in Scotland. So, when his *Tour* came before the public in the 1720s, it represented a voyage of discovery for many readers, vicariously enjoyed by those who stayed at home in the metropolis.

The Layout of This Book

The aim of this book is to provide a broad survey of the *Tour*, with a recurrent focus on the way it depicts an emerging nation. Since the work has a panoramic scale, it is appropriate to range over its contents as widely as possible. Defoe's intentions are explored along various channels: among them, those of form, rhetorical devices, political and social ideology, historiographic legacy, sources, geographic and topographic content, treatment of the communications network and folklore. Sometimes these approaches overlap, since a number of topics dominated the author's imagination. Most obviously we encounter at frequent intervals the relics of the Civil War, the rise to social prominence of the mercantile community, the aftermath of the South Sea Bubble and the fortunes of the woollen industry. New light is thrown on aspects of the work that have been ignored or neglected in previous studies. Each chapter aims to explore a facet of early modern Britain as it surfaces within Defoe's widely allusive text.

The opening part of this book pursues aspects of form and function. Chapter 1 describes a vision of nationhood, as distinct from a nationalist manifesto, that can be found in the *Tour*, with an examination of some devices employed to create the desired image of Britain, along with certain factors that made this task more difficult. The discussion follows several of the 'channels' mentioned in the previous paragraph. A cross-sectional analysis is made of a segment in Letter 2, to illustrate the range of concerns and variety of approaches found in the text. This segment also serves as a lead-in to the remainder of the book, since it touches on several topics that later chapters consider in more detail. Chapter 2 extends this line of enquiry by describing some paratextual practices in the *Tour*, as they are defined by Gérard Genette. These start with the title-page and prefatory sections, and end with appendices and indexes. Other features under review are sections embedded in the text, such as manuscripts cited, proposals reprinted from external sources, lists taken from standard reference works and so on. The argument is that separate elements of this kind serve collectively to embody a virtual representation of the nation. A topic considered in Chapter 3 is an epic strain in the *Tour*, following the model first suggested by E. M. W. Tillyard. It attempts to show how the work fulfils the requirements of the genre, as defined by Tillyard, and identifies a number of features that mimic epic properties. Chapter 4 concerns various formal elements, suggesting that Defoe builds up a regional scheme to unify his picture of the nation, parallel in some ways to the zones into which modern British highways are divided. Further, the chapter provides a comparison with the methods used in previous travel writing, and defines the originality of the work within the history of this genre by means of a semiotic square, adapted from the schema developed by A. J. Greimas.

The second part, entitled 'Time', concerns matters that relate to specific temporal issues, linked either with the subsequent legacy of the *Tour* or with events that occurred close in time to its composition. Chapter 5 attempts to show how students of history have enlisted the book for a variety of purposes, especially within the last hundred years. They include eminent writers in almost every branch of the discipline, markedly different in outlook and interests. Chapter 6 concerns a largely neglected topic, as it sets out the picture of the Jacobite Rising in 1715–16, which emerges gradually in scattered portions of the third volume of the *Tour.* Defoe's treatment of this episode is shown to underline his general approach to Scotland in the wake of the Union in 1707. The subject of Chapter 7 is the impact on the book of the South Sea Bubble, as the *Tour* draws on its author's long involvement in debates surrounding the Company. Key passages express sympathy with the directors and lament the fate of other wealthy merchants whose fortunes were destroyed in the collapse. Chapter 8 considers Defoe's profound interest in the language and mores of popular culture. It illustrates the way that the *Tour* uses the speech and activity of the people to show how each region contributes to the diverse culture of the nation, as a means of evoking the variety of Britain.

The third part, on 'Place', is made up of chapters loosely grouped by their relation to matters of space and geography. Chapter 9 analyses the use of topographic, cartographic and antiquarian sources, amplifying the influential study made by J. H. Andrews in 1960. It extends Andrews' coverage, which omitted the Scottish portions of the *Tour,* as well as supplying new evidence on the use Defoe made of maps, and offering a fuller comparison with the *Journey* of John Macky. Chapter 10 provides the first extensive commentary on a famous appendix to the *Tour* devoted to the new turnpike system, and documents the extent of Defoe's knowledge of English highways, built up over many decades and covering large segments of the nation. This chapter seeks to describe major features of the account, to indicate its timeliness, and to explain the factors which enabled Defoe to provide an unrivalled picture of the communications network of his time. His appendix furnishes a comprehensive survey of road conditions, as part of the author's overall design to show the interdependence of separate regions of the country, bound together in a circulation system centred on London. Chapter 11 is a case study concerned with a specific locality, namely the Bristol region – again, this section has never been given detailed attention before. Defoe had a solid working knowledge of the place, still second in importance to London among English cities. In particular, he had a firm grasp of the ways in which Bristol contributed to the national economy. Chapter 12 has to do with *Atlas Maritimus* (1728), a major compilation on nautical matters produced with the support of

Edmond Halley. Previous scholarship suggested that Defoe had a hand in its composition. This is the first attempt to specify the degree to which the *Atlas* is indebted to the *Tour* for almost all of its coverage of Britain, and to set out the ways in which it is made up of naked citation, metaphrase and paraphrase of Defoe's original. The signs are strong, indeed, that Defoe was himself the editor of this recension of his work.

Almost half of the items, that is Chapters 3, 4, 6, 7 and 12, have not previously been published in any form, while Chapters 1 and 8 are considerably expanded from their earlier incarnations. Other sections are made up of revised versions of articles, as listed below (pp. ix–x). Each of them has been updated and corrected where necessary: some have been reduced in size to fit the needs of this volume, and repetitions between the chapters have been stripped down to those of the barest necessity. These interlocking studies deal with some of the matters that frequently surface in Defoe's work, and it follows that a measure of overlap is unavoidable.

Some readers might wish away the regular appearance in most chapters of the name of John Macky, always to his disadvantage. But the parallels between his *Journey* and the *Tour* are too numerous to overlook. Both works first came out within a decade (respectively 1714–23 and 1724–6). Each was made up of three volumes: each constructed a survey beginning in southern England and moving northwards, before a final segment dealing with Scotland. The writers had both reached late middle age when their published travels came to an end: Defoe was about sixty-six, Macky not much (if at all) younger. They had lived lives that involved hard scrabbling, political intrigues and activity in espionage. Both had seen the inside of a debtor's prison. Both were committed Whigs and bitter opponents of the Stuart cause. In these circumstances, the most natural way to characterise the *Tour* will often involve defining by negatives. It is bound to be an uneven comparison, since Defoe was a great writer, and Macky was not. However, this does not mean that we can never gain any insight by placing the two texts alongside one another.

Defoe began his preface by promising a 'Description of the most Flourishing and opulent Country in the World', that offered 'a flowing Variety of Materials', where 'all the Particulars are fruitful of Instructive and Diverting Objects' (1: 47). Whatever the justice of these claims about the nation, the *Tour* is so rich a text that a single book cannot hope to rival the instruction or diversion it provides. This is an attempt to cover as many of its principal materials as possible. To look at early modern Britain through the lens of the *Tour* is to glimpse myriad facets of the age, not always obvious from our modern perspective. It makes up the nearest single source we have to a documentary on the subject.

PART I

Form and Function

CHAPTER 1

The Identity of Britain

Opening his massive appraisal of the Gallic environment, *The Identity of France*, Fernand Braudel stresses the diversity of the nation, geographically and humanly: 'Every village, every valley, *a fortiori* every *pays* . . . every town, every region, every province has its own distinct character – visible not only in the particular features displayed in the landscape and the many imprints man has left upon it, but also in a lived culture.' He cites a previous author who observed that 'Even for the traveller on foot . . . the landscape is always changing.' The reader who follows in Defoe's steps on his *Tour*, whether those were taken on two legs or four, or even by carriage, will find something of the same diversity in Britain. Braudel defines *pays* as meaning 'an area with its own identity, as the *pays de Bray*, *pays de Caux*'. He adds that 'not so long ago there still survived intact local privileges . . . local dialects, folklore, traditional houses . . . and local costumes'.[1] Most of these things are apparent in the *Tour*, as the work enshrines a range of customs and social practices across Britain from Land's End to John o'Groats. In the language of wines, we get the 'race' of each district – the flavour of life as it was lived in early modern days, from the Isle of Ely to the Solway Firth, from the Weald to the Pennines, from the Peak to the Brecon Beacons, from the Vale of Evesham to Strathearn.

At the start of the second volume of his *Tour*, Defoe reflects on the progress of his circuit to date. His supposed journey had got as far as Land's End, the extreme tip of the British landmass as it juts out into the Atlantic Ocean: 'My last letter ended the Account of my Travels, where Nature ended her Account, when she meeted out the Island, and where she fix'd the utmost *Western* Bounds of *Britain*' (2: 9).The syntax equates Defoe's own narrative with the 'Account' of nature herself, and prepares us for a ceremonial beating of the national bounds conducted by the author as he carries forward his description of the country's imagined corners. This sentence continues:

> being resolv'd to see the very Extremity of it, I set my Foot into the Sea, as it were, beyond the farthest Inch of dry Land *West*, as I had done before near

> the Town of *Dover*, at the Foot of the Rocks of the *South-Foreland* in *Kent*, which, I think, is the farthest Point East in a Line; And as I had done, also, at *Leostoff* in *Suffolk*, which is another Promontory on the *Eastern* Coast, and is reckon'd the farthest Land *Eastward* of the Island in general; Likewise I had used the same Ceremony at *Selsy* near *Chichester*, which I take to be the farthest Land *South* . . .. so, in its Place, I shall give you an Account of the same Curiosity at *John a Grot*'s House in *Caithness*, the farthest Piece of Ground in *Great Britain*, North. (2: 9)

In time Defoe does fulfil his last promise here – not something that applies to all the claims and protestations scattered through the text. Very near its end, the narration reaches northern Scotland and the antipodal point on the mainland from Land's End:

> Here is the House so famous, call'd *John a Grot*'s House, where we set our Horses Feet into the Sea, on the most northerly Land, as the People say, of *Britain*, though, I think, *Dungsby-Head* is as far North. . .The Dominions of *Great Britain* are extended from the *Isle of Wight*, in the Latitude of 50 Degrees, to the Isle of *Unsta* in *Shetland*, in the Latitude of 61 Degrees, 30 Minutes, being Ten Degrees, or full 600 Miles in Length; which Island of *Unst* or *Unsta* being the most remote of the Isles of *Shetland* to the North East, lyes 167 Leagues from *Winterton Ness* in *Norfolk*. (3: 273)

Even into the last pages of his book, Defoe is intent on charting limits, extent, dimensions. It is as though the subject exists only if it is defined by measurement.

The Whole Circuit

Why should Defoe have made such a fuss about the gesture of dipping feet – his own, or his horse's – into the sea? The question grows more urgent if we recall that he had probably never once ventured far into the Scottish Highlands, let alone into the remote fastnesses of the northern peninsula. (The purported correction regarding nearby Duncansby Head is a characteristic sleight of hand, drawing on material filched from maps and gazetteers). Several explanations might suggest themselves, involving, for example, the need for Defoe to give his narrative a shape by placing emphasis on these moments of arrested motion and recoil. But in the first place, the author was mimicking the ancient rites of 'beating the bounds', when local officers, accompanied often by children, would make a complete circuit of the parish. Before accurate mapping or surveying existed, this was a way in which a community could establish its borders and proclaim its identity. The ritual, commonly performed on Ascension

Day, had its religious and mystical functions, and when he projected the ceremony on a national scale Defoe carried out his own piece of sympathetic magic, as though placing feet into the water would absolve him from error, and thus confirm the claims he is making on behalf of Britain.

His first impulse as a writer was to convey a sense of precision – hence all the details about the time and place of robberies committed by Moll Flanders. Or again the way that the relentless march of the plague is charted, day by day, through London, with careful documentation of the mortality figures on a parochial basis, in *A Journal of the Plague Year*. Such attention to the minutiae of experience has been codified by critics as the 'formal realism' of his fiction. But it has its equivalent in the specificity of his political pamphlets, which regularly cite particular treaties and dates; and in the factual density of many of his historical and biographic works. Above all, his contributions to the literature of commerce play around elaborate displays of statistics: books such as *A Plan of the English Commerce*, published soon after the *Tour* in 1728, rest on a bewildering array of facts and contentions with regard to economic history. Occasionally these are quite inaccurate, as we shall see in the case of the *Tour* itself, but Defoe brandishes his evidence with an air of confidence that can easily hoodwink the reader.

Likewise, with the spatial data we have been looking at. When the *Tour* stops at London, in the fifth of its ten English sections, the principal aim of the treatment is to inscribe the centrality of the capital within the nation – politically, socially, culturally, but above all economically. In characteristic fashion, Defoe begins by taking a 'Measure' of the 'mighty' body of London. As we have seen in the Introduction, several pages are devoted to 'A LINE of Measurement, drawn about all the continued Buildings of the City of *London*, and Parts adjacent, including *Westminster* and *Southwark*, &c.' (2: 67). Nine numbered paragraphs cover the area north of the Thames, five to the south: each gives a minute street-by-street account of the city limits, accompanied by an estimate of the ground traversed in miles, furlongs and rods (as with Washington and Jefferson, it looks as if Defoe would have been happy to spend his life as a surveyor). There is even a running tally of distances carried over from page to page, testifying equally to the accountant manqué in Defoe. Several of the many guides to London in this period have maps of the city: but apart from the *Tour* only one gives a precise account of the extent of the boundaries – the parish clerks' survey, *New Remarks of London* (1732), a work that is organised entirely by parishes and sticks to the official lines of the municipal map.

Uniquely, Defoe charts more than the virtual lines of civic responsibility, though he is aware of these. He traces instead the physical margins of built-up London, and hence modern historians have sometimes used his data to compile their own models of the growth of the city, taking 1725 as their base-line.[2] As with the macrocosm, so with the microcosm of the nation which is the capital: to circumscribe the area is to define the topic. All Defoe's claims about the size and grandeur of Britain, its spectacular growth, its economic power, its competitive advantages, its opportunities for further increases in commercial and civic development, as well as personal prosperity – all these start from a vivid bird's eye view of the whole island. As we know, he had not really visited every part of the country, and some of his optimistic projections would never match the facts. But most of what he said about ongoing developments in the nation was true, insightful and even prescient.

The fictional journey derives by extrapolation from the author's own restless peregrinations during his early years, especially the travelling he did on behalf of two patrons, the important politicians Robert Harley and Lord Godolphin. Significantly, it takes Robinson Crusoe more than five years to 'make a Tour round the Island'.[3] Defoe himself would have found it impossible to hang around in this way for such a long period. In fact, the narrator of the *Tour* tells us that he had planned a more substantive sea voyage around the coast:

> I had once, indeed, resolved to have coasted the whole Circuit of *Britain* by Sea, as 'tis said, *Agricola* the *Roman* General did; and in this Voyage I would have gone about every Promontory, and into the Bottom of every Bay, and had provided myself a good Yatch, and an able Commander for that Purpose; but I found it would be too hazardous an Undertaking for any Man to justify himself in the doing it upon the meer Foundation of Curiosity, and having no other Business at all; so I gave it over. (2: 9)

He explains that his project was abandoned owing to the difficulty of finding pilots who would help him to enter all the bays, creeks and estuaries around the coast. As a result, he satisfied himself with making 'the Circuit very near as perfect by Land' (2: 10). In reality, the disparate trips that Defoe took over many years followed no consistent pattern and seldom joined up into any kind of circle. The symmetrical design of the book is entirely a matter of artifice, intended to express the fullness of the author's grasp of Britain in its variety and plenitude.

Almost eighty years ago, G. M. Trevelyan gave eloquent tribute to Defoe's value as a witness to the significant historical processes of his time. His comments on Defoe as one who 'first perfected the art of the reporter' come from one who had compiled what is still the most complete survey of England under Queen Anne:

> So then, the account that this man gives of the England of Anne's reign is for the historian a treasure indeed. For Defoe was one of the first who saw the old world through a pair of sharp modern eyes. His report can be controlled and enlarged by great masses of other evidence, but it occupies a central point of our thought and vision.[4]

Since Trevelyan wrote these words, we have had the benefit of more than half a century of increasingly sophisticated research into early eighteenth-century Britain. Recent authorities continue to quote Defoe, to cite his information and to debate his conclusions. But nothing has emerged that invalidates the central thrust of Trevelyan's comments. In the remainder of this chapter I shall try to show the ongoing relevance of the *Tour* for anyone who wishes to get a full grasp of the age, and to assess the worth of the book in the light of modern research. In turn I shall consider the significance of London in the life of the nation; the demographic issues charted in the *Tour*; the use Defoe makes of historical and topographic sources in his library; the importance of the system of transport, by land and water; and finally the vision of nationhood expressed in the book.

London

The *Tour* contains one notorious gaffe. This occurs when Defoe attempts to estimate the size of London:

> The Guesses that are made at the Number of Inhabitants, have been variously form'd; Sir *William Petty*, famous for his Political Arithmetick, supposed the City, at his last Calculation, to contain a Million of People, and this he judges from the Number of Births and Burials; and by his Rule, as well by what is well known of the Increase of the said Births and Burials, as of the prodigious Increase of Buildings, it may very reasonable to conclude, the present Number of Inhabitants within the Circumference I have mentioned, to amount to, at least, Fifteen Hundred Thousand, with this Addition, that it is still prodigiously increasing. (2: 72)

This is an absurdly high figure. London, as then defined, had grown at an astonishing rate in the seventeenth century, from 200,000 people at the start of the century to almost 575,000 at the end. By 1750 it reached 675,000, and by 1800 not far short of a million. The demographic area covered by the 'bills of mortality' included the historic city within and without the walls, together with adjoining parishes in Middlesex and the city of Westminster, as well as Southwark on the other side of the river. The boundaries of Defoe's 'Line of Circumvallation' stretch a little way in to outlying villages which had not yet been assimilated into the official returns. He observed with a certain alarm 'That *Westminster* is in a fair way to shake Hands with *Chelsea*, as St. *Gyles's* is with *Marybone*; and *Great Russel Street* by *Montague House*, with *Tottenham-Court*: all this is very evident, and yet all these put together, are still to be called *London*' (2: 66). The image of shaking hands seems benign enough, but in spite of Defoe's feelings of wonder at this explosive growth there is something sinister, too, about the 'joining' of these tentacles.

In one of the most challenging accounts of this section of the *Tour*, Max Byrd notes that 'as Defoe struggles . . . to organize the city . . . [he] turns again and again to images of the human body for his description'. Simply as 'a temporary stay', he arranged for a measure to be taken 'of this mighty, I cannot say uniform Body'. For Byrd, 'Defoe's sense of London as restless, unpredictable, devouring awakens a universal anxiety.' This is why he 'attempts to fence in the city, to erect a "Circumvallation".'[5] The sense of terror that Byrd observes seems to me slightly exaggerated, and plays down Defoe's obvious delight in the growth and grandeur that had become apparent in the metropolis during his lifetime. Nevertheless. this reading does point to genuine contradictions that surface throughout the *Tour,* where a strong endorsement of the present and faith in the future (the world of 'improvement') are sometimes cut across by a sense of the past and an evocation of loss (expressed in terms of decay and dissolution).

For one thing, he could see the process of urban sprawl working itself out beneath his nose, at the level of just one or two blocks:

> The Town of *Islington*, on the north Side of the City, is in like manner joyn'd to the Streets of *London*, excepting one small Field, and which is itself so small, that there is no Doubt, but in a very few Years, they will be entirely joyn'd, and the same may be said of *Mile End*, on the *East* End of the Town. (2: 66)

Such changes are often registered more comfortably when they do not impinge on one's own neighbourhood. To the south of the river, Newington 'is so near joining to *Southwark*, that it cannot now be properly called a Town by itself, but a Suburb to the Burrough, and if, *as they now tell us is undertaken*, St. *George's Fields* should be built into Squares and Streets, a very little Time will shew us *Newington*, *Lambeth*, and the *Burrough*, all making but one Southwark' (2: 66). Suburbs made up a largely new phenomenon in European cities, but Defoe might almost have had access to a roadmap from the 1800s. In a daring rhetorical move, he asserted that the boundaries of the city now spread further still: 'The Town of *Greenwich*, which may, indeed be said to be contiguous with *Deptford*, might be also called a Part of this Measurement; but I omit it, as I have the Towns of *Chelsea* and *Knights-Bridge* on the other Side, tho' both may be said to joyn the Town, and in a very few Years will certainly do so' (2: 72). Such a claim amounts to a radical reconceptualization of London, as it had been defined up till then. Literally, of course, suburbanisation had taken place ever since Westminster and Southwark grew up outside the walls of the ancient City. But these localities remained within sight and hearing of the older centre, and in the case of Westminster especially took on a centrality of their own. It is quite another matter with the outlying parishes in Deptford, Islington, Hampstead, and Fulham – even Defoe's own Stoke Newington. By 1747 John Rocque would be unable to squeeze any of them into his famous map of the city, which he began to survey eight years earlier. Yet they already existed in a symbiotic relationship with the inner portions of the capital, and had started to lose some of the rural appendages that gave them their character as villages. This unplanned growth presented so many challenges that Defoe was even led to propose restrictions on future building in some districts.[6]

The serious inaccuracy of his estimate of the city's population can be explained partly by a reliance on the undependable registers of births and deaths, a parochial rather than a civil responsibility. But the miscalculation also reflects Defoe's strong sense of the way London was creeping remorselessly away from its old nucleus. As we have just seen, a map of the city as little as a generation later would show that the kind of process he describes, with the assimilation of surrounding communities into the main urban mass, had already taken place. As often happens, Defoe was just a little in advance of reality. But what matters here is the nature of his exaggeration. He always tends to round figures up, but he does so most recklessly when he witnesses a process of rapid growth. His coverage of London is dominated by an awareness of the changes that had taken place in his own lifetime, and hence he lays the principal emphasis on the dynamic and accelerating pace of the transformations, which were going on under his very nose. This means that his account of relative size (between two cities, or a city in two stages of development) is nearly always correct, even though he falsifies the absolute figures by boosting them to an implausible total.

A prime rhetorical aim is to focus attention on the centrality of the capital in national life. Defoe had it altogether right here: London made up about a tenth of the population of England and Wales, whereas only one in forty of French nationals lived in Paris. Among major European cities only Amsterdam had anything remotely approaching a similar dominance, with 7 per cent of the much smaller Dutch population. Modern demographers have calculated that a sixth of the adult population (again these counts relate to England and Wales only) would reside in London at some stage of their life.[7] The metropolis had become an irresistible magnet for people of all sorts and conditions: heavy immigration took place from Scotland and Ireland, from nearby continental countries, and from further afield. For instance, a large number of Protestants fled from France in the 1680s, including Defoe's fictional heroine Roxana. But the main agency was internal migration, with a steady stream of mostly young men and women flowing in from the provinces. As a result, around 1700, a net total of some 8,000 immigrants swarmed into the city each year, a process that would continue unabated for the rest of the century. This helped to create a steady rise in population, despite a relatively stable birth-rate and initially little decline in the death-rate. The high incidence of young people in search of work had consequences which are reflected by the cautionary tales found in the works which Defoe wrote on social topics, such as *The Complete English Tradesman* (1725–7), and on the plight of London itself, such as *Augusta Triumphans* (1728).

However, the significance of London in the nation went a long way beyond its mere size. Admittedly, the city stood out as a colossus in a predominantly rural society, where only Norwich and Bristol reached over 20,000 inhabitants, with a further six towns whose population exceeded 10,000, and perhaps twenty-five over 5,000 people. The key fact grasped by Defoe was that London served as the main engine of economic activity in Britain. He saw 'the general Dependance of the whole Country upon the City of *London* . . . for the Consumption of its Produce' (1: 48). E. A. Wrigley quotes this observation in the definitive modern discussion of the subject, 'A Simple Model of London's Importance in Changing English Society and Economy, 1650–1750'. First published in 1967, but often reprinted and endlessly cited, Wrigley's article documents the ways in which the capital came almost to monopolise some crucial aspects of national life around the time that Defoe wrote. Wrigley identifies ten economic, demographic and sociological changes over the period. These range from 'the creation of a single national market' and a better transport network to 'the spread of the practice of "aping one's betters"', that is aspirational and emulative behaviour.[8] Defoe has a lot to say on these matters, as in *The Compleat English Gentleman* (written *c.*1730), while another of Wrigley's categories, the provision of more commercial and credit facilities, underlies much of the *Review* and the pamphlets Defoe wrote at the time of the Harley administration from 1710 to 1714.

Defoe concerns himself principally with London as a centre of trade and industry. He dilates upon the various markets for commodities such as meat, fish, herbs, corn, leather, coal and much more. He has a long section on the port: 'The whole River, in a Word, from *London-Bridge* to *Black Wall*, is one great *Arsenal*, nothing in the World can be like it' (2: 95). He goes into some detail on the dock facilities, and emphasises the scale of shipbuilding downriver. These sections actualise the notion of London as the great emporium of the world, which had been expressed in terms of a mythical aspiration in works such as John Dryden's *Annus Mirabilis* (1667). The Thames was, after all, the busiest thoroughfare in the city. Apart from its international shipping, London served as the base for a huge volume of coastal trade, with a high proportion of the mercantile fleet occupied in transporting coal from the northern mines around Newcastle to keep the wheels of the capital turning. In addition, Defoe writes with approval of the supply of piped water recently introduced, and discusses various support systems for business, including the customs house, the stock exchange and the insurance companies – these last also a new innovation.

But even for Defoe, trade was not everything. At the same time he celebrates the great public buildings, among them architectural monuments such as St Paul's Cathedral and Westminster Abbey. He gives an elaborate account of the palace of Whitehall, which had been the impressive centre of government in his own youth before fire had destroyed most of its structures. He even sets out a fully documented proposal, occupying several pages, to erect a new palace on the site, something which would never be realised. Along with the court and the parliamentary buildings around Westminster Hall, he mentions one nearby black spot, the only street that gives the surrounding area 'a Communication with *London*'. This was King Street, 'a long, dark, dirty, inconvenient Passage' from Westminster to the city (2: 112). But then for good measure he lists the public gaols up to a number of almost thirty: and along with these the schools, charities and hospitals, including the foundation just set up by Thomas Guy, whose progress he monitors throughout the text in appendices and addenda. Defoe's Britain is a work in progress, not least on the capital, and the structure of his book mirrors this fact.

London is the fulcrum of a machine that engages in a whirl of perpetual motion, where the spectacular growth in population and prosperity is matched by the renown of cultural institutions and noble edifices which fill the skyline of the capital: 'But the Beauty of all the Churches in the City, and of all the Protestant Churches in the World, is the Cathedral of St. *Paul*'s' (2: 81).[9] Aesthetic appreciation goes with ideological fervour: the physical grandeur of the city expresses the emergent power of the nation, which had been locked for generations in a struggle for domination with its Catholic neighbours in Europe.

In point of fact, Defoe had surplus resources for his task. If the form of his book had permitted it, he could have drawn on a large body of material that is used in his other work, especially his pamphlets on social issues. These contain discussions of matters of great interest to contemporary historians of London, for example servants, the poor law, workhouses, beggars, prostitutes, Bridewell hospital, foundlings, charities, education, lotteries, street crime, transportation, executions, the bankruptcy law, the menace of gin and so on. If his purposes had been different, he could have expiated on such topics with a flow of ideas and proposals – not all wise or feasible, but each proceeding from a well-stocked mind and a deep familiarity with London lives.

Vital Statistics

We observe the same tendency to exaggerate population figures, where they are high and rising, in other sections of the book. An extreme case occurs in Defoe's account of the wool towns of the West Riding of Yorkshire, where he describes Halifax as the most populous 'country Parish' in England. He cites a dubious source, and then commits himself to endorsing the information: 'It is some Years ago that a Reverend Clergyman of the Town of *Hallifax*, told me, they reckoned that they had a Hundred thousand Communicants in the Parish, besides Children' (3: 67). This calculation is preposterously inflated, even granting the shock which must have come to a previously remote community on the slopes of the Pennine hills as the wool trade expanded. (Defoe had visited the place for Robert Harley in 1705, and knew a local dissenting minister, so his credulity is just about explicable, if not excusable).[10] The reality is that Halifax itself would not have had much more than 5,000 inhabitants, and the cluster of villages in the surrounding valleys can barely have doubled this total. But a poetic truth lurks behind the claim: Halifax was certainly one of the largest parishes in the nation, along with Manchester, and one of the most densely populated communities outside a large conurbation. Defoe's overstatement dramatises a real social dynamic which was just getting under way. Population moved from the south and west of England to the north as industrialisation gradually shifted the main locus of manufacturing, to the detriment of the older centres of the textile trade, in East Anglia and the south-western counties. A century later, the biggest cities in the country after London would no longer be Norwich or Bristol, but places like Liverpool, Leeds and Manchester that all depended on the textile industry. What has puzzled economic historians is that Defoe sometimes writes as if this process had already reached an advanced stage, if not practically achieved completion, whereas in fact it had only just begun. As with his figures, the *Tour*'s observations bizarrely appear more accurate if we project them forward a few decades.

The same thing is largely true of what is said of Manchester. Defoe writes that the town is 'one of the greatest, if not the greatest meer Village in *England*'. This is because it has no corporation and sends no MPs to Westminster. Despite that, together with the 'Suburb . . . called – [Salford] over the Bridge, it is said to contain above fifty thousand People'. Nervously, he offers a half-retraction: 'Though some People may think this strange, and that I speak by guess, and without Judgment, I shall justify my Opinion so well, that I believe, it will convince you my Calculation is at least very probable, and much under what Fame tells us is true' (3: 129). The justification takes the form of pointing to a sharp increase in trade over the last thirty or forty years; a commensurate rise in the number of buildings; the statement by Gibson in his edition of *Britannia* that long before the parish had 20,000 communicants – to which Defoe adds an estimate of 10,000 children; and the belief of some 'antient Inhabitants' that the true figure exceeds 60,000 (3: 129–30). Of course, the number is still far too high. The population zoomed up from less than 10,000 at the start of the century to 20,000 by its midpoint and 75,000 by 1800. Thus, the account in the *Tour* foresaw an extraordinary leap in the upcoming decades, but got a little ahead of itself.[11]

We can generally rely on the comparative scale of numbers that the *Tour* provides. Defoe likes to take the instance of the tiny 'city' of Wells in Somerset, a place where he could find only a small share in the stocking industry. Wells owed its status to the presence of the cathedral, so that civic life went on around the 'dignified Clergy' in their 'very agreeable Dwellings' round the close (2: 30). Elsewhere he observes that Deptford, on the eastern fringe of London, 'is no more a separated Town, but is become a Part of the great Mass, and infinitely full of People too . . . were the Town of *Deptford* now separated, and rated by itself, I believe it contains more People, and stands upon more Ground, than the City of *Wells*' (2: 66). This time the claim is justified: Wells probably had fewer than 2,000 inhabitants with a static population, a figure eclipsed by the rapidly growing Deptford.[12] A similar comparison is used to define Frome, a nearby Somerset town engaged in clothing manufacture, which had seen a spectacular growth in the last few decades:

> The Town of *Froome* ... is so prodigiously increased within these last Twenty or Thirty Years, that they have built a New Church, and so many Streets of Houses, and those Houses are so full of Inhabitants, that *Frome* is now reckoned to have more People in it, than the City of *Bath*, and some say, than even *Salisbury* itself, and if their Trade continues to increase for a few Years more, as it has done for those past, it is very likely to be one of the greatest and wealthiest Inland Towns in *England*. (2: 32–3)

This time the comparison was not quite so solidly based, and it would be falsified in the course of time. Salisbury continued to have a fairly small and static population, but Bath (which had little more than 1,000 residents in 1660) had begun to climb as the resort grew more fashionable. The resort had its big take-off in the late 1720s, immediately after Defoe wrote, with important new building developments by John Wood the elder, so that by 1741 the town had reached 6,000. By contrast the meteoric rise of Frome spluttered to a halt, as the clothing industry migrated northwards, and it climbed only slowly to 9,000 late in the century. Though Defoe picked some unlucky examples, his calculation may just have been valid for a tiny window of time around 1710, soon after he himself visited Frome on his electioneering trips. Not that many readers in London would have spotted the error: most would have been unaware of the changes overtaking commercial towns in the provinces.

Moreover, we can place complete reliance on Defoe's descriptive terms, such as 'a Town of good Figure, and has in it several eminent Merchants' – this of Lyme Regis, taking one example out of scores of similar epithets (1: 246). Where he observes signs of decline, as with the shipping industry at Ipswich, we always find contemporary documents to support the allegation of a decay in trade and prosperity. Where he notes a swing in the competitive position of two neighbouring towns, such as the gains of Bideford on the coast of Devon at the expense of its rival Barnstaple (2: 14–16), the archival evidence confirms what Defoe had picked up, very often by first-hand observation. The detailed account he gives of the layout of some cities, such as Chester, provides a concrete basis for the assertions he makes about their size and prosperity. The facts were sacrosanct, when it came to matters pertaining to trade, even if he sometimes played fast and loose with the more striking or hyperbolic of his figures.

A Cross-section of England

Among the distinguishing features of the *Tour* are the variety of materials and the range of approaches it exhibits. Both aspects contribute to the book's readability, as the tone shifts from that used to convey solid information to that suitable for protestation, elegy or comedy. One way to make sense of these separate strands would be by means of a longitudinal survey, charting the presence through the entire work of a given element (say, market towns), and a given mode of description (say, demographic). A more convenient method used here is what might be termed a vertical cross-section, that is analysis of a part of the text by subject-matter and line of approach.

The sample chosen comes from the first volume, embracing the second part of Letter 2, in which the narrator describes the return leg of his supposed journey from Portsmouth to Southwark. It consists of about 16,000 words, just under half of the entire Letter. The route takes a north-easterly course, approximating to the modern A3 in stretches, but there are divagations to the right and left – Hampshire is treated more fully in Letter 3, but this is the only segment of the book to cover Kent, Sussex and most of Surrey. Table 1 shows some of the principal matters that come under consideration, and the mode of enquiry. A number of short passages are ignored where they simply link the narrative or provide very brief descriptions of small aspects of the landscape.

This slice of the nation is not, of course, representative of every part of Britain. Sussex and Surrey were more thickly populated and at the same time less industrialised than some other counties. They did not have the archaeological riches of Wiltshire, with its hoard of prehistoric sites, or the wild scenery of the Scottish Highlands. Nevertheless, the segment does convey something of the diversity of the *Tour*, alike in content and treatment.

Going behind the data, we can draw some conclusions about the space devoted to certain topics. It is natural that Portsmouth, with important docks, shipyard and naval business, should receive some of the fullest coverage – ten paragraphs, amounting to about 1,450 words. There is good reason too for the extensive paragraph on the fashionable resort of Epsom, which together with Banstead Downs occupies nearly 1,600 words in sixteen paragraphs, written very much in the same style as the description of Bath (2: 155–7). We can also understand that Defoe is quite brief on Southwark, with just 730 words, since he promises more in the section on London in Letter 5. However, the exceptional amount of time that he

Table 1 *Cross-section of Letter 2 (in part)*

Pages	Main contents	Mode of enquiry
173	death of Bishop Williams	anecdotal
173–4	Portsmouth docks and shipyard	topographic; economic
174–5	Portsmouth corporation; Portsea suburb	municipal; mercantile
176	roads and bridges; shipbuilding	highways; industry
176–7	stock of timber not depleted	polemical; economic
177–8	Southampton; smuggling; Bevis	trade; folklore; humour
178	limited wool manufacturing	industry
178–9	Farnham; corn market; deer stealers	trade; historical; political
179–80	Bagshot Heath; barren landscape	highways; autobiographical
180	famous verses by John Denham	literary quotation
180	aside concerning the direction of the Tour	editorial; reflexive
180	Henry VI; Cowley; Countess of Richmond	historical; biographical
181	Guildford; Wey navigation; clothing trade	commercial; transport
181–2	Hog's Back	highways; autobiographical
182–3	seats near Guildford	historical; anecdotal; humour
183–7	River Mole; 'swallows'	topographical; antiquarian; historical; autobiographical
187–9	Dorking area; vineyard; giant	horticultural; anecdotal
189	disorders at inn	social; anecdotal
189–90	Holmwood; roads	antiquities; highways; quotation
191	seats; ironworks	social; manufacturing
192	Dulwich spa	social
192	Croydon; death of Lady Onslow	antiquities; anecdotal
193	Harvey of Coombe	personal; political
193–4	seats of merchants; South Sea losses	social; political
194–6	Epsom; local seats	social; pleasure resorts
197	Kingston; Coway stakes	topography; archeology
197–8	Ham House	architecture; historical
198–9	Richmond; mansions; verse cited	eulogy; quotation
199–201	modern passion for gardening; Queen Mary	horticulture
201–3	paean to wealth and beauty of the district	social; eulogy
203	South Sea victims	political
203–5	Southwark; morality figures	historical; demographic
204	Vauxhall; Roman road; old bridge	topography; archeology

spends on Dorking, or rather on the 'disappearing' River Mole, can only be explained by Defoe's intimate familiarity with this district as a result of a long sojourn there as a boy. He was anxious to correct Camden and Gibson on the issues, and to make use of other pieces of local knowledge he had picked up. So much so that he was willing to expend more than 2,000 words on the river, with a further 1,100 on the town and its environs. If this balance seems awry, we should recall that Macky devotes over twenty pages to Epsom, that he has only the briefest 'Excursion' (eighty words) to Guildford to praise its horse racing and the clean linen for which its inns are noted, and that he evidently considers Petworth as the most important place in Sussex because the Duke of Somerset has his seat there.[13]

The facts displayed in Table 1 hold a wider significance. They show how the author managed to keep in motion a sustained fiction of travel, while discoursing across a broad spectrum of issues. Among the classic British travellers, only Cobbett comes close to rivalling Defoe, but even he has a narrower remit as he can afford to neglect large urban centres, and leaves out vast tracts of the nation. In the main series of *Rural Rides*, he never deigns to refer to a single mountain. Defoe was less prone to believe that if you could not grow crops or cultivate sheep on a stretch of ground it did not exist.

History and Topography

Defoe's version of contemporary Britain owed much to his lifelong absorption in two allied branches of literature and knowledge. These are respectively the study of antiquity, especially the earlier history of England and Scotland (he does not seem to have been well versed in Welsh antiquarian matters); and the literature of travel and topography. This is a topic investigated in more detail in Chapter 9. For now, we should note that at the start of his career Defoe compiled a volume of *Historical Collections*, never published and lost since the eighteenth century. After this, he wrote a number of books in the area of biography and historiography, and he maintained a keen interest in everything connected with travel, exploration and geography. He was evidently a close student of maps. Plenty of evidence for these obsessive concerns can be found within the text of his *Tour*, as Parts II and III of this book will document.

Our best guide to the range of Defoe's reading comes in the sale catalogue of his books, sold after his death. Unfortunately the list also embraces the collection of Dr Phillips Farewell, a High Church clergyman who died in late 1730, just a few months before Defoe went to his own grave, and many scholars have pointed to the risks we take if we assume that any given book in the catalogue belonged to either man.[14] However, we may reasonably suppose Defoe to be by far the likelier candidate in some areas, including books on history, especially those on England and Scotland (where Defoe had many links, Farewell none at all), and those on travel. From sources identified by Defoe himself in the *Tour*, we can be absolutely certain that he had access to a number of titles on the list.

More than once, the narrator emphasises his lack of interest in antiquarian lumber, and his refusal to follow previous travellers in swelling out his text with irrelevant gobbets of historical information. One passage explains his attitude more fully and openly:

> I have many times repented that I so early resolved to decline the delightful View of Antiquity . . . for the Trophies, the Buildings, the religious, as well as military Remains, as well of the *Britains*, as of the *Romans*, *Saxons*, and *Normans*, are but, as we may say, like Wounds hastily healed up, the *Calous* spread over them being remov'd, they appear presently, and though the Earth . . . has defaced the Surface, the Figures and Inscriptions upon most of these Things, yet they are beautiful, even in their decay. And the venerable Face of Antiquity has something so pleasing, so surprising, so satisfactory in it, especially to those who have with any Attention read the Histories of pass'd Ages, that I know nothing renders travelling more pleasant and more agreeable.
>
> But I have condemn'd my self (unhappily) to Silence upon this Head, and therefore, resolving however to pay this Homage to the Dust of gallant Men and glorious Nations, I say therefore, I must submit and go on. (3: 121)

In reality, Defoe stuffed the text with materials from earlier writers, especially his primary source, William Camden's *Britannia*, first published in Latin in 1586. Two versions came out in Defoe's lifetime of a new augmented translation and edition by Edmund Gibson (1695, 1722). The earlier edition duly appears in the sale catalogue as item 186, along with a reply to Camden, reissued in 1724; investigation reveals that it was the 1695 version that Defoe generally used. Scores of borrowings from *Britannia*, often quite lengthy, can be detected in the *Tour*; some are acknowledged, but many more of them are not. The presence of Camden's great book in such a dense concentration within the text provides a clue to Defoe's aims: he wished to create not just a storehouse of antiquities, but a hymn to the nation, with its roots, development and structure considered under the historical aspect. Using *Britannia* in this way enabled him to give the surface of his narrative a kind of historical undercoat on which he could paint in his own observations.

We can trace many of the other sources from which Defoe took his information, and from which he derived his sense of the nation's past.[15] He used books such as Elias Ashmole's *History of the Order of the Garter* (1715), John Aubrey's *Miscellanies* (1721), Richard Carew's *Survey of Cornwall* (1723) and the work mentioned in an earlier citation, Sir William Petty's *Political Arithmetick* (1691). Significantly, every one of these was in his library. Other books listed in the collection that are not acknowledged in the text, but possibly used in compiling the *Tour*, were antiquarian works by Richard Rawlinson, Jodocus Crull, Sampson Erdeswicke and Bulstrode Whitelocke. When the narrative reaches Stonehenge (1: 229–31), abundant evidence demonstrates that Defoe had consulted not just Camden on this topic, but also speculations by others such as Inigo Jones and John Aubrey on the origins of this monument. Taken together, these facts conclusively show that it is impossible to take Defoe at his word, as critics and historians used to do, and suppose that he had a limited interest in the history of places he visited on his imaginary journey.

Easier to spot is Defoe's fascination with topography and cartography. We can be sure that he availed himself of books in the collection such as John Ogilby's *Britannia* (1698), or *A Book of the Names of all the Parishes, Market Towns, Villages ... in England and Wales, with Maps* (1668). Surveys of Middlesex, Hertfordshire and Northamptonshire, reprinted in 1720 and 1723, would have proved highly germane to Defoe's task. As for previous British travels, one item stands out above all others. Item 950 contains John Macky's *A Journey through England in Familiar Letters*, together with its sequel *A Journey through Scotland* (1722–3). Defoe peppers the text with contemptuous references to his rival's alleged blunders, but always under the guise of 'a late author' or some variant which scornfully denies Macky a name. Unquestionably he wrote the *Tour* with one eye on the *Journey*, his gaze at once corrective and acquisitive. Defoe certainly knew, and perhaps carried with him on his trips, one of the roadbooks which gave detailed itineraries for travellers, even though none of these was sold with the library collection. The works of Emanuel Bowen, for example, had started to appear in time to be of use to Defoe in plotting routes and calculating distances. In addition, the county maps supplied by Bowen may have been of assistance, especially in remote corners of Wales.[16] Moreover, these guides show enough detail about the nature of the countryside (listing open fields, woods, hills, small streams, and so on) for an astute author to be able to stitch together a convincing description of the scenery, just as if he had recent memories of the landscape to draw on. Finally, the catalogue of Defoe's collection records 'A map of Middlesex,

Essex, and Hertfordshire, done by actual survey, six feet by four, with 728 coats of arms round the map'. Middlesex and Essex were the two counties where the author had the closest contacts, with Hertfordshire also high up on the list.[17] We might reasonably speculate that, granted some skill in draughtsmanship (and Defoe's handwriting is exceptionally neat), he could have run off such maps himself without too much trouble.

The Transport System

In Wrigley's model, we find categories such as agricultural change – a topic on which Defoe had less expertise than on trade, especially, and manufacturing, but which he does highlight in many places, as for example when he discusses sheep husbandry, something with obvious relevance to the clothing trade he knew so well. But the category which stands out for a reader of the *Tour* is that relating to 'the creation of a better transport system to reduce the cost of moving goods from place to place; to make it possible for goods to move freely at all seasons of the year'.[18] Few had fuller experience than Defoe about the rigours of eighteenth-century travel, and his book describes the scorching reflections that blinded a weary summertime traveller on the ridge called the Hog's Back in Surrey, along with the deep mud through which carts sank like stricken boats in Sussex each winter. He gives us the perils of crossing the high Pennines in a snowstorm, and (although this is most likely pure invention) the hazards of negotiating a route past the towering precipices of Penmaenmawr on the coast of North Wales. The *Tour* actualises the experience of travel. This makes for a sharp distinction from Macky and his breed, since they simply list successive towns and appear to be magically wafted from one stopping-place to another. Defoe's method here owes much to his invention of separate 'circuits', closed systems which yet form a coherent pattern, radiating out from London and Edinburgh respectively in the English and Scottish sections.

As with the course of industry and agriculture, the full transport revolution had barely started in Defoe's time. Canals lay over the horizon, and railways would not start to sweep across the land for another hundred years. Even in the case of roads, the most important technological advances came with the road-surfacing and bridge-building methods of John McAdam, John Smeaton and Thomas Telford later in the century. But the first whiff of change was in the air, and Defoe had the most sensitive nostrils to pick up this scent. He saw that better transport was the key not just to improvements in trade, but also to the creation of a more united kingdom. Indeed, the modern double sense of 'communications', with a kind of pun on two meanings (transportation/personal interaction) could have been invented to explain the underlying message of the *Tour*, with its constant emphasis on the interdependence of different regions, cities, trades and employments. At this date transport of heavy goods by water was far cheaper than land-carriage, often by a factor of three or four. Before the canals emerged, this situation placed great responsibility on natural water systems, and Defoe was quick to spot the importance of the 'navigation' acts, which enabled communities to open up links to other parts of the country, both close at hand and distant. It will suffice to cite just one example, since Defoe's first impulse when he comes to a river is always to assess its potential for navigation:

> The *Trent* is navigable by Ships of good Burthen as high as *Gainsborough*, which is near 40 Miles from the *Humber* by the River. The Barges without the Help of Locks or Stops go as high as *Nottingham*, and farther by the Help of Art, to *Burton* upon *Trent* in *Staffordshire*... .This, and the Navigation lately, reaching up to *Burton* and up the *Derwent* to *Derby*, is a great Support to, and Encrease of the Trade of those Counties which border upon it, especially for the Cheese Trade from *Cheshire* and *Warwickshire*, which have otherwise no Navigation but about from West *Chester* to *London*; whereas by this River it is brought by Water to *Hull*, and from thence to all the South and North Coasts on the East Side of *Britain* ... especially in Time of the late War, when the Seas on the other Side of *England* were too dangerous to bring it by long-Sea. (3: 14–15)

We see from this account how local measures could have regional and even national consequences. All the river improvements mentioned here had happened quite recently, and the Derwent navigation act had been passed only in 1719.

These facts enable us to scotch a persistent canard, to the effect that Defoe had got all his preparatory work out of the way years before he wrote the *Tour*. In reality, the book is commendably up to the minute on a range of topics, and nowhere more so than in the case of matters relating to transport. In one section this sense of contemporaneity rises almost to the quality of visionary insight. It comes in the famous appendix to the second volume, devoted almost entirely to the state of the English roads and to the major hope for a better future, that is the new system of turnpikes, discussed more fully in Chapter 10. These devices took the responsibility for maintenance of major highways from the antiquated and inefficient mechanism in use (unpaid labour by a gang of reluctant locals at long intervals) in favour of new trusts, operating to make a profit from the tolls charged but discreetly monitored by the presence of men like justices of the peace among the trustees. Though one or two isolated turnpikes had been set up earlier, the trend only gathered momentum in the second decade of the eighteenth century, with a rapid acceleration in the 1720s. The instances cited by Defoe include one pioneering venture in 1696, and a number of trusts which had sprung up in the ten years prior to the appearance of the *Tour*.

What is just as striking as the freshness of Defoe's information is the clarity with which he envisions the issues at stake. Overwhelmingly, these early projects were carried out along the major trunk roads leading out of London, and it was only gradually that the network spread to the minor routes scattered round the provinces. This fact suits Defoe's purposes, in emphasising the crucial position of the capital in the business of the nation. He also points out that these improvements themselves constituted 'an infinite Improvement to the Towns near *London*, in the Convenience of coming to them, which make Citizens flock out in greater Number than ever to take Lodgings and Country Houses'. Such were the advantages now that 'such Tolls are erected now on very Side of *London*, or soon will be', but he did not doubt that 'in Time it will be the like all over *England*' (2: 243).

On the turnpikes, Paul Langford has observed that 'Defoe was excited by their galvanizing effect.'[19] The writing in this appendix does indeed have an extraordinary energy, whether Defoe is lamenting the sad state of the old road system or greeting the arrival of the new promised land, fed and watered the revolutionary changes he saw in progress. Thus, he deplores the condition of the road from London to the West Midlands:

> Suppose you take the other *Northern* Road, namely, by St. *Albans*, *Dunstable*, *Hockley*, *Newport Pagnel*, *Northampton*, *Leicester*, and *Nottingham*, or *Darby*: On this Road . . . you enter the deep Clays, which are so surprisingly soft, that it is perfectly frightful to Travellers, and it has been the Wonder of Foreigners, how considering the great Number of Carriages which are continually passing with heavy Loads, those Ways have been made practicable; indeed the great Number of Horses every Year kill'd by the Excess of Labour in those heavy ways, has been such a heavy Charge to the Country, that new Building of Causeways, as the *Romans* did of old, seems to be a much easier Expence. (2: 234)

And now the prospect in store:

> Upon this great Road there are wonderful Improvements made and making, which no Traveller can miss the Observation of, especially if

> he knew the Condition these Ways were formerly in; nor can my Account of these Counties be perfect, without taking Notice of it; for certainly no publick Edifice, Alms-house, Hospital, or Nobleman's Palace, can be of equal Value to the Country with this, no nor more an Honour and Ornament to it. (2: 239)

This was quite a new way of measuring the state of the nation. Others had doubts concerning the value and profitability of turnpikes, but Defoe understood that most users would find tolls preferable to plunging into 'Sloughs and Holes' (2: 238). He saw, too, something we might miss, that better roads would facilitate not just speedier passage for passengers and goods vehicles, but also the driving of cattle and sheep over long distances, an essential part of the annual cycle in agriculture.

'Improvements made and making'. This phrase sums up Defoe's attitude to Britain, as a country in the process of rapid and mainly beneficent change. He did not get everything right, but he perceived as early as anyone that a more efficient transport network was vital to any advance in the commercial and manufacturing sphere, and by extension to wider possibilities for the national way of life. One of Wrigley's categories, we may recall, involved new habits of consumption. Defoe saw very clearly the role which markets play in economic activity, and the need to encourage consumers to find producers, and producers to satisfy consumers. He hymned the traditional activity at Stourbridge Fair near Cambridge, but he also described with a hint of reserve the new leisure resorts and spas such as Bath and Bury St Edmunds, with their opportunities for conspicuous consumption: 'I left *Tunbridge*,' he records drily, 'for the same Reason that I give, why others should leave it, when they are in my Condition; namely, that I found my Money almost gone' (1: 166).

Forging the Nation

Humour is one of the key ingredients in the book, expressing Defoe's amused and frequently sceptical take on the world he saw around him. But at other moments the work attains a plangent and even tragic tone, notably in his threnody for the losses suffered by some great mercantile figures as a result of the South Sea Bubble, just four years distant when he wrote:

> I shall cover over as much as possible the melancholy part of a Story, which touches too sensibly, many, if not most of the Great and Flourishing Families in *England*: Pity and matter of Grief is it to think that Families, by Estate, able to appear in such a Glorious Posture as this, should ever be Vulnerable by so mean a Disaster as that of Stock-Jobbing: But the *General*

> *Infatuation of the Day* is a Plea for it; so that Men are not now blamed on that Account: and if my Lord *Castlemain* was Wounded by that Arrow shot in the Dark, 'twas a Misfortune. (1: 131)[20]

This passage will be discussed more fully in Chapter 7 as it relates to the Bubble: it is cited here to illustrate one of the more profound reflections in the text. The 'Story' recurs as a main thread in the plot of the book, as it represents a perilous moment when the march of Britain towards peace and plenty nearly hit a sudden roadblock. One other recent event had similarly jangled the alarm bells, but the Jacobite rising of 1715–16 was still too delicate a subject to be met head on. A more detailed analysis of this subject follows in Chapter 6. Instead, the author generally tiptoes around the episode, except where he comes to the site of a major encounter such as Preston, scene of 'the late bloody Action with the Northern Rebels' (3: 135). In his Scottish sections, he is forced to acknowledge the existence of Jacobites and their fate. But he nearly always chooses to write without undue edge or emphasis: thus, the Duke of Gordon 'has been embroil'd a little in the late unhappy Affair of the *Pretender*; but he got off without a Forfeiture, as he prudently kept himself at a Distance from them till he might see the Effect of Things' (3: 264).

For the most part, Defoe provides adequate coverage of lowland Scotland, though never quite as convincingly as in the south and west of England. His lack of first-hand knowledge of the Highlands shows up clearly: but then the mountains and glens had not yet really been brought under the remit of the Hanoverian government, despite the Union of parliaments in 1707. (And Wales is given almost as sketchy a treatment). In that earlier phase of his life, Defoe had been employed as an agent for Godolphin and Harley, nominally as 'a person employed for the Queen's service in Scotland for the revenue, etc.', but really to promote the Union. He strongly supported the measure, but recognised that it could only achieve success with the willing consent of the Scottish people. The terms certainly satisfied the needs of the political class in the Lowlands, where Defoe was operating. In addition, he insisted that Scotland needed to develop its economy along the lines England had followed, so as to introduce improvements in trade, manufacturing, shipping, fishery and agriculture.

Already, Defoe had explored these issues in the pamphlets that he wrote during the time he spent in Edinburgh between 1706 and 1712; but he returned to them with fresh energy in the *Tour*. At Glasgow he sets out the ways in which the Scottish export trade could be boosted, despite the fact that it had been held back by the absence of profitable trade with the colonies, especially America (3: 201–4). On the coast of Fife he takes up a different aspect of the problem, and recommends that more of Scottish production should be applied to consumption at home:

> I know ... that *Scotland* is now established in a lasting Tranquillity; the Wars between Nations are at an End, the Wastings and Plunderings, the Ravages and Blood are all over; the Lands in *Scotland* will now be improv'd, their Estates doubled. The Charges of defending her Abroad and at Home lies upon *England*; the Taxes are easy and ascertain'd, and the *West-India* Trade abundantly pours in Wealth upon her; and this is all true; and, in the End, I am still of Opinion Scotland will be Gainer.

The answer is simple:

> I must add, that her own Nobility, would they be true Patriots, should then out their helping Hand to the rising Advantages of their own Country, and spend some of the large Sums they get in *England* in applying to the Improvement of their Country, creating Manufactures, employing the Poor, and propagating the Trade at Home, which they may see plainly has made their united Neighbours of *England* so rich. (3: 237–8)

Nationhood is a fragile thing, so that the creation of a truly united kingdom took several generations and never attained a perfect state. As Linda Colley has shown, many decades passed before Scotland was properly integrated into a single commonwealth, and it retained distinctive religious, educational and legal structures.[21] But at the start of the process, one prerequisite for the Union to gain acceptance (passive at least) was a clear argument on its behalf, setting out the political objectives, the economic potentiality, and the cultural benefits which might accrue. Defoe did as much as anyone to carry out this public relations exercise, and he was still promoting the agenda in his *Tour*, more than a decade after the Union came into being. In fact the case gains much greater strength in 1726: partly because he could already point to hopeful signs that the programme had begun to work, and partly because he was able to argue the case in detail with reference to particular places and trades he had encountered on his supposed journey. Above all, the instructive contrast with English experience builds up over the course of the narrative. A truly united 'whole island of Great Britain' will only emerge when the parts cohere, in a way that the design of the *Tour* brings them together as a single organic unit.

For an important analysis of the *Tour* under this aspect, we turn to the work of Betty A. Schellenberg.[22] Her basic claim is that the *Tour* attempts to portray a constructed nation, which is 'as much a reflection of Defoe's need to impose some organizing principle upon the chaotic detail of his (and his readers') experience of Britain as it is a confident "Whig" departure from traditional ordering structures'. Enlisting theoretical insights from writers such as Benedict Anderson and Homi K. Bhabha, she detects four governing models within the work, 'the nation as aestheticized landscape, the nation as body, the nation as centred circle, and the nation as network'. For our purposes, the last two of these are the most relevant. She argues that 'Defoe's concern with internal coherence is evident as well in the care with which he pushes borders beyond what is English to what is British in the aftermath of the 1707 Act of Union.' This creates a difficulty because 'Defoe's neatly temporal means of assimilating the other is apparently unable to control the destabilizing fact that the Union has made of Scotland a hinterland of London'. It follows that 'England and Scotland never quite become Britain, because Scotland has not succeeded in becoming England; or, in other words, because Defoe's image of "Britain" is in fact one of England.' This analysis reads to the conclusion that, 'Although Defoe earnestly recommends to readers his vision of "a Nation, pushing and improving," these raw edges and unruly images remain. . . . Ironically, then, the public participation that Defoe invites in imagining Great Britain leads in fact to the dissolution of his vision.'

This is one of the most searching discussions of the *Tour* to have appeared so far. In my view it exaggerates the rhetorical problems that the text displays, and overstates the 'dissolution' of the underlying vision. There is something close to circular about Schellenberg's argument that the construction of the nation reflects a need to impose an organising principle upon recalcitrant material: it would not be constructing a nation if there were no such organisation. Much of the textual detail is anything but chaotic, having been chosen and set out with careful attention to its place in the whole (to take just one instance, the way that the appendix on the highway system ties together disparate experiences that have presented as the narrator journeys along the roads). Equally, the case with regard to Scotland would be more convincing if Defoe had ducked the issues, but on the contrary Letters 11–13 repeatedly stress the need for Scotland to take up improvement in a serious way, that is to become fully integrated within the united kingdom. Far from seeing it as a mere hinterland of London, he urges the Scots to embrace their destiny, cultivate their strengths and develop their *own* resources as England had done (see for example 3: 148–9; 157–8; 190–93; 234–8). Defoe is clear that Glasgow has been doing just what he recommends, and that there is great potential for the surrounding region to outdo London, Bristol and Liverpool in some areas of trade (3: 202–3). Again, the work has acknowledged from page 1 the necessity of taking in Scotland, and the separate Introduction to these last three letters (147–9) recognises its independent situation even after the Union. Finally, Schellenberg's discussion neglects the many balanced, repeated and interlocking parts that operate throughout the entire work to provide a unifying force. The *Tour* is not primarily defining England against Scotland: if there is a shadowy other present, this would be the Catholic nations of Europe, or in some cases the Dutch, as these are the only powers able to challenge Britain's hegemony in the world.

A reading with some similar features but one that takes a more radical course is that of Trevor Speller. He argues that 'Defoe portrays plenty of spaces in the nation that need to be brought under forcible, rational control. A nation whose pockets of irrationality may at any time flare up and threaten rational political life is far less communal than anything [Benedict] Anderson suggests.' This is because 'Great Britain is a landscape of political struggle, an island that must enclose and suppress various forms of irrationality, whether philosophical, political, religious, or otherwise. These pockets of irrationality are not just limited to inhabitants; they are deeply rooted in the traditions, histories, and even the topography of the landscape.' More specifically, the argument stresses 'moments when Defoe's book makes excurses into narrative or history, when it escapes the stylistic homogeneity of mere present-centered description, and when disorder develops into anomaly, violence, and irrationality.' Speller concludes that, 'If irrationality bubbles up in certain territories, it is often at the same moment when Defoe's narrative bubbles up in excurses, or differences in genre. After all, in these moments of heterogeneity, Defoe is writing the landscape in novel ways, inscribing its relationship to reason and questioning his own sense of a new national order.'[23] As with Schellenberg, the discussion seems to lay undue emphasis on a deliberate selection of marginal and atypical portions of the text, neglecting hundreds of pages where 'the new national order' is confidently proclaimed and illustrated. The violence that has to be contained is much less pervasive in the *Tour* than a reader of this article would suppose. Nor do the admitted shifts in the manner of narration ever seem to constitute differences in *genre*, precisely.

Some oddities are apparent in what Speller writes. For one thing, though he discusses editions of the work, he completely overlooks McVeagh's now standard edition of 2001, which supplies information that might qualify his case. He is almost alone among commentators in finding the interpolated narrative of the siege of Colchester in Letter 1 as an integral and even crucial part of the overall drift of the book. This is in defiance of several facts: (1) it is the only extended passage in the entire *Tour* dealing with purely historical material; (2) it is the only long section contributed by a third person ('so good a Hand'), unidentified but very unlikely to be Defoe himself; (3) it is the only bit of the work with its own map; (4) it is never referred to elsewhere in the three volumes, nor does it establish cross-references to persons or places mentioned later, other than two very brief allusions – less than a sentence each – to General Fairfax in Letters 8 and 9; and (5) the narrative makes a sudden interruption, mid-paragraph, into an ongoing description of Colchester, which reads smoothly enough if the entire block is removed, as happened in all subsequent eighteenth-century editions. Speller also makes much of the proposed scheme to settle the poor Palatines, set against the chaos of London, marked by 'The monstrosity of the metropolis's uncontrolled sprawl';[24] but he fails to observe the restorative projects for the city described in Letter 5, notably '*A Scheme for a* Royal Palace *in the Place of* White-Hall'. by an author Defoe claims to have known, and running to almost 3,000 words – longer and far more detailed than the proposal for Palatines. In fairness it should be added that Speller makes a number of perceptive observations on the *Tour*, even if his view of the work differs sharply from the one outlined in this book.

Conclusion

Half a century ago, the introduction to my abridged edition of the *Tour* ended with what then seemed daring words: 'Out of this picture of *grandeur et décadence* there emerges not just a mirror of Britain, as the older writers put it, but a vision of nationhood.' Since that time, other writers have used similar phraseology: for example, Peter Borsay has said that 'the *Tour* is not so much a travelogue as an anatomy (even a vision) of the nation'.[25] As we have just seen, Betty A. Schellenberg has recourse to the expression. The work is available on a website devoted to 'A Vision of Britain through Time'.

What the book was intent on creating had to do with something less than nationalism in the later sense. Nationalism 'becomes pervasive and dominant only under certain social conditions, which in fact prevail in the modern world, and nowhere else'.[26] Defoe's patriotism took the form of espousing an aggressive overseas trade policy, but he saw international trade as a mutually beneficial activity rather than an out-and-out struggle to the death, or war by other means. Internally, he wanted to see Scotland properly integrated into the Union. He saw Britain evolving into a great world power, not just by military strength but by economic expansion. Trade, radiating out from its great power-house in London, would harness natural resources and, along with agriculture, take advantage of improvements devised by the innovating spirit of the people. As he made his way round the country, his report fell short of accuracy in every detail, and not all his predictions came true. But history has abundantly shown that he was more often right than wrong. The author dipped his toes into the sea at the extreme corners of the nation, and the book left its own footprint on the English imagination.

CHAPTER 2

Embedding and Embodying the Nation

Textual Practices in the Tour

Many people are familiar today with the work of Gérard Genette (1930–2018), and specifically here his book *Seuils* (1987, English translation as *Paratexts*, 1997), the foundational document in the modern study of paratextual elements in literature. Of course, previous scholars had devoted attention to topics such as the eighteenth-century title-page. What was new about *Seuils* lay in its greater theoretical clarity, as well as the comprehensive manner in which it treats a variety of techniques. At the same time a new body of work has arisen, concentrating on heteroglossia and polyphonic effects, inspired largely by the belated discovery in the West of the ideas of Mikhail Bakhtin. As far as Defoe's *Tour* is concerned, this line of thinking applies chiefly to his appropriation of material from a wide range of literary and non-literary sources, resulting in a mosaic of disparate voices within the text.

It might seem that the book is fundamentally a compilation and thus unsuitable for analysis in the terms used by Genette. The critic focuses chiefly, though not exclusively, on 'imaginative' literature; and he instances principally single-author, single-volume, single-text works. This means that he does not often instance multi-volume works, with the obvious exception of Proust, and he passes over the version of epitext which is exemplified by sequels and continuations. Further, his scheme is not designed to handle miscellaneous works or olios, such as Tonson's *Miscellanies* or Dodsley's *Collection*. Nor would it easily accommodate the collected works of Swift or the complete poems of Wordsworth, stretching over a number of volumes. But these facts can be misleading. The *Tour* does finally amount to an organic whole, even though it occupies three volumes split into thirteen separate 'letters', along with a number of peripherals. We can, in fact, apply Genette's model with a number of adjustments. Thus, the title-pages of the second and third volumes are best regarded as repeated elements, despite the fact that they obviously include minor alterations in wording and even changes in the list of booksellers involved. They do not really operate as 'intertitles', by which Genette means names that designate internal sections such as chapters and parts.[1] Rather, they serve to reinforce the message of the original title-page, modifying details in a spirit of *mutatis mutandis*. Equally, the *Tour* does constitute a single-author work, although it enlists a large array of borrowed voices to bulk out the coverage.

This chapter aims to explore certain formal devices used by Defoe to shape his work. In terms of the typology invented by Genette, some of these practices come within the branch of paratext that he names peritextual, for example title-pages, intertitles, prefaces and indexes. Some might better be characterised as *textual augmentations*, for example cuts, diagrams, tables and lists incorporated into the narrative. Some we might call *embedded* forms, for example citations from existing sources (manuscripts, reference works, antiquarian sources). By this term I have in mind not merely material planted in the text, but those instances which are in some way foregrounded, especially when the author indicates them as other than the main narrative by graphic or typographic arrangement on the page. We might describe further cases as utilising *embodied* form, for example the placing of geographical locations in textually significant locations (Land's End at the end of a structural unit – one of the 'letters' which make up the overall plan). In deploying these narratological techniques, the practice sometimes recalls earlier work by Defoe, as for example when it enlists a little of the heteroglossic form of *The Storm* (1704), with its wide range of witnesses.[2]

This chapter attempts to identify a few of these disparate practices in the *Tour*. It concentrates chiefly on the earlier portions of the work, where the method is established, and devoting proportionately less space to the narrative as it proceeds. The main emphasis lies not on theory as such, but on the ways in which they are used to create a textual version of reality, projecting the nation as a coherent yet extremely varied entity.

The Title-page

Defoe's *Tour* stands out as one of the first guide-books in English with an enduring literary interest. It occupies a place in travel literature between the popular autobiographic narratives of travellers and straight geographic descriptions. In addition, the text contains other transgeneric features – for example, it fulfils a reference function in places, and secretes information taken from manuals such as *The Present State of England* by Guy Miège, which had reached five editions by 1723, and John Chamberlayne's

Magnæ Britanniæ Notitia, whose version in that same year claimed to be 'The seven and twentieth edition of the south part, call'd England; and the sixth of the north part, call'd Scotland'.

Nobody believes any more – if they ever did – that Defoe made an extensive trip around Britain specially in preparation for his *Tour*. The evidence shows that he cobbled together impressions of various journeys undertaken over a number of years. Beyond that, much of his text, covering areas of the nation he had never penetrated, was based on a medley of blind assumptions, guesses and naked thefts from earlier writers. His book composes a virtual tour, one that derives from his brain and imagination as much as it proceeds from any recent leg-work on an extensive scale – though Defoe did have fresh first-hand material to exploit on East Anglia, suitably put to use in the first stage of his peregrination, as well as observations made on other trips around the south-eastern counties (for example, those recorded in *The Commentator* in 1720).

The word *Tour* operates first as a kind of marker, what Genette calls 'the genre indication'.[3] But it was an inspired choice. Its overtones lack the single-minded directional quality of a *journey*, which usually implies that the traveller aims at a given point, so as to get somewhere different from where he or she started. Thus we tend to speak of a journey *to* Istanbul, but a tour *of* or *round* Turkey. Circularity, as we shall see, forms a key element of the rhetorical design of the book; and Defoe sets this up in the very first noun in his title, but immediately proceeds to the prepositional phrase 'thro' the whole island of Great Britain'. *Through* gives a stronger sense of covering every base than the more easy-going term *(a)round* would do. The remainder of the phrase carries a deliberate redundancy: it denominates Great Britain, the political entity recently cemented by the Union of parliaments in 1707, but the words *whole island* emphasise a geographical entity, the mass of the British mainland.

Here we immediately encounter a departure from the methods of John Macky, Defoe's most direct model and competitor. We recall that Macky published the first volume of his *Journey* in 1714, covering the southern counties along with London. Although the three-volume layout was heralded in the dedication to this volume, nothing more happened for several years. It was not until May 1722 that the second volume appeared, still labelled a *Journey through England*, with a remark in the Preface that a third instalment was in preparation, devoted to Scotland and Ireland. (A second edition of the first part was issued by a different publisher in the same year.) By the end of this book Macky's itinerary had notionally reached Carlisle on the Scottish border; but he was diverted at this stage by a side-trip to the

Isle of Man (not covered by Defoe), and then a final chapter on the 'Excrescences of *England*', with a singularly awkward apology for areas he had omitted in the earlier text. These make up a bizarre geographic combination of the south-western peninsula, including all of Cornwall; the Isle of Wight off the Channel coast, very briefly; and right across the country in East Anglia the region of the Fens – see further Chapter 4, pp. 89–90. After this comes a discussion of the various ranks in society. All this points to a ramshackle, improvisational quality in Macky's work. When Volume I appeared in a second augmented edition dated 1724, all these features remained in place. This was despite the fact that a third instalment, entitled *A Journey through Scotland*, had come out with an imprint dated 1723.[4] Thus the promise of a third volume as imminent can still be found in the preface to Volume II, a year after its successor had found its way into print.[5] But the treatment of Ireland which the statement also promised had been quietly shelved when Volume III made its appearance. Through all these various incarnations, the title never presented the work as a unified survey of the entire British landmass.

It is plain that when Macky embarked on the first volume he had only a hazy idea of what was to follow. Crucially, he does not stress the Scottish volume at the outset, giving it a brief mention at the end of his lengthy dedication. Perhaps, as a transplanted Scot he thought it prudent to downplay this information. By contrast Defoe blazons his intentions on the original title-page. The second and third volumes did not emerge as optional sequels, *Tour 2* and *Tour 3*, even though they were published (and partly written) in the next two years. In fact, Defoe's use of updating prefaces and appendices reflects his expressed desire to keep abreast of the most recent developments in a nation that he portrays as undergoing a dynamic process of flux. He states this much near the end of his preface to Volume I, probably written around April 1724:

> Even while the Sheets are in the Press, new Beauties appear in several Places, and almost to every Part we are oblig'd to add Appendixes, and Supplemental Accounts of fine Houses, new Undertakings, Buildings, *&c.*, and thus Posterity will be continually adding; every Age will find an Increase of Glory. (1: 49)

Defoe employs an urgent-looking present tense ('Sheets are still in the Press') to augment the feeling both of rapid change in the objective world outside and of quick response within the text. We can see how elements that might be regarded as clumsy add-on features, like the supplements, are flaunted as guarantees of the book's authenticity and its closeness to what is currently happening in Britain. For Jacques Derrida, supplementarity was closely linked to the process of invagination, whereby some originary 'lack' was filled by an added element. In one way this is what the *Tour* does: Defoe's account is by definition always falling behind its appointed task, and the 'Appendixes, and Supplemental Accounts' serve to make complete something that is constantly opened up by fissures caused by new developments. What constitutes the absence here is the most immediately topical information, and the supplement exists to plug this gap.

We need to return to the title-page. The full title tells us that the tour will be 'Divided into Circuits or Journeys', an indication of the formal arrangement to come, and stressing the home-and-back basis of the supposed trip. Then comes a list of five categories of material, each 'curious, and worth Observation'. By this means the opening announcement, descriptive and denotative rather than allusive or argumentative, sets up a Baconian objective of empirical enquiry. These itemised contents are garnished with 'Useful Observations upon the Whole', another supplementary task, and stated to be 'particularly fitted for the Reading of such as desire to Travel over the Island', further emphasising the scope of coverage. Genette writes of one major purpose of the title-page: 'the function of tempting, of inciting one to purchase and/or read, is both so obvious and so elusive that it hardly prompts me to comment.'[6] The word *elusive* may apply to most modern books, especially novels and volumes of poetry, which tend to be diffident in proclaiming their own merits. In many historical texts, this was not the case. Newspaper advertisements regularly carried exactly the same information, and often in the very same words, that the book carried at its opening. Thus the ads for the *Tour* which appeared at the time of publication, for example in the *Daily Journal* on 21 May and the *Evening Post* and *Post Boy* on 23 May 1724, do no more and no less than reproduce the entire title page word-for-word, give or take a few tiny changes in accidentals along with the omission of the year from the imprint. The only addition comes at the end: 'N.B. A small number are Printed on Royal Paper for the Curious. Price 10*s*.' Plainly the title-page operates as another public notice, or advertising carried out by other means. In Genette's vocabulary, a peritextual element is echoed precisely by an epitextual element.

After this, the long title as it were, comes the authorial statement 'By a Gentleman', marked off for emphasis within rules. This was a formula retained right through to the sixth edition of 1761. In the seventh edition of 1769, the byline was changed: 'Originally begun by the celebrated Daniel De Foe, continued by the late Mr. Richardson, Author of *Clarissa,* and brought down to the present Time by a Gentleman of Eminence in the Literary World'. Even then the publishers were reluctant to forgo the claim of gentility. Within the text, Defoe remains an unspecified narrator. He does not create a persona, if we limit the term, as we should, to invented authors where there is a rhetorically significant gap between the real and assumed first-person voice. The *Tour* employs a first-person narrator for convenience, immediacy of presentation and creation of a consistent viewpoint. In a few places, as we shall see, Defoe has recourse to personal memory. But there is no attempt to give this voice any special inflection. We may assume that the writer has enough money to get around the country, and that he was comfortably enough off to have wasted some of his money gambling at Tunbridge Wells (1: 166). But we are not invited to debate whether he is like or unlike the historic Daniel Defoe, or whether his version of Britain is in any way partial or tendentious.

Finally, the imprint. This gives the names of six London booksellers, headed by George Strahan. They are listed in the less common form of presentation, with a separate line for each individual – more often, the names follow in sequence across a number of lines. Second on the list comes William Mears, who promoted the venture more actively in the press than any of his colleagues. This fact need not occasion surprise: Mears was a regular collaborator with Edmund Curll at this juncture, and his marketing strategies frequently took an aggressive turn.

Prefatory Matters

The Preface to Volume I of the *Tour* has often been cited as a guide to Defoe's ideological imperatives when he undertook the work. He does indeed itemise many of the themes of the book: the growth and variety of the nation, novelty and antiquity, the changing face of 'this *great British Empire*', another allusion to the recently united kingdom. But, more to our present purposes, Defoe lays out at the same time the groundwork for the form of his book. 'In Travelling thro' *England*', he remarks, 'a Luxuriance of Objects presents it self to our View' (1: 47). He describes his elaborate preparations for the task ahead, including 'seventeen large Circuits, or Journeys . . . taken thro' divers Parts, separately. And three general Tours over almost the whole *English* Part of the Island', along with a long period spent living in Scotland, when he 'Travell'd critically over great Part of it' (1: 49). This introduction differs markedly from Macky's longer dedicatory piece 'to the Young Nobility and Gentry of Great-Britain'.[7] This points towards the assumed audience, and explains the emphasis in the *Journey* on seats of the aristocracy and higher gentry. Macky offers a hortatory essay in patriotic vein, laying emphasis on his own knowledge of continental Europe, as a basis of comparison with the liberty enjoyed in Britain. It reads like the preface to a conduct-book. He says far less than Defoe about the actual contents of his *Journey*, and his description of its progress leans heavily on honorific adjectives like 'instructive' and 'diverting' – Defoe uses these too, but he also attempts some objective account of what is in store for the reader.

Macky sets out his itinerary as a meandering saunter through the country, starting at the peripheral town of Yarmouth, simply because the boat that brought him from Holland was forced by the weather to divert from its intended port of arrival, Harwich. He then wanders through East Anglia and what are now called the Home Counties, before providing 'the fullest Account of *London* that ever was given', an absurdly exaggerated claim, needless to say.[8] He also promises that his second volume will contain a trip through Oxford and Blenheim to Bath, from where 'an Excursion will be made into *Cornwall* and *Wales*'. As we have already seen, the intended coverage of Cornwall was postponed to a coda, following the section on the Isle of Man – a sudden cross-country leap that would have taken at the very least five or six days to accomplish in reality, and probably much more. Picking up again from south-western England, Macky's supposed journey proceeds up the west coast up to about as far as Lancaster. He then begins again in the Midlands and moves northwards to the Peak District, then doubles back to cover the East Midlands and eventually up to Newcastle, across the line of Hadrian's Wall to Carlisle. The movement is stop-start and the transitions abrupt. On top of this, Macky's coverage has some startling omissions, including all of south and mid-Wales, including important towns like Cardiff; most of Somerset and Devon; Hertfordshire, Bedfordshire and the greater part of Buckinghamshire; virtually the whole of Lincolnshire, which, as noted, has to be brought in apologetically at the end along with Cornwall; and the entire Lakeland county of Westmorland. Among the casualties are such historic towns as Stratford-upon-Avon. More seriously, by zooming directly from Newark to York (a long day's ride) he omits the West Riding of Yorkshire, with significant centres of burgeoning industrialism such as Sheffield, Leeds and Halifax, each allotted considerable space by Defoe (see also Chapter 4, p. 90).[9]

Without going beyond Macky's prefatory material, we can sense that his *Journey*, whatever local interest it may offer, will not be guided by any overall conceptual scheme, other than the desire to 'visit' textually a number of famous or picturesque spots. By contrast Defoe has a clear plan, immediately put into operation when he begins his opening 'letter':

> I began my Travels, where I Purpose to End them, *viz.* At the City of *London*, and therefore my Account of the City itself will come last, that is to say at the latter End of my Southern Progress: and as in the Course of this Journey I shall have many Occasions to call it a Circuit, if not a Circle, so I chose to give it the Title of Circuits, in the Plural, because I do not pretend to have Travelled it all in One Journey, but in many, and some of them many times over. (1: 51)

The opening ten words refer both to the start and the end, in a manner that might recall the doubling back of modern literary works such as *Finnegans Wake* or John Shade's poem in *Pale Fire.* The 'Circle' turns out to resemble the classic emblem of a completed circuit, the *ouroboros* or serpent biting its own tail, symbolising 'a close cycle of development',[10] that is commonly invoked in narratological schemes. Plainly Defoe had decided on the overall shape of his work when he wrote this opening sentence, even though he certainly had not written most of the text to come. Simultaneously, the entire paragraph (I have elided just one supporting clause at the end) concerns two orders of signification: the curve the book will describe in its textual track, and the course that the author claims to have followed in his real-world journeys.

It is obviously no accident that Defoe mentions London as his stopping-off point right at the very beginning. The *Tour* is pervaded by an insistent sense of the centrality of the capital in the nation's life.[11] The author constantly emphasises 'the general Dependance of the whole Country upon the City of *London*' (1: 48), particularly but not exclusively in terms of the economy. As a way of expressing this role, Defoe places his main coverage of London at the conclusion of the southern counties. But since the city does not lie at the geographic midpoint of England (let alone of Great Britain), he can pass on to the northern counties and to Scotland in such a way as to leave this section at the tipping point of his second volume – exactly halfway through the entire work. By choosing to organise his *Tour* in this fashion, he enables the successive letters to reflect the primacy of the capital. The first two circuits both start and end in London. The third leaves from there, and the fourth makes a return journey. After Letter 5, devoted specifically to London, the sixth and seventh revert to the pattern of out-and-back just described. These letters complete the coverage of southern England, and they also complete the first two volumes. This leaves Volume III to deal with the counties north of the Trent, together with Scotland. But this arrangement brings with it far less of the feel of an appendage than Macky's add-on third volume, which even has a new title of its own. For one thing, Defoe uses the Anglo-Scottish border as a kind of textual boundary: Letters 9 and 10 end there, Letters 11 and 12 begin there.

Thus the text enacts space: but it also sets out a more coherent temporal scheme, in which the author pursues a logical and sequential movement across the nation. Macky often wafts mysteriously from one notable locality to another without seeming to touch the ground in between – as with the sudden transition from the Isle of Man to Cornwall, mentioned just now. By contrast Defoe usually spends a good deal of time on the intervening distance between major places of interest, dilating on roads, rivers, agriculture and much else. Here we might think back to Genette's earlier work in *Figures III* (1970), in which he set out a division in narrative between 'discourse time' and 'narrative time'. For example, he shows there how Proust occasionally allots many pages to events lasting only a short time, and a short span of pages to events which occupy a long duration in the world outside the text.[12] For his part Defoe takes pains in many instances to achieve a match between the pace of his account and the ground notionally covered on his trip. Thus, in his third letter, he will remark on the fact that the ocean was in view for several miles as he made his way south from Dorchester; or describe the many byroads which crisscross Salisbury Plain, and might lead the traveller (*read* author, potentially) astray, if it were not for the presence of so many shepherds to keep him on track (1: 243, 248–9). This method draws the textual rendition of travelling much closer to the real experience of going across the country than anything in Macky, since eighteenth-century journeys were of course slower and more laborious than anything with which we are familiar today. Sometimes Defoe re-imagines the wayfarer's discomforts for his readers, as on the Hog's Back in Surrey: 'This Hill being all Chalk, a Traveller feels the effect of it in a Hot Summer's Day, being scorch'd by the Reflection of the Sun from the Chalk, so as to make the Heat almost insupportable; and this I speak by my own Experience' (1: 182).

Elsewhere the book recreates a difficult passage of the snow-covered Pennine Hills, from Rochdale to Halifax across Blackstone Edge (3: 60–67). This leg of the journey, lasting about twelve miles, takes up about 3,000 words, dense with precise observation, even before we enter into the long account of Halifax itself (3: 67–72). The account recalls a section in Defoe's recent book *Memoirs of a Cavalier* (1720), chronicling an almost Alpine trek across the Pennines, involving hunger, fear and 'terrible Fatigue'.[13] Such episodes testify to the many weary days the writer had spent in the saddle during much of his life, but they probably also draw on his study of road-books . So *Britannia Depicta, or Ogilby Improv'd* (1720), by Emanuel Bowen and John Owen, would have shown him ominously steep crags engraved in lowering outlines over the road across Blackstone Edge; and equally the maps there register a confusing medley of side-roads branching off the route traversing Salisbury Plain.[14] When it reaches places like this, the narrative must edge forward to avoid potential sloughs of despond and hills of difficulty. Valleys sometimes promise humiliation, and mountains are virtually never delectable. All in all, the *Tour* conveys the experience of *travel*, and not just a succession of localities visited.

The clarity of the intellectual design of the *Tour* is manifested in the coherence of its formal arrangements. Compared with the progress of the *Journey*, where Macky does no more than follow his nose, the narrative exhibits what we could call embodied form.

Volume I

On the threshold of his book Defoe neatly segues from the paratextual to the fully textual, with a reference back to the argument of his preface: 'I set out, the 3d of *April*, 1722, going first Eastward, and took what I think, I may very honestly call a Circuit in the very Letter of it' (1: 51). He goes on to describe the various places he visited in Essex, Suffolk, Norfolk and (unmentioned) Cambridgeshire, ending his trip 'in *Middlesex*, near the Place where I began it, leaving the Middle or Center of the several Counties to some little Excursions, which I made by themselves'. In due course the letter will announce its own finishing point: 'By this Turn I came necessarily on to *Stratford*, where I set out: And thus having finished my first Circuit, I conclude my first Letter ...' (1: 132). We witness here the characteristic technique of embodying, when the narrative loops back on itself approaching London, just as the geography completes its own circle. By this stage we are out of Genette's range of vision, but the choice of putative 'letters' to an unnamed correspondent is of immediate concern here, as it does belong to the overall packaging of the contents. Macky had likewise addressed an offstage figure, notionally living abroad, designated simply by the vocative 'Sir'.

We might have anticipated that the opening letter would emerge as the densest in coverage and the most tightly organised. For one thing, it is the only letter tied to a specific date; and as it happens, this section describes the lone trip Defoe made out of London at this juncture, which can be documented with reasonable certainty. He had good reason to visit East Anglia at this juncture: in August 1722 he was granted a lease for a large tract of property owned by the corporation of Colchester, one of a number of legal agreements connected with his business dealings in this locality over the next year. Another sign of the attention he was giving to the eastern counties lies in the jaunt that the heroine undertakes in the latter sections of *Moll Flanders*, published in January 1722. Defoe probably journeyed to Bury St Edmunds in March of the same year, to cover the notorious trial of the barrister Arundel Coke, mentioned in the *Tour* (1: 94–5). In addition, he had known Ipswich since childhood (1: 86), and Harwich from 1690 at the latest. These circumstances would lead us to suppose that his intimacy with the region was greater than in any other portion of the *Tour*, London alone excepted. Yet we find something quite unexpected.

Very early on, in the very midst of his entry on Colchester, the author inserts a 'DIARY of the most remarkable passages' in the siege of the town in 1648, which he claims to have 'had from so good a Hand, as that I have no Reason to question its being a true Relation' (1: 62). Although it had proved impossible for scholars to identify the source with certainty, no one doubts that it is an authentic contemporary account that preserves information not available in any printed source. The engraved map of the siege, folded into the pages of the text, looks as if it dates from the time of Defoe, having been perhaps made from a sketch-plan drawn shortly after the event. What has to be in question is the suitability of including such a lengthy item at this point – it runs to more than 5,000 words. Disproportionate in scale, it introduces an alternative voice into the running description with no obvious rhetorical benefit. It causes little surprise to find that this portion was excised in subsequent versions of the *Tour*, even though the editing was usually quite limited and conservative as between one recension and another.[15] The decision to include the material would make a little more sense if this had been Defoe ventriloquising, as he had done in *Memoirs of a Cavalier*; but the diary here appears to be genuinely from another hand. As we shall see, this is not the only example of what Genette would call an 'allographic' insert, but it is the least well integrated into the body of the *Tour*. It interrupts, rather than complements, the main entry – and this, as we have noted, in the coverage of a town Defoe knew particularly well. It would not surprise us to find padding in the outlying parts of Wales and Scotland that he had never visited, but scarcely in a place less than sixty miles from London. It could be argued that a leading theme of the book concerns the physical remnants and psychic repercussions of the English Civil War, but this defence hardly seems adequate.

Not long afterwards another quite substantial passage embedded within the text (1: 84–5) involves the grant of Hatfield Forest supposedly made by Edward the Confessor to one of his favourites, a Norman named Ranulf Peverel. From a strict historical angle, the story is very hazy, but Defoe would not have cared, as he took the 'merry' verses describing the grant from his major antiquarian source, William Camden's *Britannia*, as edited by Edmund Gibson in 1695. (Typically, he states simply that he was able to 'find' the material 'in the antient Records'.) He then reprints Camden's text, with only tiny alterations, in one column, together with a modernised version alongside: 'Take my Explanations with it, for the sake of those who are not us'd to the antient English' (1: 84). Words set in columns invite divided attention, but here they also create simultaneity between the medieval and the present day. The insert performs at least three functions. It adds comedy, a regular ingredient in the *Tour*. It helps to establish the author as attentive to – even expert in – antiquarian lore, an essential selling point for such a book. Finally, it diversifies the prose with a prolonged passage of verse, admittedly no more than doggerel, to supply a more varied texture to the narrative. A similar function is served by the inclusion of an epitaph to Sir John Holt, set out centred on the page to resemble an actual memorial stone (1: 104). One of the tasks that the *Tour* performs is to display antiquarian information, usually derived from authorities like Camden and William Dugdale, and to foreground these interpolated passages by means of textual commentary. The best example occurs in Letter 4, where Defoe reprints a lengthy account of Glastonbury Abbey by Dugdale, and immediately afterwards quotes Camden's observations on the supposed grave of King Arthur in the Abbey. He then provides an engraving of the inscription on the coffin – an illustration lifted directly from *Britannia* (2: 26–9).

A noticeable feature of the method lies in the habit of tabulation. Defoe frequently incorporates lists, and these are sometimes made typographically visible by the use of indentation. Among examples that we could cite are the series of 'little Observations' offered concerning the Thames estuary near the start (1: 54–6); an indented note headed 'N.B.' shortly afterwards, stressing the way in which London draws in the produce of the entire nation (1: 57); a listing of the public edifices of Colchester (1: 79); an itemisation of the factors which make Bury St Edmunds a pleasant place to live (1: 91); a roster of the market towns in Suffolk and Norfolk (1: 105); and a table of the counties whose water-courses are fed from the Wash (1: 120). This habit extends throughout the *Tour*, sometimes more prominently than in this first letter. As Defoe describes how he passed out of Suffolk into the next county, a sub-heading 'Norfolk' in italicised capitals is centred within the text (1: 104): this device would not be repeated later on.

By far the most significant element of form, in respect of the *Tour*'s overall aim, comes at the end of this letter. It comprises a two-page appendix listing some recent developments which occurred 'while these Sheets were in the Press'. Genette does not give any real attention to appendices or indexes, understandably in view of the fact that he has chiefly imaginative literature in mind. (His method is such that he would regard epilogues and codas, so important a feature in nineteenth-century novels, as belonging to the text proper.) However, these constitute a vital part of many works of non-fiction. Genette does devote two brief paragraphs to the table of contents, late in his survey: French books, of course, normally place the contents page at the end of a volume.

As suggested earlier, the 'supplementary' features of the *Tour* have a crucial purpose to serve. The introductory remarks hint at this function: 'Whoever travels, as I do, over *England*, and writes the Account of his Observations, will, *as I noted before*, always leave something, altering or undertaking, by such a growing, improving Nation as this' (1: 133). Again we see in the opening clause a merging of travelling and writing. Defoe does not merely wish to have this up-to-date information within his text: it needs to be foregrounded as a last-minute *addition*, something that could not have been present at the time he embarked on his journey or his narrative. The appendix flaunts its own supplementarity, making a virtue of its formally dissevered condition. It conveys the subliminal message that the volume simply cannot pack in everything the writer wants to say without stretching its bounds, much as a computer needs to be capable of storing further information with the help of add-on memory. The dynamism of national growth requires a dynamic expanding text.

The second letter contains many of the embedded elements we have seen in its predecessor, such as lists and tabulations, along with verses and proverbs (supplying a more demotic accent to the text, and generally taken from Camden). The first long autobiographically inflected section occurs when Defoe corrects previous writers on the supposed passage of the River Mole underground near Box Hill in Surrey. His knowledge of the matter derives from first-hand experience, since he 'liv'd in the Neighbourhood several Years,' and he recounts an episode in 1676 to prove his point (1: 184–6). This is one of the relatively few parts of the book where the real Daniel Defoe stands up *in propria persona*, i.e. very precisely not as an invented persona but as an individual who witnessed specific events at a specific date in a specific place. In general, however, the second letter is the closest approximation to a standard 'literary' version of the traveller's tale in the *Tour.* It has few digressions and no graphic devices.

The third letter provides one major embedded section. This occurs when the narrative reaches the New Forest, and it is introduced as follows:

> I cannot omit to mention here a Proposal made a few Years ago to the late Lord Treasurer, *Godolphin,* for Re-peopling this Forest, which for some Reasons I can be more particular in, than any Man now left alive, because I had the Honour to Draw up the Scheme, and argue before that Noble Lord. (1: 232)

Defoe's idea was to resettle in this area a flood of Protestant refugees to England, who had fled from the Rhineland palatinates after their native region had been ravaged during the war of the Austrian Succession and its immediate sequel, the war of the Spanish Succession. In early 1709 a large number of Protestants left their homes and made their way up the Rhine to Holland. From there a first wave of some 5,000 poor Rhenish inhabitants made their way to England in May 1709, joined by an estimated further 8,000 by August. They were forced to live in squalid tent-cities on the edge of London. The government had no experience of mass immigration on this scale and cast about for answers. Defoe offered his proposal in the *Review* in the summer, but it seems to have been ignored. In November the government gave orders for the first batch of 3,000 refugees to be sent to New York, a prospect that alarmed the governor, Swift's friend Robert Hunter, as he had no adequate accommodation or provisions ready for such an influx. Many more of the group especially travelled to America in the succeeding decades. A high proportion made their way to southern Pennsylvania, where they formed the basis of the longlasting 'Pennsylvania Dutch' community.

The proposal that Defoe set out in the *Review* is taken over with few modifications into the *Tour* (1: 233–8). It involved the creation of a model town extending to 4,000 acres, split up into portions of land each allocated to twenty families, who would provide work for a large number of servants and tradesmen. Within a generation they would flourish, and in due course would become 'all *true born Englishmen*'. Such an idealistic project may look impractical, but the model of roads laid out in a grid pattern had some parallel in the design of Savannah when an equally high-minded scheme was launched to set up a home for outcasts in Georgia, less than a decade after the *Tour* came out. Within the text Defoe includes a sketch-plan of the new town. Literally the voice does not change at this point, but the author casts himself as a survivor from the past who can look back on events as they actually unrolled. He concludes his account with the words, 'More Money than would have done this [set up the scheme], was expended, or rather thrown away upon them here, to keep them in suspense, and afterwards starve them; send them a begging all over the Nation, and shipping them off to other Countries: Where the Blame lay, is none of my Business.' He adds, 'I reserv'd this Account for this Place, because I pass'd in this Journey over the very Spot where the Design was laid out, namely near *Lindhurst, in the Road from Rumsey* to *Limington*' (1: 238). He may never have gone anywhere near the Forest for years, but the textual needs of the *Tour* demanded that embedding took place at this precise juncture.

The index to Volume I first appeared at the end of Volume II, along with the one for the second instalment. Such an aid is integral to most guidebooks and its omission would have reduced the appeal of the book by breaking the normal generic rules. Defoe or his booksellers did, however, supply a list of errata. These are generally passed over in modern scholarship, since they appear to be dispensable items, to be jettisoned as soon as corrections are made in the text. But again their presence contributes to a sense of getting things straight, and revising in the heat of the moment, a feeling that the *Tour* wishes to induce in readers.

Volume II

The third and fourth letters together comprise journeys respectively from London to Land's End and then back to London. But the third has its own little entelechy, moving steadily towards the farthest extremity of southern England. Thus the main text of Volume I ends at an outermost point of the mainland, the most distant from the capital so far reached. There follows a brief set of addenda, concerning buildings currently under construction, 'which, however, not being finish'd, cannot now be fully described' (1: 278). As we have seen, at the opening of Volume II, Defoe engages in an elaborate ceremonial to mark his position:

> My last letter ended the Account of my Travels, where Nature ended her Account, when she meeted out the Island, and where she fix'd the utmost *Western* Bounds of *Britain*; and, being resolv'd to see the very Extremity of it, I set my Foot into the Sea, as it were, beyond the farthest Inch of dry Land *West*, as I had done before near the Town of *Dover*, at the Foot of the Rocks of the *South-Foreland* in *Kent*, which, I think, is the farthest Point East in

> a Line; And as I had done, also, at *Leostoff* in *Suffolk*, which is another Promontory on the *Eastern* Coast, and is reckon'd the farthest Land *Eastward* of the Island in general; Likewise I had used the same Ceremony at *Selsy* near *Chichester*, which I take to be the farthest Land *South* . . . so, in its Place, I shall give you an Account of the same Curiosity at *John a Grot*'s House in *Caithness*, the farthest Piece of Ground in *Great Britain*, North. (2: 9)

The book, then, resumes its account just as nature by implication resumes its own account: the writer makes his way back towards the capital, seemingly drawn by a magnetic force that impels his narration.

Within this fourth letter, the heavy load of material embedded in relation to Glastonbury Abbey has already been mentioned. A little later, Defoe marks his close absorption in the wool trade around Wiltshire and Somerset with an intensive bout of listing and itemization (2: 31–7). At the Civil War battle site of Roundway Down he incorporates a lengthy descriptive of the engagement by 'one of the most impartial Historians of those Times', so far unidentified (2: 38–9). Then, at Reading, the author launches into another prolonged passage of first-hand observation of events 'to which I was an Eye-Witness'. This concerns skirmishes between the army of James II and Dutch forces supporting the invasion of William of Orange in late 1688, and especially the behaviour of some Irish dragoons as they retreated from Maidenhead via Colnbrook to London. Here Defoe takes on the role of a special correspondent to history, seeking to augment the value and interest of his book by lacing his own experiences into an account of a major episode in the nation's recent past. Of course, such passages of personal recollection must be distinguished from excerpts from the writer's previous work, such as the one about the proposed settlement in the New Forest that we considered just now. The latter might be termed *autotext*, while simple autobiographic inserts could qualify as embedded first-person text.[16]

After this the narrative reaches Windsor at Eton. Defoe tries to diversify his story by further reminiscences of time spent at Windsor, but this part of the book is heavy with borrowed information. He states that he could give full details of the Order of the Garter, including its history and ceremonial, but 'this is done so fully in other Authors, and by so many, that it would be falling into that Errors, which I condemn in others, and making my Accounts be, what I resolved, from the Beginning, they should not be, namely, a Copy of other Men's Performances' (2: 57). The contorted syntax bespeaks some embarrassment, and understandably. Defoe goes on to say, 'I shall only give you out of Mr. *Ashmole*, a List of the first

Knights who had the Honour of this Order, and who have been succeeded by so many Kings, Dukes, and Sovereign Princes Abroad, as well as Noble-Men, and Peers of this Kingdom at home.' Under this cover, the narration leaps into a series of practised raids on Elias Ashmole's *Institution, Laws, and Ceremonies of the Order of the Garter* (1672) – probably in the expanded edition of 1715. Defoe disperses throughout his extensive coverage a list of the original knights, one of the foreign monarchs and emperors admitted, and one of the current knights. By this simple means he was able to satisfy the hunger for antiquarian lore and at the same time provide up-to-date facts on the present-day ruling class. It is all copied from Ashmole, apart from the final list, which could have been cut and pasted from a more recent source (neither Chamberlayne nor Miège was up to speed here in his latest edition). In any case, the degree to which the *Tour* is composed of creative plagiarism is well known, and we are concerned in this chapter neither with the literary politics of such action nor with the identification of all the particular sources. The concluding paragraphs of this letter concern Eton College, and tabulate in turn the foundation and rules of the school, followed by a list of the present fellows and masters. This flurry of information brings the text to the threshold of London, the lodestone of the entire text.

As a born and bred Londoner, Defoe should have had no trouble in finding apposite things to say about his hometown, however pushed he may have been to bulk out the material when he found himself obliged to give an account of the wilds of Montgomeryshire. As with the inset narrative at Colchester, this is not altogether the way things go, with a great deal of contributed material folded into the text. The author begins with a remarkable sequence in which he beats the bounds of the city, in the form of 'A Line of Measurement, drawn about all the continued Buildings of the City of London, and Parts adjacent, including *Westminster* and *Southwark, &c.*' This follows the course of built-up London, district by district and street by street, over a span of nearly eighteen miles. A column on the right side of the page gives a tally of the distance covered on each leg of the itinerary, measured in miles, furlongs and rods, so that we can plot the exact location within about five yards – good enough for a modern GPS system. The grand total is added up at the end, between short type-rules, with the meticulous care of an accountant. Self-evidently, this section enacts with dramatic clarity the precision and immediacy of Defoe's grasp on his subject-matter.

After itemizing ten constitutive areas of the capital, including the city and liberties of London, Westminster, Tower Hamlets, Southwark and Deptford, the author launches into 'A Brief Description of the New

Buildings erected in and about the Cities of *London* and *Westminster* and Borough of *Southwark*, since the Year 1666' (2: 74–9). It is not particularly brief, but it does show Defoe's lifelong interest in the changing face of London, and his keen eye for detail. We see the main authorial intrusion in these two sections at the head of the letter, one organised in tabular form, the other in continuous prose (although broken by several lists). After this, the coverage is dominated by catalogues, whether of buildings, markets, docks, water supplies, statues, bars, gaols, palaces, public authorities, hospitals and much more. This information comes largely from existing sources, though Defoe adds his own tart comments in places. Overall this lends the text something of the air of a guide-book, or a reference work like *Whitaker's Almanac* and *Information Please*. There is one long insert, 'A Scheme for a *Royal Palace* in the Place of *White-Hall*,' occupying several pages (2: 103–8). Defoe claims that he 'once saw a Model' for the rebuilt palace,' and knows its author – possibly Cavendish Weedon (d. *c.*1708), a barrister of Lincoln's Inn. So the narrator vouches for the authenticity of the voice entering the text.

The sixth and seventh letters, describing a circuit from London to North Wales, exhibit a similar range of devices. In this part of the *Tour* it is apparent that the further the narrative gets from home-base, the more it is dependent on earlier sources. Defoe pads out his account with citations from Camden and Browne Willis' works on cathedrals, as well as some ingenious guesswork based on his study of maps of Wales. At Chester he pauses, giving time for a short resumptive passage on the principality. Then in the seventh letter the *Tour* embarks on a long, loopy circuit covering a large tract of the English Midlands before returning to the capital. This leaves us back where we started, just as the volume is poised to end. But as well as an index we have one further element in store, and this is perhaps the most striking part of the entire work. It consists of an appendix supplying updated information, initially with regard to Bristol, and then for most of its remaining pages focuses on the road network, with a famous account of the developing turnpike system. No passage Defoe wrote has been more frequently cited or excerpted by historians (2: 231–47). It might appear simple incompetence for such a nodal discussion to be removed to the marginal status of an appendix. But to make this assumption would be to misread the structure of the book and the rhetorical ends this serves. The *Tour* operates as a dynamic contraption whose energies perpetually require adjustments of the formal settings. Paratext defines its goals along with pure text, and apparently marginal elements are constantly invading the centre. This process creates a kind of textual instability, parallel to the unstoppable forces for change within the English nation.

Volume III

Space precludes a full investigation of the third volume, the longest and most wide-ranging. This begins with a preface, looking back to the claims made in the equivalent section at the beginning of Volume I: 'The Tour is now finish'd; and you have the Account contracted into as narrow a Compass, as, considering the Extent of Ground pass'd over, with the Number of Cities, populous Towns, and a Country infinitely Rich, Populous, and Prosperous, to be described, could reasonably be expected' (3: 3). Then come three letters describing the counties between the Trent and the Border. After this we have three devoted to Scotland, each ending in the Forth/Clyde valley in the vicinity of one of the two major Scottish cities, Edinburgh and Glasgow. Each moves through uplands (the Border hills and the Highlands) and takes in some of the coastline before reaching its Lowland base. The book is split into two virtually equal parts, and this division between the two parts of the nation is mirrored paratextually. The English section has its own introduction, and then after the break we have an inner title followed by an introduction to the Scottish segment. Each part has its own index at the end of the volume. To place southern and northern Britain between the same pair of covers, rather than hive off Scotland in a separate volume, as Macky does, is itself to replay the Act of Union that Defoe wished to bolster in his text. We recall that 'Great Britain' had been blazoned in a large typesize on each successive title-page, whereas Macky had used 'England' for his first two segments and then 'Scotland' for the last.

The same embedded features we have seen earlier on in the work reappear in the final volume. A long and heavily documented 'Account of the Town and Church of Southwell' was provided to Defoe by 'a Reverend and very good Friend and one of the present Prebendaries of the Place', who has not been identified (3: 22–8). This runs to over 2,500 words and looks suspiciously like a filler. It offers the sort of content usually found in local histories, that is details of the parish and successive stages in the evolution of the minster, along with benefactions and inscriptions transcribed from tombstones. What is less usual is a fair sprinkling of more current information, with a full register of the current prebendaries and church officers, together with a list of those who contributed to a restoration fund after bad fire in 1711 caused serious damage. Such passages can provide up-to-date facts, among which some may be unavailable elsewhere, and they collect relevant materials in a single space. However, they consort oddly with the narrator's own highly personal, dry and often sceptical tone. Some of these comments apply to two long passages from Camden, smuggled into the text in Letter 9 at Beverley (3: 106–10), and in Letter 10 at Manchester (3: 130–32), neither of which can be said to have bedded down satisfactorily within the surrounding account. The issue is not plagiarism as such, rather the absence of invisible mending.

In the coverage of Scotland, the most notable element is an increased use of the enumerative devices mentioned earlier. This appears first with four 'things needful' to bring North Britain, now incorporated within the Union, up to the same economic level as England (3: 148). There are seven instances of such tabulation in Letter 11, the most extensive of which list features of Edinburgh, namely the gates, the markets, and the churches. A similar technique is used in the entry for Glasgow in Letter 12 to set out four principal manufacturing industries in the city, and then six advantages that the Scots enjoy over the English in trade if they would exploit them properly (3: 202–3). These passages serve a larger function than that of mere lists for reference purposes: instead they form part of an ongoing argument concerned with the state of the nation. The final letter displays further examples of enumeration, among them the three ways in which Dunfermline gives an appearance of decay (3: 226–7); a comparison between the ancient palaces of the two former kingdoms (2: 228–9); and a lengthy tabulation of the goods imported and exported by Scotland (2: 235–7). Later on comes a schedule of the 'Extraordinaries of *Aberdeen*', covering areas such as the architecture, the two colleges, and the commerce and fishery (2: 259–61). More characteristic in some ways is the breakdown of northern and western Scotland into regions with their constituent shires (2: 268–9). Understandably Defoe has less to say about these remote corners of the island, some of them barely penetrable, and his tabulation seems designed to conceal the poverty of his first-hand information by imposing a formal system of description.

Conclusion

For J. M. Coetzee, Defoe appears in the varied guise of 'impersonator, a ventriloquist, even a forger'.[17] This description is plainly meant to refer in the first instance to the fiction, but it carries some suggestive quality when applied to the *Tour*, with its mosaic of revealed and hidden sources. What the various devices examined here do is create a flexible medium, into which

Defoe can insert a range of textual and paratextual messages – recycling his own work, transferring the substance and appearance of material from other writers, and enacting the shape of the nation in the constituent parts – so that volumes, letters, prefaces and appendices collectively body forth a virtual representation of Great Britain. The most thinly populated districts are not served quite as well by this method, but this is part of the message – the further from the centre, the less significant their role in the great project of improvement radiating out from London. Just how the structure operates is the subject of the next chapter.

CHAPTER 3

The Epic Strain

The last chapter dealt with elements that in terms of structure are peripheral to the main argument of the book, although important in its design. We turn now to a theme that lies at the heart of the text. Fifty years ago I ventured what may still seem an overblown claim: 'The English epic found its Augustan expression not in some strutting *Brutiad* but in the modest-looking tour through Britain of Daniel Defoe.'[1] This assertion drew on the now largely neglected writings of E. M. W. Tillyard, and specifically on his late books *The English Epic and Its Background* (1954) and *The Epic Strain in the English Novel* (1958). In order to defend this view of the *Tour*, it is necessary to say something of the author and the way in which he developed his version of epic.

When the two books appeared, Tillyard (1889–1962) was one of the most influential literary critics in the English-speaking world. His name became familiar by reason of several widely read studies of Shakespeare and Milton; he had written in 1943 an exceedingly popular short survey of *The Elizabethan World Picture* which for some years commanded the admiration of scholars and the gratitude of students; and he attained celebrity as a result of controversies in which he engaged with C. S. Lewis and F. R. Leavis. Strange as it may now seem, at this date he was actually better known in many quarters than his famous antagonists. The first work on epic enlists his background in classical studies, with its first part devoted to Greek and Latin poets and historians. Succeeding parts relate to medieval authors, the Renaissance and what was then comfortably recognised as 'The Neo-Classic Age' – we might be happier today with a label implying literature of the early modern period. Although familiar with the scholarship, Tillyard spends very little time entering into the debates of classicists with regard to the ancient theory of epic. His introduction moves briskly over issues such as 'the heroic poems' and 'neo-classic theory', with a slightly longer section on 'the epic spirit'. It is noteworthy that the formal and stylistic properties of a heroic poem are not investigated in great detail.

His working assumption is set out on the opening page, after a reference to an increasing tendency to associate the genre with early stages of civilisation: 'In accordance with this shift heroic poetry ceases to be poetry with a nominally heroic subject and becomes the narrative verse with a heroic subject belonging to the heroic age, at whatever date or in whatever part of the world that age manifested itself.'[2]

The book is a remarkable feat of compression, ranging over not just the full gamut of major ancient authors in the relevant fields, but also a wide conspectus of medieval writers including Dante and Langland; and subsequently Renaissance poets and translators in Italian, French and Portuguese as well as English. The last part of the volume contains short assessments of figures as far from the mainstream as Sir Richard Blackmore, along with *Paradise Lost*, Dryden's *Aeneid* and Pope's *Iliad.* Tillyard provides a number of surprises along the way, perhaps the greatest emerging with his willingness to appropriate *Pilgrim's Progress*, Clarendon's *History* and Gibbon's *Decline and Fall* within the tradition. In a very Defoean gesture, he introduces near the end a hook to his second book on the subject, when stating, 'Looking back on the subsequent history of the novel we can see that Defoe began the transfer of the true epic instinct from the verse narrative, once its proper medium, to the middle-class prose romance.'[3]

The opening pages of *The Epic Strain* rephrase this formulation, in stating that 'by the nineteenth century the real course of the epic had forsaken the traditional verse form for the novel'. This argument is sustained in chapters allocated to *Robinson Crusoe*, *Tom Jones*, *Waverley*, *The Heart of Midlothian* and other novels by Scott, *Vanity Fair*, *Moby Dick* and *The Bostonians*, *Nostromo*, *Middlemarch*, Bennett's *The Old Wives' Tale* and *Clayhanger* trilogy and last, inevitably, *Ulysses*. This is a much shorter study than *The English Epic*, but as can be seen it covers a considerable stretch of ground. The main thesis might be summarised in the formulation, 'The traditional literary hierarchies should be made to apply *more consciously* [italics in original] to the novel than has hitherto been the case.'[4] Since Tillyard has admitted prose to his canon, and starts his second book with a reading of *Crusoe*, this may lend more credence to my attempt here to assimilate the *Tour* to the tradition of English epic, as it evolved over the *longue durée*.

The first requisite for epic status, according to Tillyard, is 'the simple one of high quality and of high seriousness', While the *Tour* might lack the earnest moral tone that Matthew Arnold would look for, it is undoubtedly concerned with highly important historical issues. As for its quality, the material set out in this book should cause readers at least to consider whether any work offering to proceed on an epic scale can be found in the period that matches Defoe's book in scope and ambition (I exclude mock-heroic productions such as *The Dunciad*). The second criterion listed is 'roughed out' by Tillyard 'in vague words such as amplitude, breadth, inclusiveness, and so on'. Again, the comparison with other surveys of Britain such as those of Fiennes, Macky, Byng and Cobbett will demonstrate how much more ground, geographically speaking, Defoe covered. At the same time, the range of his discussion across areas of life is immensely wider, since it extends to matters rural and urban; manufacturing and agricultural; historical and topical; economic and political; social and domestic; public and private.

The third desideratum is in essence the presence of clear organisation. Rabelais and Cervantes are rejected because they are 'governed by no powerful predetermination'. Throughout this book, but most directly in Chapter 4, I seek to show that the *Tour* has an overmastering narrative drive, expressed both in its structure of 'circuits' across carefully defined zonal areas and in its use of recurring leitmotifs that connect the various stages of the journey. If epic does indeed entail 'a control commensurate with the amount included', as Tillyard insists, the design of the *Tour* might be seen as overdetermined. Defoe produces a true survey, not just in the sense of an overall assessment or gazetteer, such as the itemised list of 'places of note' around which John Senex's *New General Atlas* of 1721 is built. Instead, he creates a network of intertwined topographies, relating landscape to function, produce, climate and history. The fourth and last test that Tillyard wishes to apply is that of the 'choric', by which he means that 'The epic writer must express the feelings of a large group of people living in or near his own time.' It can hardly be denied that Defoe enlisted a broad current of national pride, connected with the aims of the Hanoverian settlement and the expansive commercial ambitions that underpinned the governing Whig establishment under Robert Walpole. Tillyard quotes Lascelles Abercrombie on the 'accepted unconscious metaphysic of the age', and while Defoe always seems conscious of what he is doing, there is a substratum of assumptions that underlie his unquestioned belief in progress, improvement and growth.[5]

Finally, his pose on the title-page as 'a Gentleman' gives his work the anonymity that most traditional epics possessed. The *Tour* is sometimes compared with more recent journeys around parts of Britain, including those of J. B. Priestley, George Orwell and Beryl Bainbridge. But we all know who *they* were. Defoe did not reveal himself as the author of *The*

True-Born Englishman, or of *Robinson Crusoe*, or of a hundred familiar books. His work is 'choric', one that every man or woman could write, if they had the skill, the insight, the experience, the energy, the cheerful outlook, the perseverance and the desire to inform us.

The Preface

Epics commonly begin with a statement of the central theme. Defoe naturally does not employ a formal invocation, but the Preface to Volume I enunciates several points relevant to the criteria just discussed. The two opening paragraphs give an indication of the shared values that the writer expects to find in his readership:

> If this Work is not both Pleasant and Profitable to the Reader, the Author most freely and openly declares the Fault must be in his Performance, and it cannot be any Deficiency in the Subject.
>
> As the Work it self is a Description of the most Flourishing and Opulent Country in the World, so there is a flowing Variety of Materials; all the Particulars are fruitful of Instructing and Diverting Objects. (1: 47)

The author goes on to state how anticipations will be met, equally 'If Novelty pleases', that is by a description of the present state of the country, especially its increasing wealth, and 'if *Antiquity* takes with you', by an account of essential features of its history. This followed by a further recital of the amplitude that Tillyard's second requirement calls for, disclaiming the almost impossible 'compleat Account of *Great Britain*', as this would take many years and many hands. The clear implication is that the *Tour* will aim for an overview unprecedented in its comprehensive scale, and this is filled out in the succeeding paragraphs which list the scope of the work. A representative passage runs like this:

> In every County something of the People is said, as well as of the Place, of their Customs, Speech, Employments, the Product of their Labour, and the Manner of their Living, the Circumstances as well as Situation of the Towns, their Trade and Government; of the Rarities of Art, or Nature; the Rivers, of the Inland, and River Navigation; also of the Lakes and Medicinal Springs, not forgetting the General Dependance of the whole Country upon the City of *London*, as well for the Consumption of its Produce, as the Circulation of its Trade. (1: 48)

In the concluding phrases here, we encounter our earliest example of a leitmotif that runs through the entire book, and helps to solidify its structure in terms of Tillyard's third demand, for 'powerful predetermination'. What is amazing about the passage as a whole, abundantly illustrating the scope called for in the second requirement, is how well Defoe managed to live up to his promises. In spite of the inevitable errors and omissions, he maintained a high level of coverage on almost all topics, even if 'Lakes' are thinly represented until we get to the Highlands in Letter 13. A little later on, the claim is further enhanced by a description of the author's numerous journeys around the island. In the process he inserts a protestation of his own originality ('he is very little in Debt to other Men's Labours', 1: 49) – this is an exaggeration, but then Tillyard did not make this attribute a *sine qua non* of the epic form.

Again, Defoe asserts the timeliness of what he has written:

> The Observations here made, as they principally regard the Present State of Things, so, as near as can be, they are adapted to the present Taste of the Times: The Situation of Things is given not as they have been, but as they are; the Improvements in the Soil, the Product of the Earth, the Labour of the Poor, the Improvement in Manufactures, in Merchandizes, in Navigation, all respects the present Time not the Time past. (1: 48)

The phrase concerning 'the present Taste of the Times' goes some way to satisfy the fourth requirement. If we go through the various aspects of national life specified, it is obvious that they reflect a significant body of broadly endorsed positives in early eighteenth-century society. The Preface ends with a paean to the new developments constantly extending the wealth of the nation.

> Even while the Sheets are in the Press, new Beauties appear in several Places, and almost to every Part we are oblig'd to add Appendixes, and Supplemental Accounts of fine Houses, new Undertakings, Buildings, *&c.* and thus Posterity will be continually adding; every Age will find an Encrease of Glory. And may it do so, till *Great Britain* as much exceeds the finest country in *Europe*, as that Country now fancies they exceed her. (1: 49–50)

Tillyard was inclined to play down the role of patriotism as a motive for composing epic, but we cannot miss the thrust of this passage, ending as it does with a crude jibe at France. Just as significant is the emphasis on continual change, demanding a textual equivalent in terms of updates at regular intervals (see Chapter 2 on this).

What the Preface establishes is the status of Britain as the hero of the work – more than a location, it becomes a theme, a political entity and an aspiration in the mind of author and readers. Rather than choosing a single male protagonist to embody the nation, Defoe personifies its values by the description of its physical, political and economic identity, emphasising both its current state and its potential for greatness in the future.

Epic Action

Horace advised writers to plunge *in medias res*. Defoe does that, but he cleverly goes one stage further. His opening to the main text in Letter 1 takes this form:

> I began my Travels, where I purpose to end them, *viz.* at the City of *London*, and therefore my account of the City itself will come last, that is to say, at the latter end of my Southern Progress; and as in the Course of this Journey I shall have many Occasions to call it a Circuit, if not a Circle, so I chose to give it the Title of Circuits, in the Plural, because I do not pretend to have Travelled it all in One Journey, but in Many, and some of them many times over; the better to inform my self of every thing I could find worth taking Notice of. (1: 51)

Of course, there was a change of plan, so that in the event London did not have to wait until 'last' to become the centre of attention, though it did follow the four letters describing the southern counties (and the traveller did return to his base at the end of this opening trip, as well as at the conclusion of Letters 2, 4 and 7). The larger point is that we are instantly located *in mediis rebus*, the place which all the English sections look towards as the heart of the national court, government and economy. As we shall see in the next chapter, the routes chosen for each circuit are defined by a zonal system that circulates centripetally from the capital. The ten letters devoted to England seem originally to have been meant to be completed in nine; none the less, they have their nodal home in Letter 5, expressing a centrality in geographic and commercial terms effectively at the midpoint of the three volumes: 'As I am now near the Center of this Work, so I am to describe the great Center of *England*, the City of *London*' (2: 65). K. W. Gransden argued that 'Structurally book VI is the pivot of the entire *Aeneid*.'[6] We can say as much of Letter 5, even though for practical reasons Edinburgh becomes the hub of the Scottish sections. Thus the opening paragraph to the book serves in place of an epic proposition, announcing a key theme of the *Tour* as it orientates the reader at the outset of all the journeys to be undertaken over the next 1,300 pages (counted in the texts of 1724 to 1726). The *Aeneid* foretold the ascent of Rome, with its golden race of men and women; the *Tour* celebrates the greatness of London and predicts that it will preside over a new age of prosperity.

Although the work deals with real places and events, it tells its story as an avowedly fictional series of tours that the author never took in precisely that form. Partly for that reason, it is possible to interpret the 'action' in traditional terms, for instance by seeking an Aristotelian unity of plot. Such a coherence is not difficult to find in the *Tour*: it is promoted by the sequentiality of the letters, the geographic logic of its routes, and the repetitive nature of its main thematic threads. As we know, epic often concerns itself with the fate of nations, as predicted by certain signs described in its text. While Defoe may not have believed in a manifest destiny, with the people of Britain comprising God's chosen race, the Preface alone is enough to show that he inherited the husks of the Puritan faith in England's special place in the divine plan, and shared in the confidence of many Whigs that the Glorious Revolution had opened the way for a glorious future. Linda Colley has called Defoe a 'committed publicist for Protestant Israel', and it is a fair judgement as long as we recall that (as Colley acknowledges) he was concerned to point out that 'there was only limited uniformity in terms of culture, custom or outlook'. It is generally agreed by historians that early modern Britain remained divided by large regional inequalities in prosperity (as it does today). The *Tour* supplies what is probably the most complete register of these disparities that was compiled at the time.

Colley notes that 'it is tempting to believe – and some historians have actually argued – that the sublime confidence running through Handel's oratorios or Defoe's political and economic writings was little more than the propaganda of an affluent and atypical minority'.[7] There is a difference with Handel, since Defoe never entered the higher reaches of the British establishment.[8] But one can see how the emphasis on wealth and improvement might lead to such a view. But it surely quite inapplicable to the *Tour*, which investigates the lives of all kinds of folk, including fishermen, artisans, the decoy-men luring ducks on the fens, the horse grooms, the humble cottagers on the heathland on Holmwood or around Halifax, the short-lived wives along the marshes on the Thames estuary, the 'Commons or Vassals' (crofters, in effect) scattered around the Highlands, the threshers of Northumberland, the 'good old Women' whom the narrator quizzed about the battle of Otterburn, the farmers in the Vale of Aylesbury and scores of other groups remote from the seats of power. Perhaps the most striking single instance is the detailed account of the subterranean lead miners in the Peak district, to which we shall turn shortly. While John

Macky seldom shifts his gaze away for long from the homes of the high and mighty, Defoe plunges into the farthest recesses of provincial Britain, unafraid to muddy his boots in back-country lanes or dirty his hands in small-town workshops.

In the end, it is Britain itself which stands in for the epic hero. Climactic moments in history parallel the triumphs and trials that such a hero would undergo: for Defoe these would include on the positive side the outcome of the wars with France and the accession of the Hanoverian monarchs; on the negative side, the Jacobite Rising and the South Sea Bubble. Meanwhile London has heroically restored itself after the destruction caused by the Great Fire (see especially 2: 86–7).[9]

One of the most familiar ingredients of the heroic genre is an epic journey, whether we apply the term to the *Odyssey*, the *Aeneid*, the *Anabasis* or the *Lusiad*. In most cases, such travels are of long duration, venture into little-known regions, involve considerable hardship and are brought to a stop in places. By comparison the individual legs of Defoe's itinerary are generally short, and they tend to follow well-trodden paths. This is, of course, less true when the *Tour* enters mountainous districts, especially in Wales and Scotland. Only a few sections emphasise the arduous passage of difficult terrain, with the most detailed account on the crossing of the snow-covered Pennines in Letter 8 (3: 60–63). Nevertheless, the collective impression of the successive circuits is more than would be given by a few casual trips: they add up to a full-scale narrative of a determined reach to achieve a specified goal. In particular, there is a palpable sense of finding a way home, each time the traveller gets back to London: 'By this Turn I came necessarily on to *Stratford*, where I set out' (1: 132).

Epic Properties

A number of devices and conventions associated with epic are mirrored in the *Tour*. The setting is on a sufficiently large scale, unlike the more limited segments covered by most travel books of the time, and embraces the entire landmass of the country. The narrative proceeds in an assumed present tense, but contains several flashbacks, by way of historical episodes. These include repeated recollections of the Civil War, with several minute descriptions of critical events, notably the siege of Colchester with the battles of Roundway Down, Newbury, Edgehill and Marston Moor. These go together with frequent references to the Dutch Wars, and a long account of 2,750 words covering the descent of William of Orange's forces on London in 1688 (2: 43–9): the narrator claims to have been an eye-witness of the events. By this means the seventeenth century becomes part of Britain's genealogy, helping to explain the course of later history, much as the lineage of an epic hero is responsible for his valour and the need to outdo his ancestors. So Defoe's celebration at the outset of 'the Situation of Affairs in this *Great British* Empire' (1: 47), meaning Britain as a whole, embodies a claim of superiority not merely spatially but temporally. We come back to the boast about the kingdom quoted earlier, that it 'as much exceeds the finest Country in *Europe*, as that Country now fancies they exceed her' (1: 50). At the same time the section incorporates a claim that the nation has built on its past to achieve a predestined greatness, which constitutes a central theme of epic.

Furthermore, we are given extensive passages in the Scottish sections concerning the struggle of contending forces in the nation's history, focusing on events such as battles from Bannockbourn to Sheriffmuir, and tracing some of the religious disputes of the 1680s and 1690s. There is a section of about 1,300 words devoted to 'that noted Story of the *Whigs* in the old persecuting Times', introduced with a characteristic formula, 'and which I must give you a short Account of, for I have not Room for the whole History' (3: 187). This relates to an attack by Covenanters on government forces in the Pass of Enterkin, which took place on 29 July 1684. The extent of detail suggests that the author may have been given a first-hand narrative of what transpired (he had already used the material in his *Memoirs of the Church of Scotland* (1717).[10] Elsewhere in the three final letters, ruined palaces and monasteries attract a good deal of space. This is in keeping with the author's aim of showing Scotland as a country which has fallen from its former glories, but which has abundant opportunities following the Union of reinventing itself as prosperous and secure (see Chapter 6 below). Now that 'the Wastings and Plunderings, the Ravages and Blood are over' (3: 237), there will be the chance to match England or France. By this means Defoe is able to align the last three letters with the methods of his earlier coverage of England, just described; and also to exploit the considerable knowledge of the history of Scotland he had acquired while living in Edinburgh.

In an age of increasing scepticism, Defoe even finds a substitute for the supernatural agents who enter the narrative in classical poetry. Like Virgil in the *Aeneid*, and Statius in the *Thebaid*, Ovid introduces the figure of Fama or rumour in the twelfth book of the *Metamorphoses* (a work that is epic in scale and concept, if not in structure), presiding over a scene where every story is repeated and augmented at each fresh hearing (12: 39–63).

The *Tour* repeatedly engages with a domesticated version, that is the store of English (occasionally Welsh or Scottish) legends that Defoe treats with scarcely disguised scorn. He refers throughout his supposed travels to the tales of local inhabitants, sometimes drawn from perennial folklore (see Chapter 8, pp. 186–89 below), but often recent myths, such as the tale of the highwayman Nicks, which he relates at length but undercuts at the end: 'but these Things, I say, I do not relate as certain' (1: 143). His attitude to much of what he hears from local people is commonly expressed in a formula such as 'They told us an odd Story . . .', or 'All the use I shall make of this unlikely Story, is this . . .' (3: 72). Or these examples: 'This I leave to those who such Stories are better suited to than I expect of my Readers' (3: 42); and 'I believe my Share of this Story' – that is, not at all (1: 108). His studied neutrality regarding one legend ('I know not what to say to the Story of *Joseph* of *Arimathea*, and his *Holy Thorn* at *Glassenbury*', 1: 155) is belied by what he says later when he reaches the town (2: 25). At Lichfield, Defoe comes on a story that had been passed on by none less than the eminent antiquarian Sir William Dugdale, 'but I conceive that to smell as much of the Legend, as the Miracles of St. *Chad* himself' (2: 200).

Such disavowals of the information that has been fed to the narrator culminate in a disproportionately long passage on 'the *Wonderless* Wonders of the *Peak*' (3: 41). Disproportionate, unless we consider how widespread the legends had become over the preceding sixty years. In all, this section occupies thirty-two pages in the first edition of the *Tour*, making it the most prolonged exercise in demystification within the text. Ilse Vickers has documented Defoe's allegiance to the methods of empirical science, as recommended by Bacon and put into practice by the Royal Society. In his description of the Peak, he defines his approach as rational mainly by means of a negative – setting himself against the 'strange long Stories of Wonders' that 'some others (I think foolishly) have done before me' (3: 32). He may have thought that John Macky's account of the wonders, while not wholly credulous, made too many concessions to the mythographers.[11] Certainly one declared aim of the *Tour* is to debunk falsities that have gained popular assent.

In the midst of this section, the narrator breaks off his account of the accredited Wonders of the Peak with two anecdotal passages. One concerns a poor old woman living with her five young children, who emerges from a cave set in the rocky hillside. He begs leave to record what he saw, 'to shew the discontented Part of the rich World how to value their own Happiness, by looking below them, and seeing how others live, who yet are capable of being easie and content, which content goes a great way to being happy, if it does not come quite up to Happiness' (3: 34). This moralistic comment, of a kind that had always been allowed to heroic poets, introduces a short apologue on the art of living simply. It is one of the places where Defoe drops his tone of assumed neutrality to offer advice to the reader.

Just a page later comes an even more graphic description of a humble existence. The traveller and his companions are amazed to see a figure scrambling out of a narrow shaft. This turns out to be a lead miner emerging from the pit where he has been working. He is described as 'a most uncouth Spectacle ... lean as a Skeleton, pale as a dead Corps'. The emotions aroused include disgust and terror: 'We that saw him ascend *ab Inferis*, fancied he look'd like an Inhabitant of the dark Regions below, and who was just ascended into the World of Light.' The party of visitors naturally quiz the miner on the conditions in which he labours and finally reward him with two shillings, more than he could earn in three days. However, they decline an invitation to go down into the pit to explore its workings at first hand. Macky had referred to the local guides living near the wonder called 'the Devil's Arse', who were willing to show travellers 'the Territories of Satan', adding that 'These People resemble the *Troglydites* or *Cunicular* Men, who ... lived under Ground like Rabbits.'[12] But the reference to infernal powers indicates that Defoe had in mind less the anthropology of human troglodytes than the stories surrounding Hades in classical myth. The tip to the miner reminds us of the *obolos* given to the ferryman Charon to gain a passage across Styx, as it ran down a gorge in Arcadia into the nether regions. The gloomy landscape recalls the Cimmerian world of the dead visited by Odysseus, but more directly the journey to the underworld in the sixth book of the *Aeneid.* In Virgil, the hero emerges from the shades, turning his back on Tartarus, to reach the Elysian fields, enlightened and empowered to rival the great deeds of Rome's founders. If the narrator's experience is less intensely spiritual after his encounter with the denizens of the Peak, it still endows him with a renewed gratitude for his privileges:

> If we blessed our selves before, when we saw how the poor Woman and her five Children lived in the Hole or Cave in the Mountain, with the Giant's Grave over their Heads; we had much more room to reflect how much we had to acknowledge to our Maker, that we were not appointed to get our Bread thus, one Hundred and Fifty yards under Ground, or in a Hole as deep in the Earth as the cross upon St. *Paul's Cupolo* is high out of it: Nor was it possible to see these miserable People without such Reflections, unless

> you will suppose a man as stupid and sensless as the Horse he rides on. But to leave Moralizing to the Reader, I proceed. (3: 38)

It is a brilliant touch to forge a comparison between the subterranean chasm in the remote Derbyshire hills with the lofty dome of the cathedral in London, completed only a few years earlier. The leap of our imagination required crystallises the distance that the narrator's travels have taken him from his home. In any case, 'Such Reflection' in a heroic poem would call for none of the self-censorship we see at the end of this passage, as they form part of a familiar epic topos. No other passage in the *Tour* enters this realm of feeling.

While there are no heroic games to describe, Defoe gets somewhere near when he gets to Newmarket: 'Here I fansy'd myself in the *Circus Maximus* at *Rome*, seeing the antient Games, and the Racings of the Chariots and Horsemen; and in this warmth of my Imagination I pleas'd and diverted myself more and in a more Noble manner, than I could possibly do in the Crowds of Gentlemen at the weighing and starting Posts, and at their coming in' (1: 118). Horse-racing is mentioned elsewhere, for instance at Epsom (1: 194), outside Aylesbury (2: 137) and in North Yorkshire (3: 89–90). In addition, Defoe refers to athletic contests such as Cornish wrestling and the 'The Game called the *Hurlers*', which he compares to the scene where Hercules slays the giant while cleaning out the Augean Stables, possibly a confusion with the story of Antaeus (2: 102).

An element common in heroic verse is the use of sententiae, pithy observations that often display the paradoxical, gnomic or antithetical form that are found in proverbs. For instance, the celebrated line in Lucan's *Pharsalia,* 'victrix causa deis placuit, sed victa Catoni', might be compared to a stock expression in English, 'Win at first or lose at last'; or we might think of a formula such as 'More haste, less speed'. As shown in Chapter 8, pp. 176–89 below, proverbs left a heavy imprint on the *Tour*, especially those that held a particular local significance. More widely, the text contains many moralistic asides, for example on the behaviour of men and women at pleasure resorts or the conduct of gamblers, though the tone is generally more regretful than harshly critical.

Episodes and Catalogues

Among the generic properties frequently adduced by theorists is the use of episodes, in the technical Greek sense of an interpolation. These are often seen as casting oblique light on the main narrative, though it seems likely that the main attraction to poets was the chance to provide something completely different, in order to diversify the mood of the work. (This is how Aristotle briefly refers to such elements in Chapter 23 of the *Poetics*.) Most of the principal digressions have been discussed in the previous chapter, as instances of 'embedded forms'. They form self-contained units but, apart from the lengthy excursus on the siege of Colchester, they do not take us into much extraneous detail. In Chapter 26, Aristotle points out that both the *Iliad* and the *Odyssey* contain a number of subordinate parts, each possessing its own scale and unity, yet all serving the wide purposes of the overall action. Applying this formula to what we have called the action of the *Tour*, it is evident that the work satisfies the demand in the *Poetics* that its size should allow the reader to comprehend at one view the beginning and the end. Defoe achieves this partly by the use of deliberate pointers at the outer limits of each letter and section, with internal prefaces and appendixes marking off the subdivisions (see also the opening section of Chapter 1, pp. 19–20 above). .

Similarly with catalogues that are such a characteristic feature of epic narrative. As we saw in the last chapter, when a number of examples were quoted, Defoe was addicted to lists. They relate to every sort of information, but those that most approach the ancient practice are those that enumerate great figures of the past, such as the schedule previously mentioned of the original Knights of the Garter. This is immediately followed by 'an Account by the Register of the Order, that are reckoned up of this Noble Company', which details subsequent creations starting with 'eight Emperors of *Germany*', along with a series of English and European monarchs. Lastly, and most significantly, 'The List of the present Knights', headed by the King, the Prince of Wales and the latter's son Prince Frederick. The sequence ends with the most recent creation, made in 1724, that of Viscount Townshend, Walpole's brother in law, and current secretary of state (2: 57–61). The effect of such collections of names corresponds to an aggrandisation of the theme wherever heroes are commemorated in traditional epic, a device that serves in both cases to enhance the status of the nation.

Much of Letter 5 consists of itemised descriptions of features of the city, whether of the various constituent parts; new buildings erected since the Great Fire; new projects that have been mooted (such as a new bridge over the Thames, unrealised until Westminster Bridge was completed in 1750); markets; docks; gaols; other notable buildings such as churches; the commissioners of the Admiralty; hospitals; the governors of St Thomas' hospital; and new edifices now erected or being erected since the previous account was written. Most of these lists involve assiduous counting. The effect is to aggrandise the scale, dignity and growth of London, suitably as the capital of a dynamic nation.

Linked to this technique is one of the ways in which the *Tour* seeks to appropriate something of the grandeur of ancient poetry: it lies in what we might call 'the enumerative sublime'. Examples abound in every letter, and sometimes they occur on several pages in succession. Two brief cases must suffice here. The first passage has already been touched on in Chapter 1, but it needs to be put into context now as part of the epic potential of the work.

> I now began to approach the town of *Hallifax*; in the Description of which, and its Dependencies, all my Account of the Commerce will come in, for take *Hallifax*, with all its Dependencies, it is not to be equalled in *England*. First, the Parish or Vicaridge, for it is but a Vicaridge; is, if not the largest, certainly the most populous in *England*; in short, it is a Monster, I mean, for a Country Parish, and a Parish so far out of the way of foreign Trade, Courts, or Sea Ports.
>
> The extent of the Parish, they tell us, is almost circular, and is about twelve Miles in Diameter. There are in it twelve or thirteen Chapels of Ease, besides about sixteen Meeting-Houses, which they call also Chapels, and are so, having Bells to call the People, and Burying Grounds to most of them, or else they bury within them. I think they told me, the Quakers Meetings, of which there are several too, are not reckoned into the Number. In a word, it is some Years ago that a Reverend Clergyman of the Town of *Hallifax* told me, they reckoned that they had a Hundred thousand Communicants in the Parish, besides Children. (3: 67)

This is the opposite of the Burkean sublime, where 'obscurity' is one of the predisposing qualities, illustrated by Milton's description of Death, in which 'all is dark, uncertain, confused, terrible, and sublime to the last degree.'[13] Size is conveyed by a pair of superlatives (largest, most populous), with one emotive word, 'Monster'; otherwise, the surprising greatness of Halifax is evoked by modes of enumeration (about twelve Miles; twelve or thirteen Chapels; a Hundred Thousand Communicants). A verb used twice in two lines is 'reckon'. Counting things up makes them loom larger.

A second instance might equally stand for many others in the text. It concerns the woollen industry in the West Country, where the author was delighted to find clothiers 'worth, from Ten thousand to Forty thousand Ouds a Man'. He proceeds:

> If I may speak here from the Authority of the Antient Inhabitants of the Place, and who have been curious Observers upon this Subject, the Country which I have now described, as principally imploy'd in, and maintained by

> this Prodigy of a Trade, contains Two million, Three hundred and Thirty thousand Acres of Land, and has in it Seven hundred Eighty-Eight Parishes, and Three hundred and Seventy-four thousand People. It is true, that this is all guess-work; but I must confess myself very willing to believe, that the Reckoning is far short of the Account; for the County is exceeding large and populous. (2: 33–4)

Note that the ordinal numbers, not the denominators such as 'millions', are capitalised. It is as if the bogus 'wonders' of legend have been replaced by the more reliably attested wonders of a growing economy. We saw in Chapter 1 how Defoe was prone to exaggerating population figures, and one reason may be his need to magnify the scale of the increase.

Conclusion

It would be idle to pretend that the *Tour* precisely matches all the attributes of traditional epic. After all, many qualifications have to be made to allow *The Pilgrim's Progress*, *The Decline and Fall of the Roman Empire* and even *Ulysses* admission to an equivalent category. For one thing, Defoe wrote his book in the middle style of prose, not in the high style of heroic verse. But if we adopt Tillyard's more elastic standards, which extended the scope of the term to include novels, that consideration ceases to appear disabling. Given that the language of *Crusoe*, not to mention *Waverley* and *The Old Wives' Tale*, is suitably high, then the idiom Defoe uses in his account of Britain should be acceptable, as it lacks formality and solemnity but it is not wholly without dignity. He seeks to attain a seriousness comparable with that of epic less by pompously straining after elevated diction than by confronting major issues.

Nevertheless the *Tour* exhibits an extraordinary eloquence in places. Among the best examples are passages quoted at length in this book, such as the lament for the victims of South Sea (1: 131); the sounding meditation on ruined cities when contemplating the disappearance of the coastal town of Dunwich beneath the sea (1: 98); or the spirited rejection of pastoral myths in favour of the poetry of modern cities (1: 208). But all through the work we come on passages of freshness and wit, even when he is near the end of his laborious task and forced to deal with an area he knew very little or not at all:

> Our Geographers seem to be almost as much at a loss in the Description of this North Part of *Scotland*, as the *Romans* were to conquer it; and they are oblig'd to fill it up with Hills and Mountains, as they do the inner Parts of *Africa*, with Lyons and Elephants, for want of knowing what else to place

> there. Yet this Country is not of such difficult Access, as to be pass'd undescrib'd, as if it were impenetrable. (3: 269)

There is a consistent power to evoke varied emotions in a short space: take this passage in deepest Wiltshire.

> As we pass'd this plain Country, we saw a great many old Camps, as well *Roman* as *British*, and several Remains of the ancient Inhabitants of this Kingdom, and of their Wars, Battles, Entrenchments, Encampments, Buildings, and other Fortifications, which are indeed very agreeable to a Traveller, that has read any thing of the History of the Country. Old *Sarum* is as remarkable as any of these, where there is a double Entrenchment, with a deep Graffe, or Ditch, to either of them; the Area about 100 yards in Diameter, taking in the whole Crown of the Hill, and thereby rendering the Ascent very difficult: Near this, there is one Farm House, which is all the remains I could see of any Town in or near the Place, for the Encampment has no Resemblance of a-Town; and yet this is call'd the Borough of old *Sarum*, and sends two Members to Parliament, *who*, those Members can justly say, *they represent*, would be hard for them to answer. (1: 221)

The agility with which this passage glides in a few quick steps from conventional archaeology to mordant satire can best be aligned with the sudden mood swings of *Bleak House* – a work that in its shifting scenes and timescales, its broad thematic canvas and its array of stylistic effects is itself surely a candidate for a place in the story of novelistic epic surprisingly neglected by Tillyard. Like Dickens and indeed Homer, Defoe can invoke the comic without undermining the fundamental seriousness of his undertaking.

An acute sense of the past pervades Defoe's observations on the contemporary world, promoting a wider temporal span and thus a larger theme. We can turn to the Preface again to see this. Even as he seems to be endorsing improvement, a sense of loss creeps in.

> The Fate of Things gives a new Face to Things, produces Changes in *low* Life, and innumerable Incidents; plants and supplants Families, raises and sinks Towns, removes Manufactures, and Trades; Great Towns decay, and small Towns rise; new Towns, new Palaces, new Seats are built every Day; great Rivers and good Harbours dry up, and grow useless; again, new Ports are open'd, Brooks are made Rivers, small Rivers navigable, Ports and Harbours are made where none were before, and the like.
>
> Several Towns, which Antiquity speaks of as considerable, are now lost and swallow'd up by the sea, as *Dunwich* in *Suffolk* for one; and others, which Antiquity knew nothing of, are now grown considerable: In a Word,

> New Matter offers to new Observation, and they who write next, may perhaps find as much room for enlarging upon us, as we do upon those that have gone before. (1: 48)

The tendency shows up even when the narrator is proclaiming his resolve not to delve into antiquarian matters. One example occurs in the two paragraphs that conclude Letter 9:

> I cannot but say, that since I entred upon the View of these Northern Counties, I have many times repented that I so early resolved to decline the delightful View of Antiquity, here being so great and so surprizing a Variety, and every Day more and more discovered; and abundance since the Tour which the learned Mr. *Cambden* made this Way, nay, many since his learned Continuator; for as the Trophies, the Buildings, the religious, as well as military Remains, as well of the *Britains*, as of the *Romans*, *Saxons*, and *Normans*, are but, as we may say, like Wounds hastily healed up, the *Calous* spread over them being remov'd, they appear presently; and though the Earth, which naturally eats into the strongest Stones, Metals, or whatever Substance, simple or compound, is or can be by Art or Nature prepared to endure it, has defaced the Surface, the Figures and Inscriptions upon most of these Things, yet they are beautiful, even in their decay, and the venerable Face of Antiquity has some thing so pleasing, so surprizing, so satisfactory in it, especially to those who have with any attention read the Histories of pass'd Ages, that I know nothing renders Travelling more pleasant and more agreeable.

This passage serves at least three ends. It places the author in the line of Camden and his editor Gibson; it relates his account to the diverse history of the British race, giving the story a kind of genealogical imprimatur; and it justifies his tour as a contribution to the literature of travel, mixing pleasure with profit, as foreseen in the opening sentence of the Preface. The final payoff is equally plangent.

> But I have condemn'd my self (unhappily) to Silence upon this Head, and therefore, resolving however to pay this Homage to the Dust of gallant Men and glorious Nations, I say therefore, I must submit and go on; and as I resolve once more to travel through all these Northern Countries upon this very Errand, and to please, nay, satiate my self with a strict Search into every thing that is curious in Nature and Antiquity. I mortify my self now with the more case, in hopes of letting the World see, some time or other, that I have not spent those Hours in a vain and Barren Search, or come back without a sufficient Reward to all the Labours of a diligent Enquirer; but of this by the way, I must, for the present, make this Circuit shorter than usual, and leave the Description of the other three Counties to my next. (3: 120–21)

This operates as a bridge to the last section on English counties, Lancashire, Westmorland and Cumberland. But uttered at the Scottish Border, where the traveller has reached Berwick, his words have the air of a retrospective glance. A page or so earlier, he had given an account of the battles of Otterburn, mentioning the famous ballad 'Chevy Chase', and Flodden Field: the effect is to connect his narrative with heroic contests of the past. He depicts himself as embarked on arduous 'Labours' involved in a prolonged quest such as the protagonist of an epic might undertake. His diligent 'Search' assumes the proportions of a selfless quest, recalling not just the stories of antiquity but also medieval sagas and Arthurian romances.

What, finally, can be said of the *Tour* in the light of the foregoing discussion? Plainly Defoe was not attempting to produce an exact replica of a heroic poem. Nonetheless the work aspires far beyond the normal remit of a guide-book, setting out dry information in a matter-of-fact series of entries. Rather it seeks to portray the greatness of the newly united Britain as a grand adventure, fit for panegyrical treatment in spite of the many challenges that the nation confessedly faces.

It is possible to see why Tillyard might have excluded the book from consideration. He argued that Britain had failed to decide where she meant to go after the Civil War and the Revolution of 1688. Consequently, 'it was only in the next century that the union with Scotland, Britain's hegemony under Marlborough, and the triumph of Newton's philosophy helped with other things to make Britain feel at ease with herself . . . England after 1667 was not propitious to epic writing. It was not an epic area like the England of Elizabeth.' To this perhaps complacent set of fortunate circumstances, Defoe would have included with 'other things' the arrival of the Hanoverians, the expansion in trade and the improvement of the nation's infrastructure. If we take account of all the factors mentioned in this chapter, it is hard to accept Tillyard's blanket statement, 'an all embracing epic was not to be expected in the ages of Queen Anne and George I'.[14] Along with many contemporaries, Defoe thought that he was recounting the story of Britain at the moment when she had just reached the point where she could live up to an epic.

CHAPTER 4

The Shape of the Nation

This chapter is concerned with the design of the *Tour*, which seems to be original with Defoe – if not in conception, then certainly in execution. Its novelty emerges if we look at some of the earlier surveys of the country. Typically they follow no strict plan, in terms of the areas they cover or the order in which these appear within the text. This does not apply to Defoe's principal trove of material, that is William Camden's *Britannia*. However, his procedure was to take each of the English and Welsh counties in turn according to the Celtic tribes as identified in Roman Britain. This arrangement makes limited geographic sense, as the account sweeps first across southern England, from Cornwall to Kent. It then shifts into a long curve, moving anticlockwise on the map, from Gloucestershire over to East Anglia, then through the Midlands westwards and northwards. A new segment covers the three Welsh tribes, stretching from Herefordshire to Flintshire. The last section covers the territory of the Brigantes, that is the northern counties of England. Camden followed the same scheme in his treatment of Scotland, except that the division is by district rather than county, while he added a more scattered account of Ireland.

In spite of Defoe's reliance on *Britannia* to provide key information, this design would not do for the *Tour.* Its main spatial categories were prescribed by the political and social realities that existed more than a millennium before. The subdivisions by county restrict analysis by other means: thus it was impossible for Camden to follow a main artery of trade across the boundaries, as Defoe does in the case of the Great North Road and other highways. Although the structure of the *Tour* looks fairly cut and dried, it allowed the author plenty of flexibility. He was able to dilate on the agricultural symbiosis between Somerset, Wiltshire, Gloucestershire and Dorset (2: 24–5); and more lengthily on the clothing trade and cheesemaking in this region (2: 32–7).[1] The text here enacts connections across the paragraphs between towns spaced out over the region, such as Frome, Wincanton, Devizes, Warminster, Malmesbury,

Shaftesbury, Beaminster, Tetbury and Fairford (twice as many places are mentioned). Throughout this passage, the wider importance of the supply of manufactures and provisions in this district is related to a national distribution chain centred on London.

In his 'circuits' Defoe follows the direction of eighteenth-century communications as they actually operated. If he writes about the course of the Severn, it is not because the river holds mythological significance, as it did for Michael Drayton in *Poly-Olbion*, but because it served as a main conduit for the internal economy of the port of Bristol. In the opening letter East Anglia is present as a complex organism: Essex, Suffolk, Norfolk and Cambridgeshire are viewed as a group, not because the remote ancestors of the people came from the same stock, but because they have vital connections established by modern commerce, older and newer migration, the development of the transportation system, the growth of overseas traffic in the ports and many other factors. To Camden not just the Roman capital Colchester but also Ely mattered more than Ipswich or Harwich. It is the other way round with Defoe, despite his personal links with the former town. The entire pattern of the *Tour* is defined by an urgent awareness of the contemporary landscape.

Defoe and His Predecessors

One of the founders of English topography, John Leland, had made up to six journeys in the reign of Henry VIII, which were later assembled to form the basis of his *Itineraries,* along with much fragmentary material. His first expedition starts from Cambridge and moves into the Midland counties and the North before returning southwards to end at Hampton Court. The second leaves London and progresses westward along the Thames past Oxford to a point near its source, before continuing down the southwestern peninsula. A break occurs around Bodmin before the narrative fills in the remainder of Cornwall and makes its way back to London. Leland does not even have time amidst his antiquarian jottings to mention Land's End, a focal point for Defoe. The fifth section begins near Thame in Oxfordshire, and traverses the West Midlands before returning to London via the Chiltern Hills. A marked contrast with the *Tour* exists throughout: the author has no obvious motive for taking a particular route, other than his underlying curiosity about relics of the past; he seems never to have visited East Anglia (Defoe's first port of call); and as his editor tells us 'what now exists of the "Itinerary" contains nothing of London itself'. It is, of course, not like that at all in the *Tour*, where the capital is almost omnipresent, exerting a strong pull over most phases of the narrative. This discrepancy owes something to the fact that Leland started and finished his routes in several different places, which means that his account lacks not just the strong centripetal energy Defoe's book commands, but any sort of clear geographical logic.

Many works by the best-known authors of British travel literature exhibit similar tendencies. This applies to the journeys of Celia Fiennes in the late 1690s and early 1700s, and equally to those undertaken by John Byng a hundred years later. Both give assiduous reports on what they saw in the course of their trips, which cover a lot of England (though by no means all). Neither ventured as far as Scotland, although Fiennes did tiptoe across the border for a few miles before scooting back into the safety of Cumberland. She was put off by the sight of idle wenches with bare legs, and by the information that there were few towns apart from Edinburgh, Aberdeen and 'Kerk' which could provide decent accommodation to travellers.[2] What these two writers produced were confessedly travel diaries, unmediated and undirected to a wider purpose. They followed their nose for likely material, just as Leland had pursued his quest for antiquities. In the case of Fiennes, this meant among other things pleasant scenery and picturesque social details, though like Defoe she was thoroughly alert to the newly emergent landscape of manufacturing and construction.[3] In that of Byng, it meant convivial company and romantic vistas.

The fact that both authors were simply writing up their day-to-day experience, as it happened, provides a charming freshness and immediacy. However, it also limits the scope of their books. Their view of the nation is dependent to a large extent on chance, according to the arbitrary route that their tastes led them to take. Rarely do they stand back to set their observations within a wider appraisal of the state of the nation, as Cobbett for instance does to such trenchant effect. In a good sense, they are trippers, bent on an enjoyable vacation. In most cases they make a once-for-all descent on a given place, commonly reached by means of a single itinerary in that region, though this applies a little less to Fiennes' earlier journeys. It is obvious that this mode of travel could not provide an overall governing framework for their peregrinations – few holidaymakers would wish it otherwise. By contrast, as we saw in the previous chapter, the epic scale of Defoe's ambitions required him to plan carefully in advance of writing.

It is noteworthy that the title promises a tour of 'the *whole* island of Great Britain' – my italics. The effect is one of repletion: just as the political state has recently been expanded to form a single unit covering the entire island, so the work will attempt to chart the complete landmass. Of course, Defoe did not handle each of the outlying areas as comprehensively, in particular when writing about Wales and Scotland. But these were marginal to his main purposes, and they are at least *there*. Few authors make a serious effort to reach the parts that other travellers have missed. We have only to think of William Cobbett's *Rural Rides* a century later. As with Defoe, Cobbett has a definite ideological programme behind his trips round the country. The trouble is that he scarcely ever got out of his comfort zone. We noted in Chapter 1 the limited regions of his concern. The main routes he followed in England all lie in the south and southern Midland counties. Cobbett gives no description of the South-west or the North-west. Later he wrote, with a certain disdain, of Scotland and Ireland from a brief acquaintance. While he was no little Englander, his portrait of the nation is heavily skewed by its narrow emphasis on the Home Counties. Because of the gravitational pull that London exerts over the economy, Defoe places it at the centre of his design, round which the remaining counties of England rotate; but he has no illusion that the capital is representative of what was going on in each corner of the country, however remote. In the *Rides*, the Wen is the agent of destruction, while in the *Tour* it is the great enabler.

Every Corner and Creek

Defoe's most celebrated rival, John Macky, had a more programmatic approach than the majority of travel writers. His work, consisting of two volumes that describe *A Journey through England*, supplemented by one through Scotland, where the author originated (1714–23), deals with a larger segment of the nation, and even outlying portions such as the Isle of Man. It has a fuller description than the *Tour* of many stately homes; and it contains much extraneous information, in considerable part relating to the history of various peerages, members of whose family owned these same seats. Unlike Fiennes and Byng, he aims at a comprehensive survey, giving the reader more sense of a serious reference function. Unfortunately, this scheme was undermined by several factors. A gap of eight years elapsed between the first and second volumes, which according to the author was occasioned by such circumstances as the death of Queen Anne and the Jacobite Rising – events that lured more into print than they deterred. The volume on Scotland was delayed a further year. This means that the entire three-volume set was never fully integrated as was the *Tour*. There is, for example, an awkward hiatus between the first and second parts, with the coverage of London split between the two.

Beyond this, the *Journey* has fundamental flaws which have a conceptual as well as a structural cause. Macky's account starts at Yarmouth, where he has supposedly arrived by boat from Holland. This lends a nice anecdotal air, but it also conveys a sense of beginning on the edges, as the traveller does not mention the town again, nor does he visit anywhere else in Norfolk apart from Norwich. One of the features of the *Tour* is extensive cross-reference: this makes for a more comprehensive account of the places that the narrator has visited, and allows readers to make their own comparisons.[4] As for Macky, though his wanderings take him back to London several times, the capital does not become a real hub, geographically or thematically. Successive letters start or end in places dotted round the country, never forming a coherent itinerary. The stopping-off points include Windsor, Oxford, Woodstock, Derby, Chester, York, Stamford, Tunbridge Wells, Bath, Northampton, Nottingham, Carlisle and Guildford. Along this magical mystery tour, the separate trips follow one another in no recognisable order. We are wafted in less than a page from Stamford to York and thence again to Newcastle, while we zoom just as fast from Liverpool to Lancaster, bypassing Manchester and ignoring the Lake District. Defoe amuses himself by pointing out this characteristic: 'From *York* we did not jump at once over the whole Country, and, *like a late Author*, without taking notice of any Thing, come out again sixty or seventy Miles off, like an Apparition, without being seen by the way' (3: 102).

Some of the omissions are startling: large stretches of the coastline simply fail to appear in the narrative. Macky claims to have made an 'Excursion' into South Wales from Ludlow, described as the capital of this district: but the southern and middle regions of the principality are conspicuous by their total absence.[5] Local centres as important in their different ways as Leeds and Taunton do not figure at all, while Halifax, on which Defoe lavishes so much space, might never have existed for Macky. Not a word is said about the fast-growing Sheffield. Even cathedral cities such as Wells and Peterborough have been expunged from the record. There is a mass displacement of market towns such as Leominster, Sudbury, Hertford, Northallerton, Penrith, Marlow, Tewkesbury, Dorking, Bridgwater, Yeovil and dozens more. Having left out from his earlier description places such as Cornwall and the Fens, together with Lincolnshire, the author unblushingly interpolates a chapter at the end of Volume II to repair this gap, assuring the reader that they have been reserved 'for your Dessert' – this while he is stuck for no obvious reason at Douglas on the Isle of Man. He allots just a few dismissive sentences to the gaggle of Cornish boroughs leading down to 'that long Excrescence, called the *Land's End*', which between them sent forty MPs to Westminster, lumping them together with terms such as 'very mean', 'very miserable', 'pitiful poor', 'a confused heap of Cottages'.[6] By contrast Defoe recognises the importance of such towns, in terms of politics or trade, and allots more than 6,000 words to these ignominious-looking settlements.

Similarly, Macky had annexed to Volume I, in the middle of his section on London, another 'little Excursion' (in more than one sense). This was after 'looking into the Map, I found by my Scheme' that Bedfordshire could not be accommodated, so that he now stuffs in the county among the 'Environs of London'. A strange touch is added: 'For the Counties of *Surrey*, *Middlesex*, *Hertfordshire*, *Buckinghamshire* and this County, are properly so, and cannot come in to the regular Tour of a Kingdom.'[7] It is hard to know what kind of a scheme can assimilate Essex and Kent, but not the shires named. In truth this is an attempt to justify the haphazard course of the *Journey*. The author's final claim, 'Now, Sir, I have finish'd to you every Corner and Creek of *England*', would seem excessive even if applied to the *Tour*, but it would not be as plainly absurd there as it is in the case of Macky's *Journey*.[8]

Along with this improvisatory, not to say casual, quality goes a pervasive superficiality in the narrator's observations. He skims over the surface of the landscape, alighting mainly at impressive mansions or historic towns. There is never any sense of being on the road, in the immediate process of covering the ground from A to B, since he is teleported over long stretches of land without the need to feel his feet on the ground, still less to dip his feet in the ocean (he gives no sign of reaching Land's End or John o'Groats). He seldom turns his gaze towards the fields or the downs he may be crossing. There is extraordinarily little about the industrial landscape, and perfunctory treatment of ports and harbours. Even where he should have had an advantage, that is in the Scottish volume, his coverage of the Lowlands provides less fresh first-hand information about the current social landscape than Defoe, a confessed Londoner, while he displays hardly anything more by way of close acquaintance with the Highlands and far north of the country. Again the coverage is sketchy on most aspects of the places visited, other than seats of the aristocracy. The text of the third volume of the *Journey* is padded more outrageously than the *Tour*, with a long list of Scottish kings and peerages, followed by thirty-eight pages setting out the coats of arms of the nobility, and then ten more on the crown jewels. Such information has its place somewhere, but it does not contribute to any deep enquiry into the state of the nation.

On most counts Defoe emerges as the clear winner. The discrepancy is most glaring in two areas. First, Defoe gives us an incomparably clearer picture of working Britain, with his account of the location of manufacturing centres, different areas of the woollen industry, the network of distribution, inland navigation, the extent of fisheries and so much more. Macky's Britain scarcely has an economy; Defoe's is largely conditioned by its operations. Second, the *Tour* is organised on rational principles. In England at least, almost every trip into the wide blue yonder has a firm anchor in the ties of the area in question to London. As Furbank and Owens neatly put it, 'We are asked to see Bristol and Norwich, Kidderminster and Birmingham, when the narrative reaches them, as knots in a web of connections, of which London is the centre and nexus.'[9] Yet each separate area has its own home key, with regional attributes colouring the texts, whether these are the dominant occupations of the people, their customs and idiosyncrasies, the physical characteristics of land, sea, forests, hills or rivers, or the presence of historical markers such as castles and fortifications (ruined or otherwise), battlefields, medieval churches, Roman roads and British earthworks.

We could schematise the relationships between different kinds of topographic literature by adapting the semiotic square made familiar by A. J. Greimas. In Table 2, modes of writing are defined along two sets of variables. In the left column, the works described are organised *temporally*, in that the text follows a sequential series of events or descriptions, usually presented day to day in the first person. Typically these take the form effectively of a journal or diary (as in Celia Fiennes' journeys, or later Boswell's tour to the Hebrides), but Defoe's use of the letter form allows him to produce a narrative of his supposed progress across the country, even though 'the gentleman' holding the pen is not exactly identified with his creator. This may be termed a *personal* mode. In the right column, the books are organised *spatially*, that is to say their manner of proceeding lies in the succession of places described, not according to the traveller's calendar. Within this category the author declines any attempt at an imaginary first-person account, and there is no suggestion of physically moving from one place to another. The manner is maybe styled *impersonal*. We see this in large antiquarian and topographic compendia such as *Britannia* and in some atlases.

In the top row, the variable is *formal*, meaning that the work has a carefully designed structure in which discrete parts are welded into a pattern. The successive stages of the volume(s) are set out according to geographic location, as counties in Camden, deriving from a historic group of tribes, or regionally, as with the zones of the nation that the *Tour* purports to visit in the series of letters. Moving across the bottom row horizontally, we have the inverse, that is *informal* presentation, where the writer follows his or her nose, with no overriding plan. Such narratives cross borders at will, and may lump together disparate regions which have little in common historically or economically. The capricious routes followed by John Macky are an obvious example; as noted, his 'journey' flits over several counties at a time, and zooms through the Ridings of Yorkshire in a trice. To the right of this row we have works such as gazetteers or atlases which divide the materials by recourse to an A to Z scheme: there is a logic, but it is not geographic, merely alphabetical. The *New Remarks* of the parish clerks is divided into sections relating to the areas covered by City authorities, but within these the order is that of the churches listed by the alphabet. In addition, the roadbooks by John Ogilby and Emanuel Bowen must be classified here, since the routes they follow are presented in no coherent sequence beyond the alphabetical order of their destination. Each is a self-contained itinerary with no particular relation to the route that precedes or succeeds it.

The only debatable case here might be Leland, since his successive journeys have a certain internal coherence. None the less, the overall course of his itineraries has a clearly impromptu quality, which means his work is best characterised as *T/I*. Even Cobbett must be placed in this category, since his rides follow in no intelligible order, though individually do have a clear sequential plan. The originality of the *Tour* lies partly in its form. Within this group, the work is the only instance of *T/F*, that is a progress along predetermined lines through the nation with a conscious, some might say overdetermined, trajectory. It borrows elements from both *T/I* and *F/I*, that is to say the methods of Macky and Camden respectively – not

Table 2 *Kinds of topographic literature*

	TEMPORAL	SPATIAL
FORMAL	first person, structured itinerary *Tour*	third person, geographic placement *Britannia*; Senex, *Atlas*
INFORMAL	regular journal-type entries Fiennes; Macky	ordered with no geographical logic gazetteers; roadbooks

coincidentally, these are the authors whose tracks can be unearthed most often in Defoe's text.

Mapping and Nation-building

The most intriguing attempt to diagrammatize the *Tour*, so as to impose a master narrative lurking behind the form, is that of Gerald Hill. His article 'Circling Defoe' (1990) starts from a highly stylised sketch-map of the supposed journeys taken by the author, which 'yields the outline "map" of Great Britain as toured by Defoe'.[10] The result is a series of closed loops representing these trips (Letters 1–2; 3–4; 6–7; 8–10; 11–12; 13). However, Hill immediately acknowledges that this involves 'applying a somewhat arbitrary closure to the curved shapes of [Defoe's] trips' and makes a damaging admission from the point of view of his own argument: 'Such a schema effaces the centrality of London to the structure of Defoe's text and to his State-of-the-Nation reading of Britain's economic and political status.' There follows a more radical form of cartographic diagram: 'The thirteen circuits, grouped according to "distance" from London, are seen as six concentric circles. Defoe's ethnography, or the narrative of where he went and his interpretation of what he saw there, extends in rays across the circles from the centre.' The Letters stretch out in widening rings, containing 1–2, then 3–4, then 6–7, then 8–10, 11–12, then 13. Further, 'These rays, consisting of Defoe's positive remarks, together act as the "high road", the route of Defoe's nation-building ideology.' The centrality of the capital reflects Defoe's privileged position as a first-person narrator, based in London, and an inbred prejudice against the outlying parts of the country: 'Defoe's shaping implies his attitude: the "closer" to London the "better".' In the remainder of his article, Hill attempts to show how the book renders textually the writer's high estimation of London and ill-repressed scorn for the further regions of the kingdom.

Though ingenious and stimulating, this reading seems flawed. As John McVeagh has pointed out, the 'loops' involve smoothing out 'what was, in fact, rather irregular toing-and froing'. This matters because the swerves often result from a conscious decision, for example the perceived need to treat the inland wool towns of Essex together, rather than lump them together with the coastal portions of the county – hence the need to announce a shift in direction (1: 82). Again, the 'schematic' depiction of the letters defies real-life geometry, since the 'concentric circles' represent journeys that did not actually centre on London – rather, those shown in the three innermost rings started and ended in the capital, while the fourth, covering Northern England, are not circuitous at all. Letters 9 and 10, relating to the fifth ring, have Edinburgh and Glasgow as their hinge point, whilst Letter 13 is again less than a complete circle. In the event, Hill leaves Scotland aside from this point as a separate entity, presumably less amenable to the case for London's gravitational pull.

The argument is a little short cut owing to the method that Hill adopts. He allots little space to large sections of the *Tour*, even within the delimited space of England, and awards much of this to London, an unexceptionable choice. After this, the coverage is highly skewed:

> Imagining London and Defoe's 'I' at the centre, then, I turn to the first of Defoe's circuits. I will combine his first two journeys since they are essentially the same 'distance', in various senses, from London. Then I will move to the tenth journey in order to observe what 'extremes' (a particularly loaded word for the moderate Defoe) he sees so far north-west of London.

This leap from the Home Counties to Lancashire means that we have no coverage at all of the intervening circuits – nothing, for instance, about Land's End, the 'extreme' point at where Defoe explains the scope of his work, or Wales, which embodies much of the extremity that Hill attributes to outlying regions. It allows him to conclude that 'In Cumberland, then, the road has ended, and his narrative has atrophied to the bare bones of a guidebook, a scant collection of curiosities, inscriptions, statistics on plague, and antiquities.' Actually the road does not end there, because Letter 12 picks up the story at just this point, as the traveller embarks on his route march through Scotland (3: 181). More seriously, the abrupt switch to Letter 10 has eviscerated the *Tour* at its heart. Since there is no exploration of the interior, it is easy for Hill to contend that there is a steady and almost attritional rise in the distaste that Defoe shows for what he sees around him, beginning very close to the capital ('Already, just a county or two away from the centre, pockets of decay, incivility, and natural disintegration have appeared').

The many gradations of tone as we move through the nation are lost: and along with this, the intense celebratory moments that occur whenever Defoe comes across scenes that draw his admiration. This occurs regularly at the sight of a prosperous community engaging in fruitful occupations, for example among the busy fishermen and polite gentry of Dorset, the rich graziers of the Vale of Aylesbury, the entrepreneurial merchants of Newcastle, the industrious clothiers of Wiltshire, or their colleagues among the workers in Halifax, where 'no Hand being unemploy'd, all can gain their Bread, even from the youngest to the antient' (3: 65). Of course, there are critical passages, describing poverty-stricken neighbourhoods, vapid amusements in expensive spa towns, or neglect by the municipal authorities. But almost everywhere he goes, the narrator lights on some notable feature of a given area, whether a handsome town, a fine building, an excellent harbour, a river with recently improved navigation, rolling fields of corn, a local charity, civilised assemblies, a dissenting meeting-house with a full congregation – or a hundred other sights to please his eye. Hill's schema has led him to distort the true picture of Britain supplied by the *Tour*.

A more sophisticated analysis is provided by Christopher Parkes, who argues that 'The "Tour" . . . is organized by circuits that use London as a reference point, allowing a complete survey with all points related in a system of intersecting lines.'[11] Further, 'It is possible to situate the Tour inside the discourse of eighteenth-century cartography, and when this critical move is initiated "Defoe the cartographer" emerges.' Parkes draws on the influential ideas of J. B. Harley to indicate that the *Tour* has a naked ideological purpose similar to that of maps described by modern historians of cartography. Indeed, he claims that the work is composed 'as map space, and throughout it Defoe draws much attention to the fact that his is a complete survey rather than a one-dimensional collection of rambles across the countryside'. This is in line with the argument presented in the first section of this chapter, and Parkes does briefly contrast Defoe's methods with those of Fiennes and Macky. The article describes some of the passages where the *Tour* eulogised trade, a feature of the book that we have already encountered in several places: 'Defoe's cartography legitimizes commerce, in general, making it the new material from which the epic pattern emerges. Trade becomes the epic struggle of nation builders, rather than the business of profiteers.' Parkes is using the term 'epic' in the modern sense, which covers 'a movie, poem, or book that is long and contains a lot of action, usually dealing with a historical subject'; but as the last chapter argued, the older and more technical sense also applies. The overall drift of his case is encapsulated in a striking claim, to the effect that 'Before anyone else Defoe saw in the discourse of thematic cartography the ability to transform physically and psychologically the landscape of Britain into a blueprint for economic development, and for this reason he can be counted among the early architects of the modern nation state.'

This article provides one of the most convincing accounts of the structural basis for the *Tour*. It gains added points from the fact that discussions of J. B. Harley's views continue to impact studies of cartography, thirty years after his death. In one respect, however, Parkes seems to exaggerate the book's maplike qualities. This relates to his contention that the text is 'written to scale like a map', as the abstract of his article asserts. In support of this case, he explores various parts of the *Tour* to suggest that textual space precisely mirrors physical space, with each letter drawn to a different scale. Thus, he compares the number of words devoted to London and Aberdeen on the basis that the entries on each place match one another, if the appropriate scale is applied to the letters in question (5 and 13). This involves a somewhat shaky generalisation: 'Simply stated, within Defoe's narrative the percentage of space taken up by the description of a town is the same as the percentage the town itself takes up in the actual geographic space encompassed by the circuit he travels.' How does this square with the facts? Staying with Scotland, and turning to Letter 11, Edinburgh occupies eleven pages out of twenty-eight in McVeagh's edition of this journey. (I am assuming that the calculation is confined to the narrow route followed, not the entire area of south-east Scotland through which this line passes and which would be visible on an ordinary map.) The supposed trip covers a minimum of sixty miles, probably more like eighty or ninety. On the other hand, the bounds of Edinburgh did not exceed three miles in any direction. So the proportion sums offered by Parkes fail to match the reality.

A similar reservation applies elsewhere. If we look at Emanuel Bowen's *Britannia Depicta* (1720), as reproduced in facsimile with an introduction by J. B. Harley, we can observe that 'the great Road' from London to Harwich, charted in the opening circuit, of the *Tour*, extends to seventy-one miles as surveyed.[12] Defoe's progress starts three miles along at Bow Bridge (1: 51), and it is interrupted by several divagations including a trip down the Thames estuary, making in all just over 4,700 words. Out of these, almost a third, that is no fewer than 1,500 words, are devoted to Colchester (once more, this excludes the long, interpolated narrative on a Civil War siege), and a quarter, that is 1,212, are allotted to Harwich. Neither of these towns occupies much space in Bowen's map, with a length of road measuring little more than a mile for the former, and half that for the latter. Chelmsford shows up on a par with Harwich in terms of area, but it gets very little coverage in the *Tour*, as having 'very little to be said' of it (1: 82). Within Letter 1, the same pattern emerges with respect to Norwich, Yarmouth and Cambridge: the scope of their coverage is out of all proportion to the space they occupy as small outcrops on the map. So it is with the remainder of the *Tour*. Nor are statements Parkes makes on Defoe's prescience with regard to enclosures and canals wholly convincing, though the broad aim of showing how the work 'represents an attempt to change the nation from an actual historical space into conceptual space in which the landscape becomes meaningful, or a nation, only when it is brought into a useable system of intersecting lines' is unexceptionable.

The scheme that Parkes establishes might best be regarded as offering a symbolic parallel, rather than a literal equivalence. It is seen at its most effective in what he says about four small rivers rising in the Cotswolds that merge near Lechlade to form the Thames, where Defoe is able to survey 'as a system' a district consisting of seventy-eight square miles, which makes up part of an integrated economic network (2: 154). What the *Tour* gives us in my view is not exactly 'a living graphic "language"', as Harley describes maps, but more of a textual simulacrum of the real world.[13] Its purpose is to enact a spatio-temporal movement as the traveller passes through a geographically plotted landscape in a supposed 'present' tense.

All round, the most satisfactory brief account of the form of the work is to be found in John McVeagh's introduction to his edition. He draws attention to various structural symmetries, where 'Text and subject coincide.' McVeagh notes the 'balancing act' in the third volume, where three northern English letters are matched by three Scottish journeys. Such uses of parallelism, the editor observes, 'reinforce our sense of the author's control over his subject'. Further, Defoe employs backward and forward glances to enhance the confidence of readers: 'Their guide knows where he is going and why.' Instancing the brief description of Stilton in Huntingdonshire, McVeagh cites it to show how Defoe 'can dance in the smallest space'. Because 'the Britain that he opens out before our view is a Britain no previous writer has seen', a large claim is possible: 'One could call the *Tour* a modern Domesday Book: it is the proprietor's documentation of a new Britain' (1: 30–35). That new nation, as evoked by Defoe, is the subject of the present volume.

A Countdown of the Entries

We can now consider not the area of towns but their population. Here some significant issues may become apparent, following on from suggestions in Chapter 1 on the way that Defoe allocates space in Letter 2. Fairly reliable figures exist for the whole island from around 1700 which can be used to plot the size of various towns described in the *Tour*, as in Table 3 and Map 2. It should be remembered that these places represented less than a fifth of the nation as a totality: the sixty-eight towns in England with more than 2,500 inhabitants in 1700 made up in aggregate less than a million people.[14]

Table 3 *Towns rated by population size*

>500k	>30k	20k–30k	10k–20k	8k–10k	4k–8k
London	Edinburgh	Bristol	Aberdeen	Birmingham	Ayr
	Norwich		Exeter	Chester	Bury St Edmunds
			Glasgow	Colchester	Cambridge
			Newcastle	Dundee	Canterbury
			Yarmouth	Ipswich	Chatham
			York	Manchester	Gloucester
				Plymouth	Hull
				Worcester	Inverness
					King's Lynn
					Leeds
					Leicester
					Liverpool
					Nottingham
					Oxford
					Perth
					Portsmouth
					Salisbury
					Shrewsbury
					Sunderland
					Tiverton

These data can be set alongside an estimate of the length of the main entry within the *Tour* for the town concerned. (I have omitted obvious digressions such as a visit to the site of the battle of Marston Moor in the middle of the entry for York.) The word 'main' here is critical, since each of the towns is mentioned elsewhere in the text, often to bring out its regional importance. London may be left aside, since it has a whole section in Letter 5 to itself. This runs to almost 27,000 words, meaning that it has a ratio of about twenty-two inhabitants per word. Obviously, in what follows, the lower the ratio, the more intensive the coverage. It will be seen that no town in Wales quite reached the critical mass to appear in the table.

Defoe writes about all these places in some detail, with two striking exceptions which appear to be sports – there is no proper entry for either Birmingham or Sunderland, although both are mentioned a number of times.[15] As regards the larger towns, the most notable feature is the high ratio for Norwich, with as many as forty-eight inhabitants per word. This will occasion some surprise, in view of the fact that Defoe had ties of family and

Map 2. Towns mentioned in the *Tour*, graduated by size in *c.* 1700.

friendship with the city: for some reason he chooses to deal with its antiquities with extreme brevity. Another place that the author knew well, namely Bristol, is treated at some length, as shown in Chapter 11; but it has a relatively high score of 22 because of the size of the city. Predictably, the fullest and most detailed entry in this group is that of Edinburgh, where Defoe had lived for a long time, resulting in an impressively low ratio of 4. Within the next bracket, Exeter does not fare particularly well, with a ratio of almost 27. Newcastle is rather more densely covered with an index of 17. Glasgow shows up well with 8, in an entry that prefaces an analysis of the opportunities for further expansion of overseas trade. Despite the fact that it had little trade, York comes out at a much lower figure, 5, a result that may be unexpected to some. The full coverage of Yarmouth reduces its ratio to 6.

Moving further down the list, we find mostly low results, pointing to Defoe's interest in regional centres just below the level of national hubs. Thus, Ipswich has less than 3, a low score boosted by an account featuring some personal recollections; Manchester 4; Worcester 7; and Plymouth 11 (I omit the account of an offshore engagement that Defoe witnessed). Like the divided entry for Colchester, where Defoe already had some business interests, the one for Aberdeen registers 6, a sign of the importance it is accorded in the book (3: 257ff). Dundee does less well on 11. Stepping down a further grade, we reach towns in a period of growth with a correspondingly plummeting ratio, such as Liverpool (6), Portsmouth and Leeds (5 each) and notably Nottingham (just 2). Chester, whose population was more static, comes out at 8. In the process of edging gradually up into next bracket, with about 7,500 residents at the turn of the century, we find Hull, which achieves a respectable 5, but this is on the basis of a highly derivative entry. A thin description is accorded to Leicester (as many as fifteen inhabitants per word); this is a case where Defoe was more interested in the rural economy of the surrounding area than in the county town itself. Somewhat anomalous are two locations with their own distinctive geographic setting, Perth and King's Lynn, each at almost 10; the inland resort Bury St Edmunds, with both antiquities and modern leisure activities to record, causing the proportion to drop significantly to 2.5; and above all St Andrews, where a wealth of historical materials brings the ratio down to one of the lowest levels at less than 1.5.

The interpretation of these figures plainly gives rise to some elements of qualification. By 1725 the industrial towns would have shown increased populations, meaning that their ratios as calculated here would have gone up; and the definition of an entry cannot be mathematically strict, so that the numbers cited do not exactly represent the degree of coverage that a town receives over the course of the *Tour*. Still, we can draw some broad conclusions from the data. It is apparent that Defoe spent a lot of time and effort on quiet shire capitals as well as greeting the burgeoning industrial centres of the north of England, whose wondrous rise he found so remarkable, as in Leeds (3: 73ff), Liverpool (3: 123ff) and Manchester (3: 129ff). Ports are generally, but not uniformly, given extra attention: see for example Whitehaven, shown in Figure 1. A resort like Bury St Edmunds is likely to be

Figure 1 Matthew Read, *Prospect View of Whitehaven, Cumbria* (*c.*1730). Defoe observes that the town had 'grown up from a small Place to be very considerable by the Coal Trade', so that it was now 'the most eminent Port in England for shipping off Coals, except Newcastle and Sunderland'. (*Tour* 3: 140). He notes the safety of the harbour, protected by St Bees Head, visible in the background. Source: YCBA.

covered at length – we see this with spa towns whose permanent population in 1700 fell just below the 3,000 limit, including Bath, Tunbridge Wells, Epsom and Knaresborough.[16] The places with the most extensive treatment are not always the ones with which the author had the closest personal links. Finally, he gave full attention to the larger Scottish cities, even those in less accessible locations that he did not know well. Together with other evidence, this brief examination of the treatment extended to towns throughout Britain indicates that the author sought to give as fair a picture as he could of the whole island.

The Information Highway

There is another way to define the manner of proceeding in the *Tour*. An initial hint is provided by one of the roadbooks that proliferated in the age, and that Defoe probably knew. *Britannia Depicta*, published by Thomas Bowles in 1720, consists of maps engraved by a young Welshman, Emanuel Bowen, with textual descriptions by an antiquarian named John Owen. This is a recension of John Ogilby's *Britannia* (1675), a work described by J. B. Harley as 'in several respects . . . a major step forward in the mapping of England'.[17] Defoe himself possessed the 1698 edition of Ogilby, and may have used it on his travels as a political agent.[18] At the head of Bowen's volume comes 'A Table of all the Roads contain'd in this Book', followed by an explanation: 'Having dispos'd all the Principal ROADS of ENGLAND & WALES into 4 Classis, under ye distinction & order following, viz. [1] Independant [2] Dependant [3] Principal & [4] Accidental Cross Roads'. The seventy-three routes are all based on Ogilby's list. They lead off with fourteen major arteries, the first class 'comprising all the Direct Independant Roads from London', a significant way of orientating the national system. In this volume all roads do lead, directly or indirectly, to London, even though the third and fourth classes describe routes from one provincial town to another. (The frontispiece to the present volume shows a section of the West Road leading from central London past Hounslow and across Bagshot Heath, an area notorious for its unattractive terrain and the bodies of gibbeted highwaymen on the roadside: see also Defoe's description in Chapter 10). By contrast Defoe ventures along byways that were effectively culs de sac, such as those branching off on to the Isle of Sheppey or St Bees Head, where no principal thoroughfare existed. You could not get to Liverpool following any of Bowen's itineraries, for instance, and you could not make your way with his aid to Whitehaven.

You would be completely lost if you wanted to cut across to the small town of Wooler to visit the Cheviot Hills, as the brave tourist does.

It will not escape attention that there are already similarities visible with the modern scheme of classification in the United Kingdom, which is divided into M, A (subdivided) and B roads, along with those that are designated 'unclassified'. In Bowen's work, the destination of these fourteen routes from the capital are set out in alphabetical order: Aberystwyth, Arundel, Barwick [Berwick], Bristol, Buckingham, St David's, Dover, Harwich, Hith [Hythe], Holyhead, Land's End, Newhaven, Portsmouth and Rye. Some features are immediately apparent. Only one map here, the second, will take the traveller north of Chester; to go further in the North-west, we must wait for the road to Carlisle, no. 18 in the list. Equally, the road to East Anglia takes us as far as Harwich. which is where the first section of Letter 1 gets us in the *Tour* (1: 85). If we need to press on to Norwich or Yarmouth, the next ports of call, we must turn ahead to map nos. 25 and 31. By contrast, there are actually three roads leading into Wales, and no less than five heading towards the coast of Kent and Sussex, as well as the one for Portsmouth. Separately, we notice that Land's End is the only destination in this group named for a physical feature, rather than for a town: this may help to explain the song and dance that Defoe makes, almost literally, when he reaches the conclusion of his journey into the West Country.

Some of those itineraries went back to Roman times and were recorded in the Antonine Itinerary during the second and third centuries AD. The progress of the *Tour* requires Defoe to spend a fair amount of time tracking the old Roman roads that still served as major routes linking different parts of the country. He was not unaware of their historic significance, and allows himself an occasional flight of fancy:

> It is a most pleasant Curiosity to observe the Course of these old famous Highways; the *Icknild Way*, the *Watling-street*, and the *Foss*, in which one sees so lively a Representation of the antient *British*, *Roman* and *Saxon* Governments, that one cannot help reallizing those Times to the Imagination; and tho' I avoid meddling with Antiquity as much as possible in this Work, yet in this Case a Circuit or Tour thro' *England* would be very imperfect, if I should take no Notice of these Ways, seeing in tracing them we necessarily come to the principal Towns, either that are or have been in every County. (2: 204)

In fact there are many references to the Fosse Way, showing Defoe's understanding of the network that branched out from the main artery. But his underlying interest (if we can put it like that) is in the present viability of the surface of the road. As we shall see in Chapter 10, he made careful observations of some stretches along the route. He also witnessed an experiment carried out, less for archaeological purposes than to learn the secret of the stability of Roman construction – it was a highway engineering project: 'This very Causeway have I seen cut into, so as to discover the very Materials with which it was built; and in some parts of the same Causway, farther *North*, where the great road has taken some other Way, I have seen the old Causway dug down to carry the Materials away, and mend the Road which was then in Use' (2: 236).

Defoe mentions these surviving stretches when he can, but of course most highways in his own day took a different course – nobody wanted to get from Uriconium (Wroxeter) to Venta Silurum (Caerwent) in 1725. The Roman divisions of the colony were governed largely by military needs, and so surrounded the hotspots where Celtic tribes had their strongholds. Likewise the more primitive road system of the Anglo-Saxon era joined not settled regions but kingdoms of the Heptarchy, who were often at odds. By Defoe's day the obligations of cartography were wholly different, since roads linked a national economy, now overseen by one parliament in the previously divided state. Moreover, the distribution of the population had changed since the Middle Ages and would change further as the location of industry shifted from its traditional centres. Migration led to growth in the number of people in some counties and depletion in others. The districts with the biggest ratio of increase in this era, especially after 1700, were those with a manufacturing rather than an agricultural economy: counties that had a fairly large population and had grown steadily in previous centuries, such as Norfolk and Wiltshire, began to lose ground. In most places there was an increase in urban residents as against rural, but the pattern was not uniform across the whole country.

What this means is that the older ways of apprehending the shape of Britain, and the dividing lines that were drawn between regions, were no longer applicable. Some of our familiar geographical labels were not yet in common use: Defoe speaks in the *Tour* once of having come forward 'to view the Midland Counties of *England*, I mean such as may be said to lie between the *Thames* and the *Trent*' (2: 192). This definition had formal implications, since Letters 8 and 9 both take off from the Trent, one ending up at the Tees, and the other at the Tweed – just as earlier Letters 1, 2, 3–4, 6–7 had each departed from and arrived at the banks of the Thames. Later, in his appendix on the highways, Defoe mentions places 'within the Compass of this Midland Circuit' (2: 241), suggesting that he had linked the term to the progression of his journeys. But this expression, 'the

Midlands', had not achieved the wide currency it has developed in more recent times. Nor were there yet Border Counties between England and Wales, while the Home Counties had to wait until 1883 to gain their modern identity.[19] The conclusion we must draw is that the author had no very obvious regional grid on which to plot his description of England in particular.

At this date, the term 'East Anglia' was only used of the historic Saxon kingdom, and naturally Defoe does not apply it to the region he surveys in Letter 1. However, it is hard to think of any earlier writer who had produced such a coherent picture of the Eastern counties. The circuit embraces the Thames estuary, fishing villages along the coast of the North Sea; the old capital of Colchester and the Roman road; major harbours including Harwich, Ipswich, Yarmouth and King's Lynn; cathedral cities, among them one second in size for a long period only to London, that is Norwich; the ancient university town of Cambridge; the great mart at Sturbridge Fair; the pleasure resort of Bury St Edmunds; the horseracing centre of Newmarket; modern mansions erected by Whig grandees; and a whole variety of trades and crafts, notably those relating to textiles, above all wool – one of the binding factors that Defoe enlists to create the sense of a homogeneous entity. No one made picturesque tours of Suffolk or Norfolk in the 1720s, but for Defoe the passage through Essex was only way he had to reach the hinterland of these counties, and this made up an area whose business ecology he knew intimately. The letter is alive with anecdote and folk tales, from the ague-ridden women of the marshes near the site of modern Southend to some medieval doggerel on Hatfield Forest, from the tale of the Dunmow Flitch to the migrating swallows near Orford, from the disappearance of the once thriving town of Dunwich to the wrecks off Winterton Ness. And nowhere do we get a stronger impression of the pull of London as on the Great Road, with its 'large thorough-fair Towns, full of good Inns, and chiefly maintained by the excessive Multitude of Carriers and Passengers, which are constantly passing this way to *London*, with Droves of Cattle, Provisions, and Manufactures for *London*' (1: 82). The prose almost falls over itself in redundancy as the capital looms into view.

If we turn back to *Britannia Depicta*, we can see that the supposed course of Letter 1 starts along route no. 8, described in the opening paragraphs as 'the Great Road' (1: 53), and later joining up with no. 31, and returning partly via no. 22. Letter 2 hugs no. 7 quite closely for stretches as it makes its way along the Thames Estuary towards Canterbury and Dover. Thereafter it takes a cross-country hop along the south coast before veering back to the capital from Portsmouth, in close parallel at times with no. 13, referred to as 'the Great Road from *London* to *Chichester*, and from *London* to *Portsmouth*' (1: 182). Near the capital there is a divagation that takes us nearer no. 12. I am not suggesting, of course, that the narrative follows the exact line of the route marked out in the roadbook. Rather, the highway supposedly taken defines a main artery through which trade circulates, and which thus leads us to a defining social and economic characteristic of the region it serves.

Zonal Marking

Many will recognise the fact that portions of the first four journeys chronicled in the *Tour* loosely correspond to the directions followed by modern trunk roads: in Letter 2, the A2, returning by the A3; Letter 4, returning by the A4; Letter 6, the A5; Letter 7, returning by sections of the A5 and A6. The itinerary joins up with the A1 at various points of Letters 6, 9 and 11. In addition, the route of Letter 10 runs close to the A6. Part of the A10 between King's Lynn and Cambridge (route no. 22 in *Britannia Depicta*) matches the return journey of Letter 1. In the Scottish section, there are fewer direct correspondences, but part of Letter 12 hovers near to the A7. However, there is a more extensive parallel within the contemporary system, as shown in Table 4.[20]

The connection will be apparent to those familiar with the road numbering scheme used across Great Britain, which has been in operation in various forms since the 1920s. Under this classification, all A and B roads are given a number containing up to four digits (for B roads, three and four digits only). The relevant area is defined by a single-digit A road marking its boundary, each spreading radially from London in a clockwise direction. It is obvious that the zones thus formed echo in many instances the layout of the *Tour*, even though they derive from a classification system that was not introduced until 199 years after its publication. Again, there is no exact one-for-one correspondence in every place, but the degree of symmetry displayed in this Table is surely striking.

We must be aware that routes which pass through more than one zone retain their original number. The roads listed in the third column do not in every case correspond exactly with those that a traveller in Defoe's time would have used: they represent the general course of the *Tour* as the narrative moves from point A to B via C. The author would probably have taken minor roads where convenient, and some routes designated today by a 'B' would have given him a more comfortable ride than others now

Table 4 *Circuits in the* Tour *and modern road zones*

Letter	Zone classification	Modern roads within the zone
1	all within Zone 1	A1, A10, A11, A12, A13
2	closely matches Zone 2	A2, A20, A21, A27
	on return skirts border of Zone 3	A3
3	almost all Zone 3	A30, A38, A303
4	mostly Zone 3	A36, A37, A38, A39
	skirts border of Zone 4	A4
5	(touches on Zones 1–6)	A1, A2, A3, A4, A5
6	almost all in Zone 4,	A1, A38, A361, A40, A41, A48, A470, A487
	last segment in Zone 5	A5, A55
7	mostly Zone 5, some Zone 6	A41, A5, A45, A607
	section of Zone 1	A1, A15, A16, A5120, A6, A605
8	almost all Zone 6, touches Zone 5	A58, A6, A60, A625, A635
	skirts Zone 1 at end	A1, A61
9	almost all in Zone 1	A1, A167, A171, A1079
	brief incursion into Zone 6	A69, A697, A698
10	almost all in Zone 5	A580, A595
	skirts Zone 6	A6, A66
11	virtually all in Zone 1	A1
12	almost identical with Zone 7	A7, A75, A71, A714, A736
	briefly into Zone 8 at end	A8, A872
13	first part in Zone 9	A9, A90, A91, A92, A96
	second part mostly in Zone 8, with side trip into Zone 9	A82, A3

Note: It is impossible to chart the itinerary of the closing section of Letter 13 at all precisely.

allocated to the 'A' category. More significant is the way in which the bureaucratically defined zones so often map areas of Britain in terms of a grid that aligns with the layout of the *Tour* (see Map 3). This seems natural to us today, but we should remember that the bureaucrats had not begun to slice up the landscape. It is thanks to works like Defoe's much reprinted guide that regions could be named, or even fully conceptualised. There was a West Country, and had been one since Saxon times; but the expression was only just coming general usage – and Defoe never uses it.

Some of the lines of diagrammatic force are clear. The first journey out of London sticks to Zone 1; the second almost entirely to Zone 2; the third (divided between Letters 3 and 4) to Zone 3; while the fourth (divided between Letters 6 and 7) mostly lies within Zones 4 and 5. The pattern becomes a little less clear when the routes do not start from London, but Letter 8 belongs chiefly in Zone 6, with Letter 9 mostly in the northern half

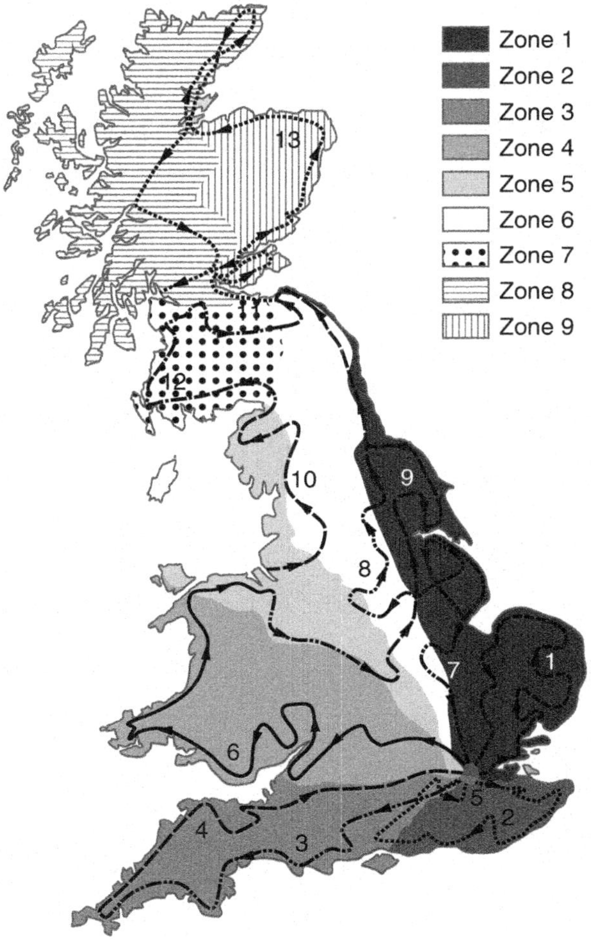

Map 3. Map showing modern highway zones and, numbered, the supposed routes of the *Tour*. Source: Gabriel Rogers.

of Zone 1, and Letter 10 in the northern half of Zone 5. Scotland is relatively straightforward, with Letter 11 in the furthest stretch of Zone 1, Letter 12 in Zone 7, and Letter 13 equally divided between Zones 8 and 9. No stretching of the evidence is required to attain these results.

While the equivalences are amazingly close, they are cited here for illustrative purposes. They suggest that Defoe had in his head a roughly equivalent set of zones, which enabled him to view regions as distinct entities while tracing their relations – economic, political, cultural – with adjoining parts of the country. His out-and-back method enabled him to textualise the pull that London, and to a lesser degree Edinburgh, exerted over the rest of the country. There are internal hinge-points elsewhere: it is seldom observed that Letter 10 starts off by ferrying over the Mersey to Liverpool from Chester, where Letter 6 had ended and Letter 7 began. Letters 8 and 9 each take off from the River Trent, notionally at Nottingham and Newark, sixteen miles apart. The two last English circuits reach as far as the border, at Berwick and Carlisle respectively: the first two Scottish circuits resume the progression at the same hubs, to use an expression from air travel. In my estimate the formal propriety of the *Tour* derives from a strong sense that Defoe had of *relational* space, which allowed him to see the country as a machine of interlocking parts. The zones enable you to fit together everything you have seen about Britain, if you know the right direction to go.

Conclusion

What is the value of these formal devices, as they express the contours of early modern Britain? An answer is provided by a major study of Europe in the seventeenth and eighteenth centuries. Tim Blanning begins his comprehensive account, *The Pursuit of Glory*, with the words 'Communication is central to human existence.' In his opening chapter of thirty-nine pages, he devotes the first eighteen to the state of the roads across the continent, followed by ten more on waterways. The latter topic is so well handled in the *Tour* that the leading authority on this subject drew his map of inland navigation by reference to its coverage (see Chapter 5). As for transport by land, Blanning states at the outset that 'it was the condition of the roads which dictated the pace of communications and the degree of mobility'. He describes how primitive these routes were physically, by comparison with what came later, and adds that 'Even the main highways would count for forest tracks today.' They were essentially as they had been left under the Roman Empire, so that 'whether in Galway or Galatia, the average speed for the majority of travellers rarely exceeded walking pace'. In the earlier part of the period, only France made headway on changing this situation, while 'The sinuous, time- and effort-consuming nature of English roads was legendary.'

All this was transformed with the coming of the turnpike system. Britain had several advantages, as Blanning notes: 'Distances between major centres were shorter, the terrain was more co-operative, commercial incentives were stronger, and capital was more plentiful.' This led to a great reduction in travel times from London to places like Bath, Edinburgh, Exeter and Manchester, a point we have touched on in the Introduction (p. 7). A wider outcome was 'the construction of a national road network in the space of a couple of generations'. This would enhance productivity, material prosperity, life expectancy and other benefits. The turnpikes were able to bring 'speed and mobility into a society previously characterized by their opposites'. Blanning also remarks on the absence of customs duties, other than the small tolls, which regularly impeded the traveller on the Continent. In passing he mentions some comments in the *Tour.*

It was, of course, Defoe, not subsequent historians, who first saw the significance of what had just begun to happen in his own time. His celebrated account of the turnpikes in the second volume of the *Tour* is the subject of Chapter 10, later in this book. Blanning's comment that in this period the traveller 'would quickly encounter incomprehensible dialects and patois' resonates throughout the text, as we will see in Chapter 8. Defoe's methods allowed a pervasive sense of the potential for 'a national road network' to seep through the entire text. He understood the need for 'commercial incentives' to accelerate the growth of the turnpikes, and no one is better at evoking the delays and frustrations imposed by the sorry state of the highways on those who made journeys either for business or pleasure. Hardly anybody was keener on bringing the material benefits to which Blanning alludes. Defoe's own narrative enacts the rigours of day-to-day travel, and incorporates solutions. He seeks out the vestiges of the Roman roads wherever he can, and he suggests ways of creating an equally durable communication system. Although the construction of better roads was not, as Blanning reminds us, 'a sufficient route to modernity', it can certainly be claimed that it was a necessary step along the way. In that sense, the *Tour* served as a signpost to a future Defoe himself would never see.[21]

There is nothing like this from the other travel writers. A good roadbook permitted you to get from one place to another, but not to collate your experience of different journeys: you cannot readily join up the separate strip maps that *Britannia Depicta* offers you, as they follow one another alphabetically. You keep leaving London, but you don't get back there unless you reverse the description of the trip, and read backwards. (A strip map is linear and unidirectional, unlike a traditional map.) And trying to navigate the land with the help of Macky's *Journeys* would be like using a GPS grid with coordinates based on the surface of the moon. On the other hand, as John McVeagh puts it, 'If the *Tour* is a map of England, Defoe makes sure it is one that we can never get lost in' (1:30).

PART 2

Time

CHAPTER 5

The Role of the Tour *in the Historiography of Early Modern Britain*

Before we explore in more detail some central themes of the *Tour*, it should be useful to indicate the continuing relevance to modern historians of its depiction of the age. This chapter seeks to bring out some of the ways in which it has proved a central text for the study of early modern Britain. If we were to describe changes that have taken place in the historiography of this period over the past fifty years, there would be no shortage of issues to consider. The new modes of social history, some derived from the *Annales* school, would furnish an obvious example. Attention to the lives of women is still growing at an almost exponential rate. Urban history has expanded from almost nothing to a major area of study. Then there is the rise and to some extent the decline of cliometrics. Constitutional history seems to have lost some ground steadily. World and transatlantic history now plays a much bigger role than it did formerly, with consequences for the way insular matters are treated, and various modes of interdisciplinarity have affected the way we look at the period. One thing has remained constant, however. Hardly anybody has managed to compose a broad sweep of the subject, especially with regard to the late seventeenth and early eighteenth centuries, without calling on the evidence of the *Tour*. Across almost all the aspects of the period considered by Penelope J. Corfield in 2011, as flourishing or ripe for development, Defoe has something pertinent to contribute.[1]

Indeed, it must be as hard to write such a survey of Britain in the early modern period without once citing the *Tour* as it is to emulate Georges Perec by composing a novel without any use of the letter e. That is to judge by the plethora of authors who have found the work an indispensable source. Of course, mere frequency of citation does not always give conclusive evidence of intellectual influence, though it is a persuasive sign that the source provides rich stores of useful material. Three things stand out when we look at the way that historians have raided the *Tour*.

Towns and Transport

The first issue is the sheer range of topics on which scholars have had recourse to its pages. Two examples, taken at random from older and newer works, will make the point. M. Dorothy George supplied four extracts in her selection *England in Johnson's Day* (1928). These covered respectively the houses of merchants arising on both banks of the Thames upstream from London; a grand country house (Burleigh); one of the growing number of spas (Tunbridge Wells); and one illustrating the pace of change, at the site of a future seaside resort, Brighton, described as '*Bright Helmston*, commonly call'd *Bredhemston*, a Poor fishing Town, Old built' (1: 167).[2] In their compendium, *London: A Social and Cultural History 1550–1750* (2012), Robert O. Bucholz and Joseph P. Ward draw on seven passages relating to such issues as 'The Socioeconomic Base', 'Riot and Rebellion' and 'Plague and Fire'. The matters under review include the decline of provincial ports such as Ipswich; the relations of court and the City of London; the layout of the capital; the growth of fire insurance; and the role of the Bank of England.[3] Further instances of this spread of interests will emerge in the discussion here.

Second, we encounter a wide array of writers in different traditions who have enlisted the *Tour* to aid their widely divergent purposes. Among these are exponents of traditional and radical approaches; popular and scholarly authors; liberals and Marxists; old-style 'literary' historians alongside their more 'scientific' peers; poets and Gradgrinds. We might not expect those who were then the young Turks from Warwick University, disciples of E. P. Thompson, to hold Defoe in much regard, considering his hardline attitude towards the poor. But in their influential collection *Albion's Fatal Tree* (1975), three contributors (Cal Winslow on smuggling; John G. Rule on wrecking; and Douglas Hay on poachers) extracted some of their information from the *Tour*. Subsequently these authors have gone to the same fount of knowledge in other publications. As for their fellow contributors, Peter Linebaugh quoted a snippet in his major study *The London Hanged: Crime and Civil Society in the Eighteenth Century* (1992), while Thompson himself used Defoe's book to build up in part his picture of Windsor Forest and its surroundings, a scene evoked with magisterial skill in *Whigs and Hunters: The Origin of the Black Act* (1975) – one of the classic accounts of the era in modern scholarship.

Third, it is noteworthy how often modern writers have used generalised observations by Defoe to buttress their own argument. Again, it is enough to give two brief instances, as examples abound. In his account of the turnpike system, *Transport and Economy* (1977), Eric Pawson notes that 'Defoe was one of the first observers to describe the centrality of London in the national system of internal trade. Indeed, it was one of the key themes in the Tour.' He goes on to quote a famous passage from the opening pages of the first circuit, which describes the way in which the whole kingdom was employed 'to furnish something ... to supply the city of London'.[4] There is a revealing footnote which should be added here. Notoriously, the weakest part of the *Tour* by far lies in Defoe's vastly exaggerated population estimates for growing towns and cities, such as London, Halifax and Frome. Yet a distinguished demographic historian of our times, Sir Anthony Wrigley, supports the case of his most famous essay with an extract from the Preface to the first volume of the *Tour*. This makes the same point as Pawson's citation, but occurs a few pages earlier in the *Tour*. Wrigley writes of 'London's importance as a centre of consumption, which prompted Defoe in 1724 to write of the "general dependence of the whole country upon the city of London"'. This statement comes from 'A Simple Model of London's Importance in Changing English Society, 1650–1750', first published in *Past and Present* (1967).[5] Ironically, Wrigley makes the citation not directly from the text of the *Tour*, but from an earlier article by the economic historian F. J. Fisher.

In the last major account of eighteenth-century London, *A Great and Monstrous Thing* (2013), Jerry White borrowed a phrase for his title (and quite a lot else) from the *Tour*.[6] In this he was simply following a line of distinguished historians of the capital who have found a need to draw materials from Defoe. They include scholars with a mainly political bent such as George Rudé and those focusing principally on economic life such as L. D. Schwartz.[7] Defoe's key ideas are found in the contributions to a volume devoted to *Londinopolis*.[8] As already noted, urban history has undergone a huge expansion in recent decades, with many of the most influential figures incurring a similar debt – to mention only a few, Peter Borsay, Peter Clark, C. W. Chalklin, P. J. Corfield and Alan Everitt.[9] Local studies of larger towns such as those of Gordon Jackson on Hull and David Hussey on Bristol have quarried the book extensively.[10] In a well-known collection on country towns in the pre-industrial era, the contributors on Ipswich and Winchester in the seventeenth century make more use of Defoe's later account than that of any single source prior to 1700.[11]

Not that this process began in late years. Early in the twentieth century students of the development of transportation including Sidney and Beatrice Webb, as well as W. T. Jackman, drew heavily on the *Tour*, although they misleadingly cited later versions which came out after the original author's death.[12] Here they were following a bad tradition inherited from the nineteenth century. We have only to look at the *Lectures on the Industrial Revolution* (1884), a posthumous publication by Arnold Toynbee (1852–83), uncle of the celebrated universal historian of the same name. This book was hugely influential, and by general consent popularised the expression 'Industrial Revolution'. Toynbee was aware that Defoe had written his 'admirable' book in the 1720s, but his repeated citations are always taken from the seventh edition (1769).[13] The practice is less common today, but still not unknown.

It scarcely needs pointing out that the authors of specialist monographs, written to replace the Webbs and Jackman on this subject, made repeated use of Defoe. Signs of this dependence are particularly evident in literature on transport in the period. Writing on *The Turnpike Road System* in 1972, William Albert remarks that observations about this topic in the *Tour* 'are of particular importance for they were made at a time when there were still relatively few trusts, and the difference between trust and parish repair, especially on the main routes, could therefore be clearly seen'.[14] In a work already cited, *Transport and Economy* (1977), Eric Pawson scours the text for seventeen references to passages across the whole of the *Tour*. Equally valuable material was mined in several works by the major historian of inland waterways T.S. Willan. For example, in a twelve-page article for the *Economic History Review* on the navigation of the River Severn, Willan turns to Defoe's book on twelve occasions.[15] Everyone familiar with the period knows that most places dotted around the country were linked by water as much as by land.

Defoe's England?

We can now return to Dorothy George's classic work on London life (1925), where she had recourse to several works by Defoe, among them the *Tour*.[16] As we have already seen, she included extracts from the work in her anthology *England in Johnson's Day* (1928). A more pervasive presence marks her study of *England in Transition* (1931), itself a phrase that encapsulates so much of what Defoe sets out to evoke. She describes him as 'Far the best authority for early eighteenth-century England'. This is at the start of a chapter entitled 'Defoe's England: London and the Country.' It may be felt that George cannot provide the last word any more on Hanoverian society, though her work on London still commands respect. Accordingly, some readers may think her praise hyperbolic: 'His famous *Tour through the whole Island of Great Britain* shows us the country as it appeared to a skilful observer with a marvellous eye for significant detail, who was also a man of business as well as a consummate journalist.'[17] George goes on to point out that, though the England of the 1720s may seem to us static, to Defoe it was a place of rapid economic, commercial and technological development. The advance in our knowledge in these areas has not totally invalidated the claims made here.

Economic historians have long shown heavy reliance on the same source, beginning with writers such as Ephraim Lipson and Paul Mantoux.[18] They were followed by a distinguished line of scholars, notably Sir John Clapham, T. S. Ashton, D. C. Coleman and Peter Mathias, who went so far as to call Defoe 'the keenest observer of economic growth of his time' in his *Tour*.[19] David S. Landes enlisted the book briefly in his influential study of industrial development, *The Unbound Prometheus* (1969). More significantly, F. J. Fisher was one of the first to recognise a facet of the *Tour*'s originality as a source for broad-based economic history. As he pointed out in his inaugural lecture in 1956, 'It is not until the very end of the seventeenth century that much effort was made by the government, or by economic interests, or by writers to bring together similar information for different parts of the country so as to afford a conspectus of the whole. It was not until the eighteenth that those efforts were crowned with spectacular success in the work of Defoe.'[20] The approach seen in the *Tour* derives its novelty in part from the author's knowledge of disparate areas of the country, most of it first-hand if not all recent. A more important factor was his ability to perceive connections, both between regions and between different aspects of the economy (production, distribution, transport, market, availability of labour and physical resources).

Others in cognate fields have grasped the continuing utility of the *Tour*'s evidence. In his survey of the improving bent of the period, the noted historical geographer H. C. Darby cited the book on more than a dozen occasions with reference to almost thirty passages.[21] Among social historians we can observe the same legacy, founded by J. L. and Barbara Hammond, and continued by G. D. H. Cole and Raymond Postgate. Cole was one of the most effusive in his admiration, offering a number of claims for the book's centrality, such as 'We can make great use of Defoe unrevised to tell us what England was really like in the early eighteenth century.'[22] The only real rival to Cole in this respect is G. M. Trevelyan, who introduced *England under Queen Anne* (1930) with an assertion that 'When a survey is demanded of Queen Anne's island . . . our thoughts turn to Daniel Defoe.' As we saw in Chapter 1, he also stated that Defoe's report 'occupies the central point of our thought and vision'. Twelve years later he recycled this paragraph at the start of a section on the early modern period in his *English Social History*, to which, like George, he gave the subtitle 'Defoe's England'.[23]

In the more munificent climate for academic publishing in the first part of the twentieth century, it was feasible to produce huge multi-author collections such as *Shakespeare's England* (1916), edited by C. T. Onions; *Johnson's England* (1933), edited by A. S. Turberville; and *Early Victorian England* (1934), edited by G. M. Young. These provided expert essays running in some cases to 15,000 words or more. The two Turberville volumes contained a chapter by H. L. Beales on 'Travel and Communications', which supplied some provocative suggestions. 'Defoe had a definite utilitarian purpose,' Beales wrote, 'to make the whole country familiar to those who lived in it.' Because of the rapidity of change, as 'new foundations are always laying', the work became all the more necessary, and 'it became the parent of a prolific stream of books with the object of guiding travellers to the places of importance'. Beales also treated the later editions with some contempt, as the product of 'hack-workers', who 'did little more than make the sprightly original into a commonplace guide-book'.[24] Further citations from the *Tour* appear in chapters from the same collection including those on 'Industry and Trade', 'Agricultural and Rural Life', and 'Town Life in the Provinces' (the last by G. D. H. Cole).

Here it is instructive to look at a volume in the old Oxford History of England, devoted to the 'Whig supremacy' in the years 1714 to 1760. The focus of the book is primarily political, but its author Basil Williams allots one chapter to the social and economic life of the people. He begins by isolating 'two remarkable records of the state of England at the opening and closing of this period'. One is that of Defoe, 'the supreme journalist, interested in every aspect of the national life', while the other, used 'to supplement' this source, is that of Arthur Young. Then Williams goes on to cite some passages from the *Tour* on the condition of the highways, drawn from the celebrated appendix to Volume II on the turnpike system. Later in this chapter he refers to Defoe's account ten times, on topics ranging from trade and agriculture to coal-mining, the port of London, Liverpool and pleasure resorts (five passages cited). The political content of Williams' book, published in 1939, has not worn altogether well, but there is little in this particular chapter that would require major adjustment today.[25]

In any case, even if some of these once highly respected authorities have lost some of their currency, the *Tour* remains omnipresent in the latest works of reference in pertinent fields. This applies very clearly in the burgeoning literature devoted to the towns and cities of early modern Britain. Thus in his chapter on the transformation of urban space 1700–1840, for the second volume of *The Cambridge Urban History* (2000), Michael Reed has occasion to raid Defoe's text on various issues, both general and particular.[26] In the same place Peter Clark, Penelope J. Corfield, Alan Dyer, Jonathan Barry, John Langton, Peter Borsay, Barrie Trinder and Gordon Jackson also cite Defoe a number of times.[27] One of the heaviest concentrations of allusions comes in Joyce Ellis' chapter on regional centres, with more than a dozen applications to the text.[28] It turns out that references are found in seven chapters out of eleven assigned to the years following 1700, all written by experts in their field. This is the more remarkable if we consider some facts: that Defoe had no modern aids, no research assistants, no scholarly library to visit, and no well-trained colleagues to consult; that he was busy writing several other books at the time that he prepared the *Tour*; and that the province of knowledge which we study today as urban history was by no means the sole facet of national life he had to cover. Elsewhere, Borsay has written that his 'first authentic view of Augustan England (*c.*1680–1730) was that captured through the pages of [the *Tour*]'; this is the opening of an essay entitled 'Urban Development in the Age of Defoe'. Later he observes, 'Few men could have known Augustan society as well as Defoe, or have been compelled by their profession to appraise it so rigorously. Even fewer could have combined both these qualities.'[29]

If anything, the density of allusion has increased in modern times. The sustained tendency can be remarked in writers as different as Christopher Hill and Nicholas Rogers, E. P. Thompson and Roy Porter, or Jeremy Black and G. E. Mingay. Porter, who seems to have known every primary and secondary source in existence, would enlist the *Tour* on several occasions to depict the changing face of England, or to illustrate 'the wonderful extent and variety of London'. In the course of evoking the creation of the modern world he returned to the same book, 'that national anthem to progress, agricultural, commercial and industrial'.[30] In the *Tour*, wrote W. A. Speck in a widely read textbook, 'Defoe set out to provide not merely a tourist guide for the early Hanoverian traveller but an economic dissertation.' Speck argues that, contrary to some claims, most of Defoe's contentions about the growth of the national economy can survive scrutiny even today.[31]

One of the most revelatory passages among all the writers just cited comes in Hill's contribution to the *Pelican Economic History of Britain*

(1969). It involves a comparison between John Leland's sixteenth-century *Itinerary* and the *Tour*:

> For Leland the important features of the landscape are castles – mostly ruinous by now, except in the North and Wales – religious houses, gentleman's seats, forests, market towns: landlords dominate, trade is local. For Defoe gentlemen's seats still matter, but castles, monasteries and forests have mostly disappeared, market towns are far less important: almost all trade that matters is with London. Both writers are concerned with transport and communication.[32]

In such formulations, 'Defoe's England' has ceased to operate merely as a toponym; it has become a historical marker, a social definition rather than a geographic entity. Hill reads the landscape of the nation through the varied descriptions of the physical environment in the *Itinerary* and the *Tour*. The books have become exemplars of their age.

Unlike most writers, Wilfrid Prest in *Albion Ascendant* (1998) gives full weight to Defoe's treatment of Wales and Scotland, and stresses that he 'depicts England as a land of great regional diversity, and marked economic specialisation'. He observes the way in which the *Tour* registers the North–South divide, not then such a familiar topic as it is today.[33] Julian Hoppit's comprehensive overview of the kingdom between 1689 and 1727 for the New Oxford History of England (2000) makes repeated calls on the *Tour* to document issues ranging from the dominance of London and the growth of Manchester to early enclosures and the discovery of Roman remains. (From that point of view, the New Oxford simply dispensed the wine of Williams' Old Oxford.)[34] In his extended survey of the turnpike system in *A Polite and Commercial People* (1989), written for the same series, Paul Langford devotes several pages to the new roads, and draws attention to the way in which Defoe 'was excited by their galvanizing effect and devoted a special appendix to a description of their consequences'.[35]

Country Matters

Defoe is not usually credited with any great knowledge of agriculture: it is one of the few branches of commercial activity in which he scarcely dabbled, though later in life he did take a ninety-nine-year lease on a spacious tract of land outside Colchester. Yet in 1984 contributors to *The Agrarian History of England and Wales*, under its formidable editor Joan Thirsk, had room for a good deal of evidence taken from his pages when it reached the early modern era – as had their predecessors on a slightly earlier period in 1967. Some of these writers touch down briefly for an odd fact or a striking quotation; but most of them raid the *Tour* gratefully and regularly.[36] Not many have more authority in this area than Thirsk herself, who once remarked that 'The identity of the clothing and dairying industries in the west country did not escape the notice of Daniel Defoe', adding that for all his digressive habits 'in fact his observation is precise'.[37] In truth, remarkably few salient facts escaped his notice. A further indication of what might be called the *versatility* of Defoe's coverage comes in another volume edited by Thirsk, *Rural England: An Illustrated History of the Landscape* (2000). Six separate contributors, out of ten who discuss 'Panoramas of Landscape', allude to passages in the *Tour*. These deal with such contrasting settings as downlands, wolds, woodlands, marshes, moorlands and common land.[38] The difficult thing would be to find a considerable historian working in the early modern period who has *not* had occasion to dip into this seemingly unquenchable fount of knowledge.

Confirmation of Defoe's grasp of the issues affecting society in a largely rural part of England comes in the work of a distinguished specialist on the history of the provinces. David Underdown devoted his last book, *Start of Play* (2000), to the early history of cricket, focusing in large measure on Kent, Sussex and Hampshire. As we know, this was the region described in Letter 2 of the *Tour*, and Underdown makes several raids on its coverage to enhance his own survey of the cultural landscape of the area, taking seriously the economic forebodings conveyed in the text. Early on, he writes, 'Daniel Defoe noted the contrast between the Weald and the lower slopes of the Downs, as he noted almost everything else worth seeing, during his wanderings through England in the early eighteenth century.' It is an intriguing thought that in laying the groundwork for his *Tour* the traveller (a student of the sports and pastimes of the English people) might have lit upon some of the earliest sites of organised cricket – though he came too soon to drop in on 'the cradle' of the game. This was the village of Hambledon in Hampshire, whose team took on the rest of England from the 1760s at its windy outpost on Broadhalfpenny Down. In 1725 Hambledon was just a sleepy backwater of 700 souls. Blink and you missed it – but would Defoe have blinked?[39] Almost exactly a century later, William Cobbett did come to the village: all he could find was 'a tumble-down rubbishy place' – the great Hambledon eleven had dispersed, and anyway Cobbett had no interest in cricket.[40]

The increasingly sophisticated study of electoral history has also benefitted from what Defoe supplied. For David Hayton and his colleagues on the volumes of the History of Parliament devoted to *The House of Commons 1690–1715* (2002), the pages of the *Tour* supply a thick body of evidence. This shows up particularly in their coverage of boroughs up and down the kingdom. In a number of cases these were spectacularly decayed, as with Dunwich, East Looe, Gatton, Hedon, Old Sarum, Queenborough and Winchelsea. But this is to leave out a much longer list, including Aberdeen Burghs, Aldborough, Beaumaris, Bedford, Boroughbridge, Boston, Bramber, Bristol, Buckingham, Bury St Edmunds, Calne, Carmarthen, Cirencester, Colchester, Dartmouth, Devizes, Great Yarmouth, Guildford, Harwich, Haverfordwest, Helston, Hereford, Huntingdon, Kingston upon Hull, Knaresborough, Lincoln, Liskeard, Lostwithiel, New Windsor, Northallerton, Northampton, Nottingham, Orford, Pembroke Boroughs, Plymouth, Preston, Richmond (Yorkshire), Ripon, Salisbury, Scarborough, Shrewsbury, Southwark, Tregony, Wigan Wilton and York (a pretty representative sample of the nation, excluding Scotland, that embraces larger and smaller towns, with a striking geographic spread across England and Wales). Among the entries for constituencies, a remarkable number find a descriptor for their opening sentence from the *Tour*.[41] An almost comparable density is found for references in standard sources such as the Victoria County Histories and the *Survey of London*.

It would be otiose to attempt a list of all the relevant scholarly studies and biographies which have been devoted to individual figures within the period. We might briefly note those on James Gibbs by Terry Friedman (sometimes citing Defoe's words from a later edition); on Nicholas Hawksmoor by Nicholas Hart; on Alexander Pope by Maynard Mack; on John Gay by David Nokes; on the Duke of Chandos by C. H. C. and M. I. Baker; on the Duchess of Marlborough by David Green; on John Theophilus Desaguliers by Audrey Carpenter; and on Handel by Otto Erich Deutsch and subsequently Donald Burrows. It is no surprise to find that historians of art and architecture, music, science and literature figure in this list. Such a spread once again reflects the scope of the work and its holistic approach.

The extraordinary fecundity of what Defoe wrote can be gauged by the range of subdisciplines it has penetrated. To give just a few instances, the *Tour* is adduced by historians of the family, old age, women, religion, shopping, weather, landscape, cartography, leisure, travel and tourism, infectious disease, antiquarianism, archaeology, gambling, the Navy, Civil War battlefields, dialect, industrial archaeology – the list could be greatly prolonged. It is referenced on the salt trade, decoy duck shooting, cave dwelling, sheep grazing, standing stones, shipbuilders' unions, coastal erosion, hop growing, whaling, smugglers and wreckers, Cornish wrestling, dockyards, Newmarket racing, mop fairs, fire insurance, the siege of Colchester, diving for treasure, navigation on the River Don, Scottish country houses, Cameronian martyrs and a hundred other topics. Defoe knew quite a lot about fisheries, as befits a man who sold oysters from Colchester. The leading authority on craftsmen and interior designers uses a passage in the *Tour* to document the career of the most important stuccoist of the period.[42]

Toponymists discuss the form that place-names take in Defoe's work; collectors of proverbs register his usages. He affected not to be interested in antiquities, but, as Rosemary Sweet has noted, he could not help taking careful notice of the remains of the past – actually he has plenty of first-hand observations in addition to his raids on Camden.[43] Even students of topography find him useful, as is evidenced by sections of *The Atlas of Historic Towns*, Volume II (1975) devoted to Bristol and Cambridge.[44] Charting 'Land Use and the Built Environment' in his social atlas (2000) of London in the 1690s, Craig Spence invokes Defoe's description of the shape of the city. Before that the historical topographer Hugh Phillips also made use of the *Tour*, which may suggest that if you wish to draw a map of London at the start of the eighteenth century you might well consult Defoe's peregrination of its bounds. Among criminal historians, we might note the well-conceived survey by Frank McLynn, *Crime and Punishment in Eighteenth-Century England* (1989), which makes some judicious raids on the *Tour*. Setting the scene for his book on *The London Mob: Violence and Disorder in Eighteenth-Century England* (2004), Robert B. Shoemaker turns to Defoe on three occasions in his opening chapter concerning street life. Few books in the language, whatever their qualities, have been so widely pillaged. Yet no collective statement of this debt has been made by historians.

Defoe's Perspective on the Nation

It may be asked, why has the text been so influential? Among possible explanations that could be suggested, we could instance the relative ease of the *Tour*'s availability in print, combined with a lack of access that until recently historians had to other primary sources. However, we should recall that, apart from brief excerpts, the work was never republished between 1779 and 1927, and after this latter date the Scottish sections were omitted from the most used reprint. The standing of the work derived partly from

Defoe's reputation in other forms of literature, and we have seen that his name was attached to later eighteenth-century editions that introduced a large number of changes into the text. As a result, he may be more cited than Celia Fiennes, who is known only for her *Journeys*, first published in the nineteenth century. However, a more persuasive reason lies in the fact that the *Tour* is so much more comprehensive in terms both of geography and information, above all on matters relating to trade, industry, transport and allied issues. This consideration applies also to the travel diaries of the second Earl of Oxford, and to accounts by foreign visitors such as César-François de Saussure and Zacharias Conrad von Uffenbach.

A further distinction lies in the far greater topical content found in the *Tour* compared with other accounts of the nation: this includes political, economic and social developments. As this book has repeatedly attempted to show, the work of Defoe's most direct rival, John Macky in his own *Journey* (1714–23), comes out unfavourably in almost every respect. His itinerary is jagged and arbitrary; his progress across the country is thin on detail regarding modes of travel; his entries are bitty and disconnected; and his information is quite as derivative as that of his rival. Only in a few scattered instances would we find it more instructive to quote his work rather than the *Tour*. Here we may look briefly at some of the factors that have made the *Tour* such a constant recourse for scholars.

In so many ways Defoe was the right author in the right place at the right time. This is most immediately apparent in respect of his discussion of the new turnpikes, considered at a more detailed level in Chapter 10. This appendix contained a sneak preview of measures under parliamentary scrutiny, not yet known to the public at large. The author was conscious that occasional mistakes would slip through, and in the preface to the second volume he offered a generous apology for some very minor errors. A work that strove to relay the latest information was naturally subject to the need for correction. We saw in Chapter 2 that the *Tour* incorporated a number of outlying paratextual elements that were demanded when the text burst its allotted bounds. In this respect, the book serves as an equivalent of the fast-growing nation.

Naturally there are omissions. The *Tour* does not mention the recent innovations of Abraham Darby I at Coalbrookdale, which lay just too far off the author's itinerary – though, as briefly noted in the Introduction, he could well have encountered Darby, a partner with a fellow quaker Benjamin Cool in the Bristol Brass Company at the very juncture (1706) when Defoe was using Cool as his local distribution agent for political propaganda.[45] Likewise, the flying shuttle made its appearance in cotton mills just too late to make its way into the *Tour*. Its inventor John Kay actually formed a partnership in 1733 to exploit his machinery in Colchester, where Defoe had owned property now passed on to his son Daniel, a merchant.

As England began to emerge from its agrarian past into the industrial age, Defoe had the percipience to comment on the wool-manufacturing methods of the West Riding, and the silk-throwing factory set up by the Lombe brothers at Derby as recently as 1717–21 – nor does he fail to point out that this was made possible by the technological innovations of George Sorocold. He does not seem to have been aware of Thomas Newcomen's steam engine, patented in 1712, and just coming into service. But this leaves plenty of crucial events of the age that the author did witness at first hand, many of them memorialised in the *Tour*, including the Great Plague and Great Fire, the Monmouth rebellion, the coming of William III, the effects of the Great Storm in 1703, the manoeuvring in Edinburgh at the time of the Union, the accession of George I, the turmoil in Exchange Alley at the time of the Bubble, the plague scare in 1720 and so much else.

Unavoidably there were some topics which he decided to exclude from his coverage. Overseas exploration and discovery for commercial purposes were matters to which Defoe had allotted a great deal of his proselytising energy, but they could not easily be brought within the scope of his *Tour*. At the same time, we need to recall other matters which Defoe left out, for various reasons of tact and decorum, though he wrote about them elsewhere: for example, the introduction of penal transportation to the colonies in 1718–20; the lives of criminals such as Jonathan Wild and Jack Sheppard (provoking fears of a supposed increase in violent crime);[46] the plague scare of 1720; the echoes of the brouhaha surrounding Wood's halfpence in Dublin; the campaign for smallpox inoculation led by Lady Mary Wortley Montagu; or conflicts within the church, most obviously the Bangorian dispute. These issues came to a head in the first decade of George I's reign, although they relate directly to events before and after.

A Changing Landscape

Moreover, the physical landscape was also in the process of change, in London especially – but public and private buildings were shooting up all across the nation. Defoe gives due attention to St Paul's Cathedral, the Queen Anne churches and the notable addition of St Martin's in the Fields, consecrated a few months after he wrote. He picks out some of the new edifices that dominated the skyline – even mentioning the yet unrealised plans of the South Sea Company to extend their headquarters in Threadneedle Street. But the stronger emphasis in this section is on the piecemeal growth of the capital outside the city walls, as the metropolis steadily extended its boundaries, and people of all classes moved towards the periphery. Beyond London, the *Tour* dilates on some new country houses in the process of construction, among them Walpole's mansion at Houghton, Chandos' palace at Cannons and Lord Onslow's home at Clandon. Along with the houses go innovations in landscape gardening: descriptions by the author of recently designed parks are often reproduced by modern scholars.[47] He had also caught the building at King's College, Cambridge, just undertaken by James Gibbs at the start of 1724 – this may be first-hand observation, since he had more business at this time in the eastern counties than anywhere else outside London. He knows that the foundations have been laid for Guy's Hospital in London. Some of these have to be slipped into the text by means of appendixes, a testimony to the kinetic energy that spreads from the nation to the composition of the book itself.

Just as up to date is the famous section on the turnpikes, which includes not just a glimpse of the latest stretches of the highway to be put in place, but some future schemes still undergoing scrutiny by parliament (see Chapter 10). The treatment of the roads here is highly characteristic, as it builds on more than half a century of first-hand experience along the length and breadth of the kingdom and demonstrates the kind of *change* which Defoe had observed on his travels – thus creating an emblem of the entire nation, as he conceived it. Less well known is his ability to keep up to date on inland waterways, which is something that can be seen in his allusions to recent measures promoting river navigation. Defoe wrote just too soon to see the rapid increase in the number of parliamentary enclosures. 'Only two inclosure acts were passed in the twelve years of Anne's reign; between 1714 and 1720 only five. But in the succeeding twenty-year periods of the century the pace began to quicken, with 67 in 1721–40, 205 in 1741–60.'[48] But he was by no means unaware of what was happening more and more around the countryside. For example, he describes 'an eminent Contest' at Tring between 'Mr. [Henry] *Guy* and the Poor of the Parish, about his Enclosing part of the Common to make him a Park'. Not far away, he once saw an enclosed field of pastureland let to a grazier near Aylesbury for £1,400 per annum – 'and knew the tenant very well, whose Name was *Houghton*', he adds with a friendly intimacy (2: 137–8).

Alert to what was going on in every corner of the land, he took the side of Newcastle keelmen, whom he may have met on frequent stops in the city, in their disputes with employers: there is a very brief reference to the matter in the *Tour* (3: 118). Equally he wrote on behalf of the poor silk weavers of Spitalfields when they protested about the import of East Indian cottons, setting up an entire journal to discourage the use of foreign materials – a campaign which helped to pave the way for the Calico Act of 1721. The wearing of calicoes instead of domestic 'stuffs', he stated with understandable exaggeration, was 'a Contagion, that ... will, like the Plague in a Capital City, spread itself over the whole Nation'.[49] Again the *Tour* makes a very short allusion to these matters (3: 148). When it came to the issues that were impacting ordinary people, he was remarkably close to the heartbeat of the nation. A great observer of the English scene, very familiar with its presentation by Defoe, once remarked that historical changes 'really come about at the *cell* level, as it were': charting these local developments will act as a corrective to 'easy generalizations that infest so many historical works on a grand scale'. The words are those of W. G. Hoskins, whose contribution to understanding the past according to Joan Thirsk was to have set 'every intimate local inquiry in a larger frame and given it place and significance in our national history'.[50] One of the great merits of the *Tour* is that its conclusions about the state of Britain are buttressed by innumerable particular observations of life lived in the biggest cities and the smallest hamlets. Whether the topic is duck-shooting in the Fens, or the subterranean homes of lead miners in the Peak District, we are persuaded that the report has come straight from the action.

Few writers convey such a sense of immediacy as Defoe. To read his book is to imbibe a strong flavour of the 1720s. It has long been on record that the author had not visited all the places he describes, that he had not been near others in decades, and that he borrowed information from all kinds of sources – antiquarian tomes such as Camden's *Britannia*, the tourist guides of writers such as John Macky, maps and atlases by Herman Moll and John Senex, semi-official handbooks such as those of Guy Miège and the burgeoning crop of newspapers. The borrowings make very little difference. His earlier tours of the nation have been to an extent reimagined as he writes.[51] The voice is always Defoe's own, confident and personal; the ideas emerge freshly minted, and the scene described is patently right there before his eyes.

As remarked in the Introduction, Defoe began his writing life with *An Essay upon Projects* (1697), putting forward a range of schemes intended to improve the public weal. His concern with innovation came not just from the perspective of an economic theorist: they were fed by his varied experience as a trader, landed proprietor and – even – projector. This fact alone helps to explain his readiness to detect change, even if he does not approve of all the developments that he observes on his travels. Hardly any commentators on the state of the nation had seen so much of the physical landscape of Britain, especially in the south, in the Midlands and on the main roads from London to Edinburgh. Even though the coverage is generally stronger on commerce than on industry or agriculture, the *Tour* allots plenty of space to all sides of the economy: much of his time had been spent in manufacturing towns, or else in the open country as he rode from place to place along 'highways' that were largely unfenced and thinly settled. Despite this, we still lack a comprehensive survey of the writer's achievement across all the fields of his interest, in his books on historical and geographical subjects, his manuals on trade, his pamphlets on social issues, his work as a journalist and a political agent, his tracts on religion and superstition and much else. Most immediately to the purpose, we have no connected account of the features of the *Tour* which explains the centrality assigned to it by so many leading authorities over the past hundred years.

Conclusion

What of the *Tour* today? For most of the period under review, historians had to make do with editions of varying merit. Often, as we have seen, they cited versions of the book from later in the century, and failed to distinguish between Defoe's own words and those of his editors. The first reprints of the 1724–6 publications began to appear in the 1920s, but their texts were not wholly reliable and one of them brought in inappropriate modernisations of spelling and punctuation. A good deal of confusion was spread by the decision of the publishers of the widely read Everyman's Library to omit the Scottish sections and issue the work in their series under the title *A Tour of England and Wales*. Dozens of historians employed this text, and many appear to have been unaware that Defoe extended his coverage into Scotland – so that they did not grasp the importance of this section to the whole enterprise, in view of Defoe's residence in Edinburgh at the time of the Union. Further editions and abridgments came out in the later part of the twentieth century, but it not was not until John McVeagh produced his version for the Pickering Masters series of *The Works of Daniel Defoe* that a full annotated text became available. This is obviously of general benefit to the scholarly community, but it has specific advantages for historians, in supplying a more determinate basis for their enquiries.

In addition, we know a lot more today about Defoe himself than was the case ninety years ago, when the well-used Cole introductions appeared. James Sutherland provided what was then the most reliable and intellectually searching account of his life in 1937, eventually supplemented by F. Bastian's more speculative narrative of the early years in 1981. In recent decades the biographies of Paula Backscheider (1989), Maximillian Novak (2001) and John Richetti (2015) have gone further in exploring the author's career. The edition of his letters by G. H. Healey in 1955 had already enhanced our understanding. As for bibliography, thanks mainly to the contributions of P. N. Furbank and W. R. Owens, we have now acquired a canon that is stripped down to more dependable proportions. An excellent book by Peter Earle (1976) brought an acute historian's eye to both the inner and outer worlds of Defoe, with especially strong coverage of economic issues.[52] There is now less excuse for mistaking the author's purposes, as has sometimes been the case, as well as more opportunity for new research following up on the lead he gives in so many areas. The challenge is to assess the overall adequacy of his picture of the way that the nation worked. This means testing his judgements on particular issues (say, the degree of social mobility among the wealthier classes), something beyond the scope of this book. But it also means forming an opinion of his attempt to portray the nation as an interlocking system, an idea crucial to the structure and rhetoric of the book. Up to now, historians have tended to pluck out isolated passages without locating them adequately within the overall ideological shape imposed by Defoe's view of the state of the nation. In his well-known study of *The Making of the English Middle Class* (1989), Earle acknowledges that he chose the period 1660–1730 for investigation, partly because 'it was the lifetime of Daniel Defoe . . . whose views on a wide range of subjects will be found scattered through the pages' (many, naturally, drawn from the *Tour*).[53]

As the evidence collected here confirms, the *Tour* is a truly central work for our understanding of Britain at a crucial stage of its transition into modernity. It is the place where Defoe's economic views, crystallised after a lifetime of observations, first took proper shape, ready for their exposition in works such as *The Complete English Tradesman* (1725–7), *A General History of Discoveries and Improvements* (1725–6) and *A Plan of the English Commerce* (1728). If we want to enter the landscape of the early Georgian era, and to discover how it struck a contemporary, this is the most fecund source that has come down to us. Although the author had no advanced method of enquiry, he had compensating qualities – practised narrative skills allied to boundless curiosity and an analytic approach to the world. For historians, the book can make more sense of the period than any other survey of the landscape of the age.[54]

CHAPTER 6

The Jacobite Rising in the Tour
Preventing the Ruin of Scotland

The Scottish sections which make up the last three segments of the *Tour* have received comparatively little attention in recent years. This is surprising on more than one ground. The *Tour* continues to engage students of early modern Britain across several fields, while social and economic historians still plunder the coverage of England and Wales comprised in its first ten sections. Equally, the author's longstanding connection with Scottish affairs, above all his first-hand observation of the negotiations for the Union of 1707, might seem to warrant careful analysis of the treatment he bestows on regions across the border. In particular, we have largely missed the extended discussion of the events and implications of the Rising of 1715–16 found in the *Tour*. This is, of course, a topic of strong contemporary interest in the scholarly world, a result in part of the widespread attention given to Jacobitism in general.[1] There is also a more general consensus on the significance of the episode. Many historians will now assent to Daniel Szechi's verdict: 'The '15 was potentially the most serious Jacobite rising of the eighteenth century. There is a deep irony in this, as it was an incredibly botched job on the part of the Jacobites.'[2]

Much has been written about Defoe's stance on political and religious issues, but very little of this relates to the picture of the Rising which emerges gradually in scattered portions of the narrative in the third volume, Letters IV to VI, that is nos. 11–13 in the continuing series.[3] Two reasons go some way to explain this neglect. One concerns the degree of first-hand knowledge of Scotland that the author was able to enlist, which gave the segment a more patchy quality than elsewhere. In Letters 11 and 12, devoted to the Borders and the Lowlands, the level of detailed observation and up-to-date information is comparable with that apparent in most parts of the English sections – indeed, it exhibits at times a stronger grasp of local affairs than does the coverage in some areas of the North Midlands and the North. This is probably because there were districts such as Lincolnshire, the North Riding of Yorkshire and Cumbria, where the author had never strayed far from the trunk roads on his visits – almost all of which had taken place at least ten years prior to the appearance of the *Tour.*

On the other hand, Letter 13 describes the whole of Scotland north of the Clyde–Forth divide – until its final paragraphs wander far enough south to offer some perfunctory comments on Kintyre, Arran and Bute. There is confessedly no treatment of the Hebrides, and whilst the circuit extends as far as the northern coast of Caithness, plus a short addendum on the Orkney and Shetland islands, it is palpably thinner on the central Highlands. We saw at the start of Chapter 1 that the visit to John o' Groats is celebrated as a significant moment in the coverage of the entire island. While Defoe is on solid ground for the nearer counties (as they then were, Fife, Clackmannan, Kinross, Stirling and Dumbarton, with much of Perthshire and Argyll), he had undoubtedly spent little time, if any, within the Gàidhealtachd. The next part of this chapter sets out the basic facts concerning Defoe's acquaintance with the regions of Scotland, and the limitations these imply for his ability to cover the material adequately.

Szechi dismissed his contribution to the campaign on behalf of the Union as the work of 'that well known government hack, Daniel Defoe', While not without any shred of justification, this assessment seriously underestimates a range of attributes he brought to his task.[4] These include the length and breadth of his concern with Scotland; his close acquaintance with leading figures on both sides of the border; his familiarity with high politics in Britain since the 1690s; the extent of his contacts with more modest local officials; his very wide experience in trade, a branch of activity he continued to pursue when he reached Edinburgh; his background as a commentator on social and economic topics; his obsessive curiosity with regard to all aspects of geography and topography; his energy, enabling him to produce a long and elaborate compilation of documents in *The History of the Union* (1709), which can hardly be described as the work of a mere 'hack'; and finally his exceptional skills as a writer. The largest cluster of his surviving letters concern the periods he spent in Edinburgh, and they contain a wealth of first-hand observation on the progress of negotiations. Many of the qualities just listed are evident in his lively treatment of the Union in the *Review*; and they shine forth intermittently through the *Tour.*

The second factor that explains neglect of the Scottish circuits might lie in distrust of the author's propagandist aims. Defoe had been sent to Edinburgh to help ease through the Union and contain problems that arose in its aftermath.[5] Unquestionably he overstated the benefits that Scotland would derive from the measure, and this deliberate bias extends to the *Tour.* The book is a nakedly pro-Union, pro-Hanoverian, pro-Protestant and pro-Whig undertaking, even though it sometimes mutes its criticisms of opposing views. In particular, the rhetoric of the Scottish segment is designed to blur the distinction between anti-Union sentiment and Jacobite allegiance. On one side of the ideological divide, we are presented with forward-looking attitudes, practical improvement and civic activity in areas such as building, landscape design and agriculture, all leading to stability and prosperity. Against this, we are shown primitive and outdated feelings of tribal loyalty, allied with religious bigotry, culminating in faction and rebellion, with the inevitable consequences of poverty, decay and dissolution. Such an approach is obviously far from objective, and it would not fit the narrative supplied by most modern students of the period. My aim here is not to offer either justification or denunciation of Defoe's aims. It is rather to demonstrate the skill with which he handled an exceedingly touchy subject. His technique involves selecting topographic and biographic data relevant to the progress of his supposed 'tour' of the region, and inscribing within this narrative his own critique of the Rising, with its failure made most clearly manifest in the fate of those who took part on either side.

Defoe's Knowledge of Scotland

There is no need here to rehearse the writer's engagement with Scottish affairs in exhaustive detail (see Figure 2 for one of his regular haunts). He may possibly have visited the country in the 1690s,[6] but we reach certain ground only when he began to work in support of the Union as a secret agent of two leading ministers, Sidney Godolphin and Robert Harley. From 1706 to 1711 he was based in the Scottish capital with a few intervals: almost certainly he never travelled there again. His duties involved perambulations of neighbouring shires in order to test the political and religious waters. We can trace his movements in his correspondence, and more fitfully in the pages of his journal *The Review*. He was willing to go further afield when necessary. Once in 1707 he volunteered for a dangerous mission into the Highlands.[7] The threat was posed by the Duke of Atholl, then regarded as leader of the 'discontented party', though he later recanted (see p. 292, n. 34). Among those summoned to a meeting was Lord Sinclair, a Jacobite from Fife whose activities turn up in the pages of the *Tour*. The offer was refused, perhaps because Harley was more concerned with battles waged by different factions in Edinburgh than with the relatively minor prospect of an insurrection in the Highlands.

Figure 2 J. M. W. Turner, *High Street, Edinburgh* (*c.*1818), showing St Giles Cathedral and the street market. The scene is as much as Defoe knew it a century before when he haunted the area. The main official and legal buildings lay in Parliament Close, to the right of the cathedral, viewed as here from the direction of the Lawnmarket (*Tour* 3: 170–71). Source: YCBA.

Defoe was never content to remain just a passive observer. He engaged in several branches of trade while in Edinburgh, with varying success. Indeed, when he came to write a resonant welcome to the Union in the *Review* on 29 March 1707, lauding 'this mighty Transaction' which will bring 'new Success, new Advantages, and the approaching Happiness of both Kingdoms', he could not refrain from a vainglorious celebration of his own activity:

> Nor am I an idle Spectator here; I have told *Scotland* of Improvements in Trade, Wealth, and Shipping that shall accrue to them on the happy Conclusion of this Affair, and I am pleas'd doubly with this, that I am like to be one of the first Men that shall give them the Pleasure of the Experiment.
>
> I have told them of the Improvement of their Coal Trade, and 'tis their own Fault if they do not particularly engage 20 or 25 Sail of Ships immediately from *England* on that Work. I have told them of the Improvement of their Salt, and I am now contracting for *English* Merchants, for *Scots* Salt to the Value of above 10,000 *l. per Annum.*

> I have told them of Linen Manufactures, and I have now above 100 poor Families at Work, by my Procuring and Direction, for the making such sorts of Linen, and in such Manner as never was made here before and as no Person in the Trade will believe could be made here, till they see it.
>
> This has been my Employment in *Scotland*.

On top of this, he took a major interest in printed journals, and tried to obtain a monopoly on distributing news. He offered to produce a new edition of the Psalms. Meanwhile his brother-in law Robert Davis was establishing a dock for boat repairs at Leith, and this circumstance underlies the section on Leith in the *Tour* (3: 176). He sought a place in the Scottish customs service, and at one stage he might have become a commissioner. Before he took up his role, he had already made the acquaintance of members of the London mercantile community who were transplants from north of the border. The most obvious example is William Paterson (1658–1719), celebrated alike for helping to found the Bank of England (from which he quickly bailed out) and for devising the ill-fated scheme to set up a colony on the isthmus of Darien. Meanwhile Defoe even brought his son Benjamin Norton Defoe along and entered him as a student in the famous university. However, a decisive proof of his involvement in Scottish affairs perhaps lies in one of his major poems, *Caledonia* (1706). One sign can be found in the list of subscribers to this work, mostly pro-Union, Protestant, Whig and Hanoverian.[8]

Due allowance needs to be made in respect of his thin description of the northernmost counties. When Defoe wrote, General George Wade had only recently carried out his first survey of the Highlands, and his plan to construct the first real roads across the region would not be realised for some years. Few Lowlanders, let alone travellers from south of the border, ventured far across the dreaded fastnesses *in partibus infidelium*. We can gauge the situation by looking at Macky's *A Journey through Scotland* (1723), a text which – as in other parts of the nation – supplies a number of instructive comparisons with the *Tour*. The author was certainly from northern Scotland, though his precise origins are obscure. Yet, in a volume of 340 pages, he is able to allocate fewer than fifteen pages to the Highlands, plus a small handful on Argyll and Bute.[9] (This count excludes the coastal strip past Aberdeen round to the Moray Firth.) As mentioned on previous occasions, Macky had begun his series with *A Journey through England* in two volumes (1714; 1722). Defoe had used these sparingly in the earlier sections of his *Tour*, despite a few barbed comments pointing out errors in his predecessor. However, there are more signs in the coverage of Scotland that he was lifting material from Macky, most often relating to the stately baronial homes which form the basis of *A Journey through Scotland.* The biggest single difference in the entirety of the two accounts lies in the heavy emphasis that Defoe places on domestic and overseas trade, a topic in which Macky shows hardly any interest.

Unsurprisingly, the catalogue of Defoe's books contains two items by Macky, the second edition of the English journey, volume I (1722), and the Scottish journey. Plainly the author of *The History of the Union* and *Memoirs of the Church of Scotland* (1717) had occasion for a compendious library, and the sale catalogue lists a large number of relevant items.[10] The collection as a whole embraces more than 150 works with a specific link to Scotland. There are numerous items in several categories, such as church history, general history, politics, monarchs, geography and topography, government and law. This is a minimum tally: several other works excluded from the count derive from Scottish authors or were published in Edinburgh, not to mention books which deal with the Rising without specific reference to affairs north of the border. One example of Defoe's interests is an important guide to natural history by Sir Robert Sibbald, *Scotia Illustrata* (Edinburgh, 1684).[11]

In any case, he had been writing about Jacobitism since early in his career, and the Rising simply brought to a head issues that had been circulating in his mind for many years – certainly from the time that he embarked on the *Review* in 1704. We can no longer attribute to him some pamphlets he was once supposed to have composed in response to the tumultuous events of 1715 and 1716, including *A True Account of the Proceedings at Perth.* Still, that leaves works such as *A Trumpet Blown in the North,* which are probably authentic, and serve to confirm the close attention that Defoe gave to the rebellion and its leading actors.

It does not appear to have been observed that the *Tour* makes direct use of certain earlier pamphlets he had written on the subject. The largest presence in Letter 12 is that of *A View of the Scots Rebellion,* published in October 1715. This was reprinted in Dublin under the rather more helpful title, *An Historical Account of the Highlanders; Describing their Country, Division into Clans, Manner of Living and Fighting; their Habit, Arms, and Government under their Lairds, &c.* The topics listed here correspond exactly with those that Defoe wrote about in the *Tour*, and the geographic details supplied are unmistakably drawn from their coverage in the *View.* Highland chieftains on both sides of the conflict are listed, and almost every one of these men will earn a reference in 1726. Moreover, that Defoe was thoroughly prepared to chronicle the events leading up to the Rising and its aftermath is demonstrated by the weight of commentary in the

Review on Jacobites or Jacobitism. More than 300 separate references are to be found in the standard index to this journal, compiled by W. L. Payne: not all of them concern Scotland directly, but a considerable proportion do.[12]

The extent of Defoe's background knowledge is illustrated by a passage which occurs near the end of the *Tour*:

> I cannot but say that his Majesty's Gift of 1,000 *l*. annually to the Assembly of *Scotland*, for sending Ministers and Missionaries for the propagating Christian knowledge in the *Highlands*, is certainly one of the most needful Charities that could have been thought of, worthy of a King, and well suited to that Occasion; and if prudently apply'd, as there is Reason to believe it will be, may in time break in upon this horrible Ignorance, that has so far spread over this unhappy Part of the Country. (3: 278)

This concerns the so-called Royal Bounty, for which the Church of Scotland and the Society in Scotland for the Propagation of the Gospel (founded in 1709) had been lobbying since the reign of Anne. The aim was to bring 'Protestant religion and morality to the Highlands', but more honestly to try to curb the hold of the Catholic faith in outlying parts.[13] It was steered through the General Assembly in May 1725 by the Earl of Loudoun, who had been present at Sheriffmuir and was known to Defoe; it was then presented to George I by the Committee for the Reformation of the Highlands and Islands. The Royal Bounty was duly granted. While in Edinburgh, Defoe had minutely followed all the doings of the Assembly, and he had taken an active role within the campaign of the SSPG. Scarcely any other Englishman would have maintained a close observation of the earlier events and equally been on the spot to witness the ongoing negotiations in the mid 1720s between the English government and the so-called Argathelian party. This group, led by the Duke of Argyle, had come to dominate Scottish politics, in combination with men like Loudoun, the King's Commissioner to the Assembly.

All in all, it is clear that the *Tour* is based on prolonged exposure to relevant matters. Defoe's own correspondence shows that he had regular dealings in Edinburgh with prominent figures involved in the Union negotiations, both pro and anti. His work brought him into contact with members of the old Scottish parliament, as well as those elected to UK parliament from 1708, and the sixteen representative peers chosen to sit in the House of Lords. He met leading members of the Presbyterian establishment, and he was in personal contact with the Principal of the University. During his stay Defoe witnessed street riots and listened to tub-thumping sermons.[14] He got around to most parts of the Lowlands and ventured a little way north. He was much less well acquainted with the Highlands and with the heads of the great clans who identified in many cases with the Stuart cause; but he knew very well who they were and what their goals were. The passage of a decade may have allowed him to speak more freely. He would no longer feel any embarrassment on account of his association with Robert Harley, Earl of Oxford, once a touchy issue in his relations with the Whigs when they regained power: his former master had died in 1724. Ill-fated renewals of the Jacobite enterprise had come and gone, such as the Gyllenbergh plot of 1716–17; the abortive Rising of 1719; and the Atterbury plot of 1721–2. What Defoe had to do in 1726 was to muster the slowly accumulated database of ideas and information he had built up over the years.

Peace and Plenty: the Hanoverians

One passage stands at the heart of Defoe's treatment of the Rising, and indeed it helps to establish a theme that runs through the entire section of the *Tour*, Volume III, that is devoted to Scotland. It occurs almost halfway through Letter 13:

> Going from Hence we took a full View of the Field of Battle, call'd *Sheriff-Muir*, and had Time to contemplate how it was possible, that a Rabble of *Highlanders*, arm'd in haste, appearing in Rebellion, and headed by a Person never in Arms before, nor of the least Experience, should come so near to the overthrowing an Army of regular, disciplin'd Troops, and led on by experienc'd Officers, and so great a General: But when the Mistake appear'd also, we bless'd the good Protector of *Great Britain*, who, under a Piece of the most Mistaken Conduct in the World, to say no worse of it, gave that important Victory to King *George*'s Troops, and prevented the Ruin of *Scotland* from an Army of *Highlanders*.
>
> From this Place of Reflection I came forward . . . (3: 250)

Such moments of contemplation are not unusual as Defoe surveys the site of a great battle. When the narrative of Letter 8 reached Towton, he had recalled how local ploughmen said that they sometimes dug up broken javelins and helmets: 'so we cou'd only give a short Sigh to the memory of the Dead, and move forward' (3: 94). Here the pause for reflection permits a sense of wonder at the fortunate preservation of the nation. A sweeping contrast is drawn between the two generals, but more widely between the armies in conflict. We are presented with the 'Rabble' of Highlanders (not, we observe, Jacobites or rebels, but savages from the outer fringes of civilisation) as against the 'regular, disciplined Troops', that is the organised forces of a modern state.

On the next page, the narrator continues to muse:

> It is a strange Testimony of the Power of Envy and Ambition, that Mankind, bless'd with such Advantages, for an easy and happy Retreat in the World, should hazard it all in Faction and Party, and throw it all away in View, and even without a View of getting more: But I must not phylosophize, any more than launch out into other Excesses; my Business is with the present State of the Place, and to that I confine myself as near as I can. (3: 251)

The 'Advantages' that the people of Scotland enjoy, as the rest of the *Tour* makes clear, include those granted by their natural situation, but more particularly the new potential for greater prosperity afforded by the Union. The failure to take these chances by boosting trade is visible in areas such as Galloway: 'They have all the Materials for Trade, but no Genius to it; all the Opportunities for Trade, but no Inclination to it. In a Word, they have no Notion of being rich and populous, and thriving by Commerce' (3: 189). An allied strategy in this portion of the work is to link Jacobitism with backward-looking attitudes, feudal behaviour and poverty, in contrast with the vigour and improving zeal of the Hanoverian leaders.

This will become more apparent if we review the treatment in the text of key individuals on either side. The 'great' general at Sheriffmuir was the Duke of Argyll, prior to his replacement as leader of the government troops by William Cadogan. However, subsequent references downplay military prowess. The Duke is the chief of the Clan Campbell, 'but then it should be noted too, that those Western Gentlemen are not so blindly to be led, or guided by their Chiefs as those in the North; nor when led on, are they so apt for Mischief and Violence' (3: 283–4). It does not need to be spelt out that the more northerly clans are those like the Mackenzies, Gordons and Macdonalds who joined the Pretender's army. Like Macky, Defoe did not adjust his itinerary to cover Inverary, the Campbells' main residence, but he does refer briefly to 'the many fine Seats and strong Castles which they were always possess'd of in the Highlands' (3: 211). No reference is made other aspects of Argyll's career, including his successes in the Marlborough wars and his often stormy life in politics. This might appear surprising: the explanation seems to be that Defoe felt some distrust for the Duke's impulsive character, while in the Whig split after the Rising he had chosen the Stanhope-Sunderland faction against the one led by Walpole and Townshend, who backed Argyll.[15]

The *Tour* is more forthcoming on other prominent Hanoverians. A good example comes in its treatment of the Duke of Roxburgh, whose brand of Squadrone politics Defoe did not altogether approve. Nevertheless he grows rhapsodic in describing the family seat near Kelso:

> His House call'd *Floors* is an antient Seat, but begins to wear a new Face; and those who view'd it fifteen or sixteen Years ago, will scarce know it again, if they should come a few Years hence, when the present Duke may have finished the Additions and Embellishments, which he is now making, and has been a considerable Time upon. Nor will the very Face of the Country appear the same, except it be that the River *Tweed* may, perhaps, run in the same Channel: But the Land before, lying open and wild, he will find enclos'd, cultivated and improv'd, Rows, and even Woods of Trees covering the champaign Country, and the House surrounded with large grown Vistas, and well planted Avenues, such as were never seen there before. (3: 218)

Here the narrator is remarkably up to date: William Adam's rebuilding of Floors was barely complete in 1726, having been undertaken in 1721. It is unlikely in the extreme that Defoe had visited the house again since he left Edinburgh in 1711 – so the phrase 'fifteen or sixteen Years' may accurately reflect the gap in time. The transformation of the 'wild' site into a cultivated and improved landscape expresses the vision of a benign and prosperous world ushered in by the Hanoverian dispensation. As Alistair M. Duckworth sees it, in his fine essay on 'Whig landscapes' in the *Tour*, 'Defoe's practical and progressive spirit, along with his sometimes chillingly functionalist view of landscapes, is most evident in [the Scottish sections].' He does not refer to the political context or to the crucial overtones of the notion of Whiggery in Scotland when the *Tour* came out.[16] The praise of improvement which Duckworth stresses has a key place in the ideology of the work, identifying its presence with Hanoverian interventions.

An equally clear instance occurs in Letter 11. The supposed itinerary has reached a point in East Lothian, not far from Haddington. We are told of 'the Marquess of *Tweedal*'s fine Park, and which is indeed, the main Thing, his fine planting at *Yester* . . . I say the Park, because, tho' there is the Design of a noble House or Palace, and great Part of it built; yet, as it is not yet, and perhaps, will not soon be finished, there is no giving a compleat Description of it' (3: 156). This time the hesitant phrasing conceals a lack of recent information: the house, designed by James Smith, had been started in 1697 and was essentially completed by

1715, too late for Defoe to have seen the finished mansion. (The 4th Marquess went on tinkering with the house and gardens throughout the writer's lifetime.) Instead, he launches into an encomium of the gardening activities of the 'old *Earl*', that is the first Marquis, who had begun to lay out the grounds in the 1680s. As well as praising 'the Plan and Design of all those Noble Walks and Woods of Trees . . . which he afterwards planted', the writer points out that 'his Lordship, and his immediate Successor, planted above 6000 Acres of Land all full of Fir-Trees; and that, wherever it was found that any Tree fail'd, they were constantly renew'd the next Year'. Further, 'As the Success of this Planting is a great Encouragement to the Nobility of *Scotland* to improve their Estates by the same Method, so we find abundance of Gentlemen of Estates do fall into it, and follow the Example' (3: 157). This is one of several places where Defoe confers a kind of moral and political virtue on planting trees, as a form of practical improvement of the estate.[17] It is no surprise that virtually all the individuals singled out for their activity in this sphere turn out to be Whigs, Protestants and Hanoverians. It is they who supply the dynamo for change.

One passage where the latent ideology behind the Scottish sections emerges with great clarity occurs early in Letter 12, as the narrator turns his attention to Dumlanrig Castle in Dumfriesshire. Defoe explains that he had the honour of knowing the late owner, the 2nd Duke of Queensberry, and enjoyed opportunities to witness his extensive service to the state under two monarchs, William III and Anne. One of his official tasks was touch with a sceptre 'the Act of Parliament, which put an End to Parliaments for ever, in that *Great Britain*' (3: 186). This moment of ceremonial splendour is further charged with symbolic power a few lines further on in the text: 'While I was at *Drumlanrig*, being desir'd by the late Duke to make some Observations on his Grace's Estate there, which is very great, in Order to some *English* Improvements, I, in particular, view'd some of the Hills to the North of the Castle.' Accompanied by a Derbyshire gentleman knowledgeable in lead mining, he proposed some means of exploiting the ore. However, the Duke's death in 1711 forestalled this 'and several other Improvements then in view'. The phrase '*English* Improvements' may look patronising to us, but in its context it is meant to suggest that landowners should not only beautify their estates, but also turn them to their own advantage through commercial use, in the English manner.

Earlier Defoe had expressed his amazement at seeing 'a Palace so glorious, Gardens so fine, and everything so truly magnificent, and all in a wild, mountainous Country'. He continues:

> [Here], in a word, we saw the Peak of *Darby* restor'd, (viz.) the finest Palace in all that part of Britain, erected under the Mountains, full of Lead-Mines, and Quarries of Freestone, and where nothing, but what was desolate and dismal, could be expected, especially if you come to it by the said Pass of *Enterkin*, or by the Mountains of *Cumock* and *Carrick*, more to the North West of the Place. (3: 184)

Drumlanrig bids fair to equal the splendid mansion of Chatsworth on the edge of the Peak District, where Defoe had similarly found 'a Palace for a Prince, a most magnificent Building, and, in spite of all the Difficulties or Disadvantages of Situation, [it] is a perfect Beauty' (3:46). Thanks to the Union, the Scottish nobility will be able, like their English counterparts, to plant edifices befitting their station in life in 'a wild mountainous Country'. Decoded, this conveys the idea that under beneficent Hanoverian rule the Scots will be able to redeem their savage past and join the modern world of progress and civility. The *Tour* even verifies the point: 'Just thus, with horrid Desart Hills embrac'd, / Was Paradise on *Euphra*'s Border plac'd.' At least Defoe has the good grace to recognise that not all inhabitants of Scotland will see matters in this way: 'whether the *Scots* will remember it [the treaty of Union] to the Advantage of the Duke's Character, in their Opinion, that must be as their several Opinions guide them' (3: 186). The *Tour* as a whole leaves us in no doubt where Defoe's sympathies lie.

As we should expect, Hanoverian figures with less political importance generally receive shorter and less effusive treatment. The Earl of Eglinton has 'an ancient House', but he is simply 'one of the richest Peers in *Scotland*' (3: 196), ignoring the fact that he had resisted strong blandishments from the Jacobite faction and raised a troop to oppose the Rising in support of the government. Part of the explanation may lie in Macky's comment, 'He hath a great Estate, and is a vast Improver, but none of his Seats come up to the Dignity of his Rank.'[18] In the same paragraph the account moves on to the home of his kinsman, the Earl of Loudoun, near Galston. 'It is a noble and beautiful Seat,' we are told, '[but] I cannot describe Houses: they come too thick upon me.' For once, Macky is almost equally brief. There is a similar hesitation in respect of the townhouse of the Duke of Montrose in Glasgow. Though the Duke's interest in the area is so great that 'he is, in a civil Sense, Governor of this City', yet 'His fine

House at the North End of the City is not finished, so I need not enter upon a Description of it' (3: 200).

Such statements regarding works under construction resonate with the underlying theme of the *Tour*, announced on the first page of the Preface: 'If *Novelty* pleases, here is the *Present State* of the Country described, the Improvement, in Culture [agriculture], as in Commerce, the Encrease of People . . . also here you have an Account of the Encrease of Buildings . . . as in the new Seats and Dwellings of the Nobility and Gentry' (1: 47). Another case in point is found in the description of the home of the Earl of Hopetoun, built upon 'a delightful Plain' west of Edinburgh:

> The House was originally a Square; but the Earl is now adding two Wings to it, which will greatly add to the Beauty of the Building; the Situation is so good, and gives so fine a Prospect, as well to the Sea as to the Land, that nothing can be finer. It is exquisitely finish'd, both within and without; and besides Family-Pieces, the Earl has some fine Pieces of Painting that are very curious. The Stables and Riding-Places are by far the finest and most magnificent in *Scotland.* (3: 178)

The Hanoverian aristocrats, having gained their victory, indulge in a measure of conspicuous consumption. But their ancestral seats also served a strategic purpose during the Rising, as we see near the end of Letter 13:

> The Earl of *Sutherland* has a Castle beyond *Innerness,* call'd *Dunrobin,* situate on the Eastern Shore, which his Lordship was sent down by Sea to take an early Possession of in the late Rebellion; and which, if he had not done, would soon have fallen into the Hands of the late Earl of *Marr*'s Party; but by his coming timely thither it was prevented, and the Country on that Side kept from joining the Troops of the *Pretender,* at least for that Time. (3: 269)

The grand mansions of the loyalists are thus justified by their providential role in providing a bulwark against the rebels.

Other Hanoverian stalwarts were busy about their estates. Thus, the Earl of Haddington, a well-known improver, had followed his neighbour Tweeddale at Tyninghame House, 'where, tho' the Trees are younger than at *Yester,* yet, they seem to follow them apace, and to thrive so much, as that they may, one Time or another, overtake them' (3: 157). The homes of the Elliot family, including Defoe's colleague in negotiations, Sir Gilbert Eliot of Stobs, were among the 'Abundance of Gentlemen's Seats and antient Mansions' that were worthy of mention along the Tweed (3: 217). There is high praise for the architecture and 'well planted' gardens of the Earl of Rothes (another hero of Sheriffmuir) at Leslie, even though the situation of the house is not exceptional (3: 231; compare the fuller account in Macky 3: 164–5).

Defoe does not mention that the Earl had been forced to retreat to Stirling early in the 1715 campaign when a troop of Jacobite soldiers captured Leslie. One of the few exceptions concerns Wemyss House, where Defoe finds fault with the 'very Romantick' description of his rival (3:238; Macky 3: 82). He admits that 'it is a very good House', and isolates some admirable features. But the situation is unduly confined, and the fir trees that have been planted 'do not thrive'. More typical is the description of a mansion belonging to the Earl of Leven, a significant figure well known to Defoe. This was Melville House in Fife, designed in 1697 for the Earl's father, termed 'a regular and beautiful building' (3: 246; compare Macky 3: 155). It was constructed close to the ruins of a medieval monastery, which aptly was left as a kind of folly – a playful gesture, unlike the unsought ruination of Jacobite dwellings. For a Unionist, Presbyterian and Whig like the Earl, as for Defoe, the replacement of an antique Catholic structure in poor repair with a spanking new home in a classical style represented the triumph of progress and civilisation.

Ruin and Decay: the Jacobites

It needs little emphasis that Defoe's first-hand knowledge of the Highlands was sketchier than that of the other parts of Scotland. In any case, the clan chiefs who took a prominent role in the Rising would never have welcomed him to their remote homes, as they were mostly implacably opposed to the Union, and his stance on the major issue of the day was no secret. Nevertheless, he encountered those who were elected to the parliament in 1710, including the Earl Marischal, and on his travels around the Lowlands came on the seats of some Stuart loyalists. As early as 1707, he was warning Harley that 'The Intollerable Boldness of the Jacobite party in the Northern Highlands is Such Now, And in some of the Lowland provinces also in the North, that Unless Some speedy Care is Taken to prevent Their Disorders The Consequences Can not but be fatall.'[19] In less than a decade, the only means to 'prevent' this calamity was to take military action. In the meantime, of course, the Pretender had launched a would-be invasion with a naval expedition in March 1708, rebuffed by the government fleet of Admiral Sir George Byng. The *Tour* charts the progress of this futile effort along the east coast of Scotland, from the Firth of Forth as far as the entrance to the Moray Firth (3: 240, 257, 262). Defoe alluded to the episode in works such as his *Memorial to the Nobility of Scotland* (1708), while it naturally figures conspicuously in the *Review* over the course of some weeks, for example on 27 March and 1 April ('And so the *French* are gone Home again, are they? And all the mighty Project is come to nothing').

It is a cause for little surprise that among the Jacobites the most frequently mentioned is the ineffectual commander of their forces, the Earl of Mar. He was already regarded by the Hanoverians as a turncoat after his transformation from a pro-Union servant of Queen Anne as secretary of state. His conduct during the Rising dismayed some of his followers, with his clansmen dragooned into action often against their will, and a scorched earth policy introduced. He lost further popularity when he hastily decamped from Montrose along with the Pretender, in whose service he remained until 1724 as a titular 'Duke', while achieving very little. Defoe had not minced words in regard to the Earl, allowing one of the pseudonymous spokesmen he employed in his pamphlets to call him 'a Master of Sedition, and a Leader of the Wicked among the People'.[20]

The only visit to Stirling by Defoe positively identified took place in 1707, but it was well within the range of his habitual fact-finding missions and he may have been here on other occasions. The entry for the town in the *Tour* seems exceptionally well informed. He admits that the Earl's house in the High Street, highly praised by Macky, offers fine prospects, but criticises its defensive situation as too near the castle.[21] His comments on the influence of the Erskine family in Stirling look equally informed, but he seems understandably to have mixed up three individuals named Colonel Erskine, two with the forename (like the Earl himself) of John.[22] He spends some time on the supposed curse which hangs over Mar's house, now 'at last forfeited to the Crown' (3: 212). A more effusive tone is adopted on the nearby family estate at Alloa, 'where the Earl of *Marr* has a noble Seat, I should have said had a noble Seat' (3: 250). One mode of phraseology that recurs takes the form 'the late exil'd Earl of Marr' (3: 208) or 'the late Earl of *Marr*'s Party' (3: 269). This usage was normal in the period, but even then it could not fail to emphasise the fact that the Earl was now effectively dead as far as his rank and honours went: 'The Seat of the present, or rather late Earl of *Marr*, the present Earl being attainted for Treason, and so dead, as a Peer or Earl, though alive in Exile' (3: 209).

Once the expression is augmented at Kildrummy, the original recruitment base for the Jacobite army, to read 'the Country, where the late unhappy Earl of *Marr* first set up his Standard of the *Pretender*' (3: 262). This is a lone oblique reference to the famous gathering on the banks of the

Dee at Braemar, held under the guise of an annual deer hunt, that set the Riding in motion. So began the ineluctable procession, as Defoe saw it, to failure and humiliation, symbolised by events at Sheriffmuir when the rebels were unable to capitalise on their numerical advantage under an inept commander: 'The Rabble of *Highlanders,* arm'd in haste ... and headed by a Person never in Arms before, nor of the least Experience.' James Edward Stuart had not yet set foot in Scotland, but the passage makes Mar his proxy, as a pretender to the qualities of leadership that a monarch should possess. The text regularly juxtaposes the two men as architects of a disaster: 'the late Insurrection of the Lord *Marr* for the *Pretender*' (3: 267).

For other Jacobites, a key word in the *Tour* is 'ruin'. This could apply to the physical condition of their properties; the state of their finances; or the hope remaining for their cause. A representative case is that of the Duke of Perth and his son, the Marquess of Drummond:

> The Family of *Montrose,* whose Chief was sacrificed for the interest of King *Charles* the First, had a strong Castle here called *Kincardin*; but it was ruin'd and demolished in those Wars, and is not rebuilt. The Castle of *Drummond* is almost in the same Condition, or at least is like soon to be so, the Earl of *Perth,* to whom it belongs, being in Exile, as his Father was before him, by their adhering to the late King *James* the Seventh, and to the present *Pretender.* King *James* the Seventh made the Father a Duke, and Knight of the Garter, and Governor to his son the *Pretender.* His eldest Son who should have succeeded to the Honours and Titles dy'd in *France,* and three other Sons still remaining are all abroad, either following the ruin'd Fortunes of the *Pretender,* or in other Service in Foreign Courts; where, we know not, nor is it material to our present Purpose. (3: 283)

The passage ostensibly deals with the demise suffered by the Drummond family, as a result of which their titles were stripped from them and they were forced to join the Jacobite diaspora across Europe. But the insistent emphasis on the Stuarts, especially the Pretender, means that the ruination falls most heavily on the cause more generally. This ominous tone befits the subsequent history of Drummond Castle near Crieff, since it escaped forfeiture in 1716 but was seized by the state after the rising of 1745–6. By contrast, Macky flatly reports that the Earl 'follow'd King *James*', while Lord Drummond 'dy'd at *St. Germains,* Master of the Horse to the Queen-Dowager; and the other Sons are in the Service of the Pretender'.[23]

Forfeiture echoes throughout the Scottish sections. In Letter 12, we encounter one of the Jacobite lords tried in London:

> The Castle in this Town [Dumfries] ... was formerly belonging to the antient Family of *Nithsdale*, the only remaining Branch of which being unhappily embark'd in the late Rebellion, and taken in Arms at *Preston*, made his Escape out of the Tower, and is now Abroad, but under Forfeiture. That last mention'd Castle has been a very magnificent Structure, though now, like its Owner, in a State of Ruin and Decay.
> (3:183)

Again Macky is less direct, saying only that Nithsdale, 'who made his Escape from the Tower, was allied to all the great Families of the two Kingdoms'.[24]

Nithsdale was not the only one of the lords attainted and condemned to death who managed to escape to the Continent. Another was Winton, who owned impressive seats near Edinburgh:

> And I must add here, the antient and noble Houses of *Seaton*, and *Winton*: Both the Palaces, for so they deserve to be call'd, of the late Earl of *Winton*, who did so many weak and rash Things, to say no worse of him, in the Affair of the late Rebellion; and the kindest Thing can be said of him now is, to leave it upon Record, that he seem'd to be turn'd in his Head. The Houses are now in a State of Ruin, and as fine an Estate, for its Value, as any in *Scotland*, all lying contiguous with itself, and valued at almost 5,000 *l.* Sterling *per Annum* besides; but all now under Forfeiture, and sold to the *York-Buildings* Company. The fine Gates and Stone-wall were demolish'd by the Government, after it had been made a Garrison by the Highlanders; who, from hence began their hairbrain'd march to *England*, which Expedition ended at *Preston*, as has been mention'd in my Account of *Lancashire*. (3: 162)

Winton alone pleaded not guilty, but though he offered some ingenious defense he was sentenced to be hanged, drawn and quartered. The observation that he seemed to be turned in his head goes back to oddities he displayed in court, when his counsel is said to have advised him, 'as the only plea he had, to act the madman, and ... he performed it to the life'. Defoe enlists the tale in order to impute the entire Jacobite enterprise as a 'harebrained' undertaking led by crackpots. Once more, Macky is more restrained, confining himself to saying that Winton 'was try'd and condemn'd at *London* for the Rebellion at *Preston*, and forfeited Honours and Estate', omitting the aftermath.[25]

Another rebel lord had a worse fate than forfeiture, as Defoe bleakly notes in his account of Carrick: 'The late Earl of *Kenmure* had some Interest here, but, as the Family was much sunk in Fortune, so, both what was left here, and in *Galloway*, is gone, and the Honour extinct in the last Earl, who being beheaded for the late Rebellion, *Ann.* 1716. left nothing behind him worth naming in this Country' (3: 194). Extinction, that is, of the individual as well as the peerage, which foretells the extinction of Jacobite ambitions for the crown. Defoe makes no mention of Kenmure's brother-in-law the Earl of Carnock, also captured at Preston and attainted with loss of his titles, sentenced to death, but ultimately granted a pardon. 'When he emerged from the Tower he found himself without property, and even deserted by his friends . . . He lived on only a further nine years.'[26] Actually Carnock survived for nineteen years, but it took another hundred before the family honours were restored.

A different fate was in store for another of the great families of the realm:

> Here in particular is the noble Palace of *Glames*, the Hereditary Seat of the Family of *Lyon*, Earls of *Strathmore*; and as the Heir in Reversion now enjoys the Title and Estate, so it very narrowly escap'd being forfeited; for the eider Brother, Earl of *Strathmore*, having entertain'd the *Pretender* magnificently in this fine Palace, and join'd his Forces in Person, and with all his Interest, lost his Life in that Service, being kill'd at the Battle of Sheriff-Moor; by his Fall, the Estate being entail'd, descended to the second Son, or younger Brother, who is now Earl of *Strathmore*. (3: 249)

On this occasion, Defoe appears to be rephrasing Macky's comments: 'The present Earl's Elder Brother sav'd the Estate from being forfeited, by being kill'd at the Head of his Regiment on *Sheremore*.'[27] In addition, the *Tour* repeats with evident relish what the *Journey* had said about the magnificent reception given to the Pretender at Glamis, with eighty-eight beds made up for his retinue. Whenever possible, an entry for a Jacobite is turned into a reproach directed at the man for whom he had risked all.

As the narrative moves forward, the northern counties yield less discussion of the physical state of Jacobite estates, probably because Defoe had never seen most, if any, of them. On the way to Montrose he touches on Panmure House, near Carnoustie, only to return several pages later to the recently improved medieval castle of Brechin belonging to the family. On the first occasion he refers to 'the noble Palace of *Panmure*, forfeited in the late Rebellion by the unfortunate Earl of *Panmure*, who was himself wounded in the Fight near *Dumblain* [Sheriffmuir], and with that Action ruin'd a noble and antient Family, and a fine Estate' (3: 257). The Earl had been captured but escaped, making his way via Arbroath to join the Pretender. He never returned to Scotland. There is no sympathy here, but unmistakably a measure of pity. On the second occasion, the tone is more businesslike: 'From this Place we went to *Brechin*, an ancient Town with a Castle finely situate; but the ancient Grandour of it not supported; the Family of *Penmure*, to whom it belong'd, having been in no extraordinary Circumstances for some time past, and now their Misfortunes being finished, it is under Forfeiture, and sold among the Spoils of the late Rebellion' (3: 282). Macky, the likely source here, is even brisker: 'This Palace hath a greater Air of Grandeur than *Penmure*, and belongs to the *York-Buildings*.'[28]

Shortly afterwards the narrative takes in a more significant figure within the Jacobite ranks, the Earl Marischal.[29] The passage concerns the spectacularly sited Dunnotar Castle, near Stonehaven: 'The Earl Marshal, of the Name of *Keith*, was the Lord of this Castle, as also of a good House near it [Fetteresso, where Mar met up with the Pretender on his arrival in Scotland], but not a great Estate, and what he had is now gone; for being in the late Rebellion his Estate is forfeited; and we are told his Lordship, making his Escape, is now in the service of *Spain*, where he commands an *Irish* Regiment of Foot' (3: 258). Defoe may well have consulted Macky: 'The last Earl going into the Rebellion with the Earl of *Marr*, his Estate was forfeited, and his Honours extinguish'd. He is now in the Service of King *Philip* of *Spain*, and is reckon'd a very fine Gentleman.'[30] Neither account does full justice to the Earl, who had already become an important advisor to the Pretender after his attainder in 1716, resulting in his appointment as a leader of the abortive 1719 invasion of Scotland. 'He remained involved in the numerous, but futile, plans to restore the Stuarts', as the *Oxford Dictionary of National Biography* puts it, and might have been named as commander of the forces of the Young Pretender in 1745 but for his strained personal relations with Charles Edward.[31] He later became a valued servant of Frederick the Great. In fact, the Earl was one of the few Jacobite leaders whose career was not totally blighted by their participation in the Rising. The same cannot be said of his castle. In 1720 Dunnotar was acquired by the York Buildings Company for about £40,000, and reduced to a shell after all the fixtures and fittings had been carried away. Defoe may not have known how ruinous its state had become by 1726.

Further north in the itinerary, the *Tour* grows increasingly vague. We see some of this when it reaches Speyside:

> Upon the Bank of this River the Duke of *Gordon* has a noble Seat call'd after his Name, *Castle-Gordon*. It is, indeed, a noble, large, and antient Seat; as a Castle much is not to be said of it, for old Fortifications are of a small

> Import, as the World goes now: But as a Dwelling or Palace for a Nobleman, it is a very noble, spacious, and royal Building; 'tis only too large, and appears rather as a great Town than as a House.
>
> The present Duke has been embroil'd a little in the late unhappy Affair of the *Pretender*; but he got off without a Forfeiture, having prudently kept himself at a Distance from them til he might see the Effect of Things. The Duke has several other Seats in this part of the Country; and, which is still better, has a very great Estate. (3: 264)

John Macky relates the key facts about the Duke in a curt sentence.[32] But we need to read between the lines a little here. As Marquess of Huntly, the 2nd Duke of Gordon had taken a major part in the early stages of the Rising and fought at Sheriffmuir, many thought with less than whole-hearted zeal; but he subsequently came to regard the undertaking as doomed to failure and he surrendered Gordon Castle to the Earl of Sutherland in February 1716. He was released from custody when the Rising collapsed and was allowed to succeed to the dukedom when his father died a few months later. Defoe could not possibly have known the full sequel: the new Duke turned his escape 'into a platform for his family's transformation from a bastion of Catholicism and Jacobitism in the Highlands into a Protestant pillar of the Hanoverian regime' (Daniel Szechi).[33] It was, however, just what the *Tour* implicitly advises all Jacobites to do. Almost alone among the Jacobites, Gordon's story has an ending other than dispossession and exile.[34]

Defoe does not always trouble to make the Jacobite connection explicit. A passage in Letter 11 begins, '*Calendar*, which seems, as well as that of *Kilsyth*, to be in its Widow's Weeds, those two Families, collateral branches both of the name of *Livingston*, having had their several Decays, though on different Occasions. The Town of *Falkirk* is near *Calendar* House, but nothing on it is remarkable, but the other old decay'd House of the Earl of *Calendar*' (3: 205). This leaves out a great deal, much of which must have been familiar to Defoe. Callander House had an illustrious history, involving Mary Queen of Scots among others. However, the 'other' house must be Linlithgow Palace, partially derelict, which had been in the care of the Earl of Callander's family for more than a century. He had in fact inherited the title of 5th Earl of Linlithgow in 1695 and had been active in Scottish affairs since then. In 1715 he attended the famous gathering at Braemar which heralded the Rising. After escaping the country in 1716, he joined the Pretender at Urbino and died at Rome in 1723. He suffered attainder and his estate was sold to the York Buildings Company, who in turn leased it to the Earl's daughter Anne Livingston. She married the Earl of Kilmarnock, who would be executed in 1746 for his part in the next major rising. On this occasion, Macky had been more forthright, acknowledging that the Earl 'was with my Lord *Mar* in the Rebellion'. and mentions the sale of his estate.[35] Defoe seems to let the decayed condition of Linlithgow stand without further comment. His rhetorical aims would have been strengthened if he could have seen into the future, as the Duke of Cumberland's army burnt down most of what remained of the palace in 1746.

Elsewhere he leaves it to informed readers to make the necessary application. At Dysart in Fife, 'the Property both of the Town and the Lands adjoining belong to the Lord *Sinclare* or St. *Clare*: But be the Estate whose it will, the Town, though a Royal Burgh, is . . . in the full Perfection of Decay' (3: 233). A dramatic life-history unreported here is that of John, Master of Sinclair (1683–1750). He had been declared ineligible to sit in the Union parliament in 1708 because he was under a sentence of death for murdering two fellow officers. With the connivance of the Duke of Marlborough, he was allowed to escape from custody; and helped by the Duke of Hamilton he was granted a royal pardon. Not chastened by these experiences, he duly volunteered to lead a troop at Sheriffmuir, but he played only a passive part in the encounter, and he became bitterly critical of Mar's leadership. Like others under attainder, he fled to the Continent. With amazing tenacity, he somehow managed to get his death sentence revoked by professing loyalty to Walpole's government, and came back to Scotland around the time that the *Tour* appeared. Defoe would have known all about him, having observed the doings of Sinclair's father. In 1707 he went on a field trip and reported to Harley that among those attending the Jacobite recruiting meeting held by the Duke of Atholl were 'the Lord Sinclear & sevll Other of the Popish and Jacobite Gentlemen on Fife Side where I Now Am'.[36]

Where a clear Jacobite connection had not been established, the *Tour* opts for discretion. Thus, there is reference to 'the late Earl of *Kinnowl*'s Son, the Lord *Duplin*', as married to the daughter of the late Earl of Oxford, that is Defoe's patron Robert Harley. The family seat is described as 'situated in a good Soil, and a pleasant Country', with adornments by the Earl's descendants and two new wings. There is no hint that, at the start of the Rising, Kinnoul himself had been imprisoned in Edinburgh Castle as possibly complicit in the Jacobites' plans, while his heir George Hay was detained in the Tower of London for several months. We are not told that his younger son John Hay would help to take Perth for the insurgents in September 1715, that he would escape to the Continent to serve as the Pretender's secretary of state, and that he would become the Jacobite Duke of Inverness. A tactful silence is observed with regard to allegations that George Hay, who had succeeded his father in 1719, was involved in the organization of the Atterbury plot in 1721–2. Behind this lies the fact that the former Earl's daughter Margaret was the first wife of the Earl of Mar. Moreover, Macky is equally reticent on this topic, merely acknowledging like Defoe that the Kinnoul peerage was granted by Queen Anne.[37]

The most ambiguous case of all was that of the 4th Duke of Hamilton. In the lead-up to the Union, Defoe clearly regarded him as the inspiration behind street protests in Edinburgh, and the hero of the mob: 'All this while Duke Hamilton was Huzza'd and followed with the blessings and prayers of the crowd following his coach every day.'[38] However, the Duke moved to London, ingratiated himself with the new Tory ministry, and sent conflicting messages about his support for the Pretender. Killed in a famous duel in 1711, an event which was widely interpreted as caused by underlying political motives, he might have jumped either way when the Rising took place. Defoe simply avoids saying anything to the purpose in the *Tour*: 'He never came to the Estate, for he was kill'd before the Duchess *Dowager* died; so that the Estate . . . being her own, remain'd in her Hands till afterward; whether his might not be the better for the present Heir, I shall not determine, let others judge of that' (3: 205). It may be that Macky was equally perplexed, since he is just as reticent, though he devotes twelve pages to the Hamilton family and their seat.[39]

In only a single case does the *Tour* have anything unequivocally positive to say about a Jacobite active in the Rising. This relates to Alexander Forbes, 4th Lord Forbes of Pitsligo:

> The Lord *Pitsligo* . . . though unhappily drawn into the Snare of the late Insurrection, and forfeiting his Estate with the rest, yet carries Abroad with him, where-ever he goes, a bright Genius, a Head as full of Learning and sound Judgment, and a Behaviour as polite, courtly, and full of all the good Qualities that adorn a noble Birth, as most Persons of Quality I ever saw. (3: 262)

Macky averts his eyes from the episode.[40] In any case, Pitsligo did not learn the lesson that Defoe wished to inculcate. He returned from exile in 1720, but though he had reached his late sixties in 1745 he took up arms once again. After Culloden he was forced to go into hiding in a cave near his former home, disguised as a beggar. The castle was sacked by Hanoverian troops and allowed to fall into a ruin. It is noteworthy that some properties belonging to Stuart supporters that came through intact after the 1715 Rising were demolished in the wake of the second great rebellion.

Here, for a moment, there is a hint of pathos, and perhaps even of tragedy. As we have seen, the single word 'unhappily' was used in connection with Nithsdale, and it chimes with terms such as 'unhappy', which was applied to the Pretender's enterprise and to its commander in chief, Mar. A near synonym, 'unfortunate', characterises Panmure. The same semantics can be employed for places: Perth was 'unhappily for some time, the Seat of the late Rebellion', even though for tradespeople in the town it was far from an unhappy period (3: 247). At Scone, the Pretender 'kept his Court, a fatal Court to the Nobility and Gentry of Scotland, who were deluded to appear for him' (3: 253). Indeed, the failure of the Rising is most frequently registered in the physical decay of Jacobite seats, mirroring the 'several Decays' of the owner's line, surviving only in its 'Widows' Weeds'. The phenomenon parallels the decline of towns like Ayr, caused by the decay of trade, itself the result of a lack of the modernising enterprise which the Union now permits. Unlike the smiling Virgilian landscape that surrounds the domain of Hanoverian grandees, the favoured setting for the Jacobites resembles the region around Lochaber:

> It is indeed a frightful Country full of hidious desart Mountains and unpassable, except to the *Highlanders* who possess the Precipices. Here in spight of the most vigorous Pursuit, the *Highland* Robbers, such as the famous *Rob Roy* in the late Disturbances, find such Retreats as none can pretend to follow them into, nor could he be ever taken. (3: 279)

It is no surprise that 'this unhappy Part of the Country' is dominated by Catholics, and urgently requires the Protestant 'Ministers and Missionaries' (3: 278) who will boldly go out into the heart of darkness supported by the Royal Bounty.

Another group of usages emphasises dispossession or exile, as a form of death. As seats are demolished or left to rot, titles are extinguished and family lines terminated. This is often the result of forfeiture, another idea which recurs throughout the text. It even crops up in a digressive passage early in Letter 13, which tells of a murder committed at Inverkeithing by Lord Balfour of Burleigh. Defoe had been 'upon the Spot' when this event took place, but it hardly seems to warrant the space he allocates it.[41] The explanation may be that it gave him an opportunity to underline a central theme of the book. Balfour was captured, but escaped from the Tolbooth in Edinburgh: 'In return for this Deliverance he appear'd in the late Rebellion, and was in the Battle of *Dumblain* or *Sheriffmuir*; but got off again; and his Estate, which, however, was but small, was forfeited among the rest. But the Murtherer is not yet brought to Justice' (3: 226). Subliminally we may be led to reflect that many of the attainted rebels who fled have themselves not been brought to justice along with their fellow criminal, Balfour.

Almost all the figures of real substance who took part in the Rising are covered in the *Tour*. A major exception is William Mackenzie, 5th Earl of Seaforth (*c.*1686–1740), appointed by the Pretender as lieutenant general of the northern forces and leader of a large force at Sheriffmuir. His father had gone into exile with James II, and he was imprisoned following an abortive rising in Scotland. There are two possible reasons for this silence. One is the remoteness of the family seat at Brahan Castle near Dingwall, the location of a siege in November 1715 when Highlanders loyal to the Earl of Sutherland took over the house as their own garrison. The second reason is that, after attainder, exile and wounds at the battle of Glenshiel in 1719, Seaforth sued for a pardon. In June 1726 the government acceded, and the penalties imposed were removed, although not the attainder. It would have been tactless for Defoe to draw attention to the Earl's history at this precise juncture.[42] Other omissions are the Earl of Carnwath, the Earl of Southesk and Highland leaders belonging to the Macdonald, Macgregor, Mackintosh, Maclean, and Macneill clans (absent from the text for reasons sufficiently explained earlier).

Conclusion

Plainly, a work organised on a topographic layout cannot provide a linear narrative of events. The *Tour* never claims to offer a connected history of 1715 and 1716. Defoe makes no pretense of analysing the clan system, as Samuel Johnson does in his *Journey to the Western Islands* (1775), or to tease out the intricate details of the divided loyalties found in some of the Highland clans. He declines to supply an etiology of Jacobite sentiment, or to dig into the pathology of the movement, as it was expressed in what Daniel Szechi calls 'the Jacobite socio-cultural milieu'.[43] Something he does supply is a remarkably coherent vision of a nation torn in two by the Rising. The rhetorical strategy he adopts is simple but highly effective in a work of political persuasion. Progress, improvement, cultivation, a settled order, success and the future are associated with the Union (as they constitute its supposed goals), as well as with the Protestant and Hanoverian cause. Defeat, displacement, disruption, ruination and the past are identified with Catholicism and Jacobitism, embodied in the divisive presence of the Pretender.

The Rising figures within the *Tour* as a disaster for the Scottish nation. Some clear parallels exist with the treatment of the South Sea Bubble, seen in the text – not quite accurately – as an English phenomenon. We shall see in the next chapter that Defoe constantly railed against the villainy of stockjobbers, and he blamed the crash on corrupt politicians and share-pushers. As a result he can regret the losses that some formerly wealthy investors suffered, though he knows it is their own fault: 'Pity and matter of Grief is it to think that Families, by Estate, able to appear in such a Glorious Posture as this, should ever be Vulnerable by so mean a Disaster as that of Stock-Jobbing' (1: 131). The Jacobites were equally 'vulnerable', either because of their religious faith, family loyalties, or their ill-founded belief in the Pretender and his commander. Their punishment is a harsh but necessary reward.

History, we need no reminder, is written by the victors. Because Defoe's sympathies had always lain with the winning side, it would be unreasonable to expect a balanced or objective portrayal of the episode. Yet, granted his limitations, he offered an account that is largely accurate on matters of fact. The *Tour* is not a primary document, in the sense that some of his earlier work can claim to be with respect to the Union. But it is the product of long familiarity with the issues, and first-hand acquaintance with numerous people and places covered in the itinerary. It imports a spectrum of feelings, ranging from a deep satisfaction with the outcome of the Rising, generally avoiding naked triumphalism, through scorn to a discreet measure of regret and compassion for the losing side. The text embraces eulogy, indignation, sly innuendo and threnody. These elements are all largely absent from Macky's *Journey*, with its flat and businesslike approach resembling the brusque coverage of highlights in a modern tourist guide. With great skill Defoe embeds his view of the Rising within the larger case of the *Tour*, as it contrasts the past and present factors inhibiting progress in Scotland with the future potential opened by the Union and the Hanoverian accession.

CHAPTER 7

The Impact of the Bubble

Another event that occurred soon afterwards went a long way to eclipse the Rising, for the nation but also for Defoe. This was, of course, the South Sea Bubble in 1720, together with a parallel and almost contemporaneous episode in France often known as the Mississippi Bubble. There is no need here to rehearse all the happenings in that tumultuous year, as its tercentenary has seen exhaustive coverage by students of financial history. Almost everyone in Britain was affected, directly or indirectly, by what went on in Exchange Alley and to a lesser extent the rue Quincampoix. A flood of pamphlets, broadsides and graphic satires deluged the country, many of them analysed in recent scholarship. The topic called out one of Swift's most characteristic poems, *The Bubble*, and one of Pope's greatest works, the *Epistle to Bathurst* (though he held his fire for over a decade, long enough to be able to set the entire fiasco in a broader context). But there was one living writer in England who had a longer and more intense involvement with the South Sea project. This was Defoe: as Maximillian E. Novak has observed, 'The effects of the South Sea Bubble remained with Defoe throughout the rest of his life; it permeates all the major fiction in which individual criminal actions of one kind or another have to be set against corporate crime and government collusion.'[1] Even more relevant to our purpose, the issue is seldom very far from the author's mind in the social and economic writings of the 1720s, and it surfaces on a number of pages in the *Tour*. Before considering these issues, we should look back at Defoe's earlier engagement with the question of further commercial exploitation in the Western Hemisphere.

Earlier Involvement

It is, and was, no secret that Defoe had a longstanding interest in extending British trade in the South Seas (the term here includes along with the Pacific coast the eastern seaboard of South America). In July 1711 he sent

Robert Harley, lately made Earl of Oxford, a detailed proposal for setting up a colony in Chile, entered on Valdivia.[2] It was once thought that this supplied the impetus for Oxford to create the South Sea Company, whose charter permitted it to operate from 1 August. It is now certain that John Blunt and George Caswall had devised a scheme in 1710 and submitted it to Harley, as he then was. With the benefit of hindsight, it is also clear that their aim had to do with making money for themselves by taking over a portion of the national debt. A viable plan to develop a trading colony, such as Defoe envisaged (however realistically or unrealistically), was not in their mind.

In any case, the author of the *Review* had repeatedly taken up from its early numbers the subject of Spanish and French trade with the Americas, and how this impacted on the British economy. Generally Defoe favoured expanding trade with the region to counter the hegemony of Europe, but he was cautious about attempting widespread colonisation on the Spanish model. He certainly saw a particular opportunity on the Pacific coast, since 'The Spaniards as if They had been Sated and Gutted with the Wealth of Peru, Never entirely Conquer'd [Chile]', but his reading of writers such as Sir Walter Raleigh left him in no doubt over the difficulties in establishing and maintaining a colony.[3] But in a *Review* paper of 4 October 1707 he had argued that 'If we were to possess the Silver and Gold of *Peru*, and the Wealth of *Mexico*, the scattering our People, and the bringing our Manufactures to be wrought in those populous Countries, would make the Gain of them be less to us, than they are now – That is, in an open Trade to *Spain*.' What he recommended instead was to use the power of the navy to seize the Spanish and French treasure ships, especially as this would weaken the French war effort in a drawn-out contest that still showed little sign of coming to an end.

Defoe's views are set out in a defence of the new Company, *An Essay on the South-Sea Trade* (1711), 'by the Author of the *Review*', which countered objections on several grounds, concerning the manner of its introduction; the method of its operation; the persons involved (the projectors like Blunt, the government and parliament); the timing; and specific parts of the scheme that had come under criticism. From the summer, a number of issues of the *Review* attempted to soften up the reading public for the new legislation, starting from the position that 'Our Eyes are all now upon the Trade to the South Seas; a Trade as proposed, few People Understand' (21 June 1711). On 28 June the writer states that he knows people have expected the paper to give its opinion on the subject, and that he is not afraid to do this, 'without respect to who *are* or *are not* for it or against it.'

He reminds his readers that in an earlier paper he had mentioned a proposal that he had laid before William III, to the effect that the war should be carried not into Old Spain but as far as New Spain, 'not into *Catalognia* but into *America*'. Whether this bold undertaking would have shortened the war is not clear. But Defoe did not lack confidence in his own rectitude, and followed up in further issues of the journal. On 17 July he sought to dispel 'gross Errors in our People, with Relation to this Trade', and stated that a design to supplant the French in the South Seas, 'and make that Profit your own, must be both agreeable and very Advantageous'. On 30 August, he tried to show how Bank stock and South Sea stock were wholly independent, with an ominous aside: 'Suppose the South Sea-Trade was quite confounded and sunk, as for all I see it will be, if these Madnesses prevail, is the Bank-Stock one Shilling the worse for it?'

Defoe never lost his enthusiasm for Britain to set up a colony to exploit the supposed hoards of Andean gold: it is the central idea behind his fictional *New Voyage Round the World* (1724), and it is still a live notion in *Atlas Maritimus* (1728).[4] Nevertheless, Defoe focused his main energies over the next few years in a different direction. Even before Queen Anne died and the Tory government fell, Lord Oxford (its leader and Defoe's patron) had alienated the most important players in the South Sea Company. When George I arrived in 1714, the court of directors gave him a warm welcome, and he reciprocated by acquiring holdings for himself and his family. The Prince of Wales became governor. From this time the institution became patently Whig in its bearings. The old guard of Tories were removed from the scene, and a variety of new faces appeared, most notably perhaps the soldier and courtier John Campbell, Duke of Argyll. When the split between the King and the Prince widened in 1717, it was the monarch who prevailed at South Sea House and became formal head of the Company. In terms of political leadership, this meant that the Whig faction led by Sunderland and Stanhope had got the better of their rivals, led by Walpole and Townshend.[5]

This should have been good news for Defoe, who was now working for Sunderland. But his attention had been diverted to other issues in recent years, most obviously the Jacobite Rising. There are occasional references in his pamphlets and newspaper articles to South Sea affairs, but they did not lie at the centre of his concerns. Moreover, he had tried to keep his relations with Walpole in good repair. His pamphlet *Fair Payment no Spunge* (1717) supported a plan by the ousted minister to establish a sinking fund to discharge the national debt by cutting the interest paid on loans and annuities. However, it was only when Stanhope sought to push through an alternative scheme by which the Company would take over part of the national debt (a role which the Bank of England thought would more naturally fall to its share) that Defoe grew uneasy. He had long worried about the workings of the market as these had been manipulated to give the Company an advantage. In 1719 his anxiety came to a head with what is perhaps the most aggressive of his shorter writings.

The work appeared in July, under the title of *The Anatomy of Exchange-Alley: or, A System of Stock-Jobbing, Proving that Scandalous Trade, as it is now carry'd on, to be Knavish in its Private Practice and Treason in its Publick* (followed by almost 150 words identifying the 'private Cheats' employed in the Alley, as well as the 'treasonable Rumours' spread there). With unsparing irony, the tract is said to be written 'By a Jobber'. The principal target is a trio of individuals running the Sword Blade Bank along with John Blunt, and as such the real financial power brokers underpinning the Company. They are called 'a true Triumvirate of modern Thieving'. In turn Defoe describes the villains of the piece, starting with George Caswall, 'a Man of Brass sufficient for much more Business than he can be trusted with, is said to manage for three Blew Ribbonds [Garter Knights], and for four or five Cash-keepers, who tell more Money than their own'. Then there is Jacob Sawbridge, who 'has twice the Head, but not half the Business that *C[aswall]* is said to have, yet he gets more Money for himself, and *C–* gets more for other folks'. Finally there is Elias Turner, who 'inherits the Face [impudence] of *C–*, with the Craft of *S–*'.[6] As far as character assassination goes, this ranks with the finest satiric denunciations in the language.

And Defoe was right about all three of them. After the crash, the bank had been forced to stop payment in October 1720. However, though a nonentity of almost eighty named Sir Roger Hill was brought in as a token governor, Elias Turner, Sawbridge and Caswall retained the most shares and the most votes in affairs of the Sword Blade company. The subsequent investigations determined that all three had acted as a channel for the transmission of bribes to MPs. In the event Caswall and Sawbridge were both expelled from parliament, along with South Sea directors, and suffered heavy fines: as a director Sawbridge was required to enter into recognisances to ensure that he would not flee the country. His securities were Elias Turner and George Caswall, not the most secure of pledges. Somehow they both survived and continued in business. Turner crept back into the obscurity from which he had emerged.

The *Anatomy* was the first prominent document to name names so directly, and to make explicit charges against key figures in the corruption that surrounded the South Sea management. Defoe had first expressed his contempt for the jobbing trade in *The Villainy of Stock-Jobbers Detected* as far back as 1701, but the new pamphlet was more pointed and precise in its allegations. He was taking a big risk, since the objects of his criticism had powerful protectors, and it was not hard to extrapolate from his criticisms to form suspicions concerning the mightiest in the land, including his own patron Lord Sunderland. But he was bold enough to predict a bad end. What he wrote near the end of his pamphlet eerily would come to pass in 1720, but also resembles the threnody contained in the *Tour*:

> The Truth is, it has been foretold by cunning Men, who often see what can't be hid, that these Men, by a Mass of Money which they command of other Peoples, as well as their own, will, in Time, ruin the Jobbing Trade. But 'twill be only like a general Visitation, where all Distempers are swallow'd up in the Plague, like a common Calamity, that makes Enemies turn Friends, and drowns lesser Grievances in the general Deluge.[7]

The nation managed to avert one 'general Visitation' when the dreaded disease arrived almost on the shores of England a year later, in a small measure thanks to the 'due preparations' that Defoe himself had urged. But the financial calamity duly took place, and though financial professionals like Caswall and Sawbridge were hauled over the coals, there were many others with no personal responsibility for the crash who suffered most acutely, as Defoe foresaw.

Mississippi and South Sea

All this while he had kept a close eye on France, observing the meteoric rise and (in due course) fall of the Scottish adventurer and gambler, turned economist, John Law. In early September 1719 Defoe produced *The Chimera: Or, the French way of Paying National Debts, laid open. Being an Impartial Account of the Proceedings in France, for raising a Paper Credit, and settling the Mississippi* [sic] *Stock*. At this juncture all seemed to be set fair for Law's ambitious project to establish a paper currency, but Defoe felt an instinctive distaste for its speculative nature. He noted the efforts of Louis XIV to elevate public credit to the level it had achieved in England under William III, but 'this Coy Mistress, call'd Credit, could never be woo'd'. As a result he predicts that the 'system' will not work, amounting to little more than a conjuring trick, or 'an inconceivable Species of meer

Air and Shadow, realizing Fancies and Imaginations, Visions and Apparitions, and making the mere Speculation of Things, act all the Parts, and perform all the Offices of the Things themselves'. The images of substance and shadow, air and apparitions, came to be widely used for the South Sea venture after the Bubble burst. Once Mississippi had run its course, Defoe returned to the case in the *Case of Mr. Law Truly Stated*, published in late 1719. This is cast in the form of a letter to the financier, running 'a short Parallel' between his management and that of the South Sea directors. He concludes that the big difference between what Law undertook in France, as compared with the directors in London, was that he did it 'openly and warily', sounding an alarm in Paris, whereas 'Our People did it subtily and privately', and so 'they were not found out till afterward'. Defoe does not try to conceal the guilt of Blunt or the now absconded cashier of the Company, Robert Knight, but he does suggest that behind them skulked 'Great Persons concern'd here, of whom Sir *John Blunt* and his Fraternity have been little more than a Shadow'.[8]

In addition, Defoe commented regularly on Law's affairs in the articles he was pumping out in the press. Unfortunately we have no means of knowing precisely which items were his work, among contributions to the papers with which he was linked at this period: the two named the *Weekly Journal* of Mist and Applebee, the *Whitehall Evening* Post and the *Daily Post.* There are naturally frequent allusions to events on the British side of the Channel alongside material dealing with the French scene. For example, late in the sequence, a piece in Applebee's journal on 12 May 1722 referred to 'those worthy Heroes of our Age, who having gamed away their Fortunes in the late Bubbling Age, and been gull'd of their Money by the *B[lunt]'s* and *A[islabi]e's*, and *L[a]w's* of the Age, have fled from the Face of Poverty by *the shortest Way*, to the Grave, and laid Violent Hands on themselves, to shun the Infamy of a mean Figure in the World' (one of numerous references to the rash of suicides that Defoe mentioned, and would touch on in the *Tour*). The phrase in italics surely points to a key episode in his own life. Much earlier, on 26 March 1720, when Mississippi stock had crashed but South Sea was still riding high, Mist's paper carried an article with a cautionary sting in its tail:

> Our South-Sea Stock has made such a consumed Noise of late, to the Terror of the trading Part of this Nation, that it has brought over many of the Quinquampoix Gentry to try their Fortunes here; and, 'tis said, that abundance of our Country Gentlemen and rich Farmers are upon the Roads from several Parts of the Kingdom; all expecting no less than to ride down again, every Man, in his Coach and Six; but, if a Friend's Advice is worth any thing, let them take Care, for, though there are some Prizes,

> they may find many more Blanks, and they may happen to lose all that in an Hour in Exchange-Alley, which the Industry and Care of their Ancestors has been scraping together for some Ages.

It would be hard to find a more characteristic example of Defoe's ideas from early in the affair. A pity that so many neglected to take a friend's advice.

We are on stronger ground in the case of two further periodicals, both essay papers issued twice weekly, that is *The Commentator*, running between 1 January and 6 September 1720, succeeded by *The Director* to 16 January 1721 (Defoe is thought to have taken over the editorship from the fifth number). The former was written in open support of the government, and a fortiori the South Sea Company, as opposed to the myriad bubble companies that had sprung up and would be suppressed by the Bubble Act in June. The author notes on 5 August that despite the Act, 'Our good Friends in *Exchange-Alley* . . . are still propagating there the *Bubble-Manufactures*, as my Friend *Daniel* well enough calls it in his Paper, entituled, *The Manufacturer*' (an unsubtle plug for his other journal). A familiar comparison is made, and a cautionary note is struck on 14 July: 'So our *South-Sea*, which upon this core we may call *Mississippi*'s younger Sister, tho' being *born of better Parents, she had a better Portion to recommend her*; yet even with all her Advantages, her Rising has been monstrous and surprizing.' When readers of the *Tour* encountered the author's laments over the calamitous course of 1720, they could hardly complain that he had not warned them enough times.

The Director is even more pertinent to Defoe's later book. It takes an unpopular line amid the bloodletting which ensued in the months following the crash, a case well summarised by Furbank and Owens: 'The "bubble" is the fault, not so much of the directors of the South-Sea Company as of despicable stockjobbers, and of sheep-like investors who ruin themselves by panic selling.'[9] The argument involves a roseate view of the dramatic falls that the market had recently experienced: either Defoe genuinely clung to this illusory belief in a rapid recovery, or more likely he thought it necessary to engage in damage limitation. One perhaps artificial distinction that he is anxious to make concerns 'the *Active* and *Passive*, according as was said of the *Directors* of the *South-Sea* Company, between the *Managers* and the *Directors*' (no. 18, 2 December). A fair amount of casuistry is required to maintain this view of the Company's operations, and to exempt so far as he can the Court of directors from *culpable* responsibility – he cannot deny their tacit consent, at the very least. In an early issue (no. 9, 31 October), the writer argues that it is not the job of the King and parliament to remedy the situation, as it is within the power of the Company to stabilise the market and bring it back up to the 'natural' price of around 400. This was a delusion: the problems had spread far beyond the narrow circle of financiers and big investors. Legislative action was needed to bring about a solution, and this happened only after Robert Walpole had knocked heads together and brokered a settlement with the Bank of England that was agreeable to both parties and sustainable over the long term. We can understand Defoe's contempt for the 'Old Women' who had taken fright too quickly and sold out when all would have been well if they had held on a little longer. But, as he must have realised by the time that he wrote about the effects of the Bubble in the *Tour*, the horse had bolted.

One other work that preceded the *Tour* deserves mention, although it belongs to an entirely different genre. This is *A Journal of the Plague Year*, published in March 1722, which can be seen as an extended allegory of the Bubble year. Other writers used the parallel between plague and financial collapse; this occurred mainly after the two phenomena became present dangers in 1720: the similitudes are fairly clear, and might have also been apparent in the case of a work Defoe issued in the previous month, *Due Preparations for the Plague.* As Novak has suggested, 'Given the anxiety about a punishment from God for the excesses of the South Sea Bubble, Defoe's publishers must have fought to get their hands on a work by Defoe dealing with so terrifying a prospect as the plague coming to Britain.'[10] But as we have seen, he had already spotted the correspondence some time before either event loomed into sight, in *The Anatomy of Exchange-Alley.* Moreover, in his articles in the press during 1720 and 1721 he regularly employs precisely the same idiom to refer to the two matters: as I have tried to show elsewhere, it is often impossible to know which is in question, if we read them 'blind' after removing any give-away expression such as dates.[11] So it is that the vocabulary of key passages in the *Tour* reflecting on the South Sea experience will echo that of the *Journal*, with its account of 'this calamitous year'.[12] Both works enlist terms conveying a sense of ruin, desolation, terror, contagion, and widely shared disaster. We now turn to some of those passages.

Pity and Matter of Grief

The first substantial reference in the *Tour* to the financial crash comes late in Letter 1, and it supplies one of the most resonant passages in the entire work. It concerns the sumptuous estate at Wanstead outside London, owned by Lord Castlemaine, who had lost a lot of his money (though by no means all) in the Bubble.

> I shall cover as much as possible the melancholy part of a Story, which touches too sensibly, many, if not most of the Great and Flourishing Families in *England*: Pity and matter of Grief is it to think that Families, by Estate, able to appear in such a glorious Posture as this, should ever be vulnerable by so mean a Disaster as that of Stock-Jobbing: But the *General Infatuation of the Day* is a Plea for it; so that Men are not now blamed on that Account: *South-Sea* was a general Possession; and if my Lord *Castlemain* was wounded by that Arrow shot in the Dark, 'twas a Misfortune: But 'tis so much a Happiness, that it was not a Mortal Wound, as it was to some Men, who once seem'd as much out of the reach of it; and that Blow, be it what it will, is not remember'd for joy of the Escape; for we see this Noble Family, by Prudence and Management rise out of all that Cloud, if it may be allow'd such a Name, and shining in the same full Lustre as before.
>
> This cannot be said of some other Families in this County, whose fine Parks and new-built Palaces are fallen under Forfeitures and Alienations by the Misfortunes of the Times, and by the Ruin of their Masters Fortunes in that *South-Sea* Deluge.
>
> But I desire to throw a Veil over these Things, as they come in my way; 'tis enough that we write upon them as was written upon King *Harold*'s Tomb at *Waltham-Abbey*, INFAELIX, and let all the rest sleep among Things that are the fittest to be forgotten. (1: 131)

At first sight, Richard Child (1680–1750), Viscount Castlemaine and later Earl Tylney, was an unlikely choice as a South Sea victim. Although he inherited a large fortune (estimated at £280,000) from the East India Company magnate Sir Josiah Child, he did not occupy an important position in the commercial life of the City.[13] He served as an MP for Essex without exercising any national authority. A convert from the Tories, he came late to the Hanoverian party, managing to buy an Irish peerage in 1718 after some hesitation among those in power. He had not taken an active role in the South Sea Company. Moreover, as Defoe indicates, he was not wiped out by the debacle as were many of his colleagues in parliament.

His inclusion here may be explained by three factors. First, his was the first grand new mansion designed by the Whigs' favourite architect, Colen Campbell, and it was the most recently completed along with show gardens in 1722. More of the victims had their estates south of the Thames, but the author could not wait for another hundred pages to compose his threnody. Second, there was a Child family who represented an influential City dynasty, and Defoe is writing about the fall of prominent commercial houses. Third, Stephen Child was a goldsmith banker in Lombard Street, at first in partnership with Benjamin Tudman, another South Sea figure whose widow married Sir John Blunt, kingpin of the entire operation. Defoe may not have realised that Stephen was unrelated to Lord Castlemaine. However, he filled the bill as a Whig and a loyal dissenter. Crucially, Stephen served as a director of the Company from 1718 to 1721, and had been fined over £40,000 after the great swindle collapsed.

Defoe's confusion extended a little further. A passage in the *Complete English Tradesman* reads:

> We have seen many trading families lay the foundation of Nobility by their wealth and opulence—as Mr. *Child*, for example, afterwards Sir *Josiah Child*, whose posterity by his two daughters are now Dukes of *Beaufort* and of *Bedford*, and his Grandson Lord Viscount *Castlemain*, and yet he himself began a mean Tradesman, and in circumstances very mean too.[14]

This is right about the two dukes, but as we have seen Lord Castlemaine was the son, not the grandson, of Sir Josiah. What the author might have added, if he had learnt it in time, was that the Duke of Bedford got married in April 1725 at the age of seventeen: his bride was a granddaughter of the great Duke and Duchess of Marlborough, further cementing the Child progeny.

If Defoe erred here, as seems likely, that does not weaken the force of his rhetoric. At a time when 'director' was one of the dirtiest words in the lexicon, he made it his business in the *Tour* to lament the fate of great captains of industry, who in his submission had been seduced into risking their fortunes on the plausible sure thing that South Sea investment represented. Again and again he stresses the comparative innocence of these men, as distinct from the actual crooks, particularly those engaged in 'Stock-Jobbing', who were responsible for devising and executing the scam. The arrow shot in the dark landed where it might, and among the individuals whose body was pierced were many belonging to a class Defoe held in high esteem – the magnates who had risen from the bourgeoisie to support the financial revolution, to bankroll the ascension of William III, and later to help set in place the Whig hegemony following the Hanoverian accession. Many were extremely wealthy; many held high office in the City corporation and the livery companies; many were MPs who provided reliable week by week backing for the Whig government, and assisted in raising trained bands when emergencies threatened the capital; many were active in charities that financed schools and hospitals. Scarcely any of these things endeared them to their Tory critics, who saw them as upstarts and mushrooms, risen from nowhere, promoting dubious projects, and deservedly brought to their knees in 1720. Defoe never saw things that way at all.

As so often, Macky's *Journey* paints a different picture. In 1722 he comments that 'The Neighbourhood of *London* is also prodigiously enlarged since the *South-Sea* Scheme . . . And indeed most Villages within a few Miles of the City, are adorned with *South-Sea* Seats.' What he means by this becomes clearer a few lines further on: 'But above all, there are Two fine Palaces, the one building by the Duke of *Chandois*, Ten Miles off, called *Cannons*; the other by the Lord *Castlemain* at *Wansted*, Five Miles off, which when finished will be inferior to few Royal Palaces in *Europe*.'[15] Astoundingly, Macky seems to believe that Chandos and Castlemaine made their money out of South Sea (both were losers), and that the Bubble era was one to celebrate on the grounds of economic expansion. We are a long way from Defoe's sober account of lives built on an apparently copper-bottomed foundation that were damaged, occasionally beyond repair.

As the *Tour* progresses, its text reverts to numerous cognate issues, some relating to the nation, some to individuals. The highest concentration naturally emerges in Letter 2, especially in the section on Surrey, where those who lost most as a result of the crash tended to have their estates. One example occurs at Carshalton: 'The other House is that of Sir *John Fellows*, late Sub-Governor of the *South-Sea* Company, who having the Misfortune to fall in the general Calamity of the late Directors, lost all his unhappy Wealth, and a good honestly gotten Estate of his own into the Bargain' (1: 193). We can see here the characteristic idiom employed in this context: words like '*Misfortune*', 'general Calamity', 'Unhappy Wealth' and 'honestly gotten' combine to lend an exculpatory air to the description. Sir John Fellowes (1671–1724), a director of the Company since its foundation, and sub-governor since late 1718, was a turkey merchant created a baronet in 1719. He had spent a great deal of money on his home, which had briefly belonged to the physician John Radcliffe, and hired Charles Bridgeman to renovate the gardens with extensive tree-planting. The great setpiece was a bathing room, fed by a tower that pumped water from the River Wandle. It was a model instance of conspicuous consumption, precisely the kind of thing that led many observers to withhold sympathy for the Bubble's victims – but not Defoe of course. Fellowes was the first of the directors to be called before the parliamentary committee of investigation in 1721. His estate was computed at around £250,000, and after his fine was imposed he was left with just £10,000. He managed to hold on to Carshalton, but he survived only three more years before going to his grave, a broken man. It was on 26 July 1724, two months after the first volume of the *Tour* appeared.

The sad tale of Fellowes is squeezed into the text among happier stories of businessmen who went through this tempestuous era unscathed. The immediately preceding sentences read:

> This Village seated among such delightful Springs, is yet all standing upon firm Chalk; and having the *Downs* close adjoining, makes the most agreeable Spot on all this side of London, as is abundantly testify'd by its being, as it were, crouded with fine Houses of the Citizens of *London*; some of which are built with such a Profusion of Expence, that they look rather like Seats of the Nobility, than the Country Houses of Citizens and Merchants; particularly those of Sir *William Scawen*, lately Deceased; who besides an immense Estate in Money has left, as I was told, One Article of Nine Thousand Pounds a Year to his Heir; and was himself since the Fire of London, only Mr. *Scawen*, a *Hamborough* Merchant, dealing by Commission, and not in any view of such an Encrease of Wealth, or any thing like it. (1: 193)

The flurry of initial capitals in this sprawling sentence seems to reflect the awe that Defoe felt, as a citizen of London and a merchant who could not leave 'any thing like' an inheritance on this scale to his children. John McVeagh gives a succinct abstract of this individual's career: 'Sir William Scawen (*c.*1647–1722), merchant, army clothing contractor and financier, who made a fortune out of the Williamite wars. He was a Whig MP, knighted in 1692. In 1720 he purchased Flancheford Manor near Reigate, Surrey, from Thomas, Viscount Windsor' (1: 320). In short – he was just the kind of man whom the Tories loved to hate. Scawen turns up a few pages later along with Sir Josiah Child, Sir Robert Clayton and other merchant princes, 'whose Beginnings were small' (1: 203). Defoe had long been aware of Scawen: subsequently, in the *Complete English Tradesman* it is noted that he married his son into the aristocracy, though the groom's ancestors, 'within the memory of the writers of these sheets, were tradesmen in *London*'; and he is mentioned in a similar context in *The Compleat English Gentleman.*[16]

The difference between Fellowes and Scawen is partly the fact that the latter heeded the advice given to prosperous tradesmen in Defoe's handbook, not to overstretch themselves when comfortably off. But it is also a matter of luck. Scawen caught a favourable wind in the 1690s: Fellowes, a man of equal accomplishment, had once been to all appearances just as securely placed, until South Sea overwhelmed everything and almost everybody.

The Reach of Disaster

Soon afterwards, we arrive at Epsom. Here the tone is more positive, with a cheerful and almost ludic quality to the entry. Such an approach is in keeping with Defoe's overall effort to present Britain in an affirmative light. To achieve this, he is forced to adopt a stance different from the one we encountered in the passage on Fellowes. The rhetorical shift is effected by a suggestion that 1720 represented a mere blip, so that members of the London business can resume their former quest for pleasure in the town. A hint of disdain perceptible in the coverage of other spas and resorts – Bath, Tunbridge, Bury St Edmunds, Buxton, Knaresborough – is absent this time.

> About four Miles, over those delicious *Downs*, brings us to *Epsome*, and if you will suppose me to come there in the Month of *July*, or thereabouts, you may think me to come in the middle of the Season, when the Town is full of Company, and all disposed to Mirth and Pleasantry; for abating one unhappy *Stock-Jobbing Year*, when England took leave to act the Frantick, for a little while; and when every Body's Heads were turn'd with Projects and Stocks, *I say*, except this Year, we see nothing of Business in the whole Conversation of *Epsome*; even the Men of Business, who are really so when in *London*; whether it be at the *Exchange*, the *Alley*, or the Treasury-Offices, and the Court; yet here they look as if they had *left all their* London *Thoughts behind them*, and had separated themselves to Mirth and good Company; as if they came hither to unbend the Bow of the Mind, and to give themselves a loose to their Innocent Pleasures; I say, Innocent, for such they may enjoy here, and such any Man may make his being here, *if he pleases*. (1: 194)

There is something unconvincing about this, especially in the concluding lines with their repetition and oddly emphasised final phrase. It is hard to square these ideas with the author's usual zeal for business, his esteem for diligence, his seldom concealed puritan attitude towards frivolous pleasure-seeking and his distrust of the activities in Exchange Alley. A flash of true feeling comes out in the phrases referring to the '*Stock-Jobbing Year*', which correspond to the vocabulary of his more familiar jeremiads on the subject.

A little later, we are back with individuals, when the text refers to a number of impressive mansions south of the city. Among these is the residence of 'Sir *Theodore Jansssen*, another *South-Sea* Forfeiture at *Wimbleton*' (1: 202). This refers to a Tudor house overlooking the

Downs. Janssen had demolished this structure but had not yet had time to erect its replacement. In April 1723 it was bought up for nearly £25,000 by the Duchess of Marlborough, who later embarked on a new building nearby. As for Janssen himself (1658–1748), he was a Huguenot émigré with a background in papermaking, naturalised in 1684. As the *History of Parliament* states, 'He became one of the most eminent merchants and financiers of his time, a founding director of both the Bank of England and its rival, the South Sea Company, as well as a founder of the new East India Company. From 1695 he was among the chief contractors for remittances to the army abroad.'[17] In 1715, as one of the first creations in the new Hanoverian reign, he was made a baronet.

At the age of about sixty he entered parliament, naturally as a Whig, but his stay would be brief, as he was expelled in 1721 because of his involvement in the South Sea scandal. Mounting his defence before the Commons investigating committee, he pleaded ignorance, and claimed that 'he had by his industry acquired an estate of near £300,000 before the late scheme was thought of; that he had no hand in the contriving or carrying on the said scheme; but often opposed the methods of proceeding in the execution thereof'.[18] The fine imposed upon an estate generously undervalued at £243,000 left him with £50,000, though in reality he may have been able to hang on to more of his assets as he regained some of his properties. John Carswell, who lists some of his diverse interests and large land holdings, was not a severe judge, but seems to think that Janssen got off lightly.[19] Defoe would almost certainly have known of Janssen's works, *A Discourse concerning Banks* (1697) and *General Maxims of Trade* (1713), but he does not appear to comment on these. The former item was reprinted in 1720, apparently as a warning against the further encroachment of the Bank of England in taking over South Sea stock.

Along with Janssen, the text once more identifies the seats of businessmen who have contrived to keep their well-gotten gains. They include the home of Sir James Bateman, another Flemish immigrant, whose son married the daughter of the first minister, Lord Sunderland, in 1720; and that of 'Mr. *Howland*'s, now the Dutchess of *Bedford*'s at *Stretham*' (1: 202), this last having come about owing to the marriage between Elizabeth Howland and the second Duke of Bedford. Unsurprisingly, Defoe singles out these same upwardly mobile alliances by children of the business community in the *Complete English Tradesman,* not once but three times, and repeats the information about the second of these marriages in *The Compleat English Gentleman*.[20]

Then, as we leave the outlying villages and approach the city through Southwark, we come to another general lament for the entire class of Bubble victims.

> It would also take up a large Chapter in this Book, to but mention the overthrow, and Catastrophe of innumerable Wealthy City Families, who after they have thought their Houses establish'd, and have built their Magnificent Country Seats, as well as others, have sunk under the Misfortunes of Business, and the Disasters of Trade, after the World has thought them pass'd all possibility of Danger; such as Sir *Joseph Hodges*, Sir *Justus Beck*, the widow *Cock* at *Camberwell*, and many others; besides all the late *South Sea* Directors, all which I chuse to have forgotten, as no doubt they desire to be, in recording the Wealth and Opulence of this Part of *England*, which I doubt not to convince you infinitely out does the whole World. (1: 203)

To forget, in this context, is almost as good as to forgive. Hodges was the son of a Spanish merchant and Whig MP who had served on the board of both the Bank of England and the East India Company. Sir William must have been a big wheel within City circles, as his lavish funeral procession was followed by forty-two coaches of the nobility. After succeeding to the baronetcy in 1714, Joseph went abroad to live in France and Spain, probably to escape debts. By the time of his death on 1 April 1722, he had managed to dissipate most of his father's fortune, estimated at seven to eight thousand pounds. It seems highly improbable that the date generally given for his birth (*c.*1704) is correct: he was the only child and his parents were married as early as 1681, while he was elected as a fellow of the Royal Society in 1717, an honour not customarily bestowed on those barely into their teens. He died in London from the undramatic cause of dropsy.

The last named in the passage was the only survivor of the trio when Defoe wrote to Johanna Cock, widow of Walter (d. 1712), a wealthy merchant with property in both Camberwell and London, who passed on his business affairs to Joanna. She had bought the manor of Camberwell in 1718, and it was her own failure as a result of the Bubble that precipitated further 'Disasters' mentioned by Defoe. We know more of the details of the career of this 'remarkable woman' thanks to the thorough research of Ann M. Carlos and Larry Neal, who describe her market activity after she 'parlayed the holdings of her deceased husband into a large-scale business, dealing in the stock of the Bank of England during the South Sea Bubble of 1720'. Carlos and Neal show that 'Johanna Cock was one of the most active in terms of purchases and sales. She acted both as a broker and as a dealer in Bank stock. As a broker, she was simply a middleman or intermediary between sellers and buyers of stock, but as a dealer (or jobber) she bought and sold shares in her own name.' The impact of the financial crash must have had a heavy impact on her dealings, even though she dealt in Bank and East India stock and did not primarily engage in the South Sea market, as she was declared bankrupt in November 1720, at which time she held £12,000 in Bank of England stock. However, her sons prospered and she was apparently still alive in 1760.[21]

An equally suggestive case is that of Beck (1679–1722), an immigrant from Holland with large interests in overseas trade and a director of the Royal Exchange, who was one of the earliest and largest of the casualties of the episode. His failure in September 1720 sent shock waves through the system. For years after his bankruptcy and death, creditors kept filing Chancery suits to try to recover what they were owed through his surviving assignee, the Dutch-born merchant Gerard Vanneck. (This is a reminder that the fallout from South Sea lasted well into the next decade.) The death of Sir Justus and his daughter within a single hour on 15 December was reported in newspapers, with the strong suggestion that the cause in his case had been suicide:

> On Sunday last died Sir Justus Beck, Bart. (the first Baronet of his present Majesty's Creation), and also his second daughter [Mary], within half an hour of each other. The said gentleman always bore a fair character; but having had the misfortune to lose a plentiful estate through the late calamity of the times, it is believ'd the same was too much laid to heart both by himself and numerous family.[22]

In *The Complete English Tradesman,* Defoe cited Beck once more, adding a little more by way of an emotive tug:

> How many City Knights, Aldermen, and some of them Lord Mayors, can I reckon up from Sir *Robert Vyner* to Sir *Justus Beck*, who have sunk from a Knighthood, and immense Wealth to the lowest Misery and Poverty: I think I can reckon fourteen within the Compass of my own Remembrance, besides some Hundreds equal to them in Wealth, tho' not honour'd with the Sir and the Gold Chain.

'These are recent Testimonies', we are told in case the point had escaped us, 'that no Prosperity in Trade is out of the Reach of Disaster.'[23]

Each of these three cases is very different. Hodges looks to be the least significant of them, as a wastrel whose money may have been severely depleted before the crash came. His humdrum departure from life warranted only a brief sentence in the press, stating that he had been 'four times Tapp'd for the Dropsie'.[24] Johanna Cock was a broker whose failure certainly resulted from the financial crisis, although perhaps not specifically because of South Sea investments. Beck, however, stands out as a classic victim of the Bubble, one deeply involved in speculation as an overseas trader, and who had close connections with the Amsterdam market, itself heavily impacted by events in London and Paris. It was he whom the crisis drove to the kind of desperate measures that older narratives (now frequently challenged) used to cite as common occurrences.

Public Debts

In Letter 5, Defoe offers a broader interpretation of the financial situation after the Bubble. It comes when the description of the capital reaches the City of London.

> Here are the *South Sea* Company, the *East India* Company, the *Bank*, the *African* Company, *&c.* whose Stocks support that prodigious Paper Commerce, called *Stock-Jobbing*; a Trade, which once bewitched the Nation almost to its Ruin, and which, tho' reduced very much, and recovered from that terrible Infatuation which once over-spread the whole Body of the People, yet is still a Negotiation, which is so vast in its Extent, that almost all the Men of Substance in *England* are more or less concerned in it, and the Property of which is so very often alienated, that even the Tax upon the Transfers of Stock, tho' but Five Shillings for each Transfer, brings many Thousand Pounds a Year to the Government; and some have said, that there is not less than a Hundred Millions of Stock transferred forward or backward from one Hand to another every Year, and this is one thing which makes such a constant Daily Intercourse between the Court Part of the Town, and the City; and this is given as one of the principal Causes of the prodigious Conflux of the Nobility and Gentry from all Parts of *England* to *London*, more than ever was known in former Years, *viz.* That many Thousands of Families are so deeply concerned in those Stocks, and find it so absolutely necessary to be at Hand to take the Advantage of buying and selling, as the sudden Rise or Fall of the Price directs, and the Loss they often sustain by their Ignorance of Things when absent, and the Knavery of Brokers and others, whom, in their Absence, they are bound to trust, that they find themselves obliged to come up and live constantly here, or at least, most Part of the Year. (2: 85)

Aside from a few flashes of Defoe's animus against stockjobbing and brokers, this is a moderate assessment of the course that the nation was now taking. And yet the behaviour that brought about the disaster has to be seen as an 'Infatuation', that is something aberrant and outside the norms of economic life, rather than an inherent feature of the cycles of capitalism.

This passage of general reflection concludes with four further paragraphs. The first presses the need to reduce the public debt, a cry which had gone up ever since credit had increased hugely in wartime conditions.

> But let the Citizens and Inhabitants of *London* know, and it may be worth the Reflection of some of the Landlords, and Builders especially, that if Peace continues, and the publick Affairs continue in honest and upright Management, there is a Time coming, at least the Nation hopes for it, when the publick Debts being reduced and paid off, the Funds or Taxes on which they are establish'd, may cease, and so Fifty or Sixty Millions of the Stocks, which are now the solid Bottom of the *South-Sea Company, East-India Company, Bank*, &c. will cease, and be no more; by which the Reason of this Conflux of People being removed, they will of Course, and by the Nature of the Thing, return again to their Country Seats, to avoid the expensive living at *London*, as they did come up hither to share the extravagant Gain of their former Business here. (2: 86)

The author goes on to foresee a time when the government will be able to pay off their existing borrowings at 4 per cent, while lending at 6 per cent, so that 'the ordinary Revenue may, as it always used to do, again supply the ordinary Expence of the Government'. It was an idealistic fantasy, never to be realised, and based on an antiquated set of economic assumptions. Defoe brings up, as he often does, the stop of the exchequer in 1672 and the revocation of the corporate charter in 1683 as failed attempts to use royal power, demonstrating that the City has now gained the ascendancy over the court, since 'the Center of the Money, as well as of the Trade and Credit of the kingdom, will be there' (2: 86–7). He exaggerated the invulnerability of the new financial institutions and the sovereignty of the credit system that supported them. That was one reason that he feared the anarchic forces ultimately leading to the great collapse in 1720, and that he sought to take away any share of the responsibility from the merchant princes who had been exposed by its sudden occurrence.

The *Tour* and the *Tradesman*

If we look ahead briefly, it is clear that Defoe's views on the crash did not greatly change. This is most obvious in respect of *The Complete English Tradesman*, no surprise in view of the fact that the two projects must have been under way at the same juncture. By the time that the second edition of the *Tradesman*, Volume I, appeared in 1727 complete with its supplement, the links could hardly be missed. Like the *Tour*, the book sets out to glorify the achievements of the trading class, and inevitably many of the emphases are the same point. Once more we find an unconcealed measure of sympathy for individuals who were generally regarded as agents of the crisis:

> To what have we seen men of prodigious bulk in trade reduc'd ... and innumerable bankers, money-scriveners, and merchants, who thought themselves as secure against the shocks of trade, as any men in the world could be? Not to instance our late *South-sea* Directors, and others, reduc'd by the terrible fate of bubbles, whose names I omit because they yet live, tho' sinking still under the oppression of their fortunes, and whose weight I would be far from endeavouring to make heavier.[25]

Once more, the responsibility is shifted elsewhere: the prudent trader needs to be 'fenced against bubbles and projects, and against those fatal people called projectors, who are, indeed, among tradesmen, as birds of prey are among the innocent fowls—devourers and destroyers'. As with the *Tour*, the idiom is often baleful: 'projects are generally as fatal to a Tradesman, as fire in a magazine of gunpowder'. In 'the late *South-Sea* calamity, for instance, the longest heads were most over-reach'd'.[26]

So, too, in the second volume, where the author hints more obviously at his verdict on the Bubble, in an awkwardly constructed sentence that may reveal his uneasiness:

> Men of the best Figures in Trade have met with a Fall, and have made a Slip at last, which at one Blow have ruin'd all their Prospects, lasted them at once, and overthrow at one Blow all their twenty Years Labour: Witness the late Directors of the *South-Sea* Company; and let their Fall be just or unjust, that is not my Business; perhaps I am not of the same Opinion with the general Clamour under which they fell. (*CET* 2.i: 90)

Again the events of 1720 are portrayed as a freak phenomenon, when 'the *South-Sea* Distractions possess'd the Nation'. The most vigorous denunciation of the evil practices comes in a passage on 'the Year *Twenty*', when 'so many honest Men turn'd K[naves] and Conscience was Bubble-ridden and Stock-jobb'd till it came under PAR, yet Time may come, in spite of Companies, and Companies of Sharpers, that *Honesty* may be able to appear upon *Change* again, whether ever it may in the ALLEY, or not, I dare not say'.[27]

The nearest to an overall judgement on the factors which precipitated the Bubble comes in the introduction to the second part of this volume:

> In the good old days of Trade , which our Fore-fathers plodded on in, and got Estates too, there were no Bubbles, no Stock-jobbing, no South-sea Infatuations, no Lotteries, no Funds, no Annuities, no buying of Navy Bills, and publick Securities, no circulating Exchequer Bills; in a word, Trade was a vast great River, and all the Money in the Kingdom ran down its mighty stream; the whole wealth of the Nation kept in its Channel, and there were no new Canals or Side-drains laid open to abate its waters, to divert its current, and to carry its stream off from the ordinary course.[28]

Defoe knew perfectly well that these good old days were never going to come back, but he could not stop himself venting his disgust for a development he regarded as preventable.

Conclusion

In combination, these references in the *Tour* hold a twofold interest. They reflect the author's perennial anxiety about the possibility of failure in business. This may seem natural, in view of Defoe's own career as a projector and merchant, littered with financial and moral reverses. However, the views he set out on the topic extend far beyond his own experience. It is obvious from numerous passages in his work that he had witnessed the demise of many commercial houses, and regarded the occupation of a trader as ineluctably a game of snakes and ladders. The title of a single chapter in *The Complete English Tradesman* shows how banal and routine the risks were: 'The *Ordinary Occasions* [italics mine] of the Ruin of Tradesmen'. Both volumes of this book recur insistently to the notion that it is never possible to achieve total safety, no matter how successful the business may seem to be: witness the passage just quoted about the wealthy families who thought themselves past 'all possibility of Danger'. In this way the *Tour* expresses a major theme of all Defoe's writings on commercial matters.

Furthermore, the references in the *Tour* to the experience of South Sea emphasise the disproportionate effect that this episode had on a particular group in society, that is the rich upper bourgeoisie connected with the City of London. A number of these individuals had originally made their money financing the war effort, especially in the reign of Defoe's hero William III. They had close connections with the new institutions of the 1690s, such as the Bank of England and the New East India Company (merged into the

United Company by Godolphin in 1708). Their Whiggish domination was so complete that Robert Harley founded the South Sea Company in 1711 partly to offset their influence, but within a few years the Tory element in governing positions had been almost entirely obliterated. This left Defoe with something of a dilemma: as late as August 1720 he was still promoting the government line on the Company in *The Commentator*, and seeking to distinguish it from the bubble companies now regarded as contaminated. When the crash came, his task was to divert blame from entities such as the royal family and court, the ministry, the Treasury officials, duped City magnates, the Whig elite generally and in the pages of *The Director* even from the prosperous businessmen who sat on the board. It was not an easy job. At the moment he was writing, more embarrassing details were coming to light. The parliamentary committee of enquiry would reveal just how deeply embroiled the City was in its collective role. As time went on, devices were invented to shield the royals, most of the government apart from the chancellor of the exchequer, John Aislabie, and some influential aristocrats. The people who weren't allowed to get away with what they had done included South Sea directors. Defoe must have reflected, 'Use every man after his deserts and who shall scape whipping?'

CHAPTER 8

Local Proverbs and Folk Wisdom

> From this Amphibious Ill-born Mob began
> *That vain, ill-natur'd thing, an* Englishman.
> The Customs, Surnames, Languages, and Manners,
> Of all these Nations are their own Explainers:
> Whose Relicks are so lasting and so strong,
> They ha' left a *Shiboleth* upon our Tongue;
> By which with easy search you may distinguish
> Your *Roman-Saxon-Danish Norman* English.
>
> Daniel Defoe, *The True-Born Englishman*

The history of a nation survives on the breath of its people. We associate the sense of a shared consciousness with German romantic writers such as Johann Gottfried Herder, whose concept of *Volkslitteratur* embraced the notion that creativity in poetry and drama derived from all classes of society. This more inclusive view of the culture of a nation soon took root, but the serious study of folklore did not properly develop in Britain until the later eighteenth century. In writing the *Tour* Defoe certainly would not have regarded himself as contributing to a well-established discipline. Nevertheless, he managed to utilise the first-hand observations of customs and language that he made on his travels to fill out his picture of the contemporary world. It is partly through their aid that he constructed such a wide panorama of eighteenth-century society and the way they lived then. He surveyed 'The Customs, Surnames, Languages, and Manners' of the people, finding relics of their activity everywhere to act as 'Explainers' of the nation.

Surprisingly little has been written about Defoe's lasting engagement with the language and mores of popular culture. As regards folk idiom, by far the best discussion of Defoe's attitude to linguistic diversity is to be found in an article by George A. Starr on 'Defoe's Tour through the Dialects and Jargons of Great Britain', which ranges more widely than its title might suggest.[1] Starr points to an attribute we have repeatedly come across in the present book, with the observation that 'the *Tour* both describes and embodies processes of circulation and exchange. The patterns of commerce—traffic, communication, and conversation in their broadest senses—become a principle of organization as well as a narrative topos.' More particularly, he notes that 'Much of the *Tour* focuses on the talk and activity of "the common People", neglected or dismissed as "low and trifling" by most earlier travel writers.' Notably, John Macky reports few contacts with individuals as he makes his way round the country. Celia Fiennes is more attentive to small details of everyday life, but she too has little time for exchanging pleasantries with bystanders.[2] On the other hand, Defoe is constantly engaging with the local populace. One index is the fact that the expressions 'they told me' and 'they [*or* the people] told us' account for forty usages throughout the three volumes. The form 'I was told' appears on fourteen occasions. Often these phrases lead into a description of a custom or behaviour in a particular corner of the world.[3] In addition, Defoe was a habitué of that quintessential Georgian nation, the coffee house, and freely engaged in talk there (if we may trust what he wrote in his paper *The Commentator* on 11 January 1720).

The narrator is always alert to what he calls at Epsom 'the general Language of the Place' (1: 194). Once he has a slightly acid conversation with his landlord at Knaresborough (3: 80); elsewhere we are privy to a secret exchange when a dissenter whispers a few words in St George's Chapel at Windsor (1: 56); sometimes in polite society he is able to witness 'the pleasant Way of Conversation', exhibited by the gentry of Dorset (1: 247). An enjoyable evening is spent dining and chatting with a fisherman at Dartmouth (1: 256). He does not just interview the wife of the poor lead-miner in Derbyshire, with the detached stance of a blasé reporter: rather, he questions her with obvious human concern (3: 34–6). When he reaches the Cheviots, he claims to have asked 'the good old women' locally if they knew the ballad of 'Chevy Chase', and of course they had it 'at their Fingers end' (3: 120; see also 221). On the edge of the Cotswolds, he engages in some mild flirtation going on with rustic maidservants, as the writer explores folk etymology:

> We were very merry at passing thro' a Village call'd *Bloxham*, on the Occasion of a Meeting of Servants for Hire, which the People there call a *Mop*; 'tis generally in other places vulgarly call'd *a Statute*, because founded upon a Statute Law in Q. *Elizabeth*'s Time for regulating of Servants. This I christn'd by the name of *a Jade-Fair*, at which some of the poor Girls began to be angry, but we appeas'd them with better words. (2: 152–3)

Tenacious legends are duly reported – as, to take one example among many, the residents of Boroughbridge have a name for some standing stones, 'which the Country People ... will have to be brought by the *Devil*, and call them the *Devil's Bolts*' (3: 88).

According to Starr, the work displays 'a sympathetic interest in odd turns of speech', along with 'a keen appreciation of proverbial and colloquial expressions'. It is this last insight that I seek to develop here, by considering the part that traditional saws and adages play in creating through speech patterns a sense of the nation in all its regional variety. As suggested in Chapter 1, the *Tour* provides a clear sense of the ways in which different parts of the country make their own contributions to its diverse culture: the 'talk and activity' of the people, as Starr puts it, help to flesh out this evocation of Britain. Proverbial usages reflect not just habits of mind among the population at large, but also the outlook of those who live in particular corners of the kingdom. In their ethnological spread, Defoe's travels possess a feeling of intimacy never found in the orthodox manuals that regularly appeared, such as John Chamberlayne's *Present State of England*. Other chapters in this book concentrate on material realities: here we enter the mentality of the race.

Sententious Wisdom

In his study of oral and literary culture in early modern England, Adam Fox has described the period from 1500 to 1700 as 'the golden age of proverbial expression'. He points out that society 'relied heavily on oral traditions', but adds the important qualifier that 'in an age of expanding formal education and the rapidly expanding technology of print, sententious wisdom assumed the status of a didactic tool and a literary tool'.[4] Defoe, of course, was born and spent the first forty years of his life within the span of years just designated. It is hard to read his work without being reminded of the 'proverbial wisdom' that Fox explores, even though he sometimes rejects the messages that a popular adage may send.

The *Tour* rejoices in the idiom of the people, paying close attention to the accents of speech, down to the dialect and the characteristics of regional language, as these might have affected users by a 'Shibboleth upon their Tongues', a phrase repeated from the verses at the head of this chapter. As he puts it in relation to the north-east of England: 'This they call the *Northumbrian* R, and the Natives value themselves upon that Imperfection, because, forsooth, it shews the Antiquity of their Blood' (3: 120). Examples include 'the boorish Country Speech' of the West Country

(1: 249–50); the indecipherable lingo of the Derbyshire lead-miner, requiring an interpreter (3:37); or the fact that the inhabitants of northern Scotland around Inverness retain 'Usages and Customs' they had picked up from Cromwell's army, so that they 'keep the Southern Accent very well, and speak very good *English*' (3: 267). 'I could give many more Accounts of the different Dialects of the People of this Country [county]', the narrator claims at Yeovil (1: 251). He actually quotes a few lines of doggerel in the local patois, one of several snatches of verse found in the text that illuminate provincial life. At any point we may come on a saw, a comic verse or a nickname such as 'Black *Barnsley*' (3: 56) that serves to identify a particular district. It is a relatively short step from this to excerpts foregrounding local documents written in an archaic language. Examples are found in the grant of Hatfield Forest in Essex, along with the long rhyming charters of King Athelstan at Beverley and Ripon. All of these appear in a wonky version of Middle English, kindly modernised by the author (1: 84–5; 3: 106–10, 85–7).

Often forgotten in discussions of the *Tour* is the second category of information promised on its title-page, which includes 'The Customs, Manners, Speech, as also the Exercises, Diversions, and Employment of the People' (1: 45). Several of the anecdotes dispersed throughout the text carry the air of a folk tale: for example the story about the woman living with husband and five children under a supposed 'giant' in the Peak District (3: 34–6), which so resembles the rhyme of the old women in a shoe; the recital of the behaviour of decoy ducks in the Fens country (2: 215–17); or the cruel treatment of a thieving dog, capped by 'witty West Country Verses' in dialect (1: 250–51), which belongs in a jestbook. As usual, the author kept his ears as well as his eyes open while he was on the road. He must have spent a good deal of time simply hanging around with the local community, unlike the run of literary travellers – again we think of Macky, who seems hardly to have spoken to anyone outside the fashionable parts of London. Along his way the narrator turns himself into something of a folklorist, and the sayings applied to various parts of the country prompt small anthropological enquiries in the field. He reports the claims fuelled by local pride, though without endorsing these, as here on the Welsh borders: 'The People of this County too, boast that they were a part of the Antient *Silures*, who for so many Ages withstood the *Roman* Arms, and who could never be entirely Conquer'd. But that's an Affair quite beyond my Enquiry' (2: 169).

Unlike Jonathan Swift, his formidable contemporary, Defoe never to our knowledge put together a collection of stock sayings and commonplace expressions. However, his work is stuffed full of traditional tags and catchphrases.[5] The first part of *Robinson Crusoe* (1719) has allusions to the Book of Proverbs and other standard biblical expressions, some of them not even annotated in most editions ('Kill the fatted calf', for example).[6] In the opening sentence of the sequel, relating Crusoe's later excursions, we read, 'That homely Proverb, used on so many Occasions in *England, viz.* "*That what is bred in the Bone will not go out of the Flesh*," was never more verify'd, than in the Story of my Life.'[7] *Moll Flanders* (1722) has phrases such as 'lay up money for a wet day', 'the devil is not so black as he is painted', 'like a bear to a stake' and 'covetousness is the root of all evil'. There is an exchange about a supposed proverb, 'When love is the case, the doctor's an ass.'[8] *The Fortunate Mistress*, or *Roxana* (1724) has the locutions, 'misfortunes seldom come alone', 'Job's three comforters', 'a dart struck into the liver', 'fire in his flax' and 'Canterbury story'.[9] These might appear to be casual usages: but a more intriguing case is provided by another of Defoe's novels, *The History and Remarkable Life of the Truly Honourable Colonel Jacque, Commonly Called Colonel Jack* (1722). This tells the story of an illegitimate boy, abandoned by his parents, who is told that he is really a gentleman, and recounts his quest for gentility as he comes to adult years. The underlying notion of the entire narrative is contained within the hero's name, suggesting as it does 'Jack would be a gentleman' (Tilley J5).

If we turn to Defoe's non-fictional works, we find a denser pattern of proverbial allusion. Here it is possible to cite only a few better-known examples from the author's immense range of writings, which on a conservative estimate run up to 250 items. His first important work, *An Essay upon Projects* (1697), begins, 'Necessity, which is allowed to be the mother of invention' (Tilley N61). Later Defoe refers to 'that proverb, a great head and a little wit', and speaks of 'more geese than swans' (Tilley H245, G369). Defoe alludes to a saying attributed to Solomon (Ecclesiastes 1. 9), and also cites the Horatian tag 'nascitur ridiculus mus'.[10] In *The Poor Man's Plea* (1698) a 'Spanish proverb', describing the devil as a doctor, is cited; and on the next page occurs '*Physicians Heal your selves*'.[11] Part I of *The True-Born Englishman* (1701) opens, 'Wherever God erects a house of prayer, / The devil always builds a chapel there', adding a footnote, 'An English proverb, Where God has a Church, the devil has a chapel.'[12] This expression (Tilley G259) has a long history and was quoted in Robert Burton's *Anatomy of Melancholy*. In fact, the title of this poem is itself a well-known form of words, if not strictly proverbial: it is used in the last line of Act I, Scene iii of Shakespeare's *Richard II*. The *Complete English Tradesman* (1725–7) is another text to cite the Book of Proverbs ('he that is a lover of pleasure, shall be a poor man'). It also contains one of Defoe's repeated maxims, apparently his own creation: 'An estate's a pond, but trade's a spring.'[13] Similarly, *The Compleat English Gentleman* (written *c.*1729) includes an allusion to the proverb 'An ounce of mother-wit is worth a pound of clergy' (Tilley O87), also used in the *Tradesman.*[14] Defoe's long-running essay journal, *The Review*, draws on Solomon again to cite, 'Give me not poverty, lest I steal', another favourite that found a place in both *Moll Flanders* and *Colonel Jacque*. And so one might go on.

A noteworthy feature of Defoe's canon lies in his frequent recourse to proverbial forms as the title of pamphlets and tracts. These include *The Remedy Worse than the Disease* (1714); *The Weakest Go to the Wall* (1714); *Strike While the Iron Is Hot* (1715); *Every-Body's Business is No-Body's Business* (1725); *Second Thoughts are Best* (1729); and *Chickens Feed Capons* (1731). One work uses a Latin phrase, *Lex Talionis* (1698). Although the expression never quite achieved the force of a proverb in English, the title *Hannibal at the Gates* translates a Latin tag, 'Hannibal ad portas', used by Cicero among others. Others employ the syntax or cadence of familiar sayings, such as *Fair Payment no Spunge* (1717), *Giving Alms no Charity* (1703), *No Queen: or No General* (1712), or *Wise as Serpents* (1712). This list omits works long attributed to Defoe, whose authenticity has been thrown in doubt in recent years, such as *Rogues on Both Sides* (1711) and *Seldom Comes a Better* (1710). There is no doubt that Defoe knew what stock of words he was enlisting. This is plain from the opening of *Every-Body's Business*: 'This is a Proverb so common in Every-body's Mouth that I wonder No-body has thought it worth while to draw proper Inferences from it.'[15]

Local Experience

Few of Defoe's books make more telling use of a branch of proverbial lore than the *Tour*. In this rich anatomy of Britain, the author shows a wide knowledge of sayings associated with a particular part of the country. Defoe could have picked many of these up from collections of proverbs, and another source to hand for some of them was Thomas Fuller's *Worthies of England* (1662), which is divided by counties and supplies proverbs applicable to each. It is possible, but by no means certain, that Defoe consulted Fuller: the book is not among the antiquarian works he obviously plundered.[16] In any case, what he offers is not a mere list such as the earlier compilers provided: rather, he draws on these traditional sayings as part of his ongoing coverage of the life of the nation. They provide 'local colour', but also bring with them something of the texture of regional experience as expressed in the hoard of domestic wisdom.

One group of proverbs refers to a specific activity or custom associated with a given place, or a legend that has grown up around this district. A good example occurs in Defoe's survey of Essex, where he tells the story of the Dunmow Flitch (1: 83). This is the most oblique of the references charted here, but his account (largely based on Camden's *Britannia* – no surprise there) essentially fills out the commonplace line 'He may fetch a flitch of bacon from Dunmow' (Tilley F375; Fuller 166–7). The passage contains one of the many homely anecdotes, meant for entertainment rather than edification, that bring with them an air of Chaucerian glee. Some of these tales the narrator hears while on the hoof, almost as they were recounted to the poet on his road to Canterbury. For instance, very early in the first trip, the modern-day traveller receives some dubious information about the dearth of women along the Thames estuary from 'a merry Fellow . . . who said he had had about a Dozen and a half of Wives, (tho' I found afterwards he Fibb'd a little)' (1: 58).

Other stories he must have heard before, but he is reminded on his travels of the credulous reception accorded to some legends attached to the local hero Guy of Warwick, and just before that at Coventry he comes on 'the Tale of the Lady *Godiva*', which is 'held for so certain a Truth, that they will not have it question'd upon any Account whatever; and the Picture of the poor Fellow that peep'd out of the Window to see her, is still kept up . . .' Despite this, the narrator's real feelings may be guessed from his dry aside: 'But Mr. *Camben* positively no body look'd at her at all' (2: 202). Celia Fiennes takes a more neutral view of the claims.[17] When they come to Stonehenge, both travellers are suspicious of the tale that it was impossible to count the number of stones twice and reach the same figure. Fiennes simply reports that she had 'told them often and bring their number to 91'.[18] This was around the usual estimate, but Defoe is more emphatic: he says that this is '*a meer Country Fiction*, and a ridiculous one too'. He attributes the difficulty to the fact that many of the monoliths are half-buried and fragmentary. Without making allowance for that, contradictory tallies will be reached, but 'I have seen then told four Times after one another, beginning every Time at a different Place, and every Time they amounted to 72 in all' (1: 229–30). This is the author at his most authoritarian in his judgements, positivist and Baconian in reporting his observations and arriving at conclusions. Since stones were often removed or reused, as McVeagh points out, the less sweeping statements by Fiennes carry more conviction.

In the second letter, we visit the once-famous Horse Fair held annually at Charlton, on the south-eastern edge of London. Defoe calls the scene 'that yearly collected Rabble of Mad People', observes that the 'Rudeness' allowed is intolerable and regrets the fact that 'The Mob indeed at that time take all kinds of Liberties, and the Women are especially Impudent for that Day ... without suffering the Censure which such Behaviour would deserve at any other time' (1: 138). Apperson 31 quotes wordplay enshrined in a proverb 'All is fair at Horn Fair'. This was 'One of the most popular fairs, until it was discontinued in 1872, famous for its obsession with horns. In its heyday in the eighteenth century, visitors flocked to the fair in their thousands carrying or wearing horns and every stall was decorated with them.'[19] The ribaldry and horseplay that went on there were connected with the cuckold's traditional horns (the most aggressive mob assembled at Cuckold's Point, which lies on the Thames nearby), an association underlined by the fact that the event took place each year on 18 October, St Luke's Day – the local parish church is named after the saint, whose attributes in art included a horned ox. Defoe was not alone in complaining about the indecencies that were permitted, but it took more than a century of opposition from evangelicals and others before the home secretary suppressed the event.

Other stock expressions are used to characterise the best-known products of a given region, and thus to establish its distinctive race – what Braudel referred to as the *pays*, an area with its own identity (see the opening of Chapter 1). For example, in Letter 1, when Defoe is writing about the environs of Woodbridge in Suffolk, he states that they are 'famous for the best Butter, and perhaps the worst Cheese, in *England*' (1: 97). 'Suffolk cheese' had become a byword as inferior, as witness *ODEP* 785; Apperson 608. During his coverage of Herefordshire, Defoe observes that Leominster, 'besides the fine Wool, is noted for the best Wheat, and consequently the finest Bread; whence *Lemster Bread*, and *Weobley Ale*, is become a proverbial saying'. Again, this came from *Britannia* (1: 690). The proverb is recorded in *ODEP* 454–5 and Apperson 360, as well as Fuller 219.[20] The alternative 'Leominster wool' was perhaps even better known, and Fuller 218 refers to this local claim to fame also. Then, having reached Derby, Defoe mentions the town's 'good Ale'. This was proverbial, sometimes in the form of a composite formulation, 'Dunmow bacon, and Doncaster daggers, Monmouth caps and Lemster wool, Derby ale and London beer' (see *ODEP* 209: in three separate pairings, Apperson 142, 171,

261). At one point or other in the text, Defoe refers to all these products of Dunmow, Monmouth, Leominster and Derby. In the process of quoting the saying, he illustrates the diversity of British industry, spread across the map. He turns to the cutlery industry of nearby Sheffield in a paragraph which begins 'leaving *Doncaster*' (3: 54). There follows an abridged version of lines from Chaucer's *Reeve's Tale*, a portion of which was quoted by Fuller 637, in his section of the manufactures of Yorkshire.

Another group of proverbs is chiefly historical in nature, summing up important proceedings in a certain part of Britain. For example, when he comes to describe the hop country of Kent, Defoe quotes an old saw in the form of a couplet, 'Hops, Reformation, Bays, and Beer, / Came into England all in a Year' (1: 152–3). Different versions have been located (Tilley H440; *ODEP* 370; Apperson 310), but they are all to the same purpose. Defoe's seems to be the only one to mention bays (baize). Such snatches of verse haunt the text, almost as the speeches of the Fool in *King Lear* are scattered with fragments of old ballads and gnomic epigrams. They go with sometimes riddling epitaphs cited in the text, such as the one for the obscure Robert Byrk at Doncaster (3: 53). Not long afterwards, the supposed traveller reaches the area in Surrey known as Holmwood. He takes another distich from *Britannia* (1: 186), although the ultimate source may be William Lambarde's *Perambulation of Kent* (1579). The lines run in Defoe's text, 'This is *Holmes Dale*, / Never Conquer'd, never shall' (1: 190). This saying (Tilley V8; Fuller 545) was supposed to allude to the defeat of the Danish forces in AD 851. The narrator here sounds appropriately sceptical. On the subject of the historic gates of London, the author writes, '*Aldgate* was very Ancient and Decay'd, so that *as Old as Aldgate*, was a City Proverb for many Years' (2: 100). This is the only citation of the expression in Apperson 466, under 'old'.

A more familiar saying crops up in Defoe's section on Lincoln. He notes that 'by the *Domesday Book* they tell it must be one of the greatest Cities in *England*, whence perhaps that old *English* Proverbial Line, Lincoln *was*, London *is*, and York *shall be*' (2: 310). This was indeed a very familiar saying (Tilley L300). In 1724 it was used by a contemporary traveller, the archaeologist William Stukeley, though his work was not published until after Defoe's death. Equally well known was a form of words that lies behind a portion of the long entry devoted to Halifax (3: 69–71), concerning 'the famous Course of Justice antiently executed here, to prevent the stealing of Cloth'. The choice of verbs is interesting, because those convicted of theft were indeed subject to beheading. Defoe discusses the punishments in some detail, as it had become known as 'Halifax Law' or 'Halifax Gibbet

Law' (Tilley L590), and gave the Lord of the Manor of Wakefield, which extended as far as Halifax, the power to execute a felon for the theft of goods to the value of 13½*d.* or more. A variant was 'Lydford law'; both forms implied 'hang first, and try later'. The material prompts a further comment from Defoe, 'Hence came that Proverbial Saying, which was us'd all over *Yorkshire,* (*viz.*) *From* Hell, Hull, Halifax, / *Good Lord, deliver us.*' This extremely well-known expression (Tilley H399; *ODEP* 367) was used by John Taylor, the 'water poet', among others, and turns up in Fuller 639. Here again there is a variant, 'Hull, Elland, Halifax', referring to a small adjoining town. It is less common and frankly much less pointed, except perhaps to residents of the neighbourhood.

The same town gave occasion for what is perhaps the most sophisticated of all the examples, in literary terms. Still at Halifax, Defoe enters into a digression concerning the Iron Maiden, used in Scotland much as the guillotine was in Halifax. He writes, 'the Engine was called the Maiden, as not having so long handsell'd, and still retains the Name, tho' it has cut off many a Head since' (3: 72). Behind the comment lies a body of folklore represented by sayings such as 'Thieves' handsel ever unlucky' (*ODEP* 811) and 'Hansell (they say) is always lucky when well wet' (Apperson 281).[21] The basic idea is that of a 'handsel' or gift bestowed at the inception of a new project, which could serve as either a favourable or unfavourable omen. This case shows how a passage offering to present a specific piece of information on local history can shade into an exploration of customs which many English men and women had in common.

Further instances concern proverbs that have some historic basis, but relate chiefly to identifiable buildings. When he gets to Salisbury, Defoe refers to the story 'according to some' that the cathedral was built on wool-packs (1: 223). This was sometimes applied rather to London Bridge (Tilley L416), but John Aubrey mentions the 'old tradition' concerning Salisbury (see *ODEP* 697). Once more, the narrator contradicts the myth. He had the support of the eminent antiquarian Richard Rawlinson, who took the expression to mean that the building was paid for out of taxes on wool imports.[22] In addition, Defoe quotes verses claiming that the cathedral has as many windows as days in the year, as many pillars as hours in the year, and as many gates as months in the year. He took this from *Britannia* (1: 116), but Fuller 604 refers to the same story, which seems to have been generally known. (Fuller describes an encounter with a countryman, surprised by the 'facts' set out in the verses.) It became a popular urban myth, if not a proverb. While in Lincolnshire, Defoe refers to another celebrated spire, quoting a line: '[I] am much of Opinion with that excellent Poet: 'Tis

Hight makes Grantham Steeple stand awry.' The excellent poet was probably John Cleveland in 1658, but the idea went back much further (see Tilley H396; *ODEP* 331). Fuller mentions it under Lincolnshire.

The comments on the bishopric of Durham mostly apply not to architecture but to the ecclesiastical revenues of the diocese. Defoe speaks of the magnificence of the cathedral, the bishop's palace and the houses of the clergy, then adds: 'I need not remind you that the Bishop of *Durham* is a Temporal Prince.' He adds that 'The church of *Durham* is eminent for its Wealth; the Bishoprick is esteemed the best in *England*; and the Prebends and other Church Livings, in the Gift of the Bishop, are the richest in *England*.' (3: 115–16). All this fills out a belief enshrined in the saying, 'Too dear for the Bishop of Durham' (Apperson 171).

Myths and Legends

Some popular phraseology, of course, serves to identify customs, habits or social practices. One of the best examples in the *Tour* occurs in a passage commenting on parts of Surrey where homes of summer residents abound: 'They are shut up, and as it were strip'd of their Inhabitants in the Winter, who return to Smoke and Dirt, *Sin* and *Seacoal*, (as it was coursly express'd) in the busy City' (1: 202). As the italics indicate, this was a stock expression, but there is no record in *OED*, standard dictionaries of proverbs, or the works of Eric Partridge. It is found from the mid-seventeenth century onwards, in plays by Thomas Shadwell (1673), James Carlile (1692) and Henry Higden (1693), and subsequently in the *Spectator* (1712). Examples can be located in the Victorian era from Theodore Hook and a contributor to Dickens' *Household Words* (1851). If Defoe had a particularly coarse instance in mind, this may be a book called *The Northern Atalantis*, published by Edmund Curll in 1713: 'Marching further into this Sink of Sin and Sea Coal, we met Whores and Rogues, as thick as Fools in *Thursday* Market [in York], looking as modest as *Newgate* Saints Canoniz'd at the *Old Baily*.'[23] In a simpler case, Defoe comments on the marriage habits of the West Country gentry: 'From whence they say, that Proverb upon them was rais'd, (*viz.*) *That all the* Cornish *Gentlemen are Cousins*' (1: 263). He probably found this in Richard Carew's *Survey of Cornwall* (1602), an acknowledged source for this portion of the *Tour*. It was evidently more widely known (Tilley G78). On his return trip along the northern coast of the peninsula, the traveller refers to the distinctive style of Cornish wrestling, and mentions 'that Closure, which they call the *Cornish Hug*' (2: 102). This term is described in more detail by Fuller 88, who mentions a metaphoric sense of double dealing under the pretence of friendship. Defoe ignores this implication (see also Tilley H804).

At times the text draws on the proverbial associations of a region with dubious qualities: typically the author refrains from a strong endorsement or rebuttal of the implied claim. During his progress northwards through Lancashire, he inserts a passage reading, 'The People are gay here, though not perhaps the richer for that; but it has by that obtained the Name of *Proud Preston*' (3: 135). This is the first instance of the phrase quoted in *ODEP* 651 and Apperson 511, but there are later citations, sometimes in the form 'Proud Preston, poor people'. It is most unlikely that Defoe invented the expression. We can more easily detect a double-edged intent when we come to remarks made in the Calder valley, concerning the reputation of Yorkshiremen for sharp practices in business: 'Whether the Scandal rais'd upon this Country be just or not, *(viz. Shrinking Cloth and sharping K[nave]s)*, that I will not take upon me to determine' (3: 58). This is a particularly sly mode of reference: we get a better idea of what the author really thought in other books. Behind the text lies a proverb once well known in a number of variant forms, such as 'Cold weather and crafty knaves come out of the North', or 'Three great ills come out of the North: a cold wind, a shrinking cloth, and a dissembling man.' The saying was chiefly applied to the 'Country' (county) of Yorkshire, and it was paralleled by expressions such as 'He is Yorkshire' (a sharp fellow) and 'To come Yorkshire on' (to cheat or dupe): see *ODEP* 926 and Apperson 718. In spite of his simulated doubts here, Defoe felt no qualms about applying the phrase in other contexts, for instance *Complete English Tradesman*: 'If he has been a cunning sharping, biting, over-reaching Wretch; if he has put *Yorkshire* upon the World all his Days, and set up Craft for Honesty' (2. i.211). In *Col. Jacque*, the hero's trickster colleague the captain has no success with his schemes in Leeds and Wakefield, and decides that the North Country people are 'all Thieves', too 'sharp' to be victims of his con game.[24]

Elsewhere conventional sayings are drawn on to allow the writer to test their reliability, with a positive or negative outcome. According to Defoe, '*Darlington*, a Post Town, has nothing remarkable but Dirt' (3: 115). He was clearly remembering a phrase 'Dirty Darlington', recorded from 1658 (Apperson 135). By contrast, he was sceptical about the story of Hell's Kettles in County Durham, 'so much talked up for a Wonder' (3: 115). Previous authors such as William Harrison in his *Description of England* (1577) had indeed made much of these pits, and the phrase 'deep as the hell kettles' evolved (see Apperson 297).

Two allied proverbs emerge as the *Tour* moves northwards on the way to the Scottish border, where Defoe remembers the 'old verse' he found in Camden, that is 'Inglebrough, Pendle-hill *and* Penigent, / *Are the highest Hills between* Scotland *and* Trent' (3: 136). This inaccurate statement is found in a slightly different form in *Britannia* (2: 972), and in sources such as John Ray (see Tilley P184 and *ODEP* 404). Fuller quotes it under Cumberland. The second occurs a few pages later where Defoe has: 'Here we saw *Skiddaw*, one of those high Hills of which, wherever you come, the People always say, they are the highest in England' (3: 140). In reality he was recalling a rhyme quoted in *Britannia*, 'Skiddaw, Lauvellin, and Casticand, are the highest hills in all England' (2: 1,006). On this common saying, see Tilley S498 and *ODEP* 740. Neither Skiddaw nor Helvellyn is actually the highest mountain in the area: for 'Casticand', an outlier of Helvellyn, see Chapter 9, note 8.

One unclassifiable item remains. Making his way anxiously past the rugged crags of Merioneth, a journey Defoe may well never have attempted, the narrator observes, 'Some think 'tis from the unpassable Mountains of this County, that we have an old saying, that the Devil lives in the *middle of Wales*, tho' I know there is another meaning given to it; in a word, Mr. *Cambden* calls these Parts the *Alps of Wales*' (3: 180). No earlier source has been traced, and the hidden implication is vague – perhaps this is simply crude prejudice against the native Welsh in their fastness among the secluded hills. Three paragraphs later, the text resumes: 'Here among innumerable Summits, and rising Peaks of nameless Hills, we saw the famous *Kader-Idricks*, which some are of Opinion, is the highest Mountain in *Britain*, another call'd *Rarauvaur*, another call'd *Mowylwynda*, and still every Hill we saw, we thought was higher than all that ever we saw before' (2: 180). Camden had recognised that Snowdon reached a higher elevation than any of the peaks named by Defoe, merely observing that '*Kader Idris* is probably one of the highest mountains in Britain' (2: 784). In this section Defoe appears more credulous in regard to the information that locals seem to have fed him, most likely because he had never actually encountered a local in Merioneth.

Fewer popular expressions appear in the Scottish sections of the book, which may be partly because Defoe was treated with more suspicion on his travels.[25] He may well have had less acquaintance with the hoard of Scottish proverbs than at least two contemporary writers, Jonathan Swift and John Arbuthnot (himself a Scot, of course), display. Among the exceptions we should note a passage as the narrative reaches Queensferry: Defoe quotes 'that homely Piece of Proverb Poetry' (3: 177), namely a distich about the Earl of Fife. There is an old ballad with this title, but it does not contain the verses cited.[26] Equally puzzling is an old inscription on the Earl of Mar's house at Stirling, described as a 'Distich in a *Scots* Dialect', reading 'Speak forth, and spare nocht, / Consider well, I care nocht.' As Defoe remarks, 'The Words seem to want a Paraphrase', which he duly attempts (3: 212). In the course of the *Tour*, a number of inscrutable signs defy interpretation by the traveller.

Taking these examples seriatim, they may appear simply to provide evidence that Defoe had a large command of popular sayings at his disposal. Collectively however, they show that he did more than observe the nation with the 'sharp modern eyes' that Trevelyan remarked on. He also *listened* to what the people were saying.

Conclusion

Apart from all else, then, Defoe was a pioneer in the literary use of folklore, and his use of regional proverbs contributes to a sense of engagement with the localities visited in the *Tour*. Again, we have noted that he wrote at a time when scholarly study in this area was only just beginning, and some of the material which would have been helpful to him (for example that of John Aubrey) remained largely unpublished. One thing he did not lack, however, was an ear, as the racy dialogue of his novels and conduct-books amply shows. The *Tour* renders Britain in its fullness, and the attention its author pays to proverbial lore (even if it is sometimes in a sceptical or critical vein) plays a part in this textual representation of the nation – its history, geography and people.

PART 3

Place

CHAPTER 9

The Uses of Topography

The most cited essay on the sources of the *Tour* has remained current for more than sixty years. It was an early work by the distinguished historical geographer J. H. Andrews, a man with whom Defoe's cast of mind clearly resonated.[1] Andrews (1927–2019) spent most of his career at Trinity College, Dublin, and became the leading authority on maps of Ireland, as well as a major figure in debates set off by J. B. Harley on the history of cartography. His study of the *Tour* comprised the first full analysis of the issues, and it has never been supplanted. This chapter seeks to amplify what Andrews says about two aspects of the subject: the use that Defoe made of maps in compiling his work, and his recourse to the text of topographic volumes, including atlases and guides. Its scope is largely confined to determining particular sources and identifiable borrowings from earlier writers. It does not seek to enter into wider issues concerning Defoe's understanding of the nature of maps, analysed by Christopher Parkes, or his sense of geography explored most prominently by Jesse Edwards.[2]

As Andrews and many other scholars have recognised, the principal source for the *Tour*'s coverage of places described in the text is William Camden's *Britannia* (see also Chapter 4 above). There is no evidence that Defoe consulted either the Latin version, first issued in various forms between 1586 and 1607, or the English translation by Philemon Holland (1610; revised, 1637). It can be demonstrated that he consistently relied on the English edition prepared by Edmund Gibson (1695, revised and expanded in 1722). This is a source that he explicitly acknowledges on more than twenty occasions, starting with an allusion very near the opening of his travels: 'Mr. *Camden*, and his learned Continuator, Bishop *Gibson*, have ransacked this Country for its Antiquities, and have left little unsearched; and, as it is not my present Design to say much of what has been said already, I shall touch very lightly where Two such excellent Antiquaries have gone before me; except it be to add what may have been since discovered' (1: 53). Camden himself is mentioned by name at least seventy times, although the raids are much more frequent than this figure suggests. The incidence is highest in the sections devoted to northern England, where the author's information was generally less recent. What remains uncertain is which version of Gibson's edition Defoe used. The 1695 edition was listed in the sale catalogue containing Defoe's book collection, and he may well have had this version to hand in compiling the *Tour*.[3] However, it is not impossible that he also had access to the 1722 text.

The main limitation of the study by Andrews is that he omitted almost all notice of the Scottish sections of the *Tour*. He quotes from the old Everyman edition, which at that date excluded Scotland. Moreover, his useful maps of places known to be visited by Defoe ('Sources' facing 270) do not extend beyond the Scottish border. Consequently, most of the discussion here is confined to the opening ten letters of the *Tour*, making incidental references only to the last three, which raise separate issues.

Maps

Regarding the first aspect of the topic, Andrews comments briefly on signs that Defoe may have consulted printed maps to glean information for the *Tour*:

> Defoe cannot be accused of using maps to invent plausible 'circuits.' He makes several passing references to maps, apparently to Robert Morden's county sheets of 1695, but his routes – and place-names – seem to be entirely his own. Only in South Wales, between the Black Mountain and 'Monuchdenny hill' . . . can he perhaps be suspected of reading a 'journey' off Morden's maps.[4]

In fact, all the reference to particular maps are to Morden, as printed in the two versions of Camden's *Britannia* edited by Gibson. The most noteworthy of these concerns a passage on the River Mole in Letter 3, where Defoe corrects both Camden and 'the Right Reverend and Learned Editor of the Additions,' noting that 'the Map of the County of *Surrey*, plac'd in Mr. *Camden*' provides a misleading broken course for the river (1: 184; *Britannia* (1722) 1: 187, with map facing col. 180). There is also an allusion in Letter 4 to the fact that 'Mr. *Cambden*, in his Writing, and his Map-maker also, calls it *Herculis Promontorium*; but the honest Sailers, and after the, the plain Country People, call it, in down right modern *English*, *Hartland Point*, or *Harty Point*' (2: 13; *Britannia* 1: 44–5, with map facing col. 28). This shows that Defoe shifted his gaze between text and map, in an effort to distance himself from the mythologizing bent of his predecessor. Vaguer references to maps (2: 32, 38) also indicate that he had looked at the toponyms used by Morden.

None the less, elsewhere within the *Tour* we can gauge the author's dependence on maps a little more precisely. It has been argued that parts of wild Wales beyond the area mentioned by Andrews, especially in Powis and Gwynedd, reveal a similar dependence on cartographic aids.[5] Occasionally this caused Defoe some confusion, as indeed happened in the Welsh sections. Another hilly section where the text has to stray off highways occurs in Letter 10: 'The River *Eden* . . . rises in this Part out of the Side of a monstrous High Mountain, called *Mowill Hill*, or *Wildbore Fell*, which you please' (3: 138). The immediate source would appear to be Gibson's expansion of Camden's observation, 'The noble river of *Eden* . . . rises in Westmorland, <at a place called *High-seat-Morvill*, or *Hugh-Morvels* hill>' (*Britannia*, 2: 988). However, Morden's map facing col. 984 did little to clarify the situation for Defoe. In depicting Mallerstang Common south of Kirkby Stephen, close to what was then the border of Westmorland and Yorkshire, the map correctly shows Wildbore Fell to the west of the valley, with Hughs Seat to the east, and Mowill Hil appearing some way further to the east. In fact the two elevations facing one another are now named Wild Boar Fell (2,323 feet or 708 metres) and High Seat, just 3 feet higher. Hughs Seat or Hugh Head is a peak on the same massif, while Morvill is simply an alternative name for this eminence, rather than for Wild Boar Fell. In his work *The Theatre of the Empire of Great Britaine* (1612), after p. 85, John Speed shows only 'Huseat Mouill Hill' at the head of the valley. Likewise Herman Moll in *A New Description of England and Wales* (1724), facing 316, identifies Wildbore Fell and further south Hutton Morvell Hill. The maps of England by John Senex in *A New General Atlas* (1721) are not detailed enough to supply information on particular counties. However, Defoe could have looked at the different map of Westmorland by Morden found in *A New Description and State of England* (1704), facing 166, which has both Wildborefell and Morwill Hill.[6]

In this part of the world, he was not able to draw on any of the various roadbooks which were issued as updates of John Ogilby's seminal work of 1676. They naturally concentrated on the main highways, starting with the arterial routes serving London, and they left out most of the crossroads. The itinerary from Kendal to Keswick and Cockermouth might be shown, but most of the Lake District was *terra incognita*. The road from London to Carlisle followed much of the route of the modern A6, via Shap and

Penrith, bypassing Appleby. Kirkby Stephen remained a backwater even when the turnpikes belatedly reached Kendal and Appleby in 1761. The passage across Mallerstang Common is still only served by a minor road, B6259, and in the early eighteenth century it was not much more than a drovers' track, most heavily used at the time of the annual fairs. The *Tour* itself describes 'the Hills of *Mallerstang* Forest' as 'in many Places, unpassable' (3: 137). However, Wild Boar Fell is a conspicuous landmark, visible from the Lake District mountains, the Pennines, the upper Yorkshire Dales and the Howgill fells. It is possible Defoe caught sight of its flat summit from the nearby Roman road, approximately on the line of the A66, which he mentions running west across Stainmore Forest by Brough to Appleby and Penrith (3: 138–9).[7] The evidence suggests that, whether or not he personally sighted the hills, Defoe was alerted to the existence of Mowill by the addition that Gibson made to Camden's text. He then consulted Morden's maps, and somehow amalgamated the two peaks. While he may not have 'read' his journey from Morden, as Andrews puts it, he included Wild Boar Fell in his itinerary because he found its cartographic presence within the pages of *Britannia*.

In a modern guidebook it would be surprising to find that only one Cumbrian mountain appears by name, as happens in Defoe's narrative. This is Skiddaw, easily picked out on Morden's map, and described in *Britannia*. The narrator mentions with scepticism the claim that this peak overtops all other English mountains, an idea which comes from a distich in *Britannia* (2: 1,006): 'Skiddaw, Lauvellin, and Casticand, / Are the highest hills in all England'.[8] However, Morden identifies very few other eminences, notably 'Hard Knott Hill', which is called in the text 'a steep ragged mountain; on top of which were lately dug up huge stones, and the foundation of a Castle; which is very strange, considering the mountain is so steep, that one can hardly get up it' (2: 1,003). We can hardly blame Camden and other antiquarians for not inspecting the site, which lies at an elevation of over 800 feet (250 metres) on Hardknott Pass beneath Harter Fell. If they had done so, they would have discovered the castle was in fact a Roman fort, Mediobogdum, built in the second century AD. The *Tour* refers accurately to '*Derwent* Fells' as a place where copper and gold were once mined (3: 140), but what Morden didn't map Defoe commonly leaves out of his account.[9]

A negative sign indicating that Defoe took some of his material from books of maps is found in the final pages of the *Tour*. This is one place where the Scottish sections help to explain what was going on in the work as a whole. The author managed to bulk out Letter 13 with several pages devoted to coverage of the Highlands, although he had almost certainly never ventured far into the Grampians. However, he does not mention a single mountain by name. The likely explanation is that his principal source, Camden, is equally sketchy in this precise regard. For the purposes of *Britannia*, Gibson had gone in 1695 to Morden's correction of Robert Gordon's map of Scotland, issued separately in 1687 – a beautiful and informative piece of work, but not one which would enable a user to locate Munros. After the Union, it was replaced in 1722 by two engravings by Andrew Johnston. These failed to show Defoe certain hills in the Southern Uplands that he mentions in the text, such as Merrick ('Mairock') and Soutra, let alone the high Grampian peaks on which he never set eyes. Moll does not cover Scotland in his *New Description*: it would have been necessary to search out his *North Part of Great Britain called Scotland* (1714 and later editions). Senex uses a larger scale for his maps of Scotland than for England in the *New General Atlas*, but as with the other representations of the country these identify regions, towns and villages along with physical features such as bays, capes, glens, the mouths of rivers and lochs – but not individual peaks. Without such an aid Defoe could not offer even an approximation of the names of mountains, such as he had done in Wales and northern England. What he would have made of Gaelic names we can only guess.

Spelling may sometimes provide a clue. One example occurs in the coverage of Lancashire. Gibson's translation and additions consistently use the spelling 'Forness' for the peninsula, abbey and fells of Furness (*Britannia* 2: 977–8). The *Tour* boils this down to a single sentence, but uses the spelling '*Fourness*' (3: 137). It comes as no surprise to discover that the latter version is the one which appears in Morden's maps for Lancashire, Westmorland and Cumberland.

We can tell that Defoe was a critical rather than an inert user of cartographic aids from a passage such as the following:

> The Author of the *Geographical Dictionary* places this Town upon the Bank of the River *Spolden*, which Mr. *Cambden*'s Continuator . . . takes notice of as a Mistake, and so it is; but I suppose 'twas occasioned by this: There is a River named *Spodden*, not *Spolden*, which rising under *Blackstone Edge*; runs into the *Roch* at *Rochdale*, and so losing its name in the *Roch*, runs into the *Irwell*, about *Ratcliff*, six or seven miles above *Manchester*, and, in some Maps, they have made not the *Spodden* lose its name in the *Roch*, but the *Roch* in the *Spodden*, and so give it yet its own name after it joins the *Irwell*, and on to *Manchester*. (3: 133)

This mistake is not made in Morden's map, which shows the Spodden entering the Roch prior to the latter's junction with the Irwell. The confusion occurs in Edmund Bowen's *Geographical Dictionary* (1688), sig. Ff 2^{r}, s.v. Manchester; Gibson had pointed it out in the 1695 edition of *Britannia* (2: 798), but the comment was deleted in 1722 – one of the hints that Defoe had the earlier version in front of him.

Works on Topography

The other matter that Andrews addresses is that of the raids made in the *Tour* on earlier topographic and chorographic sources, including guides and atlases:

> A second kind of borrowing, which Defoe never acknowledged, was needed not so much to obtain specialized topographical information as to include places, or periods, outside the range of the author's own experience. John Senex's 'New general atlas' (1721), for example, is mentioned only in a couple of passing references, both derogatory . . . but in fact it provided the 'Tour' with a good deal of miscellaneous guidebook information about places that Defoe had probably never visited, notably Wales, West Cornwall and the East Riding, including Hull, as well as contributing to his accounts of several towns in Derbyshire, Dorset and Somerset. ('Sources' 274)

Andrews is right that Defoe refers disparagingly to 'our late famous *Atlas-maker*' and 'some ignorant Writers, particularly the late *Atlas*' (1: 99, 186).[10] But elsewhere he alludes to the same source in a more oblique manner: 'The Passage from this Town of *Padstow* to *Ireland*, is called, by Writers, to be no more than Twenty-four Hours, but not justly' (2: 11). This seems to indicate *A New General Atlas* (187), even though the ultimate source is probably Gibson (*Britannia* 1: 23). Soon afterwards comes a more contemptuous observation on the arches of Bideford Bridge: 'But as for saying one of them is so big, that a Ship of 60 Tons may sail under it, *&c.* as a late Author asserts, I leave it where I find it, for the People of *Bidiford* to laugh at' (2: 15). The errant passage occurs in *A New General Atlas* (187), but again it derives from Gibson's additions to *Britannia* (1: 45). Wherever possible, Defoe takes the opportunity to show superior first-hand knowledge of a given place. It is often hard to know which of the books that Defoe had available is referenced, but he seems more prone to criticise rivals such as John Macky and Senex rather than Gibson, understandably since his debt to *Britannia* is too obvious to be concealed.

The wider claims made by Andrews are somewhat vague, and less easy to verify. His statement that the long entry in the *Tour* for Hull (3: 110–13) relied on the Senex volume seems to lack support in the text. All the major features of the city follow the coverage in *Britannia* (2: 893–7), and there is nothing in the single paragraph found in *A New General Atlas* (228–9) which could not have emerged from that source. At one point Defoe actually confuses the first mayor, who was Lord Chancellor Michael de la Pole, Earl of Suffolk, with his father, the merchant Sir William de la Pole. The *Atlas* makes no such mistake in degutting Camden. As for the remainder of the East Riding, the entry for Beverley comes straight from *Britannia*, as Andrews was the first to point out. Equally, the description of Hedon paraphrases what Camden and Gibson had written (*Britannia* 2: 898), with no reference whatsoever to the *Atlas*. The latter source simply gives up on Holderness, alluding to unnamed towns 'for which we refer to *Camden*' (229). Defoe does little better, but he does at least mention Spurn Point by name, before moving on to Bridlington, where he does not trouble to pick up the single sentence of information found in the *Atlas*.

As is its method generally, the volume passes no comment on the countryside between towns in the East Riding (nor does the small scale map of England by Senex display any conventional marks of hills here), and Defoe's brief description of the Wolds appears to derive from his own observation. Earlier, in Letter 7 of the *Tour*, he had given an account of a trip he took crossing from Lincolnshire into Yorkshire:

> A little farther within *Humber* is *Barton*, a town noted for nothing that I know of, but an ill-favoured dangerous Passage, or Ferry, over the *Humber* to *Hull*; where in an open Boat, in which we had about fifteen Horses, and ten or twelve Cows, mingled with about seventeen or eighteen Passengers, call'd Christians; we were about four Hours toss'd about on the *Humber*, before we could get into the harbour at *Hull*; whether I was Sea-sick or not, is not worth notice, but that we were all sick of the Passage, any one may suppose, and particularly I was so uneasy at it, that I chose to go round by *York*, rather than return to *Barton*, at least for that time. (2: 211)

Of course, Defoe could have made up this entire episode. But it is plausible that there really was such an occurrence on one of his journeys from London to Edinburgh: we know that he sometimes strayed from the direct route, and in 1712 he had stopped at Gainsborough on his way to Newcastle. His circuitous mission for Robert Harley in 1705 had seen him travel from York and Hull to the same town.[11] In the light of these facts, Andrews seems unduly confident in his belief that Defoe needed to consult the *Atlas* to conceal the lack of first-hand knowledge in places such as East Yorkshire.

There is even less to go on in the case of Dorset. The *Atlas* simply lists twenty-five 'Places of Note' (189–90), with entries ranging from a brief paragraph to a single sentence. Defoe refers to thirteen of these localities within the compass of more than 5,000 words that he devotes to the county (1: 238–49). The coverage embodies extensive first-hand observation and personal anecdotes, as well as much fuller discussion of the economic life of a given area. When the narrator comments on the encouraging sight at Dorchester of 'Church of *England* Clergymen, and the Dissenting Minister, or Preacher drinking Tea together, and Conversing with Civility and good Neighbourhood' (1: 241), we might recall that the agent Defoe had recruited for Harley was Baruch Nowell, minister at the Presbyterian chapel for fifty years up to his death in 1739. In 1712 a close observer called him 'a man of good sense and of generous principles. He was easy and genteel in his conservation, well acquainted with mankind and the world, and was well known and respected'.[12] Once more, the *Tour* contains something naturally lacking in the *Atlas*, given its aims – that is impressions of the roads and the landscape that the imaginary traveller has crossed on his route. The antiquarian material, as almost always, comes straight from *Britannia*, with no direct debt to the *Atlas*.

Much the same is true of Somerset, which is mainly treated in Letter 4 (2: 18–33), with the exception of a full entry on Bath in Letter 6. The coverage is filled out to 6,000 words with a long passage on Glastonbury, avowedly taken from Dugdale's *Monasticon*, and a digression on the wool trade which embraces Wiltshire, Dorset and Gloucestershire as well as Somerset. The *Atlas* provides basic facts on thirty-seven noteworthy places, including Bath and Bristol (190–92). Ten of these are covered in the *Tour*, which supplies a variety of information that goes well beyond anything in the *Atlas*, especially on topics such as the cheese industry around Cheddar. (As usual, the *Atlas* merely paraphrases *Britannia* on this matter.) The only passage in the entire section which might have been suggested by the *Atlas* occurs near its end, where the author comments on the recent growth of Frome (2: 33). But Defoe did not need to be told about such matters by the *Atlas* (191): the town lay at the centre of an area he had explored for Harley in August 1705, and he emphasizes the increasing size and importance of Frome more than once elsewhere.[13] He had probably first seen this part of the county during his foray in support of the Monmouth invasion in 1685, although he does claim to have drunk the waters at Bath 'more above fifty Years ago' (2: 156). Throughout his life he had numerous contacts with the South-west, and he mentions a relative in Martock (1: 249) – a place that does not appear in the *Atlas* – which may explain his ability, unlike his predecessors, to describe nearby Yeovil. He also had a number of Harley's agents spread through Somerset from the Devon border to Bath and Bristol, with dissenting ministers and merchants well represented. One was a master at the Presbyterian academy founded in Taunton by Matthew Warren in 1687, which lends credibility to comments on the school in the *Tour* (2: 21). It is fair to deduce from such instances that he probably had a closer knowledge of the region than the compiler of the *Atlas*.

As for Derbyshire, the *Atlas* has little more than a page (218–19) of skimpy information. Defoe did not know the county well, but he had plenty of sources for the so called 'Wonders of the Peak' – or as he terms them 'the *Wonderless* Wonders of the *Peak*' (3: 41). The authors that he mentions are Charles Cotton, Thomas Hobbes and Charles Leigh. These writers were extensively cited in the first volume of Thomas Cox's *Magna Britannia et Hibernia, antiqua & nova* (1720), and this could have been a handy source for Defoe. It is possible that he came on the legend concerning the building of the tower of All Hallows Church in Derby (now the cathedral) from the *Atlas*, but it was a time-honoured tale that many authors had retold. The only passage here that seems to derive from the *Atlas* is one in Letter 8 on the Barmote Court at Wirksworth (3: 32): there are considerable embellishments, but that was comfortably within Defoe's power. Since the *Atlas* does not contain original research, there may be a common source not so far discovered; but experience suggests that Defoe would have added something of his own, even if such a tertium quid were to be found.[14]

The situation is a little different in respect of West Cornwall, even though the assumption that the author was groping for information on West Cornwall seems to rest on a single circumstance – Defoe's report on his journey in 1705 covers no town beyond Liskeard, Bodmin and Launceston. However, this does not rule out further excursions. In the appendix to Letter 3 of the *Tour*, the writer claims to have witnessed a sea battle off the Lizard 'during the War with *France*' (1: 275). From the details supplied, this can be identified as probably occurring in March 1709. More plausibly, he writes of encountering 'several Engineers and Projectors' experimenting with diving equipment to carry out salvage on wrecks (2: 274). It is well established that Defoe invested in such projects, and supported the efforts of his brother-in-law Robert Davis, who had limited success in raising silver bars off the coast at Polpeor Cove, close to the very tip of the Lizard Point, and who accompanied Defoe on some of his travels. Consistent with this, the Cornish sections show the usual heavy dependence on *Britannia*, with occasional raids on Richard Carew's *Survey of*

Cornwall, which had been reprinted for the first time in 1723.[15] However, in this case, there are signs that Defoe looked into the *Atlas*.

Even without such aids, he was well informed about the south-western coast from first-hand observation on his trips to the region. Two paragraphs are devoted to Henry Winstanley's design for Eddystone lighthouse, and its destruction along with the loss of its builder in the Great Storm of 1703 (1: 258). In this account Defoe borrows material from reports printed in his collection on *The Storm* (1704). The topic would arouse Defoe's interest on several grounds, given his obsession with natural disasters, his ever-present awareness of shipwrecks following his unhappy plunge into marine insurance during the 1690s, his knowledge of navigation, his familiarity with construction methods, and his admiration of men like Winstanley, an engineer, merchant and entrepreneur (see Figure 3).

We have already noted the places where Defoe wrote contemptuously of the '*Atlas-maker*'. A further instance of likely influence is found at Liskeard, where Camden for once was insufficient, and the details concerning the town's main features (1: 262) are suspiciously close to those in the *Atlas* (286), excepting comments on the dissenting community which must surely have come from the author himself. Other fleeting instances occur in the entry for Mounts Bay, where a single phrase, 'was sometimes used as a Prison of State' (*Atlas* 185), finds an echo (1: 271); and at Truro, concerning the Lord Warden's stamping tin (*Atlas* 186: *Tour* 1: 268). Overall, the coverage in the *Tour* is more fresh and first-hand, that is closer to concrete features of the landscape, than the remote naming of places that appears in the *Atlas*.

Other Sources

Andrews was a shade dismissive regarding the way that Defoe employed topographic writers other than Camden and Dugdale: 'Several other historians and antiquaries are mentioned, but this was more to give the *"Tour"* an air of erudition than because Defoe had made much use of their work' ('Sources' 273). While there may at times be an element of display to impress readers, the motives seem to be more complex. Defoe wanted to lend authority to his account, to admit some borrowings to cover up for others that were concealed and to include genuinely informative passages. It was Charles Leigh's *The Natural History of Lancashire, Cheshire, and the Peak in Derbyshire* (1700) which provided the basis of his description of the 'wonders' of the Peak. Richard Carew's *Survey of Cornwall* (1600) was regularly enlisted, though rather more for anecdote than analysis (there is

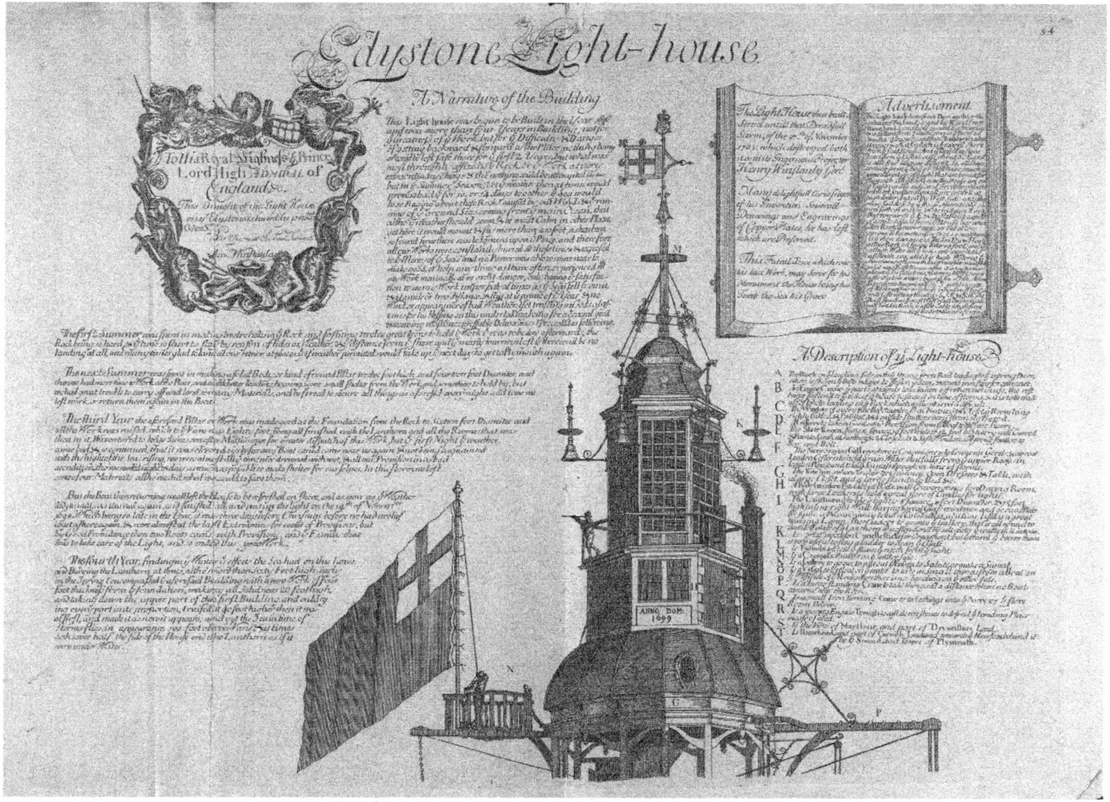

Figure 3 Henry Winstanley, *Edystone Lighthouse* (*c.*1700). Defoe describes this engineering feat prior to its destruction in the hurricane of 1703, as a work constructed 'with great Art and Expedition' that 'stood to Admiration, and bore out many a bitter Storm' (*Tour* 1: 258). Source: YCBA.

an open admission at 1: 165). Defoe cites Robert Plot's *Natural History of Oxford-shire* (1677) on Woodstock (2: 149), and Plot is one of the antiquarians cited on the Rollright Stones (2: 152) – but the section on this monument, including references to Camden and Walter Charleton, is actually a skilful paraphrase of the long and involved argument in the *Natural History* (337–41). These open admissions conceal the fact that elsewhere he borrowed heavily from Plot, for example on the mop fair at Bloxham, and the peaceful parish of 'Brightwell', perhaps a slip for Broadwell (2: 153). His reference to Robert Thoroton's *Antiquities of Nottinghamshire* (1677) is characteristically self-exculpatory: 'But the learned Dr. *Thoroton* . . . having copied all the Epitaphs and Inscriptions in this Town [Nottingham]; if I should repeat them, it would look as if I wanted matter to fill up; just the contrary of which is my Case to an Extreme' (3: 18). However, he does not acknowledge the fact that his coverage of the Willoughby family and their tombs at Wollaton two pages later is also taken from Thoroton.[16] On Cambridge (1: 128) he appears to have had recourse to a compilation entitled *The History and Antiquities of the University of Cambridge* (1721).[17]

Even where he does no more than point to a work, rather than cite it, the reference might be useful to curious readers: 'There is a long account of the Antiquities of this Place lately Published, to which I referr, Antiquities as I have observed, not being my Province in this Work, but a Description of things in their present State' (2: 126). The book in question was William Bedwell's *A Briefe Description of the Towne of Tottenham*, first published in 1631, and reprinted in 1718 together with Richard Butcher's survey of Stamford. (This volume was in the Defoe sale catalogue, and he quotes from Butcher at 2: 221.) For London the writer had more sources; he mentions John Stow twice, disavowing any intent to 'make an Abridgment of *Stow* and his Continuators' (2: 73), but he certainly derived factual information from John Strype's edition of 1720, even though this work was mostly completed by 1707 and missed out many of the recent changes that Defoe proclaimed with relish.

This is not an exhaustive list, but it indicates that the *Tour* draws purposefully on the burgeoning work of antiquarians.[18] There were still relatively few county histories, and, as Rosemary Sweet has shown, Butcher's work, originally published in 1646, was among the very earliest urban histories in Britain.[19] With most cities, the author was on his own. If anything, he is to be congratulated for having managed to find so many valuable sources of local history, in an age when public libraries did not really exist, and when a professional writer would struggle to locate private libraries that would open their resources. Contrary to what Andrews says, there is more subterranean use of these tools than surface display.

Among undeclared sources which have not been identified may be [S. Midgley?], *The History of the Famous Town of Hallifax in Yorkshire* (London, 1712). This contains a reissue of *Halifax and its Gibbet-Law* (1708), printed for John Bentley at Halifax. Defoe's long account of the punishments inflicted in the town (3: 69–72) goes well beyond anything found in Gibson's additions (*Britannia* 2: 853–4), and may be an imaginative infilling of Midgley (1: 69). On the title-page of Midgley we encounter the old proverb, 'From Hull, Hell, and Halifax, good Lord deliver us'; Defoe cites this too (3: 71), reversing the order of Hull and Hell. The presumed author is Samuel Midgley, thought to be a physician, who died in 1695 while a prisoner in Halifax gaol, where he had been incarcerated three times for debt. The odd aspect is that the engraving of the scaffold which was first used in the 1695 additions to *Britannia*, labelled 'Printed for & Sold by F: Bentley in Halifax', appears as the frontispiece in Midgley, with this part of the inscription deleted. This suggests a common source I have not been able to trace.[20]

Another possible source of materials that Andrews mentions briefly is the newspaper press. He alludes to a story about extensive flood damage in Chester, 'which had also been reported in one of Defoe's papers' ('Sources' 272). His endnotes supply a more precise reference, Mist's *Weekly Journal*, 31 December 1720. This issue does indeed contain an account of the flood, but the text of the *Tour* (2: 190) draws more heavily on the much fuller treatment in a letter from Chester which appeared in Applebee's *Weekly Journal* on the same date.[21] These days we are more cautious about ascribing articles in these papers to Defoe. But whether or not he had any hand in their publication, we can be confident that this was the route by which he heard of the events. A similar reliance may be surmised in other cases, such as an attempted murder by a barrister named Arundel Coke on the first day of 1722 (1: 94–5). Defoe had a lengthy acquaintance with Bury St Edmunds, the scene of the crime: he sent Moll Flanders to the town in a book published in January of that year, he claims to have set out on his East Anglia journey just days after the date of Coke's trial and execution (1: 50), and his agent there for Harley in 1705 had been John Morley of Halstead, a largely self-educated man of business who built up a large collection of books and provided information on local history to the historian of Essex, William Holman. Since he was not on the spot when the attack took place, Defoe surely had to take his information from a local informant, from one of several pamphlets on the subject, or from the newspaper press. His phrasing in the *Tour,* 'unheard of Act of Barbarity', echoes that of a column in Applebee's *Journal* on 21 April 1722, 'unheard of Barbarity'. Again we cannot be sure if Defoe was behind the newspaper article.

The *Tour* and Macky's *Journey*

As previously mentioned in the Introduction, Defoe's principal competitor and sometimes stalking horse is John Macky, author of *A Journey though England.* Andrews is right to point out that he 'never mentions Macky except to depreciate his work', in spite of the fact that he lifts several pieces of information on country houses and picture galleries from the earlier writer. However, a further comment is misleading: Andrews states that the *Tour* 'seems to have been inspired . . . by the publication of the *Journey* in 1722, and Defoe seems to have invented his five years' tour to justify the appearance of a rival travel book that was actually based on materials older than Macky's' ('Sources' 273). In fact, the first volume of the *Journey* came out in 1714; it was a second edition, with a modicum of revisions, and a new volume that were published in 1722. There was a further edition in 1724. Meanwhile, the third volume devoted to Macky's native Scotland was published in 1723. As regards Volume I especially, the *Journey* relies in many places on observations that may be at least as distant as those of Defoe. In 1722 Macky did not update his observations on Harwich, for example, whereas the *Tour* contains several observations on developments of the previous decade (1: 80–82).

Other instances could be quoted: two may suffice. Macky refers in a familiar way to 'Sir *Theodore Janssen*, the *French* Banker', more accurately a Flemish merchant and financier, who became a director of the Bank of England and the South Sea Company. According to Macky, he 'hath a very pleasant Seat in the Village' of Wimbledon.[22] In fact, Janssen had been fined and deprived of public offices in the aftermath of the Bubble; he had already been forced to start disposing of his assets, which included the house he was building on the site of a Tudor mansion. In 1723 it became one of the pickings of the crash bought up by the Duchess of Marlborough. Defoe notes briefly, 'Sir *Theodore Janssen* another South-Sea Forfeiture at *Wimbleton*' (1: 202). The reason for this discrepancy is clear: a running theme of the *Tour* is the fall of prosperous merchants as a result of the Bubble. At Coleshill, all that Macky can observe is 'the delicious Prospect of . . . several fine Seats', the staple content of his whole itinerary.[23]

Landscape for him is a kind of static backcloth to the world of society. With Defoe, people and places interact in a setting moulded by the course of events. He comments on the high-flying politics of this town, with its Jacobite lord of the manor Baron Digby, its former vicar John Kettlewell, who had been deprived of the living, and a later curate Thomas Carte, the non-juror and friend of Bishop Atterbury. The sardonic comments in the *Tour*, 'They told me there was but one Family of Whiggs, as they call'd them, in the whole Town, and they hoped to drive them out of the Place too very soon . . . Their Instructors being such, 'tis no Wonder the People have follow'd their Leader,' have all the hallmarks of the bitter struggles that the author had encountered in nearby Coventry, the subject of the next entry (2: 201).

Defoe is more topical than Macky, and not just because he is less reliant on stale observations unaffected by the passage of time. He also has greater alertness to the political and economic ramifications of what he sees. For him, topography encodes ideological issues. Where Macky skims from one landmark to another, zooming over the ground to reach the next port of call, Defoe stops to characterise the countryside, many of the villages, the small towns, the cities, the mills, the rivers, the docks and above all the people, reporting on their occupations and their conversation. The *Journey* gives extended coverage to the old county towns, but misses out the rising industrial centres. York has seven pages, but you would not know there were places such as Leeds or Halifax. It is true that the author mentions Liverpool, but not Manchester, since he wishes to power ahead to Preston and Lancaster:

> You may reasonably ask me, that since I was in *Lancashire*, when at *Leverpool*, why I did not proceed through that large County, before my Return to the Midland ones; and so proceed by the *West* Shore to *Carlisle*? The Reason, upon the strictest Enquiry, was, that, except a very noble Seat of the Earl of *Warrington*'s, there is not any thing remarkable in *Lancashire*, but good Neighbourhood and Plenty; and more of the Roman Catholick Religion in this County, than in any three others in *England*.

He also refers to 'the little County of *Westmorland*, where there is nothing remarkable'.[24] Of course, Lancashire was not yet a hotbed of manufacturing. Still, on his way northwards to Carlisle, Defoe manages to find something to say about many places, and not just Manchester, which he describes at length with the aid of a long, practically verbatim quotation from *Britannia* (ii. 963–4).[25] He treats of Warrington, Chatmoss, Bolton, Ormskirk, Wigan, collieries, a burning well, Kirby Lonsdale, Appleby, Windermere, the Lake

District fells, gold, copper and lead mines, a Roman road, St Bees, Whitehaven coal trade, a supposed pearl fishery, Cockermouth, Skiddaw, Penrith and much else.

It is at moments like this that we realise just how innovative the *Tour* was in its coverage of topographic elements, compared to the existing tradition of travel literature with its heavy emphasis on antiquities, churches and seats of the nobility. Even the sharp-eyed John Leland had passed over most of the local lore that Defoe takes pains to explore. His observation of regional proverbs and dialect, as this last is evidenced in Somerset (1: 249–51), aligns his work with that of John Aubrey and Thomas Fuller. Nor should we imagine that he is alone in drawing on the help of earlier writers. Macky allots no less than eighteen pages, that is over 3,500 words, to an account of Epsom, inserting this despite the fact that it is written 'in a more florid Style than what I can express my self in'. The unnamed source is John Toland's *Description of Epsom* (1711).[26]

Ultimately, it is a species of category error to align Defoe and Macky as travel writers. The *Journey* portrays the nation as an almost abstract space, dotted with disconnected sites of interest. The *Tour* conveys the sense of a physical entity, full of human activity, and linked by routes on land and water; it forms an expanse whose crossing involves time and effort. One book provides a jagged itinerary which hardly ever becomes an intelligible chorographic statement. The other gives us a connected anatomy of the nation, in which topographical information is underpinned by historical understanding and social commentary.

Conclusion

This review of the evidence suggests that much of the pioneering survey by Andrews has stood up well to the passage of time. On the first issue, the evidence corroborates what he suggested about the use of maps in the *Tour*, but it shows that Defoe enlisted their aid more widely than previously suspected. On the second point, Andrews tended to understate Defoe's acquaintance with counties such as Dorset, Somerset and East Yorkshire. As a result, except for parts of Cornwall, he exaggerated the degree to which the author relied on *A New General Atlas*. Some other sources that he did not consider have now surfaced. Inevitably an article dating from 1960 needs to be reconsidered at times with information that has become available in subsequent years, most importantly the bibliographical studies of P. N. Furbank and W. R. Owens, along with the biographies of F. Bastian, Paula Backscheider, Maximillian E. Novak and John Richetti.[27]

Overall, we can assent to most of the conclusions reached by Andrews. In a comment that is still valid, he argues that we should not exaggerate the significance of the borrowings from other sources in the *Tour*:

> [In] a work of some 350,000 words these debts are of marginal importance. Nine-tenths of the 'Tour' was wholly original, including of course, the whole of the author's very characteristic outlook, as well as almost all his general ideas and almost all his information about industry and trade. . . . More than this, he commanded documentary sources beyond the scope of the conventional topographical writer. The 'Tour' reveals him as a keen though unsystematic reader of press reports, parliamentary bills and petitions, and reports by parliamentary committees on industry, trade and navigation. ('Sources' 274)

In fact, the more we probe into the subterraneous ore out of which Defoe mined a lot of his materials, the more we are struck by the skill and imagination which went into the creation of the book. It seems fitting to leave the last words to a writer eminently qualified to pronounce an opinion: 'In spite of its weaknesses the 'Tour' remains a great pioneer work of economic geography' ('Sources', 275).

CHAPTER 10

Road-testing the First Turnpikes
Defoe's Account of English Highways

> The Roads are the Arteries that convey, and the Manufactures, Provisions, and Produce of the whole, flow thro' them, to the general Supply of every Part
>
> *Review*, 9 July 1709.

As described in Chapter 4, the *Tour* draws on extensive familiarity with the highway system. This is among the reasons that the work can be seen as the one in which Defoe is most truly himself, and in some respects most effectively a writer for our times. As well as displaying his intimate knowledge of the commercial and economic activity of the nation, both internal and external, the book feeds on a lifetime of journeys across his homeland. The testimony of many historians cited in Chapter 5 shows that no other source presents early modern Britain in such fullness and detail, with a sprinkling of arresting first-hand observations. Perhaps the best example occurs in a famous appendix to the second volume, where Defoe gave an account of the state of English roads. It remains a trove of information and insight, especially for those concerned with the early history of the turnpike system. Students of the subject still find it profitable to explore the appendix, unrivalled in its up-to-the minute coverage of a revolution in transport, written in the very time and place where it was going on.

This segment came before the public on 8 June 1725, while internal evidence suggests it was compiled no earlier than March or April of that year. The portion concerned with highways comprises the last 6,800 words of this appendix. Though cited on countless occasions for almost three centuries, the text has never been properly edited with detailed attention to its coverage of the newly emergent method of maintaining roads through the establishment of turnpike trusts. This chapter attempts to describe major features of the account, to indicate its timeliness, and to set out the factors which enabled Defoe to provide an unrivalled picture of the communications network of his era. Numerous aspects of his career made him the right author for the job, at the right time and in the right place. The appendix carries even more weight because it fills out a comprehensive survey of road conditions throughout the text, as part of the author's overall design. His aim was to show the interdependence of separate regions of the country, bound together in a newly enhanced circulation system (see Map 4).

A leading modern authority, William Albert, has described the *Tour* with perhaps unnecessary caution as 'probably the most informative contemporary account of the turnpike trusts in the eighteenth century'.[1] In fact the work provides the only full analysis of what the roads were like across the nation at the key moment of genesis for the turnpike system. Its historic value can easily be underestimated, since recent scholarship has tended to veer away from the formative years of the system, and has concentrated on a limited range of economic indicators at the expense of other issues. It is Defoe who takes us closest to the experience of using the roads, and brings out most vividly the contrast in many parts of the system to the chaotic highways found in the age of unpaid statute labour supplied by unwilling rural parishes.

Background

Serious study of the evolution of English turnpike trusts began with two works published around the start of the First World War. The initial impetus was provided in 1913 by Sidney and Beatrice Webb, with a volume in their massive series on *English Local Government* (11 vols., 1903–29), entitled *The King's Highway.* This book was reviewed by a Canadian scholar, W. T. Jackman, who subsequently produced his own comprehensive survey, *The Development of Transportation in Modern England* (2 vols., 1916), drawing on graduate studies he had carried out at Harvard.[2] The Webbs devote one major chapter to 'The Turnpike Road', while Jackman has one dealing with roads and road legislation from 1500 to 1750, followed by another on roads and their improvement in the period 1750–1830. Each work traced the development of the turnpike system as it replaced older forms of highway maintenance under statutory parish labour. Both books have been republished in more recent years.

For a long time that was effectively that. Studies of local turnpike trusts abounded, but no systematic account was attempted of how the system affected Britain's national economy, or how it prepared the way for a growth in communications central to the Industrial Revolution. This

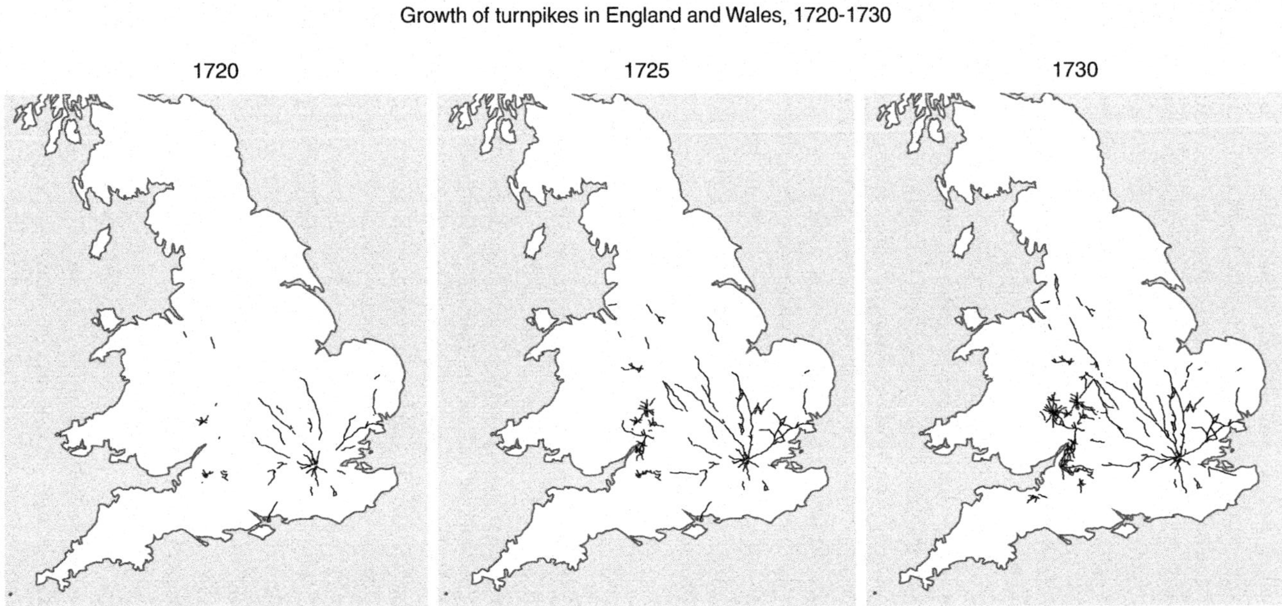

Map 4. Turnpike system in 1720 and in 1730. Source: Rosevear, A., Satchell, A. E. M., Bogart, D., Shaw Taylor, L., 'Turnpike roads of England and Wales,' 2017.

lull continued for about sixty years. As had happened in the case of the Webbs and Jackman, the rise of modern scholarship in this area would be marked by the appearance in close succession of two monographs. First came William Albert with *The Turnpike Road System in England 1663–1840*, issued in 1972. It was based on doctoral study at the London School of Economics, an institution co-founded by the Webbs, and like Jackman's book it was published by Cambridge University Press. The year 1977 saw a second work on a closely allied topic, *Transport and Economy: The Turnpike Roads of Eighteenth Century Britain*, by Eric Pawson. As the 1970s witnessed some of the heady days of cliometrics, it is not surprising that both Albert and Pawson provide much more sophisticated quantitative data than did their predecessors.

Subsequently, most attention has been given to the long-term impact of the turnpikes on transport costs. A growing proportion of scholarship has considered the effect which the system had on the rate of investment in transport. More widely, concern has lain in the profitability of trade and industry in the late eighteenth and early nineteenth centuries, prior to the displacement of turnpike roads in the mid-Victorian era, once railways, trams and the telegraph opened up new avenues of communication.[3] It is generally agreed that Britain would never have become the first industrial nation in the Western world, had it not been for the aid provided by a better means of transporting people and goods. The precise contribution of turnpikes to this process remains a more open question for scholars.

This emphasis may lead to an unspoken assumption that we can leave aside as prehistory everything before the burst of trusts created during the 'turnpike mania' of the 1750s. Moreover, it privileges the consequences for trade and industry of the newer sorts of transportation costs. These matters obviously constitute an important issue, but metrics in this area should not obscure the human and social dimension of the changes brought about by the spread of turnpikes. We should take notice of the comfort and convenience of travellers, whether they were engaged in journeys for business or for pleasure. We need to get a sense of their reactions when they first encountered the improved Holyhead road, bereft of its former windings along precipitous ridges over bays and rivers. Defoe wrote too soon to see anything like the full extent of such changes. But his account does give us the earliest shock of recognition. As well as the facts about measures affecting individual stretches of highway (for the most part, given very accurately), Defoe supplies abundant first-hand testimony regarding the conditions of travelling across large sections of England – predominantly, though not exclusively, in the Midlands and South-east, with a natural emphasis on the routes around London.

All four scholars mentioned above make extensive use of the *Tour*. However, the Webbs and Jackman regularly cite the *Tour* from its 1748 embodiment, the fourth of nine eighteenth-century editions. This means that the reader cannot know which of the comments quoted come from Defoe and which from his editor, the printer-novelist Samuel Richardson. More seriously, Richardson carried out a heavy abridgment of the appendix in the second edition (1738). As Godfrey Davies pointed out long ago, one consequence for the Webbs of restricting themselves to the 1748 version was that 'they missed altogether the only consecutive description that Defoe gave of the roads – in the appendix to Book II, published in 1725' – and the same applies to Jackman.[4] This was a disabling lapse in two remarkable studies that broke considerable new ground. Happily, Albert and Pawson displayed a greater alertness, which meant they were able to draw significant observations from the appendix to substantiate their argument.[5]

In the interim, a number of authorities had recognised the importance of what Defoe says about the road system. The prolific Labour historian G. D. H. Cole began the introduction to his edition of the *Tour* (1927) by claiming that the work was little read, even though 'almost every social or economic history of the eighteenth century makes some reference to it; and there are half a dozen passages from it that everybody knows'. Nonetheless, he found the treatment of roads 'illuminating', and praised Defoe for paying proper attention to 'the difficulties of transport'; equally, he endorses the view of earlier writers that improvements to the highways were under way well before the Industrial Revolution took off. In another essay on 'Roads, Rivers, and Canals', Cole again pointed out Defoe's enthusiasm for 'the immense improvements that had recently been made in the facilities of travel'.[6] In Chapter 5 of this book, reference was made to G. M. Trevelyan's *English Social History* (1942), and in particular a section that he entitled 'Defoe's England'. Among Trevelyan's many citations to the *Tour*'s coverage of the nation are a number concerning highways and inland waterways.[7] We also noted Paul Langford's use of the section on turnpikes as part of his volume in the New Oxford History of England, and his observation on their galvanising effect on Defoe. Langford went on to quote a resonant passage on the way in which the public value of the improved roads exceeded that of noblemen's palaces, but attributed this to Richardson's 1742 edition (3: 249).[8] In reality, the passage appears in the first edition, and it is indeed a highly characteristic example of Defoe's rhetoric on such topics (2: 239).

On the Road: Defoe's Travels

If 1725 was an opportune moment to supply a freeze frame of the turnpikes as they came into full prominence, then Defoe was an ideal person to carry out the task. His qualifications were many and various, but for present purposes they can be divided into two broad categories: those relating to his experience of the English roads and those relating to his interest in the workings of the economy. A natural first step is to look at his history as a traveller.

By the date he wrote the *Tour*, he had been traversing English roads for well over half a century, having spent some of his early years outside London, principally round about Dorking in Surrey. Initially he knew the south-eastern corner of England best, and his business career led him in due course to put down roots in an area along the Thames estuary, where he set up a brick factory. However, his journeys had already begun to take him further afield, with visits to towns such as Bath. In 1685 he joined the Duke of Monmouth's rebellion in the South-west, in what capacity precisely we do not know. Later he seems to have made a number of visits to the Cornish peninsula, once in connection with experiments with a diving bell carried out off the Lizard by his brother-in-law. Then in 1705 he conducted a whirlwind tour of the nation as a political agent on behalf of his patron Robert Harley, the secretary of state for the Northern Department. This took him down to the West Country again, then up through the Midlands and Welsh Border to the north of England as far as Manchester and Leeds, after which he returned to London via the East Midlands and East Anglia. His extensive list of contacts in the provinces included friends in places such as Norwich, the main town in East Anglia and still by population the second city of England, where his son Benjamin would settle for a while. From 1706 he spent long periods in Edinburgh for Harley, attempting to promote the Union with Scotland. This involved trips which made him very familiar with the Great North Road – we can trace hints of this experience not just in the *Tour* but also in his journal *The Review* (1704–13), in his correspondence with Harley and in novels such as *Col. Jacque* (1722), where the characters tread in his footsteps.

Moreover, he had a well-developed interest in the exploits of 'gentlemen of the road', though he probably did not write many of the accounts of highwaymen that used to be attributed to him.[9] It is no secret that many of his best-known novels deal with the exploits of criminals in various categories, such as the pirate Singleton, the courtesan Roxana and the soldier of fortune Jacque. The most familiar case is that of the thief Moll

Flanders, whose picturesque marital career includes her union with a dashing highwayman. In *Augusta Triumphans* and *Second Thoughts are Best*, both from 1728 under the pseudonym of 'Andrew Moreton', he would grapple with the new problems in law enforcement caused by the speed of urban growth. Dedicated to the king, *Second Thoughts* concludes with 'some thoughts for suppressing robberies in all the publick roads of England'. His idea was to station troops of horses at the outskirts of London, to provide a convoy for all the vehicles in need of protection, adding, 'This may be likewise practised from Town to Town all over *England*', so that the roads would be as safe as the roads in the city. On top of this, 'For those who walk on Foot to the adjacent Villages, Parties of Foot may be station'd in like Manner.' The army would supply the manpower and robbers, if caught, would be prosecuted at the public expense. As well as the account of the daring ride of Nicks, the topic surfaces briefly in the *Tour* with a plangent description of the gibbets on the edge of Guildford, where those guilty of highway robbery would be executed in the sight of townspeople (1: 182).[10]

The pace of travel slowed down a little after Defoe settled in Stoke Newington, then a village just to the north of the metropolis. One of the local responsibilities he assumed in 1717 as a gentrified citizen was that of a parochial surveyor of the highways. This post involved helping 'to organize the repair and building of the streets and roads, collecting money and recruiting laborers from parish residents'.[11] But he did not sit around in his own patch of the city. As we have seen, his property investments led him into East Anglia, and journalistic trips in the same direction may lie behind the peregrinations described in *Moll Flanders* (1722). Some legends associate him with Bristol, suggesting that it was there he met the mariner Alexander Selkirk, a fairly distant model for his own hero Robinson Crusoe. This story is probably not true, but there are signs of his familiarity with the city (see Chapter 11). Near the end of his life he underwent a sort of internal exile in Kent. This was after he had composed the *Tour*, but he may well have chosen his place of concealment because of time spent there earlier.

The Timeframe

Some of the authorities quoted at the start of this chapter mention, but do not stress, the early date at which Defoe wrote. If he had attempted to produce the *Tour* two decades earlier, when he already had absorbed much of the material that would make up the brunt of his narrative, there would have been very little he could say about turnpikes. Not until the middle years of Queen Anne was the first trust was set up, to replace the former method of oversight by the local Justices of the Peace. Significant legislation followed, including the Highways Act of 1715 (2 Geo. I, c. 52). By such measures the powers of the Surveyor, previously an ill-defined role in the days of statute labour, were more clearly set out. There had been only four new turnpike acts in the 1690s; between 1700 and 1710 this rose to thirteen, and between 1711 and 1720 it reached twenty. The average mileage for each trust was less than fifteen. After this came the deluge, with just over fifty such acts between 1721 and 1730, when the mean mileage grew to twenty-seven. This was followed by a comparative lull in the following decade. Moreover, 'Before 1720 there was little turnpike activity in areas remote from the metropolis'.[12] This obviously made it easier for the author to get a hold on what was happening. Things began to change around the mid 1720s, with an increasing number of trusts based close to provincial towns in regions such as the West Country. But at the time that the first volume of Defoe's book came out, there were still fewer than fifty projects approved, and many of them had not been fully constructed.

All this was hot news in 1725, or still lying in the womb of futurity. Not everyone had yet grasped the promise that these new arteries held. Just one year later, the Swiss traveller César de Saussure – generally, a careful observer – evidently assumed that the system was nationwide and long established:

> The journey on the high roads of England, and more especially near London, is most enjoyable and interesting. These roads are magnificent, being wide smooth and well kept. Contractors have the care of them, and cover them when necessary with that fine gravel so common in this country. The roads are rounded in the shape of an ass's back, so that the centre is higher than the sides, and the rain flows off into the ditches with which the roads are bordered on either side. It is not the custom here, as it is in France, for the poor peasants to be forced to make and keep up the high roads at their own expense and care. In this country everyone who makes use of roads is obliged to contribute to the expense of keeping them up. At even distances there are barriers on the roads called 'Turnpikes', where you have to pay a penny per horse. The keeper of these turnpikes gives you a ticket and a leaden mark, so that you need not pay a second time on your way back that same day. If you journey on foot you pay nothing; but I am certain all these details bore you, so let us talk of other things.[13]

Saussure obviously did not understand the old system of parish labour still widely in operation, and so he failed to see the scale of improvement to the highways that had now been made possible.

By contrast, Defoe had quickly gained a clear grasp of the pace of development, and had caught up with many local schemes. He mentions the earliest turnpike between Wadesmill and Royston (15 Car. II, c. 1), dating from 1663 and renewed in 1692, together with further segments on to Stilton. By this means 'these Roads, which were before intolerable, are now much mended' – but not yet of the standard reached by the road from London to Colchester (2: 237). He also describes the Stony Stratford section of Watling Street, on the road to Birmingham, administered by the very first trust set up in 1706 (6 Anne, c. 4): again, good results had been obtained 'where the Way was exceeding bad before' (2: 239).[14] Further back along the same route, the stretch between Dunstable and Hockliffe began to be repaired in 1710 (9 Anne, c. 34), with the result that 'the most dismal Piece of Ground for Travelling, that ever was in *England*' had now been 'handsomly repair'd' (2: 239).

Much of the early history of the system relates to the Great North Road, 'the longest and one of the most heavily travelled roads in the country'. Albert notes that five acts were passed on this route before 1720, with five others by 1730 and further supplementation in the 1730s.[15] Defoe indicates not just the earliest schemes around Ware and Royston, but by implication other parts that were extended in the reign of George I. He refers explicitly to one of the last measures dating from the previous reign (12 Anne, c. 19), that is the innermost portion of the road from Shoreditch to Enfield (2: 241). Sideroads just off the main artery also receive attention, such as one at 'the Turnpike at a Village very just called *Foul Mere* near *Cambridge*, for the repair of the particular Roads to the University, but those Works are not yet brought to any Perfection' (2: 238). The legislation was very recent, passed in the year that this volume of the *Tour* was published (11 Geo. I, c. 4). Defoe may have been up to date on this district because of an extensive tour of East Anglia he had made in 1722, probably stopping off in Cambridge, which provided considerable material for the opening part of his *Tour*.[16]

He was still more conversant with the Harwich Road, making reference to the original measure of 1695 (he says 'about the Year 1697') which started the process of improvement (7 & 8 Wm. III, c. 9), and looking forward to plans afoot for the commissioners to erect further turnpikes, something that was realised in part by the passage of 12 Geo. I, c. 23, just a year after the appendix was composed. On his trip in 1722 Defoe had leased a large tract of land near Colchester in Essex, and began to conduct a number of businesses, including selling oysters, which must have obliged him to take the road up to the east coast, even though his warehouse lay near

Tower Dock in London. As will emerge in the next section of this chapter, his ambitions as a trader – unsuccessful as they often were – meant that he spent much of his life travelling along the highways and byways of the nation. In this case he was able to report that the roads through Essex, 'formerly deep, in time of Floods dangerous, and at other times, in Winter, scarce passable ... are now so firm, so safe, so easy to Travellers, and Carriages as well as Cattle' (2: 237).

Defoe waxes lyrical about some of the sections of the highway which had undergone improvement, notably a stretch from South Mimms to St Albans dating from 1715 (1 Geo. I, c. 12). Here the work of mending the existing roadway was 'so well done, the Materials so good, so plentifully furnish'd and so plentifully applied ... here the Bottom is not only repair'd, but the narrow Places are widen'd, Hills levell'd, Bottoms rais'd, and the Ascents and Descents made easy, to the inexpressible Ease and Advantage of Travellers, and especially of the Carriers, who draw heavy Goods and hard Loads, who find the Benefit in the Health and Strength of the Cattle' (2: 240). Along with improving the surface of the road, the introduction of turnpike trusts brought with it some innovatory forms of highway engineering to make the routes more rapid and convenient means of getting people and goods about the country. Equally a section from Barnet to Highgate across Finchley Common, initiated in 1711 (10 Anne, c. 4), drew the author's praise: 'this Work is also admirably well perform'd, and thro' a Piece of Ground, which was very full of Sloughs and deep Places before' (2: 240). Palpably, Defoe was able from his own experience to contrast the former state of the road with its renovated condition. He is more vague when it comes to work on the Kent Road, noting progress on the innermost portion (4 Geo. I, c. 5, 1718), which incorporated a plan for stretches further down the route – in the event, these had to wait several years to be actualised.

The writer was all too well aware that much remained to be done, including work on the final portion from Highgate to the centre of London. He welcomed a recent act obtained for a turnpike now erected at Islington, since some of the roads around the capital were 'to the last Extremity run to ruin' and 'were before almost a Scandal to the City of *London*' (2: 240–41). The measure in question was 3 Geo. I, c. 4, passed in 1717. Fanning out in other directions from the metropolis were roads where turnpikes had been erected near Paddington as well as at Newington in south London (see Figure 4). As a result of work associated with the latter route, 'this Undertaking has been very well prosecuted, and the great *Sussex* Road, which was formerly unsufferably bad, is now become admirably

Figure 4 Paul Sandby, *The Bayswater Turnpike* (*c.*1770s). This was one of the earliest roads around London to be turnpiked, with parliamentary approval in 1715, and running from Paddington to Uxbridge. The route passed through a corner of Middlesex that Defoe extolled as 'made Rich, Pleasant, and Populous by the Neighbourhood of London' (*Tour* 2: 136), part of his attempt to show how the new roads enhanced trade radiating from the capital and spawned residences for rich citizens. Source: YCBA.

good' (2: 241). This is a slightly more roseate account than some travellers initially gave: it evidently rests on measures dating from 1697 (Reigate to Crawley), and 1718 (Southwark to Sutton), but some intervening portions had to wait until 1755. Defoe recognised that black spots survived: in parts of Sussex 'the Country indeed remains in the utmost Distress for Want of good Roads'. As ever, he is mindful of the effect on trade and agriculture: 'So also all over the *Wild of Kent* and *Sussex* it is the same, where the Corn is cheap at the Barn, because it cannot be brought in' (2: 243).

Defoe mentions improvements to Watling Street 'farther down', including those already mentioned, carried out some years earlier around Stony Stratford, Dunstable and Dunchurch, and those more recently underway, e.g. 9 Geo. I, c. 11 (1723) and 10 Geo. I, c. 15 (1724). He looks forward to further developments in the direction of Coventry and Coleshill, with the promise held out of making these routes 'within a few Years . . . compleatly sound and firm' (2: 241). In the event some highways here remained unimproved into the 1750s, but this did not interfere with the rapid rise of Birmingham and its environs as an industrial centre (the population of the city almost quadrupled from around 6,000 in the first half of the century). Other parts of southern England singled out were roads leading into Bath, where improvements began in 1707; the one descending Birdlip Hill into Gloucester (1698, renewed 1723); and a hilly section of the Oxford Road 'near *Beaconsfield* in *Oxfordshire*' [*recte* Buckinghamshire] which came in 1719. All these replaced segments of the road system previously labelled 'bad' or even 'a terrible Place for poor Carriers and Travellers' (2: 241).

Had Defoe passed along every stretch of the turnpiked roads that he greets so warmly? Probably not. What is true is, first, that he had travelled on most of them in their unregenerate state at some point in the first sixty years of his life; second, that he had almost certainly tested many of the routes closest to London after they had come under the control of the new trusts; and third, that he kept his eyes and ears open, which enabled him to get an unusually close sense of plans that had not yet come to fruition when he drafted the appendix. He gives us a hint of imminent events as he is writing:

> And for farther Confirmation of what I have advanc'd above, namely, that we may expect, according to this good Beginning, that the Roads in most Parts of *England* will in a few years be fully repair'd, and restor'd to the same good Condition, (or perhaps a better, than) they were in during the *Roman* government, we may take Notice, that there are no less than twelve Bills, or Petitions for Bills, depending before the Parliament, at this time sitting, for the Repair of the Roads, in several remote parts of *England*, or for the lengthening the Time allow'd in former Acts; some of which . . . give us hopes, that the Grants, when obtain'd, will be very well manag'd, and the Country People greatly encourag'd by them in their Commerce; for there is no doubt to be made, but that the Inland Trade of England has been greatly obstructed by the exceeding Badness of the Roads. (2: 245)

Scrutiny of parliamentary journals will confirm much of this prediction. A concrete result was the passage of fourteen acts in 1726, followed by ten in 1727. No larger tally appeared for an individual year until the great turnpike mania erupted in 1752.[17]

In one respect Defoe was caught out by the swift march of events. He gives no sign of recognising that there might be opposition to the turnpikes from local groups who feared for their livelihood. The first recorded riots took place in Somerset, Gloucestershire and Herefordshire, most famously the series of actions taken by the Kingswood miners in 1727. The colliers were described as 'a set of ungovernable people, regardless of consequences. They extort money of people as they pass along the road, and treat them very rudely unless they give them some'. Their aim was to deter import of Welsh coal from Swansea, in which they were at least partially successful. In this year the gentry of Bristol obtained leave to establish a trust, pleading among other things hazards to life and limb of animals under conveyance. The opposition of the colliers in the district just east of the city, who tore down gates and threw one into the Avon, meant that the scheme had to be put on hold, and the desired improvements had still not been made in 1731.[18] Defoe can hardly be blamed for not anticipating this cloud on the horizon, even though he knew Bristol well, as the next chapter will reveal. He must have heard about the reputation of the colliers, who had rioted previously, citing other grievances.[19]

On the Road: Materials, Construction and Repair

Needless to say, Defoe could not undertake his journeys tucked away in a comfortable conveyance with his head stuck in a book, let alone a phone. The motive for his travels was always to *observe* something about the spot he was visiting, whether his aim lay in collecting information on political, commercial or social activity. He went mainly on horseback, sometimes perhaps shorter distances on foot, and occasionally in the springless carriages that bumped along the roadways – these roads were still unregenerate, across most parts of the country, in 1725. On his rare forays into the remoter corners of the nation, he may even have gone by mule. This circumstance lends immediacy to his descriptions of the highway, since he has a close, indeed almost tactile, feel for the ground under his own feet or those of his horse. Modern travellers speeding along the motorway or on the intercity train have no occasion to consider the geology of the terrain over which they pass. For Defoe the issue was basic. In his first comments in the appendix, he makes this plain:

> It has not been taken Notice of, though it very well deserves Mention; That the Soil of all the Midland part of *England*, even from Sea to Sea, is of a deep stiff Clay, or Marly kind, and it carries a Breadth of near 50 Miles at least, in some Places much more; nor is it possible to go from *London* to any Part of *Britain, North*, without crossing this clayey dirty Part. (2: 233)

He gives instances from the course of the Great North Road, starting with a portion that stretches from Cambridgeshire up almost to Bawtry in Yorkshire, where 'the Country is hard and sound'. On the parallel route past Dunstable 'you enter the deep Clays, which are so surprisingly soft, that it is perfectly frightful to Travellers, and it has been the Wonder of Foreigners, how, considering the great Number of Carriages which are continually passing with heavy Loads, those Ways have been made practicable' (2: 234). Two other routes, stretching westwards on the way to Coventry and Worcester, are further instanced, with a fairly precise location given of the deepest sections.

After this Defoe turns to the construction of road surfaces, with particular attention to the Romans in Britain. As the Webbs described, there had been little interest over recent times in improving the quality of roads by the application of scientific principles. Rather, the authorities preferred to introduce legislation limiting the size of loads or the breadth of wheels: 'Instead of the modern purpose of providing such roads as secure the maximum mobility of men and commodities, our great-grandfathers aimed at preserving their highways from anything beyond the minimum wear and tear.'[20] But Defoe, long before Telford and McAdam, was deeply interested in how the surface of the road should be built and maintained:

> The Causways and Roads, or Streetways of the *Romans*, were perfect solid Buildings, the Foundations were laid so deep, and the Materials so good, however far they were oblig'd to fetch them, that if they had been vaulted and arch'd, they could not have been more solid: I have seen the Bottom of them dug up in several Places, where I have observ'd Flint-stones, Chalkstones, hard Gravel, solid hard Clay, and several other Sorts of Earth, laid in Layers, like the Veins of Oar in a Mine; a Laying of Clay of a solid binding Quality, then Flint-stones, then Chalk, then upon the Chalk rough Ballast or Gravel, 'till the whole Work has been rais'd six or eight Foot from the Bottom; then it has been cover'd with a Crown or rising Ridge in the Middle, gently sloping to the Sides, that the Rain might run off every Way, and not soak into the Work: This I have seen as fair and firm, after having stood, as we may conclude, at least 12 or 1600 years, as if it had been made but the Year before. (2: 235)

Again, a specific instance is provided: Defoe mentions three surviving portions of Roman roads, all of which he seems to have believed to be part of the Fosse Way, though the last was actually on Iter VIII, near Castleford in Yorkshire. He goes on to assert that he had seen 'this very Causeway' cut into, to discover the exact materials employed (2: 236). What is most striking about the extended passage of which I have given a précis here is its concrete and almost physical nature. While he had no specialised background in highway design, or engineering of any kind, he had a strong urge to know how things were made; and in addition he was fascinated by the relics of ancient civilisations which had survived into the modern world, as innumerable passages in the *Tour* reveal.

Again, he understood that materials for repair were not equally available in every part of England. This comes through in an extract such as the following:

> One great Difficulty indeed here, is, that the Country is so Universally made up of a deep, stiff Clay; that 'tis hard to find any Materials to repair the Ways with, that may be depended upon. In some Places they have a red sandy kind of a Slate or Stone, which they lay with Timber and green Faggots, and puts them to a very great Expence; but this Stone does not bind like Chalk and Gravel, or endure like Flint and Pebbles, but wears into Clay from whence it proceeds; and this is the reason why they cannot expect those Roads can reach up, however chargeable the repairs are to the goodness of the Roads in *Essex*. (2: 238)

He knew, too, that many regions of the country had still not acquired many turnpikes, and might face special difficulties because of the local topography.

In fact, Defoe had shown his practical awareness almost thirty years before in his first major work, *An Essay upon Projects* (1697). This book contains a number of innovative and ambitious schemes, ranging from a pension office to an academy for women. One of the most cogent cases is the fifth proposal, relating to highways. This was clearly the basis of what Defoe later wrote in his appendix to the *Tour* (to take the example closest to hand, he uses the same portion of the Fosse Way near Cirencester to illustrate his point). He gives a precise description of the roads that he wishes to see improved; of the methods to be used; of the dimensions of the roadway; and of the need not to 'repair' the existing surfaces but rather to 'perfectly build them as a Fabrick', that is freshly from the ground up. He is equally assured in proposing methods of funding, by which private undertakers would be allowed to carry out the construction on terms set by parliament. It has to be admitted that one aspect of the project may seem less palatable today, when Defoe suggests that an agreement should be made 'with the *Guinea*-Company to furnish 200 *Negroes*, who are generally Persons that do a great deal of Work' (he means the Royal African Company, in which he was seemingly an investor). But this apart, the proposal is admirable in its clarity and concise organisation: for example, when he writes of his own patch in Islington:

> There lies through this large Parish the greatest Road in *England*, and the most frequented, especially by Cattle for *Smithfield*-Market; this great

> Road has so many Branches, and lies for so long a way through the Parish, and withal has the inconvenience of a Clayey Ground, and no Gravel at hand, that, modestly speaking, the Parish is not able to keep it in Repair; by which means several Cross-Roads in the Parish lie wholly Unpassable, and Carts and Horses (and Men too) have been almost buried in Holes and Sloughs; and the main Road itself has for many Years lain in a very ordinary condition, which occasioned several Motions in Parliament to Raise a Toll at *Highgate* for the performance of what it was impossible the Parish shou'd do, and yet was of so absolute necessity to be done.[21]

As we already saw, this turnpike would be approved in 1717 and it was duly noted in the appendix to the *Tour*.

Many passages in the *Essay* are directly recalled in the appendix. One that obviously goes back to Defoe's own youthful experience in Dorking is this:

> I have seen in that horrible Country the Road 60 to 100 Yards Broad, lie from side to side all Poach'd with Cattel, the Land of no manner of Benefit, and yet no going with a Horse, but at every step up to the Shoulders, full of Sloughs and Holes, and covered with standing-water. It costs them incredible Sums of Money to Repair them; and the very Places that are mended, wou'd fright a young Traveller to go over them: The *Romans* Master'd this Work, and by a firm Causeway made a High-way quite through this deep Country, through *Darkin* in *Surry* to *Stansted*, and thence to *Okeley*, and so on to *Arundel*; its Name tells us what it was made of; for it was call'd *Stone-street*, and many visible parts of it remain to this day.[22]

The proposals in the *Essay* lack for nothing either in boldness or specificity:

> First, That an Act of Parliament be made, with Liberty for the Undertakers to Dig and Trench, to cut down Hedges and Trees, or whatever is needful for ditching, dreining and carrying off Water, cleaning, enlarging and levelling the Roads, with Power to lay open or inclose Lands; to incroach into Lands, dig, raise, and level Fences, plant and pull up Hedges or Trees, for the enlarging, widening, and dreining the High-Ways, with Power to turn either the Roads, or Water-Courses, Rivers and Brooks, as by the Directors of the Works shall be found needful, *always allowing* satisfaction to be first made to the Owners of such Lands, either by assigning to them equivalent Lands, or Payment in Money, the Value to be adjusted by Two indifferent [i.e. impartial] Persons, to be Named by the Lord Chancellor, or Lord Keeper for the time being.

Defoe seems unable to restrain his enthusiasm for the accomplishment of his schemes: 'What a Kingdom wou'd *England* be if this were perform'd in all the Counties of it!'[23]

Defoe and Economic Geography

A second advantage that the author possessed, to equip him for the task in hand, was a comprehensive vision of Britain, most especially England and Wales. Part 1 of this book described the ways in which he was able to perceive an interlocking system of trading regions that focused on London.[24] Defoe's strength in this regard came initially from his experience in commerce. If his career did not by any means achieve uniform success, it did display an astonishing versatility. His original vocation was that of a wholesaler in the hosiery trade, but he soon branched out in a wide range of other business ventures. He traded in wine, beer, cloth, shellfish and other goods; he invested in ships engaged in the Transatlantic trade, and perhaps in marine insurance, both of which may well have involved some journeys to coastal regions and to ports such as Bristol or Harwich. When in Scotland he sold horses, and made a pretence at least of engaging in linen manufacture, shipbuilding, salt manufacture and glassworks, as well as the work of a fish merchant. In old age he was operating a business that sold cheese, honey, oysters and anchovies. His purchase of land outside Colchester was partly an investment, but it may also have been born of a desire to end his days as a gentleman farmer.

In the mid 1720s, as we saw in the Introduction to this book, Defoe embarked on a series of works which collectively formed a survey of the economic geography of the nation, including historical issues and aspects of the subject affected by international trade. These include the *Tour* itself, followed by *The Complete English Tradesman*, and several other works. Some of these necessarily discuss matters relating to the transport system of the country. *A Plan of the English Commerce* invites the reader to take an imaginative tour of key areas of economic activity, with directions such as 'Let the curious Enquirer travel a little further, and look into the Countries [i.e. counties] adjacent to these Towns.'[25]

But Defoe had taken his own advice in a more literal survey of the nation. As he explains in *The Great Law of Subordination Consider'd* (1724), 'I travell'd in three or four several Tours, over the whole Island, critically observing, and carefully informing myself of every thing worth observing in all the Towns and Countries through which I pass'd.' Supposedly these journeys took place between 1684 and 1688, when he was certainly beginning to extend his acquaintance with the length and breadth of England. His travelling companion, who served as 'a walking Map' through the regions they traversed, was the son of 'a very great Clothier in the *West-Country*'. In due course, his son took over:

> [He] went into the *North* and *North-East* Parts of *England;* as first, into the *West-Riding* of *York-shire,* bordering on *Lancashire,* and after that into *Lincolnshire,* and *Norfolk;* and that his Business was chiefly buying of *Lincolnshire,* and *Leicestershire* Wool, which by the way, is the best and fittest for Manufacturing in *England,* and by this trading moving kind of Life, *added he,* I came to converse among the Poorer sort of People, Farmers, and Manufacturers of every kind, from *Lancashire* and *Westmoreland,* in the *North;* down to *Lincolnshire,* and *Leicestershire,* and thence into *Norfolk, Suffolk,* and *Essex.*[26]

By similar means, Defoe augmented the knowledge of inland trade and communications that he picked up through his own business affairs.

All these myriad experiences came together in the appendix to the *Tour*. Right through from his opening exposition, he emphasises the importance of good roads as an essential requirement for trade to expand, and for England to reach its economic potential:

> The Reason of my taking Notice of this Badness of the Roads, through all the Midland Counties, is this; that as these are Counties which drive a very great Trade with the City of *London*, and with one another, perhaps the greatest of any Counties in England; and that, by consequence, the Carriage is exceeding great, and also that all the Land Carriage of the *Northern* Counties necessarily goes through these Counties, so the Roads had been plow'd so deep, and Materials have been in some Places so difficult to be had for Repair of the Roads, that all the Surveyors Rates have been able to do nothing; nay, the very whole Country has not been able to repair them; that is to say, it was a Burthen too great for the poor Farmers; for in *England* it is the Tenant, not the Landlord, that pays the Surveyors of the Highways. (2: 234)

In this paragraph Defoe succinctly pinpoints deficiencies of the statute labour system that the Webbs and Jackman were the first to analyse at length. At the same time, he shows his awareness of the economic needs which underlay the provision of a viable transport network. So as he proceeds he sets out the advantages of better roads in terms of matters such as easier passage of packhorses; readier transportation of the hundreds and thousands of sheep and cattle who thronged the highways and byways of early modern England; new opportunities in carrying goods such as cheese; opening up drains and building bridges (he instances 'eleven Bridges wholly new-built in ten Miles length' between Southwark and Croydon, 2: 243); greater safety for the mail service and for those riding post; and many other improvements which will have an effect on 'Branches of Inland Commerce, which would be quite alter'd for the better, by this restoring the Goodness of the Roads' (2: 245).

Conclusion

With hindsight, we can perceive that Defoe may have been unduly optimistic in his vision of a new national highway system, both as regards the pace of its implementation, and as regards the unmixed blessings it would bring to all those affected by the coming of the turnpikes. Nevertheless, his account was prescient as well as astonishingly accurate, in view of the recency of the key events, and the continuing flux which marked the irregular installation of new gates. He did not know there would be anything quite as clear-cut as the phenomenon which is so familiar and unsurprising to us under the name of the Industrial Revolution. But his work shows again and again that he recognised the possibility for a considerable take-off in economic activity, and he plainly asserted that a crucial enabling factor would be better roads.

The appendix stands out for a number of reasons: its timeliness, its scope, its precision, its awareness of the history of highways and its recognition of what might lie ahead across the whole of the nation. However, two features help to account for its lasting value. One is its first-hand quality, derived from the many years that Defoe had spent as an observant road-user. We can see the difference if we look once again at the accounts of a contemporary traveller such as John Macky, whose rival description of the nation has been regularly quoted in this book. On his hedgehopping trips across the landscape, Macky seldom deigns to mention the state of the roads. This is about as near as he gets:

> I took the *Winchester* Stage-Coach, and crossing the *Thames* at *Stanes*, dined at a small Village, called *Egham*; and from thence through the worst heathy Country I ever saw, in Eighteen Miles more got to *Farnham*. If a Stranger should be brought a-sleep out of *London*, and awake in the Forest, as they call it, he would think himself in *Westphalia*, it being all over Heath and Furz as there, and not a House to be seen all the Way, except a hunting Seat of the Earl of *Anglesea*'s, called, *Farnborough*, which makes the better Appearance, standing in so course a Country, and being very well planted with Trees.[27]

There is virtually no sense of physical immediacy here, with Macky cocooned inside his snug seat on the coach. The sleeping traveller is not aware of any discomfort, and he does not even realise that this was perhaps the most notorious site in the land for highway robberies – rarely a month went by without newspapers reporting an incident there. Hence John Gay's cautionary words in his 'Epistle to the Earl of Burlington': 'Prepar'd for war, now *Bagshot-Heath* we cross, / Where broken gamesters oft' repair their loss.'[28]

Contrast this with what Defoe says in his parallel journey across Bagshot Heath, where the traveller shows much more recognition of possible threats:

> Here is a vast Tract of Land, some of it within Seventeen or Eighteen Miles of the Capital City; which is not only Poor, but even quite steril, given up to Barrenness, horrid and frightful to look on, not only good for little, but good for nothing; much of it is a Sandy Desert, and one may frequently be put in mind here of *Arabia Deserta*, where the Winds raise the Sands, so as to overwhelm whole Caravans of Travellers, Cattle and People together; for in passing this Heath, in a Windy Day, I was so far in danger of smothering with the Clouds of Sand, which were raised by the Storm, that I cou'd neither keep it out of my Mouth, Nose or Eyes; and when the Wind was over, the Sand appear'd spread over the adjacent Fields of the Forest some miles distant, so as that it ruins the very Soil. This Sand indeed is checked by the *Heath*, or *Heather*, which grows in it, and which is the common product of Barren Land, even in the very *Highlands* of *Scotland*; but the Ground is otherwise so Poor and Barren, that the Product of it feeds no Creatures, but some very small Sheep, who feed chiefly on the said *Heather*, and but very few of these, nor are there any Villages, worth mentioning, and but few Houses, or People for many Miles far and wide. (1: 179–81)

This passage achieves such a vivid effect partly because of the sharp recollection of a single personal experience, culled from one of many occasions on which Defoe crossed 'the great *Black Desert*' (1: 182). It is easy to miss the fact that Defoe has kept an eye on the agricultural potential of the land, not just its lack of aesthetic appeal and fearsome aspect.

The same qualities are carried over to the appendix, and here we touch on the second feature that marks off the treatment of roads. This is the interplay between the appendix and the remainder of the *Tour*. As suggested earlier, the controlling vision of Defoe's book derives from a sense of the economic, geographic and cultural interdependence of the various parts of the country.[29] In our reading of the section on highways, we trust the author more fully because his observations are backed up by what he has said over the course of several hundred pages about the travelling conditions he encountered up and down the nation. We recall not just the dust storm on the road from Farnham, but also the long haul over the Pennines in a snowstorm (Defoe calls the way a mere 'track', but roadbooks of the time do show a route across Blackstone Edge, rough as it would have been); or the 300 droves of turkeys passing in one season across a bridge over the River Stour on the Essex border; or the area round Lewes, the 'deepest, dirtiest, but many ways the Richest, and most Profitable Country in all that part of *England*', where the traveller witnessed 'an Ancient Lady . . . drawn to Church in her Coach with *Six Oxen*' (1: 166).

More widely, we see that generalisations in the appendix about the principal routes for commercial and agricultural traffic are supported by local evidence in the main text. Nor was it only humans who would benefit from an easier passage:

> The fat Cattle will drive lighter, and come to Market with less Toil, and consequently both go farther in one Day, and not waste their Flesh, and heat and spoil themselves, in wallowing thro' the Mud and Sloughs, as is now the Case.
>
> The Sheep will be able to travel in the Winter, and the City not be oblig'd to give great Prizes to the Butchers for Mutton, because it cannot be brought up out of *Leicestershire* and *Lincolnshire*, the Sheep not being able to travel: the Graziers and Breeders will not be oblig'd to sell their Stocks of Weathers cheap in *October* to the Farmers within 20 Miles of *London*, because after that they cannot bring them up; but the Ways being always light and sound, the Grasiers will keep their Stocks themselves, and bring them up to Market, as they see Cause, as well in Winter as in Summer. (2: 242)

It would be pleasant to assume that humanitarian care for animals might underlie this passage, but the author was clearly thinking of economic benefits. And when he goes on to speak of 'Holes and Puddles' that are 'sometimes able to bury both Man and Horse', we know whose fate most concerns him.

Defoe contributed to many subdisciplines within historical study that did not properly exist in his time – urban, regional, demographic, landscape, environmental, leisure, for example, and of course transport. His reports have to be scrutinised carefully, to make allowances for bias, limitations of contemporary knowledge, absence of a developed methodology and of course simple ignorance. They remain an invaluable source because of compensating qualities that the writer brought to his task – among them wide experience of the world, abundant curiosity, a clear-headed understanding of monetary affairs and a gift for trenchant exposition of his ideas. The fact that modern historians rely so heavily on his testimony suggests that he got more things right than wrong. As noted above (p. 127), W.G. Hoskins remarked that historical changes 'really come about at the *cell* level, as it were'. Charting these local developments will act as a corrective to 'easy generalizations that infest so many historical works on a grand scale'.[30] The *Tour* is made up of thousands of detailed observations, set out in a nucleated pattern of local cells.

Close examination of the text confirms the standing of the appendix. Nothing as detailed would appear until the time of Arthur Young and William Cobbett – and these writers, for all their virtues, had not been present to see the birth of the turnpikes. The system was so familiar to them that they seldom allude to it. Only one author was there to leave a substantial record, and through good fortune he happened to be an observer of consummate gifts and unrivalled qualifications for the task. As no other source does, the survey gives us access in the twenty-first century to a world we have lost – that of the changing roads of England in the 1720s, when the turnpikes began to spread across the country.

CHAPTER 11

Defoe on Bristol
The Text with an Introduction and Annotation

It should be useful to move from general assessments of the *Tour* to a detailed case study of one particular region. In a few areas of the country such as East Anglia, the author had an especially close knowledge. Some of these were based on personal connections, family ties (for example, through the activities of his brother-in-law, a shipbuilder), clients in several branches of trade, political contacts established when travelling the land as an agent for Robert Harley, or relationships in Scotland that came into being when he was working to cement the Union, as described in Chapter 6. While Defoe did not have quite such intimate dealings with the city of Bristol, he had been following events in the surrounding district over several decades. He understood its role in the national economy as well as anyone. This, of course, means that he knew a good deal about international trade conducted through the port, although this figures less prominently than the connection with the rest of Britain and Ireland (see also the comparison with Liverpool's Atlantic trade, 3: 124–6). There are not many places in the book where the coverage of a particular locality benefits so obviously from the author's grasp of the fundamental forces that drove the wheels of an increasingly commercial Britain.

The section on Bristol comes in the second volume, published in 1725, as part of a supposed journey described in Letter 6. It amounts to 1,200 words, and occupies four printed pages in the first edition, a sizeable chunk reflecting the importance of the city; there is also a short section of updates in an appendix at the end of the volume. The itinerary leaves London in the direction of Oxford and reaches the West Country before entering the Border counties and Wales. Defoe's imaginary narrator has just visited Bath and moves on soon afterwards to Gloucester. The central function of this chapter is to provide a full commentary on the author's coverage of the city, as it relates both to the history of Bristol and to the themes found in his *Tour* as a whole. It takes the form of an introductory discussion followed by a fully annotated text, and a brief conclusion. Writers have repeatedly drawn on this entry since its first appearance almost 300 years ago, often without acknowledgement. But we can detect three reasons to re-examine this particular portion.

The first concerns citations of the text. Many sources attribute to Defoe material found only in subsequent editions of the work appearing after his death, that is the second to ninth, which came out between 1738 and 1779. These recensions promise 'great additions and improvements', but the entry for Bristol (like others) continued to relay much of what Defoe had originally written. Thus the ninth edition (2: 258) still records, 'There were, when I was in Bristol, no less than fifteen glass-houses in it', which simply repeats the information Defoe had given more than half a century before in his appendix (2: 231).

Secondly, there has never been a proper analysis of the section on Bristol. Three annotated editions of the work have been published in recent years, but between them they offer only three short notes on this passage, two of them concerned with the Tolsey.[1] Here I have endeavoured to supply a more detailed gloss on the entry, a necessary step towards any analysis of the merits and limitations of what Defoe says about the city. It should be noted that much of the material was reproduced verbatim in *Atlas Maritimus & Commercialis* (1728), a work whose connections to Defoe are reviewed in Chapter 12.

Thirdly, his supposed connections with the Bristol region have long been occluded by a number of persistent legends, some of which continue to appear in print and on the web. We need to clear away this mythology before investigating what actually goes on in the *Tour*.

Alexander Selkirk, Woodes Rogers and the Bristol Merchants

One of the most durable tales concerns the mariner Alexander Selkirk, discovered on the island of Juan Fernández by Woodes Rogers. The privateering expedition consisted of two ships provided with official letters of marque enabling them to prey on Spanish shipping in the Pacific. It was under the command of Rogers, the son of another sea captain, and a Freeman of the city, now approaching thirty. He had lived since his teens in the parish of St Mary Redcliffe. By this time his father had bought a double plot on the south side of the newly projected Queen Square and planned to erect a 'substantial mansion'. Rogers senior died in 1706, around the time the house was completed. Backing the South Sea venture were a number of leading merchants in the city, with the largest subscriber acquiring thirty-six shares valued at £3,762 – this came from the Quaker

Thomas Goldney. The ships would leave Bristol Quay in June 1708, to be towed down the Avon preparatory to their departure for the high seas two months later.[2]

In February 1709 the expedition came on Selkirk at Juan Fernández, who had been abandoned on the island by William Dampier's crew almost five years earlier. When the party returned to England in October 1711, Selkirk became an instant celebrity, as well as getting a substantial share of the profits from the journey (though not as much as Goldney, who recouped almost £7,000). Rogers was less fortunate: he did not cover his outlay, and his wife had to move out of Queen Square when her husband stayed in London while he faced bankruptcy proceedings. To recoup his losses, he published his famous *Cruising Voyage Round the World* in June 1712. Another member of the party, Captain Edward Cooke, had already brought out his own narrative, and together with an article by Richard Steele in December 1713, these are the accounts which made Selkirk's adventures on his island famous, and supposedly gave Defoe the idea for *Robinson Crusoe*, whose first part appeared in 1719.

A tenacious myth grew up subsequently that Defoe had not just read about Selkirk, as he must have done in order to incorporate a few details in the tale of his shipwrecked sailor, but that he had actually purloined a copy of Selkirk's memoirs dealing with his sojourn. More, it was claimed that the writer had interviewed Selkirk in the city of Bristol while they were both in Bristol. This story has little substance, other than the presence of a small array of similarities between the novel and the published narratives of Selkirk's time on Juan Fernández. Crusoe's experiences parallel those of several other castaways, reported in books which Defoe, as a voracious student of works on travel, probably knew and may have owned – his library, for instance, held a copy of Robert Knox's *An Historical Relation of Ceylon* (1681), a captivity narrative thought to have influenced *Robinson Crusoe*.[3] All the rest of the legend derives from posthumous gossip. Though it surfaced in the middle of the eighteenth century, with allegations that Defoe had obtained papers illicitly, the Victorian biographer Thomas Wright gave the Selkirk connection its most prominent expression:

> As soon as his singular story was made known in England, Selkirk became an object of curiosity, and was visited by a great number of persons. Defoe, ever on the *qui vive* for what was odd and unusual, and what he fancied could be turned to account, made a journey from London to Bristol apparently for the express purpose of seeing him. The date of this journey is not known,

> but it was probably late in 1711 or early in 1712. The interview occurred in the house of a friend of Defoe's named Mrs. Damaris Daniel, who lived in a corner house in St. James's Square (Bristol), the corner originally opposite the entrance from the Barton. St. James's Square . . . was begun about 1707, consequently Mrs. Daniel's house at the time Defoe visited it must have been only recently built. The result of the meeting was that Selkirk, as he subsequently told Mrs. Daniel, placed in Defoe's hands all his papers. When Defoe commenced his famous 'Robinson Crusoe', which was founded on these papers, it is impossible to say, but the probability is that nothing was done, or very little, before his great illness of 1715, when his tongue was loosed, and when he would be struck with the remarkable analogy between the isolated life of Selkirk on his island in the Pacific and the isolated life of Daniel Defoe in the island of Great Britain.[4]

Certain as he was that the interview took place (he included a fuzzy photograph of Mrs Daniel's house), Wright denied that Defoe surreptitiously appropriated the papers. Rather, 'they were handed over by Selkirk simply as a matter of business. Not that it is likely that Defoe gave much for them'. The source is named as papers apparently in the possession of Mr. Richard Champion Rawlins, 'a descendant of Francis Rogers, one of the twelve merchants of Bristol who fitted out the *Duke* and the *Duchess*'. None of these papers has since emerged into the world.

All this is highly suspect. Damaris Wade (1694–1766) was married and widowed three times, with her most recent wedding to Thomas Daniel occurring in 1752, forty years after the supposed meeting. Favouring her part in the story are the facts that her father was 'Major' Nathaniel Wade, a prominent citizen who (as we shall see) could perhaps have been known to Defoe; that she did live at a local address, 16 St James Square, a speculative building operation erected between 1707 and 1716; and that her first marriage was to a Bristol merchant and shipowner, John Coysgarne (d. 1740), later master of the Merchant Venturers. Moreover, Francis Rogers, a trader from a Cork family known to William Penn, with interests in the sugar business, was indeed among the twelve merchants backing the expedition He acquired twenty shares costing £2,070; and he also served as ship's husband, charged with fitting out the *Duke* and *Duchess.* Francis was apparently not related to his namesake Woodes. His daughter Elizabeth (d. 1745) would marry Joseph Champion (1714–94), another Quaker and a member of one of the most prominent mercantile families in the city. For that matter, Francis was a friend and a relative of his fellow Quaker, Thomas Goldney, another man who knew Major Wade. There is no doubt that a tight-knit circle of business acquaintances existed, built on family ties and religious allegiance, as has been abundantly documented in modern scholarship. What is lacking is any convincing proof that Defoe had close links with such individuals.[5]

The legend was later amplified to include stays by Defoe at the Star Inn in Cock and Bottle Lane, on the north side of Castle Street. This lay where today Castle Park is located on the site of buildings demolished following heavy damage during the Blitz in 1940. In reality, the story has no basis in solid fact, though frequently repeated. It is a pity to have to scotch the tale, since Defoe would have been close at the Star to noteworthy landmarks, including a former sugar refinery adjoining St Peter's church, part-owned by Edward Colston and known as Norton House, which had become a workhouse just before 1700. There was also a nearby meeting house of the Quakers (see p. 238), a sect in which Defoe held a lasting interest (even impersonating a member of the Friends in print), while it would only have been a short step to places that he later wrote about, including the Tolsey.[6]

However, the facts leave little room for dispute. We have only Mrs Daniel's testimony, given years after the event, to indicate that Selkirk and Defoe met anywhere, let alone in Bristol. That she and the writer were friends is not otherwise documented: nor is her acquaintance with Selkirk. The connection suggested with her father is hazy. Defoe may have known some of the Quaker businessmen, as we shall see in the next section of this chapter. But on closer examination the story lacks credibility. In 1711–12, the date Wright assigns for the meeting, Damaris (aged seventeen or eighteen) had not yet married Coysgarne, who as it turns out did not move to St James' Square until 1715. No proof exists that Selkirk possessed any kind of papers relating to his sojourn on the island, or that he spent time in Bristol at this juncture. There is nothing to indicate that Defoe paid a visit to Bristol in 1711–12, and it is improbable he could have done so; he was still travelling up to Scotland on business of the secretary of state Robert Harley, and his journal the *Review* (which often gives a clue to his movements and concerns) lacks any references to the city. No one has ever located a transaction in which Defoe paid for materials he used in his books. The implausibilities continue to mount.

Some Bristol Contacts

If the Selkirk legend, then, relies on speculation and supposition, there exists concrete evidence to show that Defoe did have first-hand knowledge of Bristol, and mixed with leading members of the manufacturers and traders of the city.[7] This is not surprising, since before he began to write seriously his career had led him into a sphere of life where Bristol held a special prominence. He had after all engaged in many branches of commerce, particularly in textiles at both London and Edinburgh. Much of his activity during his earlier years had to do with matters such as the import/export business, as well as coastal shipping. His experience included spells importing Spanish wine. This naturally gave him an insight into the role of Bristol at the time it emerged as unquestionably England's second port. In addition he had been a shipowner and an investor in overseas ventures to Europe and the American colonies; but French privateers had ruined his own maritime efforts. We know that he had contacts with individuals in domestic ports such as Whitehaven and King's Lynn. His brother-in-law Robert Davis was a shipwright who took part in demonstrations of a new diving bell (in which Defoe apparently had shares), off the coast of Cornwall, where Defoe spent time in the early years of the century on a journey through the West Country. One of his other schemes to get rich quickly was to sell to the Admiralty some land he owned on the Thames estuary near Tilbury Fort (where he had lost money on a brick and tile company), for the construction of a naval dockyard. More widely, he had been interested in the shipping industry since a boyhood visit to Harwich and Ipswich around 1668, if we may trust his account in the *Tour* (1: 86).

The most conclusive evidence relates to one journey that Defoe made around the West Country on electioneering business purposes for Robert Harley. In September 1705 he comments on the political complexion of several towns in the region, and specifically notes that 'Bristoll, Gloucester, and Bath are Entirely Reform'd Cittyes and the Moderate Intrest prevails amain.' By this he means that Whigs had taken control of the city government, something that had been carried out in Bristol in the last years of the previous century. Here, the Tories had been ousted from the corporation, and though they had put up a candidate in the election held in June 1705 (Edward Colston Jr., nephew and heir of the famous merchant and philanthropist), he was roundly defeated. In a letter to Harley shortly afterwards, Defoe records two visits he had made to Bristol, stating that 'The history of the Revolution of this Citty is large and Edifyeing and I have an Exact scale of the people, their Trade, and Magistracy. Stay'd here 4 dayes.' Defoe makes the same claim of 'a perfectly Reforms and New Modelled' corporation. An informant on this point was 'Mr. Wade, Bro to Major Wade of Bristoll'.[8]

Not long afterwards, perhaps in April 1706, Defoe sent Harley a list of distribution agents around the country for a political pamphlet he had written. For Bristol, he names two: 'Benja Cool, Quaker' and 'Mr Wraxall,

Mercha.', both of whom he had almost certainly met on his visit in the previous year.[9] The identity of these men suggests that he had made some penetration into the upper ranks of the Bristol mercantile and manufacturing classes. Benjamin Cool(e) (1664–1717) was a founder and partner in the Bristol Brass Company, set up on the River Frome in 1702, north-east of the city at Baptist Mills, very close to where the end of the M32 now debouches into Newfoundland Way. In 1706 the firm became a joint stock company and opened two more plants at Keynsham. The original partners were members of the Society for Friends, including Edward Lloyd (d. 1718), wine merchant, and Nehemiah Champion, (1678–1747), tobacco merchant, who was soon joined by his brother Richard. These men belonged to a close-knit group among whom intermarriage was common.[10] The leading technological input was the work of an incomer from Birmingham, Abraham Darby I (1674–1717), prior to his momentous decision to leave the company and move to Coalbrookdale. At Bristol he would launch his iron-smelting business in 1709, one of the key dates in British industrial history. In this venture Darby had the support of Thomas Goldney II (1664–1731), already mentioned as one of the merchants backing the expedition of Woodes Rogers. The Goldney family remained the principal shareholders in the Coalbrookdale firm right up to 1770, maintaining a close link between Bristol and activities in Shropshire.[11]

As for Cool, originally from Devizes, he was among the most influential figures within the Friends' community, having taken a leading part in the management of the Society's new workhouse, built in 1699 on land bordering the Frome that formerly belonged to Nathaniel Wade. He worked in conjunction with William Penn (whose second marriage he attended), and wrote a number of tracts on controversial subjects. He became known as 'the Quakers' chief Preacher at Bristol'. In 1716 he had the honour of reading a loyal address from the Friends to George I, indicating that he continued to maintain the Whiggish line that would have been expected of him in 1706. The fascinating possibility opens up that Defoe may have had first-hand dealings with men like Darby and Goldney in 1705, although we have no certain proof.

The identity of Defoe's other informant is a little less clear-cut. By the time that the second volume of the *Tour* came out in 1725, the best-known individual in Bristol so named was Nathaniel Wraxall (1687–1731), a member of one of the leading mercantile families in Bristol. He was an American trader, sheriff in 1723, warden of the Merchant Venturers in 1722–3 and grandfather of the writer Sir Nathaniel Wraxall. But he would seem to be too young, since in 1706 he was only on the point of marrying and starting his business career. A much more likely candidate is John Wraxall, a linen draper, whose will dated 8 November 1712 survives in Bristol Record Office. A man with the same name made a marriage settlement in 1713 and was Master of the Mercers and Linen Drapers' Company of Bristol in 1723.[12] John II (d. 1768), who had long occupied a shop on Bristol Bridge, became bankrupt in 1750 and was appointed to the traditional compensatory role of city sword bearer (as happened to Nathaniel's son in 1776). The dates indicate that John Wraxall I would be the only one of the family in a position to give information to Defoe in 1705. It is possible that Defoe kept up a correspondence with Cool and Wraxall, as he did with others on the distribution list, such as the Norwich merchant John Fransham and the Newcastle printer Joseph Button; but if so it has been lost along with the bulk of his letters.

As for the contact in Gloucester, this is perhaps John Wade of Frampton (d. 1715) or less likely Thomas Wade of Filton (d. 1716), both recorded as brothers of the Major (all three were sons of the Cromwellian general John Wade).[13] Nathaniel (*c.*1666–1718) was trained as a lawyer and had taken part in the Monmouth rebellion, serving at the battle of Sedgmoor, where Defoe may or may not have seen action and which is described in the *Tour* (2: 22–3). After confessing to his disloyalty, and fingering some of Monmouth's other supporters, he obtained a free pardon. He was then sent to Bristol to remodel the corporation and became town clerk of Bristol for a brief period, and subsequently steward of the sheriff's court. In 1709 he led the city militia deputed to put down a riot of Kingswood colliers, and five years later he again took a prominent role in putting down riots after the coronation of George I. For this he received praise in a pamphlet once attributed to Defoe, but now thought to be the work of John Oldmixon. Though not himself a Quaker, as he shared a background in the Independent sect with Defoe, both his wives had a background among the Friends. Since Wade owned land which saw development from 1711 on the east of the city, along the Frome, he could have given Defoe valuable information for the Bristol entry, but evidence of their contact is lacking. All that can be stated with certainty is that Defoe knew of Nathaniel Wade, and believed that his informant in Gloucester was the major's brother.

By the time that Defoe's narrative reached Bristol, he had already given an extensive commentary on the city's place within the British economy. He compares it to ports such as Yarmouth and King's Lynn (1: 109, 116), and refers to the new mills for manufacturing sites for brass (1: 267). In particular, when describing the economic life of Wiltshire and surrounding counties, he emphasises more than once the role of Bristol in the wool trade. Later, as he embarks on his progression northwards, he remarks that 'great part of *Bristol* is in the bounds of *Gloucestershire*, tho' it be a County of itself' (2: 160), a status that the city has been able to claim since a charter was granted in 1373 (confirmed by 47 Edw. III). Defoe stresses the way in which, through waterways such as the Severn, the Wye and Warwickshire Avon, Bristol played an important part in the wider economy stretching into the Border Counties and West Midlands (2: 160).[14] He remarks how Bristol merchants load ships at Chepstow to export corn to Europe (2: 171–2); and notes that Glamorgan supplies its neighbour with salted cheese (2: 174). Offering an extended comparison between the two cities that runs to some 700 words, the narrator avers that Liverpool has grown so rich and populous that it may be called 'the *Bristol* of this Part of *England*', and he accurately predicts that Liverpool would soon outdo its rival in commercial activity and population (2: 188–9, 3: 124–6). Not all Defoe's projections came true, but one of his comments reads like a proleptic survey of the course of British industrial history in the decades to come:

> As for the Cities of *Bristol, Exceter*, and *Norwich*, which are large and very populous, and in some things drive a prodigious Trade, as well in Merchandise as Manufacture, we shall find them matched, if not out-done, by the growing Towns of *Liverpool, Hull, Leeds, Newcastle*, and *Manchester*, and the Cities of *Edinburgh* and *Glasgow*, as shall be shown in its place. (3: 14)

As Table 3 shows, only Newcastle of the five growing English towns mentioned had a population of more than 10,000, less than half that of Bristol and Norwich, and considerably less than Exeter (while Birmingham, Nottingham and Sheffield were in the same situation).

The entry for Bristol itself follows.

The Text

> Following the Course the River *Avon*, which runs thro' *Bath*, we come in Ten Miles to the City of *Bristol*, the greatest, the richest, and the best Port of Trade in *Great Britain, London* only excepted.
>
> The Merchants of this City not only have the greatest Trade, but they Trade with a more entire Independency upon *London*, than any other Town in *Britain*. And 'tis evident in this particular, (*viz.*) That whatsoever Exportations they make to any part of the World, they are able to bring the full returns back to their own Port, and can dispose of it there.[1]

[1] For the nature and scope of commerce in the period, a balanced account is that of W. E. Minchinton, 'Bristol – Metropolis of the West in the Eighteenth Century', reprinted in *The Early Modern Town: A Reader*, ed. Peter Clark (London, 1976), 297–31, which cites the present

This is not the Case in any other Port in *England.* But they are often oblig'd either to ship part of the Effects in the Ports abroad, on the Ships bound to *London;* or to consign their own Ships to *London,* in order both to get Freight, as also to dispose of their own Cargoes.

But the *Bristol* Merchants as they have a very great Trade abroad, so they have always Buyers at Home, for their Returns, and that such Buyers that no Cargo is too big for them. To this Purpose, the Shopkeepers in *Bristol* who in general are all Wholesale Men, have so great an Inland Trade among all the Western Counties, that they maintain Carriers just as the London Tradesmen do, to all the Principal Countries and Towns from *Southampton* in the *South,* even to the Banks of the *Trent North,* and tho' they have no Navigable River that way, yet they drive a very great Trade through all those Counties.[2]

Add to this, That, as well by Sea, as by the Navigation of two great Rivers, the *Wye,* and the *Severn,* They have the whole Trade of *South-Wales,* as it were, to themselves,[3] and the greatest Part of *North-Wales;* and as to their Trade to *Ireland,* it is not only great in it self, but *is* prodigiously encreas'd in these last Thirty Years since the Revolution, notwithstanding the great Encrease and Encroachment of the Merchants at *Liverpool,* in the *Irish* Trade, and the great Devastations of the War; the Kingdom of *Ireland* it self being wonderfully encreas'd since that time.

The greatest Inconveniences of *Bristol,* are, its Situation, and the tenacious Folly of its Inhabitants; who by the general Infatuation, the Pretence of Freedoms and Priviledges, that Corporation-Tyranny, which prevents the Flourishing and Encrease of many a good Town in *England,* continue obstinately to forbid any, who are not Subjects of their City Soveraignty, (that is to say, Freemen,) to Trade within

passage from the *Tour,* and fills out Defoe's comments on matters such as inland trade, distribution, and relations with London. See also Minchinton, *Trade of Bristol,* ix, for Bristol's status as second port in the nation by 1700. In this work some of the observations Defoe makes about the methods of traders can be found documented, e.g. with regard to Irish trade (p. xii), the combination of wholesale and other mercantile roles (p. xvii), and the city's competitive advantage over London in some branches of trade (p. 134). For the way in which the occupation developed in the preceding period as the city moved towards its greatest prominence, and an overview of its members, see P. V. McGrath, *Merchants and Merchandise in Seventeenth-Century Bristol* (Bristol, 1955), ix–xxxii.

2 Defoe wrote just too soon to know of an undertaking carried out from 1725 until its completion in December 1727, that is the navigation between Hanham and Bath, though the original act to permit this had been obtained as far back as 1712. This ultimately became part of Kennet and Avon Canal, whose inception at the eastern end by an act of 1721 is mentioned by Defoe (2: 38).

3 For the way in which the regional economy of South Wales was controlled from Bristol, while that of North Wales would come to be dominated by Liverpool, see Derek Gregory's article on 'Three Geographies of Industrialization', in *Historical Geography of England and Wales,* ed. R. A. Dodgshon and R. Butlin (London, 2nd ed., 1990), 383.

the Chain of their own Liberties; were it not for this, the City of *Bristol,* would before now, have swell'd and encreas'd in Buildings and Inhabitants, perhaps to double the Magnitude it was formerly of.[4]

This is evident by this one particular; There is one remarkable part of the City where the Liberties extend not at all, or but very little without the City Gate.[5] Here and no where else, they have an Accession of New Inhabitants; and abundance of New Houses, nay, some Streets are built, and the like 'tis probable wou'd have been at all the rest of the Gates, if liberty had been given. As for the City itself, there is hardly room to set another House in it, 'tis so close built, except in the great Square,[6] the Ground about which is a little too Subject to the hazard of Inundations: So that People do not so freely enlarge that way.

The *Tolse* of this City, (so they call their Exchange where their Merchants meet,)[7] has been a Place too of great Business, yet so straighten'd, so crowded, and so many ways inconvenient, that the Merchants have been obliged to do less Business there, than indeed the Nature of their great Trade requires; They have therefore long solicited, a sufficient Authority of Parliament, empowering them to

[4] An exceptionally clear and detailed account of the power wielded by the corporation of Bristol is found in another venerable but still unsupplanted source, Sidney Webb and Beatrice Webb, *English Local Government from the Revolution to the Municipal Corporations Act: The Manor and the Borough* (London, 1908), 2: 443–64. For the way in which the Whig oligarchy weathered challenges in the late Stuart era and then found that 'the good times were on the way back', see Timothy Mowl, *To Build the Second City: Architects and Craftsmen of Georgian Bristol* (Bristol, 1991), 11. 'When 1714 came and the Council felt constrained to celebrate the accession of German George, they were able to set to with all their old tipsy abandon: fifty-three gallons of port and fifteen each of sherry and claret were swilled down.'

[5] Defoe refers to the expansion eastwards of the city past Lawford Gate in the outparish of St Philip and St Jacob. This had been underway for a considerable time, for the city council had attempted to stop building there in 1660, with little success. The district 'soon became the most populous, as it was also the most disorderly, of the suburbs' (John Latimer, *The Annals of Bristol in the Seventeenth Century* (Bristol, 1900), 300). It was also the most plague-ridden part of the city, while one in nine of the parishioners was in receipt of alms in 1696. The district verged on the largely uncontrolled heathland of Kingswood (see note 27). Rioting took place here in 1728 and 1729. It remained a suburb until the time of the Reform Bill. Much of the development came on either side of West Street, now absorbed into the A420, east of the Old Market roundabout. A very few seventeenth-century buildings survive in modern St Philip's.

[6] Queen Square, begun in 1700 and mostly built by 1710, but not completed until 1727. It was constructed on marshy land which remained vulnerable to flash floods from the rivers Avon and Frome, both tidal. before being dammed to form a new harbour. William Goldwin, master of Bristol Grammar School, rhapsodized over the transformation: 'This handsome Square from heaps of Rubbish grew, / And, tho' past Years the marshy Bottom saw / Thick drizling Fogs from steamy Nature draw, / No vap'rish Humours left . . .' (*A Poetical Description of Bristol* (London, 1712), 18). One later scheme to improve flood defences would have turned the square into a floating basin. However, efforts were made to raise to level of the ground so that even high tides did not flow over it (as noted by Defoe in the Appendix to this volume, 2: 231).

[7] Not to be confused with the separate Mayor's Tolzey. The old Merchant's Tolzey took the form of a covered colonnade on the north side of Corn Street. It was located opposite All Saints church, close to where the High Cross originally stood, and removed in 1782.

build a Royal Exchange; by which, I mean a Place suitable and spatious, fit for the Accommodation of the Merchants, and for the Dispatch of Business; and to be. impowered to pull down the adjacent Buildings for that Purpose: But there is not much Progress yet made in this Work, tho' if finish'd it would add much to the Beauty of the City of *Bristol.*[8]

The *Hot Well,* or, the Water of St. *Vincents Rock,* is not in the City, but at the Confluence of the two little Rivers, and on the *North* Side of the Stream. It is but a few Years since this Spring lay open at the Foot of the Rock, and was covered by the Salt Water at every Tide, and yet it preserved both its Warmth and its Mineral Virtue entire.[9]

The Rock tho' hard to admiration, has since that been work'd down, partly by strength of Art, and partly blown in pieces by Gunpowder, and a plain Foundation made for building a large House upon it, where they have good Apartments for entertaining diseased Persons. The *Well* is secur'd, and a good Pump fix'd in it, so that they have the Water pure and unmix'd from the Spring it self.[10]

8 The new exchange on the south side of Corn Street, near the corner with the High Street, was finally built by John Wood the Elder in 1740–43. For the efforts from around 1717 to obtain this legislation, see John Wood, *A Description of the Exchange of Bristol* (Bath, 1745), 6–9. Wood cites a preliminary measure granted to the corporation in 1721. In fact the bill received the royal assent on 12 February 1722. In the Appendix Defoe mentions the act as passed in 1723 (2: 231). For the history of construction, which was in part underwritten by Ralph Allen, using his own Bath stone, see Mowl, *Second City*, 43–5. Two structures which had to be demolished to enable construction were the Coopers' Hall and the Barber Surgeons Hall.

9 The springs were found on the slopes of the Avon Gorge, some way downstream from the confluence with the River Frome. In 1692 the Society of Merchant Venturers, who had owned a share in the Manor of Clifton since 1676, leased the springs to two entrepreneurs, who built a pump room with accommodation for guests at the foot of the cliff in 1696 (demolished in 1816) at a cost of £50. St Vincent's Rock, a craggy escarpment slightly downstream from the Hot Wells House, was the site of the largest spring. Water with a temperature of 76°F (24°C) emerged at a rate of almost 60 gallons per minute. The chronicler William of Worcester described the rocks, spring and a chapel dedicated to Vincent in the late fifteenth century. The connection of the third-century martyr St Vincent of Saragossa with the locality is unknown, and the chapel may be mythical.

10 For a contemporary reaction, see Alexander Pope's letter to Martha Blount, 19 November 1739: 'Passing still along by the River you come to a Rocky way on one Side, overlooking green Hills on the other; On that rocky way rise several white Houses, and over them red rocks, and as you go further, more Rocks above rocks, mixd with green bushes, and of different colourd stone. This at a Mile's end, terminates in the House of the Hot well, whereabouts lye several pretty Lodging Houses open to the River with Walks of Trees. When you have seen the Hills seem to shut upon you & to stop any further way, you go into the House & looking out of the Back door, a vast Rock of 100 foot high, of red, white, green, blue & yellowish Marbles, all blotch'd & variegated strikes you quite in the face, & turning on the left, there opens the River at a vast depth below, winding in & out, & accompanied on both sides with a Continued Range of Rocks up to the Clouds, of a hundred Colours, one behind another, & so to the end of the Prospect quite to the Sea. But the Sea nor the Severn you do not see, the Rocks & River fill the Eye, and terminate the View, much like the broken Scenes behind one another in a Playhouse' (*The Correspondence of Alexander Pope*, ed. G. Sherburn, 5 vols (Oxford, 1956), 4: 201).

The Water of this *Well* possess'd its Medicinal Quality no doubt from its Original, which may be as Antient as the Deluge. But what is strangest of all is, that it was never known before; it is now famous for being a Specifick in that otherwise Incurable Disease the *Diabetes;* and yet was never known to be so, 'till within these few Years; namely, Thirty Years, or thereabout.[11]

There are in *Bristol* 21 Parish Churches, many Meeting-Houses, especially Quakers, one (very mean) Cathedral, the reason of which, may be, that it is but a very modern Bishoprick.[12] It is supposed they have an Hundred Thousand Inhabitants in the City, and within three Miles of its Circumference; and they say above three Thousand Sail of Ships belong to that Port, but of the last I am not certain.[13]

'Tis very remarkable, That this City is so plentifully supply'd with Coals, tho' they are all brought by Land Carriage, that yet they are generally bought by the Inhabitants, laid down at their Doors, after the Rate of from Seven to Nine Shillings *per Chaldron*.[14]

11 A claim elaborated by the miscellaneous writer John Shebbeare, then resident at Bristol, in *A New Analysis of the Bristol Waters; together with the Cause of Diabetes and Hectic, and their Cure, as it Results from those Waters* (London, 1740), 5–36, attributing the curative property to qualities of the limestone where the spring issued. Local legend credited the discovery to boatmen on the river, and assigned its popularity to 'the case of a man named Gagg, a broker, living in Castle Street in 1680, being afflicted with diabetes, although despaired of by all who knew him, dreaming that he drank of the Hotwell water, he followed the dictates of his vision and repaired thither, found it to relieve him, and finally became totally cured' (*Chilcott's Stranger's Guide to Bristol, Clifton, and the Hotwells* (Bristol, n.d.), 97). A more likely impetus for visitors came when Queen Catherine of Braganza made the trip from Bath in 1677. William Goldwin asserted that 'The sov'reign Virtues of the healing Flood / Check the salt Humours of scorbutick Blood' (*Poetical Description*, 20). By 1711 the Hotwells were listed in a guide called *A Natural History of the Mineral Waters of Great Britain.* It was not until 1775 that Matthew Dobson, Hester Thrale's Bath physician, identified sugar as the key component in the diagnosis of diabetes.

12 In the appendix to this volume of the *Tour*, Defoe revises the figure down to seventeen parishes and nineteen churches (2: 231), which is line with other counts. Celia Fiennes agreed on the number of churches. She also found that 'the Cathedrall . . . has nothing fine or curious in it' (Fiennes, 237). The cathedral is medieval in origin, but lost its nave when Henry VIII dissolved the abbey in 1539. The diocesan bishopric, which dates from 1542, was among the worst endowed in England, valued at £383, a tenth of that of Winchester.

13 A massive overestimate of the number of residents: with a population generally thought to be approaching 25,000 to 30,000, Bristol overtook Norwich as the second-largest town in England during the decade that Defoe was writing. Some modern estimates have revised the figure upwards, suggesting an increase from 27,000 in 1700 to one of 45,000 in 1720, but even with populous suburbs such as St Philip it could not have been close to 100,000. It is hard to quantify the number of vessels, large and small, belonging to the port. We know that 450 ships left Bristol in 1698–9, and the number steadily rose (Minchinton, 'Bristol – Metropolis', 298).

14 Apart from domestic use, coal was needed for glass-making, soap-boiling, brewing and other industries. During the seventeenth century speculators had invested in the Kingswood Chase mines, covering the former royal forest in parts of Easton, Stapleton and Mangotsfield. Local landowners leased out the mining rights to master colliers, who brought in a considerable force of casual labourers. By 1700 there were up to seventy small mines there. The miners were fiercely independent: in 1709 and 1714 they were accused of participation in the Bristol riots, and from 1727

The Situation of the City is low, but on the Side of a rising Hill. The Ground Plat of it is said very much to. resemble that of Old *Rome,* being Circular, with something greater Diameter one way than another, but not enough to make it Oval. And the River cutting off one small part, as it were, a Sixth, or less from the rest.[15]

The Bridge over the *Avon* is exceeding strong, the Arches very high, because of the Depth of Water, and the Buildings so close upon it, that in passing the Bridge, you see nothing but an entire well built Street.[16] The Tide of Flood rises here near 6 Fathom, and runs very sharp.

They draw all their heavy Goods here on *Sleds,* or *Sledges* without Wheels, which kills a Multitude of Horses; and the Pavement is worn so smooth by them, that in Wet-weather the Streets are very slippery, and in Frosty-weather 'tis dangerous walking.[17]

were involved in the destruction of turnpike gates, attacking the very innovation in road construction that Defoe greeted so warmly in his Appendix to the *Tour.* Goldwin referred to them as 'A tatter'd Brood of rough laborious Souls', who 'Thro' darksome Caves a Miner's Labour bear, / And Magazines of Coals from Nature's Bosom tear' (*Poetical Description*, 4). The extensive mining area known as the Bristol Coalfield did not emerge until the end of the eighteenth century; while transportation was inhibited by the fact that the Avon was not navigable as far as Bath until 1727 and the Frome not navigable by commercial vessels, despite a measure in 1700 (11 & 12 Wm III, c.23) designed to improve their waterways. From this time coal came increasingly from South Wales, primarily from Newport.

15 The portion south of the Avon, including Redcliffe (prior to the construction of the New Cut in 1804–9). The 'rising' ground refers to the elevated land north of the city centre, including St Michael's Hill, Brandon Hill and Kingsdown.

16 The stone bridge built in 1247 was lined with twenty-seven mostly Tudor houses with shopfronts, up to five stories in height, until its replacement in 1768. Alexander Pope's letter to Martha Blount gives a vivid picture of the city, corroborating much of the detail in the *Tour*: 'The River winding at the bottom of steeper banks to the Town where you see twenty odd Pyramids smoking over the Town (which are Glasshouses) and a vast Extent of Houses red & white. You come first to Old Walls, & over a Bridge built on both sides like London bridge, and as much crowded, with a strange mixture of Seamen, women, children, loaded Horses, Asses, & Sledges with Goods dragging along, all together, without posts to seperate them. From thence you come to a Key along the old Wall with houses on both sides, and in the middle of the street, as far as you can see, hundreds of Ships, their Masts as thick as they can stand by one another, which is the oddest & most surprising sight imaginable. This street is fuller of them, than the Thames from London Bridge to Deptford, & at certain times only, the Water rises to carry them out; so that at other times, a Long Street full of ships in the Middle & Houses on both sides looks like a Dream' (*Correspondence*, 4: 201).

17 Many streets and alleys were so narrow that coaches and carts could get wedged between the houses. As reported by Webb and Webb, 'Goods were therefore conveyed about the Town almost exclusively in trucks drawn by dogs, or, if horse-drawn, moving, not on wheels, but on long runners which smoothed even to a high polish the stones with which all the thoroughfares were paved.' The same authorities cite a number of sources, including the 1748 edition of the *Tour* (virtually unchanged from 1725) on this matter. They add: 'The fact that there were no carts to be seen "in their streets, but all sleds," was noticed by visitors in 1568 and [by Celia Fiennes] 1695 . . . By order of the Common Council of 1615, no cart having wheels bound with iron was allowed to enter the City . . . "No cart is suffered in the streets of Bristol for fear of damaging the pavement" (*Travels of Tom Thumb over England and Wales* (1736), p. 23) . . . The use of iron in these sledges was forbidden in 1705 (MS. Minutes, Corporation of Bristol, 12th December 1705). The employment of

Extract from the Appendix

The Appendix to Volume II is one of the most celebrated portions of the *Tour*, on account of its groundbreaking survey of the road system, above all the newly created turnpikes, described in the previous chapter. Before Defoe embarks on this section he provides an update on Bristol. This concludes with a short passage (omitted here) on St Mary Redcliffe, citing the monumental inscriptions for William Canynges and Sir William Penn, 'the Father of the great *William Penn*' (2: 233).

> On a more exact Enquiry into the particular State of the City of *Bristol*, I find it necessary to mention first, That there are but seventeen Parishes in the City, tho' there are nineteen Churches, including the Cathedral and the Church of St. *Mark*.[18] There are, besides those Churches, seven Meeting-Houses, two Presbyterian, one Independent, two Quakers, one Baptist; also one or two other meetings not to be nam'd.[19]
>
> As to the Exchange design'd to be built, and for which an Act of Parliament actually pass'd, *Ann.* 1723, it was at first intended to be built where the *Tolsey* now is;[20] but so many Buildings both publick and private (and one Church, namely *Christ Church*, at the Corner of *Vine-street*,

packhorses, and of sledges instead of wheeled vehicles, was not entirely abandoned at Bristol until the beginning of the nineteenth century.' See Webb and Webb, *Manor and Borough*, 2: 446–7; and Fiennes, 236.

18 St Mark's is the medieval church on College Green, formerly known as Gaunt's Chapel, and then from 1722 as the Lord Mayor's Chapel, and much frequented at this date by the Huguenot community.

19 It is estimated that among the residents of the city there were at this date about 4,000 dissenters in comparison to 2,000 Quakers. The meeting houses included a Presbyterian chapel in Tucker Street, of which the minster had been Strickland Gough senior (d. 1718), a strong Hanoverian loyalist and a former pastor at Lewin's Mead Chapel. The chapel in Tucker Street was a target for the high Church in the 1714 riot (see p. 298, note 27). In 1725 the minister was William Fisher (d. 1732). Lewin's Mead Chapel was founded on the site of the Franciscan Friary in 1693, and had a congregation of 1,600. Later in the century it became a fashionable Unitarian church. Its minister in 1725 was Samuel Bury (1663–1730). The Independents had met since the Cromwellian era at Castle Green; from 1689 their minister was Isaac Noble (1659–1727). The Quakers built a meeting house on the site of a Dominican Friary off Rosemary Street in 1670, rebuilt in 1747, which was said to hold the largest congregation in England. On the other side of the river was another one, erected on the west side of Temple Street in 1677. There were two Baptist chapels, one from 1671 in Broadmead (formerly occupied by the Friends) and from the 1650s one in the Pithay. The minister at Broadmead from 1707 to 1727 was an Irishman named Peter Ketterell, while Emanuel Gifford (1673–1724) had been pastor at the Pithay until shortly before his death. Information in this note is taken from numerous sources, but most pervasively from Kenneth Morgan, 'The John Evans List of Dissenting Congregations and Ministers in Bristol, 1715–1729,' in *Reformation and Revival in Eighteenth-Century Bristol*, ed. Jonathan Barry and Kenneth Morgan (Bristol, 1994), 63–73. The cryptic reference to meetings 'not to be nam'd' may be a characteristic way for Defoe to allude to the activities of the Jesuit mission in the city, now known to be extensive: see Kenneth Hankins, 'The Jesuits and the Rebirth of the Catholic Church in Bristol,' *British Catholic History*, 26 (2002): 102–31.

20 The private act is 8 Geo. I, c. 5, and its text can be found in the records of the House of Lords, HL/PO/PB/1/1721/8G1n20.

standing so near, as that they would crowd the Place too much, the first measures were chang'd, and now the intended Place is the Meal Market, between *Vine-street* and *St. Mary Port*, being on the north side of the Tolsey;[21] but the citizens do not seem so hasty to build, as they were to get the Act of Parliament pass'd to give them power to do it.

There are no less than fifteen Glass-Houses in *Bristol*, which is more than are in the city of *London*: They have indeed a very great Expence of Glass Bottles, by sending them fill'd with Beer, Cyder, and Wine to the *West Indies*, much more than goes from *London*; also great Numbers of Bottles, even such as is almost incredible, are now used for sending the Waters of St. *Vincent*'s Rock away, which are now carry'd, not all over *England* only, but, we may say, all over the world.[22]

The ground is now so rais'd in *Queen*'s Square, (that which was formerly call'd the *Mead*) that the highest Tide does not flow over it, and all the sides of the Square are now fully built and inhabited, except one House only.

Conclusion

This section in the *Tour* is the most frequently cited of all contemporary descriptions of Bristol in this era, as the city consolidated its power and mercantile influence. One reason for such a steady growth was the opportunity for more lucrative contracts for transporting slaves, after the ending of the monopoly of the African Company in 1698 and further deregulation by the expiry of the earlier act in 1712. Defoe knew all about that, as his major patron in the immediately preceding years was Dalby Thomas (*c.*1650–1711), a merchant, writer and official in the company, who was the dedicatee of *An Essay on Projects* in 1697. Defoe apparently held shares

[21] The Perpendicular building of Christ Church, on the corner of Broad Street and Wine (sic) Street, was demolished in 1786, as the fabric had become unsafe, and it was replaced by the present structure. It had been commandeered as a barracks by the parliamentarians in the Civil War and suffered considerable damage. The meal market, built in 1572 to protect meal and flour from inclement weather, lay on the north side of Wine Street; it had been used as a guard house in the Civil War. St Mary Port was an ancient church, possibly of Saxon origin, destroyed by bombing in the Bristol Blitz of 1940, although the fifteenth-century tower still stands. In reality the alternative site for the Exchange suggested in the *Tour* was not the one used.

[22] For the glass industry as 'the most important of Bristol's manufactures', see Minchinton, 'Bristol – Metropolis', 301. He quotes a directory of the city published in 1794 to illustrate the point, but the passage cited is mostly a paraphrase of what Defoe wrote almost seventy years earlier. These comments in the *Tour* receive a striking endorsement from the experience of one glassmaker in Temple Street, Humphrey Perrot: 'Receipted bills show that he was supplying customers in Bristol, Stourbridge, Market Drayton, Warwick, and throughout South Wales, Somerset, Devon and Cornwall; sales are also recorded . . . to a customer in Brunswick, New England. Some of the sales were of bottles filled with water from Hotwells.' See J. H. Bettey, 'A Bristol Glassworks c. 1730', in *A Bristol Miscellany*, ed. Patrick McGrath (Bristol, 1985), 15–20 (16).

in the Company himself, and defended its operations in *An Essay upon the Trade to Africa* (1711) and in commentaries written for his journal *The Review* in that year. Some regarded him as a hired publicist employed by his master Harley to defend the unpopular company.[15]

The account is far more personal and detailed than those in guides and travel books of the time: once again, the coverage in the second volume of Macky's *Journey* (1722) comes across as skimpy and lacking in precision – certainly by comparison with what the *Tour* provides (though Macky does agree on the meanness of the cathedral). His entry comprises not much more than 400 words, only a quarter of the size of the one that he supplies on Bath, whereas Defoe's coverage is slightly longer on Bristol than on its neighbour. This discrepancy tells us a good deal about the conflicting aims of the two writers: Macky emphasises the 'gay and serene' life of the pleasure resort, while Defoe supplements his account of these things with a fuller review of the thriving commercial life of Bristol.[16] Nor do other topographic works such as the roadbooks of the day supply much that Defoe drew on, although *A General Atlas* (1721), with maps by John Senex, may have given a very few pointers (it mentions the sledges briefly). That he valued this section is indicated by the fact that the entry for Bristol is reprinted almost verbatim, the longest such sustained word-for-word borrowing, in *Atlas Maritimus & Commercialis* (1728). As described in the next chapter, the treatment of Britain in this compilation is almost entirely a rehash of the *Tour,* probably carried out by Defoe himself.[17]

In several ways he was uniquely qualified for the task in hand. He may or may not have spent time in Bristol since his visit in 1705, but he had retained enough of what his well-placed informants told him to have a solid understanding of civic affairs. For the most part his entry is admirably up to date, and where he had missed a very recent development the Appendix filled the gap. His varied experience of life came in useful in odd places. To take one example, his remarks on the glass industry benefit from the time he had spent from 1695 to 1699 as accountant to the commissioners to administer the tax on glassware plus earthenware and stone bottles (7 Wm III, c. 18), where his boss was Dalby Thomas, and from his careful observation of the 'Bottle-house' at Leith, when he and his brother-in-law were active in the commerce of that town (3: 163). Another significant fact in relation to his comments on the price of coal is that he had long taken a special interest in the coal trade, notably the 'poor Keelmen' of Newcastle, whom he defended in the *Review* on 1 July 1710, and mentions in the *Tour* (3: 118). He opposed the imposition of the

London coal duty in 1694, and argued that prices were kept artificially high through the activities of middle men.[18]

Above all, he had a firm grasp of the ways in which Bristol contributed to the national economy. This owed much to his wide knowledge of the mechanisms of inland and overseas trade, acquired over a lifetime. He took into account not just the processes of manufacturing and selling, but also the supply chain, the local resources, and the conditions affecting the market in a given region. We have abundant evidence in the *Tour* of his almost unparalleled comprehension of the transport infrastructure of Britain, which would serve as an enabling factor for its take-off towards the first industrial nation in following decades. (Abraham Darby and his family were, of course, among the prime instigators.) It is amazing to find how far-seeing, and equally how accurate, Defoe was, bearing in mind the tools of research available today that he totally lacked.

CHAPTER 12

Atlas Maritimus

The Case for Defoe's Authorship

These days we cannot even agree whether Defoe wrote *Moll Flanders*, so it is not surprising that a number of less celebrated books assigned to him remain in limbo. A large segment of the deattributions made by P. N. Furbank and W. R. Owens seem to have been silently accepted by most of the scholarly community.[1] One can accept the need for a rigorous approach to the items that are still open to serious debate, as Ashley Marshall has eloquently argued.[2] However, some of the sceptical arguments against Defoe's authorship of a given work have neglected external evidence in the shape of his known presence or activities which match information in sources such as the *Review*, the letters or indeed the *Tour*. Such is the case, I believe, in one particular instance to be assessed here.

Prominent among the dubia is a large, ambitious and comprehensive survey of the coasts, ports and harbours of the world entitled *Atlas Maritimus & Commercialis*, running to more than 600 elephant folio pages in two columns. The original aim of the volume (henceforth *AMC*) was to promote a new globular projection for maps as an aid to navigation, for which a small group of entrepreneurial figures had obtained a royal warrant in 1721. Among the undertakers of the scheme were the cartographer John Senex and the bookseller William Taylor. Others involved were the mathematician Henry Wilson and the engraver John Harris.[3] In their *Critical Bibliography* of Defoe, Furbank and Owens were unable to reach a firm conclusion on the question of authorship.

The work carries a prefatory section 'To the Reader', recommending the charts provided since they employ a projection 'which in this *Atlas* is very different from any that has hitherto appeared' (*AMC* i). The author of this preface was none other than Edmond Halley, best known today as an astronomer, but also a student of navigation, member of the Board of Longitude and hydrographer who had carried out marine surveys on his Atlantic cruises.[4] Halley supported the venture from the outset, and his endorsement was mentioned on the title-page ('The Use of the Projection

Justified by Dr. HALLEY'). The coverage begins with Europe, and first of all with Great Britain. Then come in turn Asia, Africa and America. A second portion of the volume, with a separate title-page and pagination, is devoted to *A General Coasting Pilot; Containing Directions for Sailing*, by Nathaniel Cutler. The *Coasting Pilot* is a largely irrelevant to the present enquiry: its method of proceeding is different, and the ascription to Cutler has gone unchallenged. We now have a clearer idea of how *AMC* evolved between its inception in 1719 and its eventual appearance in print nine years later. This enables us to gain a clearer sense of what was required from the compiler, as the emphasis of the project moved beyond the new system of projection to a broad survey of world trade.[5]

It has often been suggested, but never conclusively demonstrated, that a principal role in this work was that of Daniel Defoe. In this chapter we shall be exploring a portion of multifarious evidence that supports Defoe's involvement, since this has never been properly assembled. I shall first consider previous scholarly discussions of the authorship. Most of what follows will be devoted to the opening segment of *AMC*, in order to show that the coverage of the British coastline is based almost entirely on Defoe's *Tour*. There is not room here to explore in detail later sections of the book, even though it can easily be demonstrated that these repeat material found in other books Defoe wrote at this period, notably *The Complete English Tradesman*, *A General History of Discoveries and Improvements* and *A Plan of the English Commerce* – not to mention further echoes of the *Tour*. More widely, it will emerge that the attitudes of the compiler throughout *AMC* match those of the books and journalism of Defoe, stretching back as much as thirty years prior to its publication.

Previous Discussions

Until John Robert Moore claimed the work for Defoe in 1956 and included it in his *Checklist* in 1960, no one appears to have suspected Defoe's hand. Moore asserted that 'the preface and the main body of the letter-press (340 folio pages in double column, running to about 600,000 words) are obviously written by Defoe – when not compiled by him or under his direction'.[6] Although Moore's observations about the contents of *AMC* are largely accurate, his argument is perfunctory and neglects to follow up on some of the most significant clues. He begins by noting that in a tract published in 1729 Defoe 'referred seven times to a recent book which he knew intimately and admired very much', namely *AMC*. Here we are close to the notorious chain of assumptions rightly stigmatised by Furbank and

Owens, since the pamphlet in question, *The Advantages of Peace and Commerce*, is given only a provisional entry by these scholars in the *Critical Bibliography* (1998).[7]

Moore devoted to *AMC* just the last two of fourteen pages of his article, and much of this was taken up with 'previously unknown sources for two of his principal narratives', i.e. passages in *AMC* that prefigure scenes in Defoe's fiction. One concerned the discovery of Bermuda, pointing towards *Robinson Crusoe*, and the other an episode near the coast of West Africa which anticipates a similar story in *Captain Singleton*. For the rest, Moore's comparisons are unspecific, referring to 'many scores, probably hundreds, of ideas which Defoe presented earlier or later' in a number of places. For once, Moore understated his case with regard to the prime exhibit he could have called on. A single sentence is all he offers: 'Here we have the editor borrowing whole passages from Defoe's *Tour*, and putting scattered fragments together in a way possible only to one who knew the materials of the *Tour* intimately.' No one has explored the overwhelming bulk of evidence which supports this statement.

Unsurprisingly, the destabilisation of the canon which has occurred in recent years has cast doubt on Moore's statement describing the entire text as 'obviously written by Defoe', and made such claims appear unduly confident. However, as noted, Furbank and Owens felt obliged to list *AMC* among the 'Unresolved Problems in Attribution' appended to their bibliography. Admitting that there were facts 'which might seem to support Moore', they set out grounds for linking Defoe with the authorship of the volume:

> There are extensive borrowings from Defoe's *Tour* (also from *A General History of Discoveries and Improvements* (1725–6), though this is only a 'probable' attribution to Defoe); and though the work, as the preface makes clear, is avowedly a compilation from many different sources, it is noticeable that, whereas extracts from Tournefort, Ralegh, Henry Maundrel, Dellon and Magaillon, etc. are indicated as being quotations (and are assigned to their author), there is no such indication in the case of Defoe.

This is well reported, as far as it goes. However, it leaves out of account many parallels with other books acknowledged to be the work of Defoe, and its reference to 'extensive borrowings' from the *Tour* is misleading – this suggests the debt is casual and intermittent, rather than virtually omnipresent and *systemic* in the opening section. As for the borrowings from *Discoveries and Improvements*, one that has gone unremarked involves a characteristically sly allusion in *AMC* (241): '*Hanno*, whom a certain Author calls the *Raleigh* of *England*, as on another Account he calls Sir *Walter Raleigh* the *Hanno* of *England*' (241). The certain author was the one who coined these descriptions in *Discoveries and Improvements* (106, 125). Furbank and Owens also noted the parallels with Defoe's fiction that Moore had spotted. In their conclusion they maintained a studied neutrality: 'It seems probable that Defoe had some connection with the *Atlas Maritimus*, but to suppose him the main author and compiler of this enormous and expert work seems implausible. There is a problem here which we cannot claim to have solved.'

In this connection Ashley Marshall has commented, 'Furbank and Owens point out that "Several passages from the *Tour* are reproduced without acknowledgment in ... *Atlas Maritimus* (1728)" ... an illustration of the fact that the appearance of passages from a "Defoe" work does not constitute solid evidence for an item's authorship.' This is a statement with which I concur, *verbatim et literatim*. It does not however cover the reality we encounter in *AMC*. Here we have not just the reproduction of passages from Defoe's works, something that occurs throughout the text. We need to look especially at two key segments under this aspect, the opening chapter (not so designated, but that's what it is), *AMC* 1–20, and the later 'Account of the Trade of Great Britain', *AMC* 100–113. Both are largely taken straight from the *Tour*. The former portion of the volume is entirely dependent on this source, with no more than tiny additions. Moreover, the text is presented word for word only in a few instances. More often, as we shall see in detail as this chapter proceeds, the precise words of the *Tour* are cleverly reworked by way of alternative phrasing, metaphrase, paraphrase or précis. It is one thing to reserve judgement when book B reprints isolated fragments of a work known to be Defoe, book A. It is quite different when B proves to be no more than a recension of A over long stretches of its text.

Two further considerations are relevant at this point, documented elsewhere in this chapter. First, *AMC* repeatedly draws on other works from the same period related to trade that are generally accepted as by Defoe (no contrary case has ever been mounted, and they meet some of the criteria Marshall proposes in terms of early attribution). Second, *AMC* uses the same passages from sources, especially in the literature of travel and exploration, that Defoe employed elsewhere and, even more telling, that were in some cases present in his own library. In other words, we are talking about something more than casual 'reproduction' of a few easily found quotes from Defoe. If for heuristic purposes we invent a putative editor with the text of the *Tour* in front of him or her, such a convenient fiction requires that several other items in the canon are also available for minute inspection, and that the job is carried out with such assiduity that the compiler is able to skip hundreds of pages in the three volumes of the *Tour* to insert an apposite sentence from the coverage of a totally different part of Britain. It is not a convincing theory.[8]

The Case of Bristol

Few scholarly articles have been devoted to *AMC*.[9] In one of these, dating from 1993, Jeffrey Hopes allots considerable space to the treatment of Bristol, which, as we have seen in Chapter 11, represents a key segment in the *Tour*. Hopes goes a good deal further than Furbank and Owens when he accuses Moore of reading the text from a single perspective, designed to establish Defoe's authorship.[10] Admittedly, Hopes does acknowledge the possibility that Defoe took some part in creating the book, but stresses the absence of clear proof. He cites a prefatory admission by the editor that 'The Work is a Collection; it could not possibly be otherwise . . . The Compiling is ours' (*AMC* i) and criticises Moore for claiming the entire work for Defoe, 'malgré cette declaration on ne peut plus claire' (despite this statement, which could hardly be clearer). Notwithstanding the use of a conventional first person plural by the narrator, the preface merely states that the volume has been put together from existing sources, not that a team of compilers has been employed on the task. In any case the writer soon moves into the singular. He refers to his own procedures (as, 'I have study'd Impartiality thro' the Whole'), and then asserts, 'The Author has indeed seen several of the Countries, Coasts, Cities, and Sea-Ports which he has describ'd' (iii), which could be a valid claim in Defoe's case. But he makes no pretence of first-hand observation everywhere, acknowledging his distance from remote places in remarks such as 'The great Square here [at Lima] is the noblest I have ever heard of' (320).

Hopes goes on to ask, 'Qui étaient donc les auteurs de l'*Atlas*?' (who, then, were the authors of the *Atlas*?) After listing those who were behind the new system of projection, he considers only one possible candidate for this role. Just as Moore had done, he notes a few parallels with what Defoe wrote elsewhere, mostly broad similarities in ideas and concerns, but he seems inclined to minimise these. Wishing to locate correspondences with other works in the canon, he observes that 'Une occasion nous est fournie par la description des villes côtières britanniques' (we are given an opportunity by the description of British coastal towns), since these passages can be compared to those found in the *Tour*. It is a pity that the analysis of the issues which follows has serious defects, suggesting that Hopes read the text with inattention along with a resolve to throw doubt on Moore's claims. This discussion ignores most of the relevant evidence to be found in the text.

Hope's account begins with misstatements about the coverage of some large cities:

> Pour certaines (par exemple Liverpool) il n'y a aucune ressemblance. Pour d'autres (Glasgow) nous retrouvons certaines formulations du *Tour*. Ce n'est que dans la description de Bristol que nous avons sensiblement le même texte, mais avec des variations qui sont significatives. D'abord la typographie et la ponctuation diffèrent, le texte de l'*Atlas* étant plus soigné. Puis l'*Atlas* corrige parfois le texte du *Tour*; le nom de la bourse de commerce de Bristol, donné comme 'Tolsey' dans le *Tour*, est corrigé en 'Tholsel' dans l'*Atlas*, qui fournit aussi une étymologie du mot. Enfin l'*Atlas* représente une mise à jour du *Tour*.
>
> (In the case of some cities, for example Liverpool, there is no resemblance. With others, such as Glasgow, we recognise certain wording from the *Tour*. It is only in the description of Bristol that we have more or less the same text, but with significant variations. In the first place, there is a difference in typography and punctuation, with a more careful text in the *Atlas*. Furthermore, the *Atlas* sometimes corrects the text of the *Tour*; the name of the Exchange in Bristol, which the *Tour* gives as 'Tolsey', is corrected to 'Tholsel' in the *Atlas*, which also serves to provide an etymology of this word. Lastly, the *Atlas* supplies an update of the *Tour*.)

Actually, the section on Liverpool, though it contains more fresh information than most of the entries, does echo the phrasing of the *Tour* at several points (compare for instance the description of the wet dock, *AMC* 17, *Tour* 2: 189). In the case of Glasgow, there is far more than the seemingly casual repetition of 'certaines formulations': for example, the opening paragraph on the bridge as it was recently endangered by a severe flood simply compresses the earlier account (*AMC* 17, *Tour* 3: 189). The paragraph beginning '*Glasgow* is a City of Business' (*AMC* 17–18) condenses the one in *Tour* (1: 200) that starts with the same words. Comments on the cathedral and the university fix on identical details and more than once employ identical words.

As for Bristol, Hopes is correct in observing the total dependence of this long entry in *AMC* (14–15) on the one in *Tour* (2: 157–9), which was the subject of the previous chapter. However, to put it that way conceals the fact that this account of the city is largely made up of fifteen successive paragraphs taken bodily from the source (*AMC* 14–15, *Tour* 2:157–9). There are tiny changes in accidentals and particles, but otherwise the reproduction is verbatim. Only two remotely substantive additions, noted by Hopes, are found, first where *AMC* changes 'in these last Thirty Years since the Revolution' to 'these last 30 or 40 Years'; and second where the compiler adds a short phrase referring to an act of parliament obtained by the merchants of the city to build a new exchange. This bill had received the royal assent in February 1722, but in the appendix to Volume II (2: 231) Defoe notes its passage in 1723, remarking as *AMC* does on the lack of progress on the scheme – the edifice would not be built until after his death.

Hopes ends by saying, 'Tout indique donc que pour ces paragraphes sur Bristol l'*Atlas* reprend, corrige et actualise le texte du Tour, ce qui ne prouve pas que cette révision soit de la main de Defoe. À présent tout ce que nous pouvons affirmer, c'est que l'*Atlas* est une œuvre de collaboration et de compilation, et que, si la participation directe ou indirecte de Defoe est possible, voire probable, sa nature et son étendue restent incertaines.' (Everything then indicates that in these paragraphs on Bristol the *Atlas* picks up again on the text of the *Tour*, while correcting it and bringing it up to date, which does not prove that it came from the hand of Defoe. All we can assert at the moment is that the *Atlas* is a collaborative compilation, and that if Defoe's direct or indirect participation is possible, or even likely, its essential nature and scope remain in doubt). As a result, Hopes asserts, 'L'identité des auteurs reste floue' (the identity of the authors remains hazy). This would appear a sound conclusion, based on the materials that have been cited. However, the judgement has been reached without any examination of the main core of the British section in *AMC*. Scores of entries, many dealing with smaller towns and coastal features such as harbours, have been left out of account.

Meanwhile the community of Defoe scholars remains divided. The best short statement of the genesis of *AMC* remains that of Paula Backscheider in her biography, even though this was published in 1989, prior to the date at which Furbank and Owens directed their sceptical assault on the increasingly fragile canon established by Moore. Backscheider describes *AMC* as 'surely one of [Defoe's] profitable undertakings', and sets the work comfortably among his enterprises in the mid-to-late 1720s.[11] But as late as 2001 Maximillian E. Novak asserted with confidence that Defoe 'was chosen to write the commentary' on 'the places of the earth and their products' for *AMC*, and to see the section on British trade as 'more or less, an encomiastic reworking of what he had said in his *Plan of the English Commerce* [also 1728]'.[12] This last comment is entirely accurate, although it overlooks the fact that many echoes of the *Tour* are also to be found in the section to which Novak alludes (*AMC* 100–113). One case in point is the description of Halifax (109), where the compiler cribs all of his facts from *Tour* (3: 67), but characteristically alters a small detail, 'There are in it twelve or thirteen Chapels of Ease, besides about sixteen Meeting-Houses' to 'within which Parish there are reckon'd 15 or 16 Chapels of Ease, besides at least as many Meeting-Houses'.[13]

One exceedingly obvious clue in the section on British commerce seems to have gone unobserved. In his assessment of fisheries, the compiler of *AMC* turns to the trade in mackerel:

> One Year I was Eye-witness to their being sold 100 for a Penny on the Coast of *Dorset* and *Devonshire*, particularly at the Towns of *Abbot-Bury, Bridport*, and other Places on the *Dorsetshire* Coast; where the Magistrates placed Guards, or Watch and Ward, on the Sea Coast, to prevent the Farmers buying *Mackarel* of the Fishermen to dung the Land with, which the Justices of the Peace thought might endanger the Health of the Country, and cause an Infection. It is to be observed also in these particular Cases, that the Fish are always the largest, fattest and best tasted. (104)

Compare this to the source passage in the *Tour*, where Defoe is concerned with the area around Bridport and Abbotsbury:

> As soon as the Boats had brought their Fish on Shore, we observed a Guard, or Watch, placed on the Shore in several Places, who we found had the Eye not on the Fishermen, but on the Country People, who came down to the Shore to buy their Fish; and very sharp we found they were; and some that came with small Carts were obliged to go back empty, without any Fish. When we came to enquire into the Particulars of this, we found, that these were Officers placed on the Shore by the Justices and Magistrates of the Towns about, who were order'd to prevent the Country Farmers buying the Mackerell to dung their Land with them, which was thought to be dangerous, as to Infection: In short, such was the Plenty of Fish that year, at the Mackerell, the finest and largest I ever saw, were sold at the Sea side a Hundred for a Penny. (1: 245–6)

Plainly *AMC* furnishes nothing more than a paraphrase of the earlier account – quite close, but with minor tactical substitutions. This is what happens consistently, page after page, right the way through the British entries at the start of the volume. Especially noteworthy is the manner in which the compiler insinuates himself into the first-hand observation of the original narrator.

By an amazing stroke of fortune, the compiler also shared another experience of Defoe further along the south coast when he witnessed fishing for pilchards. He reports, 'I once saw a whole School or Shoal of them come driving with the Flood-Tide into the Haven of *Dartmouth*' through the narrow entrance to the harbour (104). He adds that they 'swim so near the Surface, that they are discern'd by the rippling of the Water at a great distance'. In the *Tour* the narrator describes how he went out to the harbour at Dartmouth as the tide came in, and watched the fish 'skip, and play upon the Surface of the Water' (1: 257). We could accept the fact that the industrious compiler had purloined his data from Defoe, since the material conforms so closely with the *Tour*'s account for several paragraphs. But is it plausible to imagine that he could have extemporised so freely on a particular episode in a particular place?

Despite the presence of such clues elsewhere, the portion of the work at the start of *AMC* dealing with the coast of Great Britain is the place where we can locate the most significant pointers to its possible authorship. The following parts of this chapter will offer close examination of the text in this segment.

Internal Evidence

The compiler of *AMC* almost gives the game away when he accomplishes his circumnavigation of the coastline at the Pentland Firth: 'And thus I have made the Circuit of the Whole Isle of *Britain*' (18). It would be hard for an alert reader in 1728 not to catch the echo of *A Tour thro' the Whole Island of Great Britain, Divided into Circuits or Journeys*, a title whose completed text had come before the public less than two years earlier. The very first paragraph of the *Tour* explains the writer's use of 'Circuits' as a key to his method (1: 51). Previous travel writers had not generally used this term in relation to the progress of their narrative. John Macky employs the word just twice in a casual manner throughout his *Journeys* (1714–23): but Defoe twenty-three times in the *Tour*, most often in a passage describing the rhetorical scheme of his supposed journeys. This concluding gesture by the compiler gives readers a further nudge: if they not already realised it, the entire basis of the text in *AMC* is a close paraphrase of the relevant entries in the *Tour*. Defoe's work is not in any ordinary sense a source: it is a palimpsest, whose traces are detectable in almost every paragraph of the British segment in the volume.

A key word in the title is '*Commercialis*'. None of the promoters of the atlas had any special interest or expertise in matters of trade or commerce. Their concerns lay with cartography, navigation, nautical affairs, mathematics (especially as regards the geometrical issues involved in constructing systems of projection), engraving and book production. They had no record as a commentator on matters relating to trade. It hardly needs stressing that this was the central theme of Defoe's writing as well as a key component of his career in the outside world. Well over a decade before, he had put out what he called *A General History of Trade* in four instalments (1713).[14] This was rather a survey of Britain's commerce, domestic and especially international, and the first issue contained a section on navigation, which dwelt on coastal features such as harbours and piers – almost all of them covered by *AMC* in the entries for the respective port. There the compiler is particularly well informed on the provision of keys and warehouses at Leith (6), as the author of the *Tour* had been (3: 176). This is readily explicable: not only had Defoe himself become familiar with the dockland area while living in Edinburgh, but, as mentioned previously, his brother-in-law Robert Davis had also set up a shipbuilding operation there. It was this same man who travelled with Defoe on occasions, who was his partner in an enterprise on the Thames estuary, and helped to bail him out of prison. While at Leith, Davis even tried to sell Robert Harley a diving bell that he had demonstrated off the coast of the Lizard Point in Cornwall, where he sang the hundredth Psalm under water.[15]

Such an area of specialisation had come to a head with a series of books that Defoe wrote in the 1720s, enumerated in the Introduction, pp. 9–10. But the bent of the author's mind in this direction is clearly visible in the *Tour*, varied as its portrayal of the nation may be. His intelligence-gathering trips for Robert Harley in the early part of the century were described by J. H. Andrews, himself a distinguished historical cartographer, as 'field research in political geography', while the pages of the *Review* 'provide something like a serial economic geography of England'.[16] In the same light we can describe the *Tour* as a survey of the economic life of Britain, scattered through a wider topographic description that incorporates social, political, historical, demographic, architectural, antiquarian and folkloric content, along with much anecdotal material.

'We must speak like a Geographer and Historian, when we are giving the Geographical and Historical Description of Places,' the preface to *AMC* tells us. Further, 'We must use the Terms of Art that have obtain'd among Merchants and Tradesmen, when we are treating of Commerce' (ii). Few contemporaries were so well qualified as Defoe in this regard, as he had devoted much of his career to bringing the subjects mentioned into collision with one another. After all, he had engaged in several branches of business – as a wholesale hosier, a shipowner, an exporter, a tobacco importer, an investor in diving bells (Halley held a patent for this device), a projector, a linen merchant in Edinburgh and very much more. Even a brick and tile factory on which he spent so much time and money stood near the banks of the Thames. He married the daughter of a prosperous tradesman who acquired extensive property around London: one of his sons became a merchant in Cornhill, to whom the father assigned his agricultural estate in Essex. On his trips for Robert Harley he had established a distribution network involving several merchants: the largest number of political tracts sent out by this means would go to Plymouth, Exeter, Bristol, Newcastle and Norwich – this could explain why Exeter and Norwich, not coastal towns and in any case ports of secondary importance, get full treatment in *AMC* to rival that of the major centres of the shipping industry.[17] In fact, the entire area of maritime and commercial life had been Defoe's bailiwick for decades. We recall that in his 'farther adventures' Robinson Crusoe learnt enough about the commercial routes of trans-Siberia, through little known posts such as Tobolski or Astrakhan, almost to have written the section on the trade of Muscovy with Europe and Asia in *AMC* (127–32).

We can now understand why an unexpected delay occurred between the completion of the maps by July 1724 and the appearance of the work almost four years later. The promoters of the scheme, with all their varied attributes, were in no position to compile the massive survey of the coasts of the world that the composition of *AMC* required. Nor did they possess the detailed acquaintance with hundreds of localities that could only be assembled by long acquaintance with a wide range of sources. Initially, they had aimed to demonstrate their new method of projection. What they now lacked was a compiler able to carry out the hard literary slog of producing the accompanying text. Such an individual seems to have appeared around 1725 to 1727, that is the time at which the author of the *Tour* brought his undertaking to a conclusion in August 1726.

Comparison of Texts

The man who was chiefly responsible for the text of *AMC* (he refers to himself in the third person as male) possessed some marked characteristics which fitted him for the role. In its way his work, for the British section especially, is as distinguishable as that of the noted Compositor B who helped to print Shakespeare's First Folio. To give him a notional identity separate from Defoe, I will call him Compiler X. His skills lie in a variety of methods used to rehash an earlier text, specifically here the *Tour*. They include (1) straightforward verbatim repetition; (2) a form of metaphrase which reproduces intact many features of the original (key expressions, word order, syntax and so on), but introduces small changes, many of them concerning relatively inessential aspects of the passage; (3) a looser paraphrase, in which important details are taken over from the host text, generally with the use of identical words, but with more effort to conceal the act of borrowing, e.g. by interpolating additional phrases, or altering the order of elements in a passage; (4) a more oblique manner of précis, which takes significant items from the original but states them differently or surrounds them with added content. The first of these methods is the simplest to document. The last calls for less comment, as it has limited value in any effort to assign authorship (although it provides useful supporting evidence in some cases). In the case of metaphrase, paraphrase and précis, a central objective was naturally to curtail the length of the original.

Over the course of twenty densely packed pages allocated to Britain, *AMC* provides entries for more than a hundred locations. This count includes cities, towns, villages, rivers, harbours, bays, small islands and stretches of country such as Romney Marsh. It omits passing references in lists where no description is given, for example when the principal towns on the banks of the Thames are set out in tabular form (18). Some of these places had been more fully described in the *Tour*. The passage mentioned here occurs in a final resumptive section on 'The Course of the River Thames', which contains a slightly higher proportion of new material than is found in the preceding itinerary. Out of the entries as a whole, at least seventy embody the types of borrowing enumerated above. Many entries are padded out, but there are very few completely new entries. The most notable exception is the treatment of Sunderland (4), where three paragraphs have no equivalent in the *Tour*. The narrator goes on to provide fresh information on South Shields, though Defoe had briefly mentioned the salt pans there, and slightly augments the coverage of Newcastle, even if most of the entry is dependent on his habitual source (*AMC* 5–6; *Tour* 3: 117–19). No obvious reason exists why Compiler X should be so far in advance of Defoe in this limited area. It is possible that Defoe simply omitted by inadvertence the material he had collected on Sunderland.

A more betraying instance occurs in Leith. The compiler manages to add many details about the port of Leith, including the appearance of houses on the quay, and the erection of a glass-house and a sugar-baking house 'or as *the Scots* call it, a *Sugaree*' (*AMC* 16). Few English men or women had been anywhere near Edinburgh, let alone Leith. We can look at what Defoe says about Leith in *Tour* (176–7) and place it alongside what Compiler X writes on the port (6). As already indicated, there is a high degree of overlap in these accounts. We may then ask, did any other traceable author of this precise era have intimate connections with Leith, for example by living there; working there; starting businesses there of the sort mentioned in the text; having a close family member engage in trade there; writing a careful analysis of a project to improve the docks there (as Defoe did to Harley in 1710); giving an account of a riot fomented by seamen from the town (as Defoe did in his *History of the Union*); printing a narrative of a Jacobite demonstration on the pier (as Defoe did in the *Review*); describing the fortification of the port by Mary of Guise (as Defoe did in *Memoirs of the Church of Scotland*); having a fictional hero take up work there (as Colonel Jacque does); referring to the Leith glassworks, as in *The Complete English Tradesman* (2.i.63); and more generally, displaying a keen interest in seaports in a variety of books about trade; or otherwise showing particular intimacy with the doings of the town? When the answer in each instance turns out negative, we may reasonably ask at what point the evidence can be said to converge, pointing away from any alternative candidates and towards Defoe. How lucky were Taylor and his colleagues if they found a compiler readily available who possessed just one of these qualifications!

The other major additions occur in passages on offshore islands: *AMC* is fuller on the Shetlands and Orkneys, which also crop up with some self-repetition in a later portion of the text entitled 'A Description of the Coasts of the Northern Islands' (49–50). The section here on the Orkneys seems to supplement the description in Camden, the basic source as so often, with James Wallace's *Account of the Islands of Orkney* (1700), a book which appears in Defoe's library catalogue.[18] *AMC* is marginally stronger, though still hazy, on the Hebrides, and much better in its coverage of the Isles of Wight and Man, where Defoe had made no sort of effort. The passages just mentioned are the only substantive cases in the section on Britain where Compiler X has a clear advantage in all respects over his predecessor.[19]

Against this, there are a number of locations in which the *Tour* is thorough and comprehensive, where *AMC* is sketchy or non-existent. It takes fierce abridgement to contract the loquacious and digressive six pages on St Andrews in the source (3: 240–46) to half a column in the revisal (7), though every single item of information is taken from what Defoe had written. Typically Compiler X shifts one or two phrases to cover his tracks, moving the phrase 'looking into its Grave' (3: 242) from St Salvator's College to the cathedral, but retaining the surrounding details on each site. This is a typical pattern: the entry for Plymouth (13) deguts the one provided by the source text (1: 257, 259–90), while preserving many of the precise phrases found there. The *Tour* supplies superior coverage on a number of ports, such as the group of Minehead, Porlock and Watchet (2: 21–2), where *AMC* resorts to some brisk paraphrase of what Defoe observed at these towns. For that matter the coverage is skimpy on towns along the Kent coast, though the few things that are said about Milton and Faversham (20) come largely from *Tour* (1: 150–52). Further on Compiler X (11) omits Brighton, evidently sharing Defoe's opinion that it was merely 'a Poor fishing Town' (1: 167).

In the same way, a long stretch of the coastline in Galloway and Carrick is passed over with the comment, 'There is nothing to be seen here worth naming' (17), while the *Tour* used a description of this region to comment at length on its backward economic life (3: 189–96). Several coastal towns are left aside by the compiler, beginning on the first page with Aldeburgh (simply named in a list without any detail) and Orford, completely ignored, whereas the *Tour* treats both in brief paragraphs. Between Berwick and Leith *AMC* skips over many small places on the Firth of Forth, notably Dunbar and Musselburgh, while the *Tour* allots several pages to the ports along this stretch of the coast, with particular emphasis on their trading activities.[20] Apparently the need for brevity obliged Compiler X to curtail his material where the ports covered by his source held little trading importance. Consequently, he resorted to a mere listing of Cornish towns such as East Looe and Fowey, despite their 'very good Harbours' (13). By contrast Defoe had enjoyed the leisure to expatiate on these places (*Tour* 1: 263–6).

Perhaps the most striking single departure in *AMC* is the decision to omit Ipswich, presumably on the grounds that it lies several miles up the Orwell estuary. Defoe had spent five pages on this locality, emphasising its role as a port where ships of a considerable burthen could 'come up very near this Town', describing the large ships build there that he had seen launched, and expatiating on the role of Ipswich as regards international trade and maritime matters generally (1: 78–92). Again Compiler X may have felt constrained by the very small amount of space he had at his disposal in the opening section, compared with the much fuller scope of the *Tour*.

Direct repetition of the source is much more pervasive in the opening section of *AMC* than we would suppose from previous discussions. The longest unbroken segment of the text copied verbatim from the *Tour* occurs in the Bristol entry already discussed, forming a section of 1,150 words interrupted only by a very few tiny adjustments of phrasing. But an equal measure of dependence is visible in other places. The entry for Aberdeen (7–8) is entirely drawn from *Tour* (3: 258–62), with slight linkage provided: otherwise the text consists of portions of Defoe's prose, unaltered except in its omission of details about the cathedral and the colleges. These cuts amount to little more than 350 words out of 1,650 in total. The new rendition follows Defoe's itemised scheme minutely. Such examples of prolonged word-for-word transcription from the *Tour* are largely confined to the longer entries on considerable towns. They appear to represent a labour-saving device, unnecessary in short entries where Compiler X was happy to engage in close paraphrase with small alterations in wording, possibly designed to conceal the origin of his material.

Metaphrase is frequent throughout the text of *AMC*. Two characteristic examples will serve to illustrate the technique in a short space. Here is what the compiler says about the docks at Portsmouth (11):

> As to the Strength of the Town by Land, there is a large Horn-work on the S. side, running out towards *South Sea-Castle*: there is also a very good Counterscarp, a double Mote and Ravelins to cover the Curtains; besides several advanc'd Works in every Place where it is requisite, and double Pallisadoes round the whole Place.
>
> The Dock and Yards which are to the N. of the Town, were before secur'd by the Strength of the Harbour, and by the Town: But the late King *William*, not satisfy'd with that Cover, order'd them to be particularly fortify'd, and new Lines and Bastions drawn round the whole Place: Which Works are now perfected, and the Dock and Yard is now a particular Strength distinct from the Town; and they cover and strengthen one another so, that the Dock and Yards cannot be attack'd till the Town is taken.

This description of 148 words circles round the precise expressions that are found in Defoe's equivalent passage of 146 words:

> As to the Strength of the Town by Land, the Works are very large and numerous, and besides the Battery at the Point aforesaid, there is a large Hornwork on the South-side, running out towards *South-Sea Castle*; there is also a good Counterscarp, and double Mote, with Ravelins in the Ditch, and double Pallisadoes, and advanc'd Works to cover the Place from any approach, where it may be practicable: The Strength of the Town is also considerably augmented on the Land side, by the Fortifications raised in King *William*'s Time about the Docks and Yards, which are now perfected, and those parts made a particular Strength by themselves; and tho' they are indeed in some sense independent one of another, yet they cover and strengthen one another, so as that they cannot be separately attack'd on that side, while they are both in the same Hands.

Leaving aside small cosmetic changes, such as omitting 'in the Ditch', the new version follows its source in minutely similar detail. It is a technique found in dozens of places throughout *AMC*, in every sort of geographical location. We cannot regard this as paraphrase in the ordinary sense: it is too heavily dependent on the exact ordering of the material and the turns of phrase found in the original. In his next sentence Defoe writes that 'The Docks and Yards are now like a Town by themselves', while in the following sentence Compiler X strays no further than to speak of the increase in buildings 'in the Town, and especially in the Dock-Yards, which are now become a kind of Town by themselves' (this refers to the new suburb known as the Common, which grew up in the first decade of the eighteenth century, and would later be known as Portsea). Many elements of the entry for Portsmouth show an equal reliance on the *Tour*.

The coverage of Boston in Lincolnshire illustrates the same kind of working that goes on in numerous other cases. Its brevity does not disguise its total dependence, not on a single source. The description of the town in *AMC* (3) derives not from any old topographical work that lay to hand, but on the particular formulation of ideas that are found in *Tour* (2: 212). Several close verbal echoes are embedded within the paraphrase, especially regarding 'the antient Name [Title in *Tour*] of a Mart' along with a small number of other towns. Elsewhere the *Tour* mentions the usage 'Mart' not merely in its account of Beverley (3: 105), but also in relation to Howden, listing the same towns, while adding 'tho' of late they begin to lose the Word' (3: 94). The reviser has inserted '*Heydon*' (the nearby town of Hedon) incorrectly for Howden, and the only explanation is that he relied on a memory of the passage on this last-named place. It is a mistake more likely to proceed from the author of the *Tour*, since the compiler had no need to consult the inland locations.

At many points in his narrative, Compiler X uses the same device of blending close metaphrase interspersed with a slightly more distant paraphrase. A good example occurs where the story is told of a destructive storm off Yarmouth Roads (3). The passage in *Tour* (1: 113) begins, 'About the Year 1692 (*I think it was that Year*)'. *AMC* substitutes the formula, 'About the Year 1696'. Both accounts are wrong: the episode seems to have taken place in September 1695. Hesitant as Defoe is about his dating here, he had used some of the details to flesh out Robinson Crusoe's first shipwreck, which happens in this exact vicinity near the start of the novel and prefigures the course of later events.[21] Most of the content here in *AMC* is an abridged copy of the *Tour*, with the usual trivial variants ('250 Sail of Ships' in the former, where the latter had stated 'above 200 sail of Ships'. However, there is a closer congruence at the climax of the story. Defoe had written that 'some [ships] run away for *Lyn Deeps*, but few of them, (the Night being so dark) could find their way in there, some but *very few* rid it out, at a Distance ... and very few of the People on Board were sav'd'. Compiler X takes his cue from the source, when he observes that some of the ships 'made shift to get back into *Yarmouth Roads*, others run at all hazard into the Mouth of the *Ouse*, which they call *Lyn-Deeps*, some one way, some another; nor were any of the Men sav'd, or but very few'.[22]

The routine form of paraphrase used in *AMC* could be exemplified from every page and column, indeed for long stretches almost every paragraph. A representative case is the following, which deals with the Thames between London and Reading (19):

> It is particularly remarkable, that there are abundance of Mills at and near these two Towns of *Marlow* and *Wickham*; not for Corn only, but for other Business, and the most of both that are to be seen any where in so small a Compass; as,
>
> 1. Corn-Mills very many.
> 2. Paper-Mills eight or ten.
> 3. Oyl-Mills two.
> 4. A Thimble-Mill, a most exquisite Piece of Art, and merits well to be mention'd; and to be describ'd if we had room for it.
> 5. Three Coppcr-Mills for the hammering of Brass into Battery; and with them a Foundary for melting Copper with the *Lapis Calaminaris*, and for making that extraordinary Plate-Metal call'd *Black-Latin*, always, till it was made here, brought from *Holland* and *Germany*.

We might wonder if it is purely coincidental that all the industrial concerns here are specified and carefully enumerated in *Tour* (2: 49–50), or if the information might derive from a lost common source. The likelihood of this is greatly diminished by the peculiar regularity with which Compiler X follows in the verbal tracks of Defoe, especially on the 'Three very remarkable Mills' near Bisham, which convert brass into '*Battery Work'* with the help of a foundry where 'by the Help of *Lopis* (sic) *Caliminaris*' they convert copper into brass. Some confirmation is supplied by a passage in *Brief Observations on Trade and Manufacture* (1721), which is accepted as 'probably' by Defoe in the *Critical Bibliography*. In that work the author discusses the manufacture of metals in Britain, citing lapis calliminaris (otherwise known as calamine), battery work, copper plates and black Latin among the products of the industry.[23]

Even closer to the barely disguised source is what the *Atlas* says about Duncansby Head (*AMC* 273), which reiterates many aspects of the account in *Tour* (1: 272–3), including the facts that it is possible to read small print at midnight in summer; that the cape points straight towards the tail of Ursa Major in the zenith; that the ancients looked on the area as the Ultima Thule; and that travellers commonly set their horses' feet in the sea at John o' Groats, as Defoe claimed his own party had done. These scattered details are not thrust together in any other source that has been located. In the same way, the entry for Dundee (*AMC* 7) is little more than a reduction of the much longer coverage it receives in *Tour* (3: 255–7), with the comparatively few direct echoes muffled by skilful recourse to elegant variation and neat periphrastic expressions – as in the account of the Pretender's brief reign as 'Sovereign' or 'King' in this part of Scotland.[24] If we turn to the description of 'owlers' of Romney Marsh (11), referring to those who ran illicit wool to France, this offers a more impersonal précis of a lively passage in the *Tour* (1:161; see also 1: 152); but the topic had become an *idée fixe* in Defoe's work. It is mentioned in *The Complete English Tradesman,* and again in tracts such as *An Humble Proposal to the People of England, for the Encrease of their Trade* (1729), where the author writes of 'a clandestine, smugling, pernicious Trade' – compare 'that Smuggling Country call'd *Romney-Marsh* . . . A pernicious Trade (*AMC* 11).[25]

Sometimes the paraphrase strays into such close proximity to the original that the identity of the narrator in the *Tour* and that of Compiler X simply merge. For example, Defoe says about Cheshire cheese: 'I am told from a very good Authority, the City of *London* only takes off 14000 Ton every Year; besides 8000 Ton which they say goes every Year down the Rivers *Severn* and *Trent*' (*Tour* 2: 191). Remarkably, the compiler personally received the same information: 'of which they told me, and with very good Authority, that *London* alone takes off yearly 14000 Tons, and the Navigation of the *Trent* and the *Severn* carries off near 8000 Ton more' (*AMC* 17). He computes the total output of the county as 'at least 30000 Ton of Cheese a year'. Defoe had made the same calculation in *The Complete English Tradesman* (2.ii: 31), except that he set the figure at 'near 3000 ton'.

A final example in this category may be found in the entry for Harwich, the first town mentioned on the itinerary charted by *AMC* (1). Most of this passage rests on the customary blend of abridgment and précis: thus, a paragraph on the packet boats from this port to Holland, noting the recent loss of coaches to and from London, is scaled down to a couple of sentences. But though Compiler X is able to shorten his predecessor's voluble treatment of the 'petrifying' spring in the town (*Tour* 1: 81), he cannot help repeating a few telling expressions from this excerpt. Thus, Defoe had written of the locals, 'They boast that . . . their Streets [are] pav'd with Clay'; the new volume for once is a little fuller: 'The Streets and Walls of *Harwich* having been pav'd and built with this petrifying Earth, gave rise to that Saying, that *Harwich* was pav'd with Clay'. A good example of skilful reworking occurs near the start in a passage on the inland trade of King's Lynn, enabled by rivers such as the Great and Little Ouse (*AMC* 3; *Tour* 1: 115–16). The facts are the same, but the words are disposed in a different order, and different names are used (the Mildenhall for the Lark, and Cam for the 'Grant' (Granta).

The sections in *AMC* which utilise straightforward précis are unremarkable, except for the fact that they seldom go without any recollection of the particular wording found in the text of the *Tour*. A single instance among many concerns the district around Inverness (8), where the narrator describes the Anglicised nature of the far north in Scotland, after it had been colonised by Cromwell's soldiers. The result was that southern practices in husbandry had been taken over and a less rich provincial brogue was heard – Defoe had wondered that the local population 'speak perfect *English* . . . nay, some will say that speak it as well as at *London*' (3: 267). Other representative cases are the short entry for Dumfries (compare *AMC* 17 with *Tour* 1: 182), and the treatment of Bideford and Barnstaple (*AMC* 14; *Tour* 2: 14). In both these examples, the material deployed by Compiler X is identical with that found in Defoe, even if abbreviated, but there is little by way of direct verbal echoes.

The Fall of Carthage

Four passages supply positive, indeed blatant, indications regarding the likelihood of Defoe's involvement in the compilation of the British section of *AMC*, as well as the later segment on British trade. Each of these clues is hard to miss, and one or two might have been apparent to readers in 1728. They offer more than the vague 'fingerprints' of authorship that scholars such as Furbank and Owens rightly dismiss.

The first is the most striking case, since it involves what is as thoroughly a Defovian passage as anything in the entire text. It concerns Norwich, a city with which Defoe had many contacts, but more to the purpose it reflects on the fate of Carthage and Corinth. In fact, Defoe's belief that the destruction of places like Carthage represented a major disaster in human history can be seen as the most idiosyncratic feature of his ideas on the history of commerce. In several places the *Atlas* meditates on the fall of these cities and their ruins (78, 185, 241, 265). Defoe had a marked tendency to insert into his works a lament on the tragic long-term consequences of the disappearance of great centres of the ancient world, especially Carthage, Tyre and Corinth. He repeatedly deplores the loss of trading satellites set up by these cities, asserting that the impact on global commerce was so vast as to constitute 'the greatest Loss to the World that ever happen'd in it' (*AMC* 265). Even by the standards of Defoe's frequent recourse to hyperbole, this is an extreme claim. The fullest expression of his views comes in *A General History of Discoveries and Improvements* (1725–6), which contains what P. N. Furbank has called 'a history and eulogy of, and eventually a lament for the extinction of the Phoenecians'.[26] The main theme of this book might be described as the fatal effects on trade and navigation of the overthrow of the great cities. It makes much of the way in which exploration and discovery were slowed as a result of the Romans' disinclination to move beyond military conquest and subjugation of local peoples.

A particularly eloquent meditation on the destruction of Carthage and Corinth occurs in the *General History* (123–4). The topic is resumed in *A Plan of the English Commerce* (1728), which celebrates at some length the centres of commerce in antiquity (312–17). The line that leads to *AMC* becomes clear if we juxtapose the treatment of a single notion in three sources. In the *General History*, Defoe writes that 'Commerce receiv'd a mortal blow in the destruction of *Carthage*; the whole World felt the shock' (164); in the *Plan* this becomes 'when these two Cities of *Corinth* and *Carthage* fell . . . Trade receiv'd a mortal Wound; I may say the whole World did so' (314); in *AMC* 'really the World received a mortal Wound in the Overthrow of the *Carthaginian* Empire . . . the whole Trade of the World might be said to sink with them; At least it felt a Shock' (239).

Other phrases recur within these texts. For example, the *General History* has this: 'I can not say that the Genius of the *Romans* lay so much for Trade, and Discoveries or Improvements, as that of the *Carthaginians*, and the *Phoenicians* did, and therefore Navigation and the building of Ships, as also the Commerce of the World, rather receiv'd a Check for some time by the ruin of *Carthage*' (44). Slyly the author of the *Plan* commends his predecessor: 'It is true, as has been observed by a well informed Writer on this Subject, that the *Romans* . . . were no Friends to Trade . . . Instead of encouraging Trade and Navigation, they murther'd the Merchants, burnt their Ships, and carry'd away the People, which are the Life and Support of Manufacture and Trade' (312–13). *AMC* reverts to a closer rephrasing of the original: 'tho the *Romans* were great Encouragers of Learning . . . yet their Genius did not lie to Trade, or to the Discovery of foreign Countreys, or settling Colonies for Commerce in new-found or remote Places; nor did they encourage Navigation or Plantation . . . as the *Carthaginians* and *Phoenicians* had done before them' (265). The surrounding argument to each of these quotations displays further congruence.[27]

AMC even manages to come up with an unlikely echo of the *Tour* in its threnody for lost cities. The compiler craves leave '*to drop a Tear* over the Ruines, not of the City of *Carthage* only, but the whole *Carthaginian* Empire, whose Monument and Grave are together seen in the Heaps of faded Glory, huddled together where that flourishing City once stood' (239). This involves a conscious adaptation of Ovid's lines from the first of the *Heroides*: 'Tum [*recte* iam] Seges erat [est], ubi Troja fuit', that is 'there were cornfields then where Troy stood'. Most apposite to the argument here, the writer observes:

> But I return to *Carthage*. In our way from *Algier* to *Tunis*, we see the ruinous Heaps where that famous City once stood, the Haven of *Biserta*, of little use, and almost choak'd up with Sand; the numberless Villages, like the *Bastides* of *Marseilles*, which contain'd the Country Lodgings, or Summer Retreats for the Citizens, are now left off and reurn'd to their original wild Condition, namely, into plow'd Fields and Forests, and not so much as a Remembrance that any such Habitation had been there. (239)

A particularly cogent parallel emerges here. The reference to the *Bastides* recalls a page in the *Tour* where Defoe touches on the residences of prosperous merchants outside London, calling them 'Houses of Retreat, like the *Bastides* of *Marseilles*, Gentlemen's meer *Summer-Houses*, or Citizen's *Country-Houses*' (*Tour* 1: 202). It has not proved possible to find one single use of the keyword in any other English source (excepting translations from French) during the first half of the eighteenth century.

Carthage was not the only city whose loss Defoe lamented. He refers more than once to the destruction of Tyre, citing the words of the book of Ezekiel on its rise and fall (*Plan* 9–10, 31; *General History* 41, 86–7, 99–100). It is no surprise that the same biblical prophecy is quoted to the same effect in *AMC* (185). A similar pattern can be found in respect of Corinth. However, it was the demise of the Carthaginian empire, with its baneful effects on trade, navigation and discovery, that haunts the pages of the works most regularly. The echoes linger on throughout *AMC*.

If we go back to the British sections of *AMC,* these characteristic accents reappear in the account of Norwich (2):

> In all, or most of the antient decay'd Towns or Cities in the World, whose Walls show their former Extent, and whose Glory has suffer'd decay by the Injuries of Time, Wars, removing of Courts, of Trade, of Navigation, and the like, we find the Ruins of their antient Grandeur generally appear in one thing or other; *Carthage* shews the Heaps of Marble Columns fallen down upon one another, *Troy* the Remains of the Temples and Palaces of their Gods and Princes; *Corinth* shews the vast extended Suburbs and destroy'd Temples at a distance from their City; and *Rome* it self shews not only the great Extent of their old Walls, but how the Vacancy within was fill'd up; here the Amphitheatres, there the Obelisks; Triumphal Arches on one side, vast Aqueducts on the Other; the Baths of some Princes in one Quartcr, the Pavements of others in another: but in *Norwich,* the plow'd-up Fields show no Urns, no *Roman* Coins or *Mosaick* Pavements; nor do the enclos'd Fields shew the Ruins of antient Buildings, but, in all probability, those Fields were Fields from the beginning, and have remain'd so to the present Days.

Such feelings for the remnants of ancient cities are equally characteristic of the writer of the *Tour.* A sounding reflection occurs a few pages before the entry for Norwich:

> The Ruins of *Carthage*, of the great City of *Jerusalem*, or of antient *Rome*, are not at all wonderful to me; the ruins of *Nineveh,* which are so entirely sunk, as that 'tis doubtful where the City stood; the Ruins of *Babylon*, or the great *Persepolis*, and many Capital Cities, which Time and the Change of Monarchies have Overthrown; these, I say, are not at all Wonderful, because being the Capitals of great and flourishing Kingdoms, where those Kingdoms were Overthrown, the Capital Cities necessarily fell with them; But for a private Town, a Sea-Port, and a Town of Commerce, to Decay, as it were of itself (for we never read of *Dunwich* being Plundered, or Ruin'd, by any Disaster, at least not of late Years); this I must confess, seems owing to nothing but to the Fate of Things, by which we see that Towns, Kings, Countries, Families, and Persons, have all their Elevation, their Medium, their Declination, and even their Destruction in the Womb of Time, and the Course of Nature. (1:98)

The comments on Norwich in *AMC* instantly recall other passages in the *Tour*, where Defoe casts himself back into the ancient past, fancying himself 'in the *Circus Maximus* at *Rome*' (*Tour* 1: 118). In *AMC* the writer pauses only briefly to touch on the decay of Rome, explaining that 'It would perhaps require as much room to give a full Account of the Ruin of the *Roman* Empire, as it has done to write the Rise of it' (78), a line that might almost have inspired Gibbon.

Following the Tracks of the Compiler

The second clue is slighter, but still indicative. It relates to a mistake Compiler X makes at King's Lynn, when he refers to 'a very handsom Statue of the late K. *William*' that graces the market square (3). In fact the statue, erected in 1686 and demolished around 1831, commemorated James II. This error comes straight from *Tour* (1: 116), where Defoe blundered further by stating that the king was mounted on a horse. None of the likely immediate sources for *AMC*, such as Macky's *Journey*, the Senex *New General Atlas*, or Moll's *New Description of England and Wales, with the Adjacent Islands* (1724), refer to the statue. It may be a contributing factor that both *AMC* and the *Tour* take every opportunity to laud the memory of William.

A third pointer occurs when the narrative reaches Hull (4). Here Compiler X launches into a paragraph of almost 300 words with almost no relevance to the main theme of his work, that is the commercial and maritime life of ports around the coastline. The subject is an episode at the start of the Civil War in 1642 when the town's governor, Sir John Hotham, refused to allow Charles I and his entourage to enter Hull. In this case Defoe (who may well have never visited Hull personally) does seem to have copied Edmund Gibson's edition of Camden as well as Senex, for most of his entry – but unsurprisingly he omits the Hotham story in *Tour* (3: 110–13). However, it was an incident that clearly possessed a durable hold in his memory. Not only did he bring this event into *Memoirs of a Cavalier* (1720), 169–70, but he also introduced it, we might feel even more *à propos de bottes*, during a discussion of violent acts and retribution in his *Serious Reflections of Robinson Crusoe* (1720).

The most blatant of the four clues occurs at the start of the section devoted to the Thames:

> The tedious old Tale of the River *Isis* keeping its Name till it meets the River *Tame*, which coming out of the Vale of *Aylesbury*, joins it at *Dorchester*, where the two Rivers are marry'd together, and from that Conjunction call'd *Thamesis*: This Tale, I say, I omit as a fabulous Gingle, and leave it to the old *British* Poets; tho Mr. *Camden* is so very fond of them, as to give us their antient Poetry upon that Subject at large. (*AMC* 18)

Defoe's scorn for such fables shines out in several works. But this particular inclination shows itself in two places within the *Tour*. One occurs as the supposed journey approaches Oxford: 'I observe that most of our Historians reject the Notion that Mr. *Cambden* makes so many Flourishes about, of the Marriage of *Thame* and *Isis*; that this little River was call'd the *Thame*, and the other, the *Isis*; and that being join'd, they obtain'd the united Name of *Thamisis*: I say they reject it, and so do I' (*Tour* 2: 138). A more highly coloured version appears at the start of Letter 3, setting out the author's utilitarian goals:

> I shall sing you no Songs here of the River in the first Person of a Water Nymph, a Goddess, (and I know not what) according to the Humour of the ancient Poets. I shall talk nothing of the Marriage of old *Isis*, the male River, with the beautiful *Thame*, the female River, a Whimsy as simple as the Subject was empty, but I shall speak of the River as Occasion presents, as it really is *made glorious* by the Splendor of its Shores, gilded with noble Palaces, strong Fortifications, large Hospitals, and publick Buildings; with the greatest Bridge, and the greatest City in the World, made famous by the Opulence of its Merchants, the Encrease and Extensiveness of its Commerce; by its invincible Navies, and by the innumerable Fleets of Ships sailing upon it, to and from all Parts of the World. (*Tour* 1: 208)

No one familiar with what Defoe wrote could miss his rhetorical touch in such a context, but the author's scorn for the 'Jingle' in *AMC* is as great as that for the 'Whimsy' here. The passages just quoted from the text of the *Tour* are among the most typical samples of Defoe's high style, and each of them has a close echo in *AMC*.

Such selective quotations cannot bring out the density of allusion to the *Tour* which pervades the new volume. Nor does a brief summary make clear the agility with which Compiler X found his way around the massive text he was following, to delve into its labyrinthine nooks and crannies. Regularly he has to jump from letter to letter in the original to adjust his steady progress around the island, in order to meet up with Defoe's more jagged itinerary. First he goes anti-clockwise, as seen on maps with an orientation to the north, taking him from the Thames estuary to the Pentland Firth; then he changes tack and perambulates the west coast from Kent to Cape Wrath (or loosely there, as Compiler X is as vague as Defoe on the geography of northern Scotland). This does not make a neat match with the course of the *Tour,* where coastal regions are placed according to the route of a primarily inland voyage. Yet the compiler has no trouble about finding his bearings within the source. On occasions he leaps across large gaps in the text: for example, the paragraph about rock salt production near the River Mersey, yielding 'Salt upon Salt' (17; information repeated 108), is taken not from what Defoe says about the salt industry in Cheshire (2: 191–2), but from his coverage of Devon three letters earlier (2: 15). Equally with the treatment of some Thamesside towns in the conclusion of this portion of the atlas (18–20), which makes brief raids on entries in the first five letters of the *Tour*.

Compiler X sometimes 'corrects' Defoe, though not invariably with success – *Tour* (1: 100) describes the battle of Southwold Bay in 1662, while *AMC* 2 wrongly substitutes the date of 1666. Often figures are slightly amended, either because new information was available or (more likely) because the compiler wished to conceal his borrowing. This happens with the count for herrings caught at Yarmouth, either 50,000 barrels, including Lowestoft (*AMC* 2), or 40,000 (*Tour* 1: 108, also *Plan* 237).[28] Similar minor discrepancies are found regarding the bridge at Glasgow, with seven arches (*AMC* 17) or correctly eight (*Tour* 3: 199), although the account of the flood that threatened the structure obviously takes its cue from Defoe's first-hand report, which may derive from his visits during the anti-Union riots of 1706–7. Others may come from misreading the source or inadvertence: Tilbury Fort had a battery of 106 cannons, each carrying from 24- to 46-pound balls (*Tour* 1: 56), or one of 'near 100 of 24 to 48 pound Ball' (*AMC* 20). At Scarborough, the narrator states, 'Here we saw Turbets of three quarters of a hundred Weight' (*Tour* 3: 114); the reviser converts this to a mention of 'large Turbets, of which they frequently take some weighing 50, 60 to 80 Pounds each' (*AMC* 4). Nothing in these disparities suggests the presence of a vigilant independent observer. Very rarely does the revision take issue with its predecessor. However, in the entry for Southampton, a neat job of invisible mending that rephrases the source, the writer does amend a claim that there is 'much Smuggling' in the port (*Tour* 1: 177) with a more prudent statement that 'too much of the Brandy [trade], that is the Smuggling, has been discover'd hereabouts, but 'tis now much abated' (*AMC* 12).

It is easy to see what Compiler X could do. He managed to write an entry for Sunderland entirely in Defoe's manner, in respect of content and wording. On the hurricane in 1703, he was able to draw freely (10) on the information Defoe supplied in *Tour* (159–60) or with more specific detail in *The Storm* (1704).[29] Implausibly, he shared the first-hand experience of counting huge numbers of ships in the Pool of London (*AMC* 19; *Tour* 2: 96). He had the capacity to improvise a passage in Defoe's idiom on the ruins of Carthage and Corinth, one of the author's most recurrent themes, in a section on Norwich where the *Tour* had no such interjection. Without any apparent effort the compiler could move around his host text, shifting from letter to letter and even volume to volume for the material he needed. He inserted passages of dubious relevance that Defoe had included, and generalised confidently on matters of trade, whether internal or external.

He had the journalistic knack of slipping in topical additions, such as the episode concerning George I. In places it looks as if he might have had access to Defoe's working notes. One example occurs in the account of the bridge at Barnstaple, 'built, as Mr. Camden relates, by one *Stamford*, a Citizen of *London*', where *AMC* (14) follows *Tour* (2: 16), except that Defoe had concealed his indebtedness to *Britannia* (1722 edition, 1: 46). The compiler does not generally signalise his use of Camden or other authorities in this part of the volume: it is highly suspicious that he was in a position to name the source here.

Conclusion

The time may have come to acknowledge that *AMC* relies on more than 'extensive borrowings' from the *Tour* and other works by Defoe. As regards the British section, in particular, the evidence is overwhelming. Here the fiction of Compiler X as a separate identity cannot be sustained. It comes down in the end to *aut Defoe, aut diabolus.* The objections by Furbank and Owens to any use of 'Defoe against the world' reasoning seem flimsy: sometimes it is precisely by excluding other possible authors that we narrow down the plausible likelihoods. We would need to disinter some nameless author with a range of attributes known to be possessed by a single writer of the day. Defoe was on the spot, working at his most prolific on cognate tasks, well proven as a deliverer, familiar with all aspects of the material, skilled in rehashing earlier sources, as for instance in *A Journal of the Plague Year* (1722). When the project was launched, he was Taylor's most successful author. Furbank and Owens understandably felt nervous about confirming Defoe's responsibility as 'the main author and compiler of this enormous and expert work'. But he generally chose to work alone, even on vast enterprises such as *The Review*, and was capable of fast production. As for expert status, no one alive had a stronger background in writing on the issues of world trade, geography and discovery.

Recently J. Paul Hunter has listed 'navigation charts and records' together with 'travel and exploration narratives' among the diverse literary models that went into *Robinson Crusoe.*[30] The castaway took care indeed to rescue from the shipwreck 'three or four Compasses, some Mathematical Instruments, Dials, Perspectives, Charts, and Books of Navigation, all which I huddel'd together, whether I might want them or no'.[31] Always alert to practical needs, the author of the novel required no assistant to produce '*A General View of the World, so far as Relates* to *Trade and Navigation*'. This task did not require the talents of a Halley. Above all,

Defoe was primed to revisit the substance of a long book he had recently brought before the public, which contained almost all of what was called for in the opening section of *AMC*. Why would the individuals behind the new system of projection look anywhere else?

Atlas Maritimus is an important book, still of interest in the context of historical geography. Its aim ultimately was not just to promote the specific scheme endorsed by Edmond Halley, but to advance the aids to navigation by providing a huge array of information on coasts around the globe – to do little less indeed than supply the 'General View of the World' which was blazoned in the largest type used on the title-page. We should recognise the contribution that Defoe made to it, not as the host for some parasitic reviser but as the author himself.

Notes

Introduction

1. Inevitably the same quotations sometimes appear in the two books, but their use is always inflected by their appearance in the course of a different argument.
2. The interval of years has made it possible to explore in depth issues that keep coming up in more recent scholarship, for example, by giving the first full analysis of the relation of the *Tour* to a compilation from 1728, *Atlas Maritimus*. The final chapter of the present book sets out a much more detailed review of the evidence to confirm Defoe's presence as all but undeniable.
3. Nicholas Rogers, 'Money, Land and Lineage: The Big Bourgeoisie of Hanoverian London', in *The Eighteenth-Century Town: A Reader in English Urban History 1688–1720*, ed. Peter Borsay (Harlow, 1990), 268–91 (280).
4. Joan Thirsk, *Horses in Early Modern England: for Service, for Pleasure, for Power* (Reading, 1978), 24.
5. *Letters*, 98–102.
6. There is no afflatus in the claim of Michael Shinagel, 'So far as we know, no other living person had anything like Defoe's immediate and comprehensive sense of his country and his society.' See *Daniel Defoe and Middle-Class Gentility* (Cambridge, MA, 1968), 202. The aim of the present book is to determine what form exactly this 'sense' took, and the ways in which it is expressed in the *Tour*.
7. For fuller details, see my article, 'Defoe's Distribution Agents and Robert Harley', *English Historical Review*, 121 (2006): 146–61.
8. *Letters*, 276. Defoe seems to mean North Britain, that is Scotland.
9. Maxine Berg, *Luxury and Pleasure in Eighteenth-Century Britain* (Oxford, 2005), 22.
10. Peter Earle, *The World of Defoe* (London, 1976), 45.
11. *CET*, 2.ii: 61–71; compare *Tour*, 2: 167, 3: 186. For a passage almost equally dense in its citation of chapter and verse, see *Plan*, 154–90, and on imports 190–244.

12. See my article, 'Daniel Defoe's Knowledge of Essex: The Evidence of *A Tour thro' the Whole Island of Great Britain*', *Essex Society for Archaeology and History Transactions*, 4th Series, 9 (2020 for 2018), 127–41, at 135–7.
13. See Tim Hitchcock, *Down and Out in Eighteenth-Century London* (London, 2007). Hitchcock refers to the 'degraded and suffering poor', who 'are part of that dystopia of social disorder found in the work of Daniel Defoe, William Hogarth and Henry Fielding' (xvi).

1 The Identity of Britain

1. Fernand Braudel, *The Identity of France, vol. I: History and Environment*, tr. Siân Reynolds (London, 1988), 37.
2. See Chapter 5 for discussion of writers (among them Dorothy George, George Rudé, Jack Lindsay, L. D. Schwartz, Craig Spence, Roy Porter, Douglas Hay and Nicholas Rogers) who have explicitly named Defoe's account as the basis for their own account of the changing topographic and social space of London in this era.
3. *Robinson Crusoe*, ed. Evan R. Davis (Peterborough, ON, 2010), 162.
4. G. M. Trevelyan, *Illustrated Social History, vol. III: The Eighteenth Century* (Harmondsworth, 1964), 18–19. The text is that of Trevelyan's *English Social History* (1944). Note that the map of 'London in the Reign of George I' (276–7) appears to have been drawn at least in part on the basis of the information supplied by Defoe
5. Max Byrd, *London Transformed: Images of the City in the Eighteenth Century* (New Haven, 1978), 8–17 (quotations from 14, 17).
6. After quoting some of what Defoe says on this topic, L. D. Schwarz comments, 'Even as he was writing, the building boom in London was breaking. Building deeds reached their peak in Middlesex in 1725 and did not return to that level for forty years' (*London in the Age of Industrialisation* (Cambridge, 1992), 79).
7. See E. A. Wrigley, 'A Simple Model of London's Importance in Changing English Society and Economy, 1650–1750', in *People, Cities and Wealth: The Transformation of Traditional Society* (Oxford, 1987), 133–56 (137).
8. Wrigley, 'A Simple Model', 151–2.
9. Defoe's fullest arguments regarding the centrality of London are found in the *CET*, 2.ii.111–47, where he asserts, '*London* consumes all, circulates all, exports all, and at last pays for all, and this is Trade' (142). He repeats his exaggerated estimate of the population (112, 122).
10. *Letters*, 112, 117. For the contacts that Defoe made on his trips and their recruitment, see my article, 'Defoe's Distribution Agents and Robert Harley,' *English Historical Review*, 121 (2006): 146–61. Some of these individuals would

have been useful sources of local information that went into the *Tour*. To take just a single example, Samuel Done, who hosted Defoe at his house in Castle Hill at Liverpool, was heavily involved in municipal affairs, and owned several properties. A dissenter, he had a prominent business role in supplying goods or services on the Pool, for example to clean and refit ships in 1696 (National Archives, numerous documents in ADM 106/502). He also served as muster master for the Royal Navy from 1696, bailiff of Liverpool in 1704 and land tax commissioner in 1705. With so many fingers in the pie, he could have told the visitor almost everything he wanted to know about the town. He was known to Sir Thomas Johnson, a leading citizen and MP for the borough from 1701 to 1723, who was largely instrumental in the construction of the first dry dock in Liverpool, mentioned in the *Tour* (2: 126).

11. Just how remarkable the rise was that Defoe anticipates is shown by a striking fact. Among towns of 10,000 or more across Europe, only four out of 259 moved up more than one category (that is, a division by size, such as less than 10,0000; 10,000–20,000; 20,000–40,000; 40,000–80,000) in the period from 1750 to 1800. These four were Leeds, Manchester, Plymouth and Sheffield. The *Tour* dilates upon the growth of each of them, when their development was at a relatively early stage. See Jan de Vries, *European Urbanization 1500–1800* (Cambridge, MA, 1984), 133.
12. Once the comparison goes the other way, when Defoe writes of Peterborough, 'This is a little City, and indeed 'tis the least in *England*; for *Bath*, or *Wells*, or *Ely*, or *Carlisle*, which are all call'd Cities, are yet much bigger; yet *Peterborough* is no contemptible Place neither' (2: 217–18).
13. Macky, 1: 103–6, 108–29, 132.
14. *Libraries*, xxi–xxii. See the perceptive introduction, most relevantly here the section on 'Some Defoean Subjects', pp. xvii–xxviii, as well the extensive indexes, pp. 133–209.
15. Further confirmation comes from several books not listed in the sale catalogue which crop up regularly in the *Tour*. For fuller documentation, see Chapter 9. The most important items include William Dugdale's *Monasticon Anglicanum* (1655–73), John Stow's *Survey of London* (1598, 1603), and Robert Plot's *Natural History of Oxfordshire* (1677).
16. For possible use of *Britannia Depicta* in mid-Wales, see Chapter 9.
17. All three counties are among those into which the circuit described in Letter 1 strays. See my study, 'Daniel Defoe's Knowledge of Essex: The Evidence of *A Tour thro' the Whole Island of Great Britain*', *Essex Society for Archaeology and History Transactions*, 4th series, vol. 9 (2020 for 2018): 127–41.
18. Wrigley, 'A Simple Model,' 151.
19. Paul Langford, *A Polite and Commercial People: England 1727–1783* (Oxford, 1989), 396. Significantly Langford discusses the turnpike system first in his

section on 'New Improvements', and devotes considerable space to the topic (391–410).

20. Compare this with a passage in *CET*, 1.i.200. Oher parallels exist, for example *Tour* 1: 203 with *CET*, 2.i: 95.
21. Linda Colley, *Britons: Forging the Nation 1707–1837*, 2nd ed. (New Haven, 2005), 12. This is the most important study of the creation of the 'united' kingdom.
22. Betty A. Schellenberg, 'Imagining the Nation in Defoe's *A Tour Thro' the Whole Island of Great Britain*', *ELH*, 62 (1995): 295–311 (297, 305, 306).
23. Trevor Speller, 'Violence, Reason, and Enclosure in Defoe's *Tour*', *Studies in English Literature, 1500–1900*, 51 (2011): 585–604 (586, 599–601).
24. Speller, 'Violence, Reason, and Enclosure', 591.
25. Peter Borsay, 'Urban Development in the Age of Defoe', in *Britain in the First Age of Party*, ed. Clyve Jones (London, 1987), 195–219 (195).
26. Ernest Gellner's formulation, quoted by Gerald Newman, *The Rise of English Nationalism: A Cultural History 1740–1830* (London, 1987), 52.

2 Embedding and Embodying the Nation

1. Gérard Genette, *Paratexts: Thresholds of Interpretation*, tr. Jane E. Lewin (Cambridge, 1997), 294–318.
2. After four short introductory sections, the remainder of this book is mainly taken up with first-hand accounts of the hurricane by a large number of eye-witnesses. See *The Storm*, ed. Richard Hamblyn (London, 2003). Defoe also makes extensive use of lists and tables (see 146–7, for example).
3. Genette, *Paratexts*, 94–103.
4. The position is complicated by the fact that John Pemberton and John Hooke, one or both of whom appear in the imprint of all editions published in the 1720s, advertised a third edition of both the English volumes, first in the *Evening Post* on 15 January 1723. The same advertisement announced that the volume on Scotland would appear 'in a few Days'. As usual when this formula is used, the publication was delayed a little longer: the book was first announced as published 'this Day' in the *Daily Post* on 22 February.
5. The fourth edition of Volumes I and II of the *Journey* was first advertised by Pemberton and Hooke in the *Evening Post* on 4 June 1724. This was exactly two weeks after the same journal had announced the publication of the first volume of Defoe's *Tour* – an indication of just how tight the commercial competition was between the two ventures.
6. Genette, *Paratexts*, p. 91.

7. Macky, 1: i–xix. The volume on Scotland was dedicated to 'The Nobility and Gentry of Great-Britain', 3: i. Defoe singles out Macky's concentration on seats of the aristocracy in the Introduction to his own Scottish segment (3: 154).
8. Macky, 1: xii.
9. The reader will look in vain for Manchester, Leeds, Sheffield or Halifax in the pages of Macky. There is one fleeting reference to Liverpool as a port in his second volume.
10. Jean Chevalier and Alain Gheerbrant, *A Dictionary of Symbols*, tr. John Buchanan-Brown (London, 1996), 728.
11. On this topic, see Cynthia Wall, 'Defoe and London,' *The Cambridge Companion to Daniel Defoe*, ed. John Richetti (Cambridge, 2008), 158–81.
12. See Gérard Genette, *Narrative Discourse: An Essay in Method*, tr. Jane E. Lewin (Ithaca, NY, 1983), 86–112.
13. [Defoe], *Memoirs of a Cavalier* (London, [1720]), 258–9.
14. Bowen, 241, 223.
15. The diary does however appear in an unauthorised reissue in parts by George Parker as *Curious and Diverting Journeys, thro' the Whole Island of Great Britain* (1734), which presents the text almost word-for-word but significantly omits many of the paratextual elements such as prefaces. See my article, 'George Parker, Defoe and the Whitefriars Trade: A "Lost" Edition of *A Tour thro' Great Britain*,' *The Library*, 7th series, 8 (2007): 33–59.
16. Note that such autotextual passages do not amount to intertextuality in the strict sense. We should restrict this concept to cases where material from an external source is alluded to or appropriated, and the passage exhibits some significant difference when reused, as compared to its earlier context. Simply to quote an excerpt from a previous writing, unaltered in the new context, is not necessarily a case of intertextuality.
17. J. M. Coetzee, 'Introduction' to *Robinson Crusoe* (Oxford, 1999), vii.

3 The Epic Strain

1. Daniel Defoe, *A Tour through the Whole Island of Great Britain*, ed. Pat Rogers (Harmondsworth, 1971), 33.
2. E. M. W. Tillyard, *The English Epic and Its Background* (London, 1954), 1–15 (1).
3. Tillyard, *English Epic*, 496.
4. E. M. W. Tillyard, *The Epic Strain in the English Novel* (London, 1958), 5, 21. A modern and well-received study by Henry Power charts the way in which classical epic was reappropriated by the Scriblerian satirists and then by Henry Fielding. Power has only two brief references to *Robinson Crusoe*, contrasting its 'excited sprawl' with Fielding's 'symmetry and polish': see *Epic into Novel* (Oxford, 2015), 136. He does not mention Tillyard's work.

5. Tillyard, *English Epic*, 4–15 (5, 6, 8, 9, 12, 13).
6. K. W. Gransden, *Virgil's Iliad: An Essay on Epic Narrative* (Cambridge, 1994), 32.
7. Linda Colley, *Britons: Forging the Nation 1707–1837* (New Haven, 2nd ed., 2005), 16, 32–3.
8. It is symbolic, if not something more than that, that Defoe lived on the outskirts of the city, far from the polite quarters of what we now call the West End. By contrast, Handel's home in Brook Street lay close to most of the major institutions of London, and to the residence of important figures in national culture. See Ellen T. Harris, *George Frideric Handel: A Life with Friends* (New York, 2014). The map that Harris provides (9) is designed to show where close acquaintances such as Mary Delany and Anne Donnellan lived: but it also reveals how close at hand were St James', Hyde Park, Piccadilly, Burlington House, Bond Street, Leicester Fields and many more places of interest. A high proportion of the movers and shakers had their homes in this small area. Defoe never did.
9. For whatever reason, he avoids the subject of the Plague (except in reference to deaths in Colchester, 1: 77), even though he continued to write about it in later works, mentioning briefly the 1665 episode and the Marseilles outbreak in *Atlas Maritimus* (1728), 67, 146–7, 151, 190, 206; and *A Plan of the English Commerce* (1728), 259–60, 267.
10. On this episode, see my article, 'Some Concealed Allusions in Defoe's *Tour*,' *Notes & Queries*, 264 (2019): 87–90. I am indebted to Dr Mark Jardine for information on this topic: no precise source has been located.
11. Macky, 2: 178–202.
12. Macky, 2: 198.
13. Edmund Burke, *A Philosophical Enquiry into the Origin of our Ideas of the Sublime and Beautiful*, ed. Adam Phillips (Oxford, 1990), 55.
14. Tillyard, *English Epic*, 470; *Epic Strain*, 26.

4 The Shape of the Nation

1. The scale of the woollen industry amid the counties adjoining the Cotswolds was a major obsession with Defoe: see for instance *CET*, 2.ii. 58–9. He did not foresee that their heyday was over.
2. Fiennes, 204–5. She adds that most who travel in the region go from one nobleman's house to another, where the inhabitants 'live great, tho' in so nasty a way,' that 'one has little stomach to eat or use anything'. Even supposing Defoe had baited his journeys in such a place, he could not afford to be quite so fastidious. It is not at all clear what town she was referring to as 'Kerk'.

3. The neatest comparison in terms of the two writer's interests is that of Christopher Morris: '[Like Defoe, Fiennes] too had all the Nonconformist, unromantic tastes and virtues. She too admired what was utilitarian and up to date. She too was sober, matter-of-fact, plain-spoken, trenchant and direct. There is, however, a warmth and charm in her Puritan piety and in her enthusiasm which keep her human and retain our sympathy' (Fiennes, xliii). In spite of Morris' use of the limiting 'however', which may be intended to exclude Defoe, I believe that the entire passage applies equally well to both writers. The big difference is that Fiennes came from the Cromwellian aristocracy and Defoe from the world of 'middling men', that is small merchants in the City.
4. One example may be given out of scores that permeate the text. At Shrewsbury we are told, 'This is really a Town of Mirth and Gallantry, something like *Bury* in *Suffolk*, or *Durham* in the *North*, but much bigger than either of them, or indeed than both together' (2: 194). We have already visited Bury in Volume I, and Durham will follow in Volume III: these tiny capillary vessels circulate meaning throughout the text.
5. Macky, 2: 139.
6. Macky, 2: 231, 234–5.
7. Macky, 2: 301.
8. Macky, 2: 236.
9. Defoe, *A Tour through the Whole Island of Great Britain*, abridged and ed. P. N. Furbank and W. R. Owens (New Haven, 1991), ix.
10. Gerald Hill, 'Circling Defoe,' *Arion*, 21 (1990): 69–84.
11. Christopher Parkes, '"A True Survey of the Ground": Defoe's *Tour* and the Rise of Thematic Cartography', *Philological Quarterly*, 74 (1995): 395–415.
12. Bowen, no pagination.
13. Quoted by Paul Laxton in his Preface to J. B. Harley, *The New Nature of Maps: Essays in the History of Cartography* (Baltimore, 2001), xiii.
14. P. J. Corfield, *The Impact of English Towns 1700–1800* (Oxford, 1982), 8. Other figures are drawn from a variety of sources, including E. A. Wrigley, *People, Cities and Wealth: The Transformation of Traditional Society* (Oxford, 1987), 160–61. Certain towns might be added to the list, including Reading (already 5,000 by 1660); Whitehaven (4,000 by 1713); Northampton (4,500 by 1675); and Carlisle (4,300 by 1688). See Christopher Chalklin, *The Rise of the English Town 1650–1850* (Cambridge, 2001), 77–8. The *Tour* covers each of these.
15. In the case of Sunderland this seems to be a simple oversight, as a highly Defovian entry is provided in *Atlas Maritimus* (see Chapter 12).
16. Bath and Tunbridge Wells came just below the cut-off line. So, too, did Scarborough, though Defoe is brief in his entry here (3: 114), most likely because he had never visited the town.

17. J. B. Harley, 'Introduction', in Bowen, 3.
18. *Libraries*, 13.
19. According to *OED*, the phrase derives from the Home Circuit of assize courts, first recorded in 1737.
20. It should be noted that the course of the modern A1 though to the A6 corresponds to the main Post Office routes established in the seventeenth century.
21. Tim Blanning, *The Pursuit of Glory: The Five Revolutions that Made Modern Europe 1648–1815* (London, 2007), 3–4, 9–12, 17. In his opening chapter (37), Blanning also describes postal innovations, including the penny post of William Dockra (*Tour*, 89–90), and the cross posts pioneered by Ralph Allen, unfortunately too recent to make it into the text.

5 The Role of the *Tour* in the Historiography of Early Modern Britain

1. Penelope J. Corfield, 'British History: The Exploding Galaxy', *Journal for Eighteenth-Century Studies*, 34 (2011): 517–26.
2. M. Dorothy George, *England in Johnson's Day* (London, 1928), 9–15, 222, 225. George uses modernised spelling: I revert to the original.
3. Robert O. Bucholz and Joseph P. Ward, *London: A Social and Cultural History 1550–1750* (Cambridge, 2012), 89, 304, 319, 330–31, 338.
4. Eric Pawson, *Transport and Economy: The Turnpike Roads of Eighteenth Century Britain* (London, 1977), 18.
5. Reprinted in E. A. Wrigley, *People Cities and Wealth: The Transformation of Traditional Society* (Oxford, 1987), 33–56 (147). The Preface with this famous passage has been anthologised more than once, most recently in *Travel Writing 1700–1830: An Anthology*, ed. Elizabeth A. Bohls and Ian Duncan (Oxford, 2005), 105–8. Favourite passages on the Peak District and the Pennines are also included.
6. Earlier, Jack Lindsay had produced a similar echo in the title of his book *The Monster City: Defoe's London, 1688–1730* (London, 1978). Defoe is cited on numerous occasions, and the author conducts his own 'tour' of the city. John Brewer's splendid work of cultural history refers to Defoe's account of London, once citing the phrase 'prodigious Thing' (actually applied to the trade of Halifax, 3: 60): see *The Pleasures of the Imagination: English Culture in the Eighteenth Century* (London, 1997), 11, 31, 51. In her copiously illustrated book *Londoners* (London, 1987), Celina Fox reproduces Defoe's comments on the markets in the capital (139). An alternative designation for the period is used in Derek Jarrett, *England in the Age of Hogarth* (London, 1976), but the *Tour* still makes an appearance (15, 58).

7. L. D. Schwartz, *London in the Age of Industrialisation: Entrepreneurs, Labour Force and Living Conditions, 1700–1850* (Cambridge, 1992), 79. Citing two paragraphs from Letter 5, Schwartz comments, 'Defoe, writing during the mid 1720s, would wax eloquent on London's growth.' The *Tour* is the prime source for Rudé's opening description of the growth of the city, and it is cited almost a dozen times in all: see *Hanoverian London 1714–1808* (London, 1971), esp. 1–18 .
8. *Londinopolis: Essays in the Cultural and Social History of Early Modern London*, ed. Paul Griffiths and Mark S. R. Jenner (Manchester, 2000), 162. Another frequently cited passage concerns the homes of wealthy citizens outside the capital: see William M. Cavert, *The Smoke of London: Energy and Environment in the Early Modern City* (Cambridge, 2016), 220.
9. Chalklin, for example, quotes from the *Tour* thirteen times in his introductory chapter to *The Provincial Towns of Georgian England* (London, 1974), 6–24.
10. The *Tour* is the first authority cited by Jackson, followed by four more citations and five from *A Plan of the English Commerce* (1728): see *Hull in the Eighteenth Century: A Study in Economic and Social History* (London, 1972). It is the first contemporary source quoted by Hussey in his opening paragraph: see *Coastal and River Trade in Pre-Industrial England: Bristol and its Region 1680–1730* (Exeter, 2000).
11. See *Country Towns in Pre-Industrial England*, ed. Peter Clark (New York, 1981). Similar findings apply in the case of several contributions to *Crisis and Order in English Towns 1500–1700: Essays in Urban History*, ed. Peter Clark and Paul Slack (London, 1972); *The Early Modern Town: A Reader*, ed. Peter Clark (London, 1976); *The Transformation of English Provincial Towns 1600–1800*, ed. Peter Clark (London, 1984); *The Eighteenth-Century Town: A Reader in English Urban History 1688–1820*, ed. Peter Borsay (London, 1990); and *Provincial Towns in Early Modern England and Ireland: Convergence and Divergence*, ed. Peter Borsay and Lindsay Proudfoot (Oxford, 2002). Of course, this list is not exhaustive.
12. Sidney and Beatrice Webb, *English Local Government: The Story of the King's Highway* (London, 1913); W. T. Jackman, *The Development of Transportation in Modern England* (1916; 3rd ed., London, 1966). The most important discussion of the later editions, and an argument that they deserve more respect than they have been given, are to be found in Katherine Turner, 'Defoe's *Tour*: The Changing "Face of Things"', *British Journal for Eighteenth-Century Studies* 24 (2001): 189–206. Even granted Turner's strong case, this does not justify scholars in attributing to Defoe by name some passages written long after his death.
13. Arnold Toynbee, *Lectures on the Industrial Revolution*, 2nd ed. (London, 1887), 60.

14. William Albert, *The Turnpike Road System in England 1663–1840* (Cambridge, 1972), 140.
15. In what remains a standard work on the subject, the same author cites the *Tour* on twelve occasions also: see T. S. Willan, *River Navigation in England 1600–1750* (1936; reprinted London, 1964). His map of 'Navigable Rivers, 1724–7 (Defoe)' is based on the *Tour* (68).
16. M. Dorothy George, *London Life in the Eighteenth Century* (1925; reprinted New York, 1965), 255, 231.
17. M. Dorothy George, *England in Transition: Life and Work in the Eighteenth Century* (Harmondsworth, 1969), 29–42. See also the lengthy quotation in the next chapter on the woollen industry of Halifax (44–6).
18. Paul Mantoux, *The Industrial Revolution in the Eighteenth Century*, tr. Marjorie Vernon (1906; London, 1966), 50–56, conducts a peregrination of the woollen industry on the basis of numerous passages in the *Tour.*
19. Peter Mathias, *The First Industrial Nation* (London, 1969), 161. In one of a number of references to the book, Ashton observed that 'Defoe had an eye for whatever was striking and unusual, and sometimes he ran to hyperbole; but it is impossible to ignore the picture he presents' (*An Economic History of England: The Eighteenth Century* (London, 1955), 33). Clapham quoted Defoe seventeen times in fifty pages on industrialism, and seven times in nine pages *A Concise Economic History of Britain: from the Earliest Times to 1750* (Cambridge, 1963).
20. F. J. Fisher, 'The Sixteenth and Seventeenth Centuries: The Dark Ages in English Economic History?', *Economica*, 24 (1957): 2–18 (9).
21. See 'The Age of the Improver 1600–1800', in *A New Historical Geography of England*, ed. H. C. Darby (Cambridge, 1973), 302–88. A map on the distribution of the cloth industry (339) is based on Defoe's work. Another eminent historical geographer, J. H. Andrews, concluded that 'In spite of its weaknesses the 'Tour" remains a great pioneer work of economic geography': see 'Defoe and the Sources of his "Tour"', *Geographical Journal* 126 (1960): 268–77 (275). For a discussion of the reliability or otherwise of the *Tour* on relevant issues, see Derek Gregory's chapter on '"A New and Differing Face": Three Geographies of Industrialization', in *An Historical Geography of England and Wales*, ed. R. A. Dodgshon and R. A. Butlin (London, 1990), 351–99. He concludes that the book 'remains an indispensable source for the mood of much of early-eighteenth-century Britain' (394).
22. Cited from Cole's *Persons and Periods* (Harmondsworth, 1938), 23, a collection of essays including one on Defoe generally and one on 'Defoe's England'. Further applications to the *Tour* appear in sections of this book on 'London – One Fifth of England' and 'Roads, Rivers, and Canals'.

23. See *England under Queen Anne: Blenheim* (1930; reprinted London, 1965), 13–14; *Illustrated Social History* (1944; reprinted Harmondsworth, 1964), 3: 17–18. The expression 'Defoe's England' gained fresh currency more recently when used as the heading of a section on the *Tour* in Douglas Hay and Nicholas Rogers, *Eighteenth-Century English Society* (Oxford, 1997), 114–15.
24. *Johnson's England*, ed. A. S. Turberville, 2 vols (Oxford, 1933), 1: 128–9.
25. Basil Williams, *The Whig Supremacy 1714–1760* (Oxford, 1939), 93–143.
26. Michael Reed, 'The Transformation of Urban Space 1700–1840,' in *The Cambridge Urban History of Britain*, vol. 2: *1540–1840*, ed. Peter Clark (Cambridge, 2000), 615–40.
27. In a momentary aberration, Clark twice allocates Defoe's 'gloomy picture' of Scotland to the 1730s ('Small Towns 1700–1840', in *Cambridge History*, 754–5).
28. In her useful survey, *The Georgian Town 1680–1840* (Basingstoke, 2001), Ellis again cites the *Tour* more than any other contemporary source. The references occur in all seven chapters, devoted respectively to 'The Urban Prospect', 'Urban Growth', 'Making a Living', 'Urban Society', 'Landscape and Environment', 'Identity and Community' and 'Towns and Change.' There could scarcely be a more convincing or concrete demonstration of the value of the work across a wide range of issues connected with urban history – just one of the aspects of national life that Defoe illuminates.
29. See *Britain in the First Age of Party*, ed. Clyve Jones (London, 1987), 195–209. Borsay also cites the *Tour* in his essay 'A County Town in Transition: The Great Fire of Warwick, 1694', in *Provincial Towns in Early Modern England and Ireland*, ed. Peter Borsay and Lindsay Proudfoot (Oxford, 2002), 151–70 (162)
30. Roy Porter, *English Society in the Eighteenth Century* (London, 1990), 214; 'The Wonderful Extent and Variety of London', *London 1753*, ed. Sheila O'Connell (Boston, 2003), 9–17; *The Creation of the Modern World: The Untold Story of the British Enlightenment* (New York, 2000), 40.
31. W. A. Speck, *Stability and Strife: England, 1714–1760* (Cambridge, MA, 1977), 120. See also the comment by Angus McInnes, citing a passage from the *Tour* on Catholics in Durham, '"Daniel Defoe, a keen observer and one of the most skilled journalists of the period": The Revolution and the People,' in *Britain after the Glorious Revolution 1689–1714*, ed. Geoffrey Homes (London, 1969), 80–95 (81). McInnes also devotes space to the famous episode when the narrator encounters the leadminer in the Peak District (87).
32. Christopher Hill, *The Pelican Economic History of Britain*, vol. 2: *1530–1780, Reformation to Industrial Revolution* (Harmondsworth, 1969), 21.
33. Wilfrid Prest, *Albion Ascendant; English History 1660–1815*, The Short Oxford History of the Modern World (Oxford, 1998), 110–15.

34. Julian Hoppit, *A Land of Liberty? England 1689–1727* (Oxford, 2000), which contains nine references. J. A. Sharpe's social history of *Early Modern England in the Period 1550–1760* (London, 1997) paraphrases Defoe's findings in the *Tour* ('so familiar a source') with regard to the extent of manufactures prior to the Industrial Revolution (146–7). Maxine Berg makes several citations from the *Tour* on industries, both in their growth and their decline: see *The Age of Manufactures 1700–1820*, 2nd ed. (London, 1994).
35. Paul Langford, *A Polite and Commercial People: England 1727–1783* (Oxford, 1989), 391–408.
36. Near the start of their enquiry into class mobility in the early modern period, Lawrence Stone and Jeanne C. Fawter Stone cite several passages from Defoe's 'tour of England', and conclude that his 'description of how merchants entered the gentry is entirely accurate' (*An Open Elite? England 1540–1880* (Oxford, 1986), 6–17). They draw on the work in further excerpts from their book.
37. Joan Thirsk, 'Industries in the Countryside', *Essays in the Economic and Social History of Tudor and Stuart England*, ed. F. J. Fisher (Cambridge, 1961), 70–88 (74–5).
38. Defoe's comments on tree planting are used by Keith Thomas, *Man and the Natural World: Changing Attitudes in England 1500–1800* (Harmondsworth, 1984), 209.
39. David Underdown, *Start of Play: Cricket and Culture in Eighteenth-Century England* (London, 2001), 4. Alternatively, the traveller could have witnessed race meetings on the Down, or even a political affray there a few years earlier that involved Jacobites, among them Pope's friend John Caryll (101). The references are to the reprint by Penguin Books.
40. Quoted by Underdown, *Start of Play*, 193.
41. These examples come in addition to many citations from entries on the shire constituencies and on the members.
42. Geoffrey Beard, *Craftsmen and Interior Decoration in England 1660–1820* (London, 1986), 244 (other references: 146, 151).
43. Rosemary Sweet, *Antiquaries: The Discovery of the Past in Eighteenth-Century Britain* (London, 2004), 314–16. In an earlier work Sweet had remarked that 'it is very common to find passages on the town [Norwich] lifted almost verbatim from Defoe' (*The Writing of Urban Histories in Eighteenth-Century England* (Oxford, 1997), 268). This comment applies to surveys of many other towns. Sweet calls attention to Defoe's 'prescient' sense of the manufacturing town in her *Introduction to The English Town, 1680–1840: Government, Society and Culture* (Abingdon, 2014), 17. See also the comparison between the *Tour* and Stukeley's *Itinerarium Curiosum* (1724) in David Boyd Haycock, *William Stukeley: Science, Religion and Archaeology in Eighteenth-Century England* (Woodbridge, 2002), 112–13.

44. Significantly Jeremy Black quotes a key passage from the preface to vol. I of the *Tour*, 'a book whose publication reflected a widespread interest in the country': see Jeremy Black, *Historical Atlas of Great Britain: The End of the Middle Ages to the Georgian Era* (Stroud, 2000), 51. Black's book is organised in terms of the way that Britain was mapped over time, a matter of great relevance to Defoe, who was a keen collector of works on geography and chorography, and evidently used roadbooks as one of his sources. The prominent cartographer Herman Moll supplied maps for vols II and III of the *Tour.*
45. *Letters*, 116.
46. On this perception and its consequence in terms of more severe government measures, see J. M. Beattie, *Policing and Punishment in London 1660–1750: Urban Crime and the Limits of Terror* (Oxford, 2001), 256. Defoe's comments on the situation appear chiefly in his pamphlets on social themes written around this date. The former attribution to him of lives of criminals such as Jack Sheppard and Jonathan Wild in 1724–6 is no longer regarded as safe.
47. See, for example, comments on James Johnston's new-fangled garden at Twickenham, quoted by D. D. R. Chambers, *The Planters of the English Garden: Botany, Trees, and the 'Georgics'* (New Haven, 1993), 130.
48. Williams, *Whig Supremacy*, 103.
49. *The Manufacturer*, 30 October 1719.
50. W. G. Hoskins, 'Foreword', *Crisis and Order*, vii; Thirsk, 'Introduction', *Rural England: An Illustrated History of the Landscape*, ed. J. Thirsk (Oxford, 2000), 14. For the use by Hoskins of the *Tour* in his most famous book, see *The Making of the English Landscape* (London, 1985), 140–41, 151–52, 215, 219, 222.
51. For an insistence that Defoe relied on his earlier journeys, see Andrews, 'Defoe and the Sources', 271–3; and F. Bastian, 'Defoe's Tour and the Historian', *History Today*, 17 (1967): 845–51. There are in fact more signs in the text of recent knowledge than either of these writers admits. See also Chapter 10 below.
52. Earle makes free use of the 'great Tour' in *The World of Defoe* (London, 1976), noting that modern writers miss the conservative element in Defoe's economic theory when 'they seize on the *Tour* as a superb description of England on the eve of the Industrial Revolution, which of course it is' (17, 108).
53. Peter Earle, *The Making of the English Middle Class: Business, Society and Family Life in London, 1660–1730* (London, 1989), xi. In the sequel. *A City Full of People: Men and Women of London 1650–1750* (London, 1994), Earle alludes to the *Tour* more sparsely.
54. Many bibliographies of the period place Defoe's book at the head of their list. For example, the opening section of 'Source Material' in one list of almost 300

entries contains three items: the first is Cobbett's *Parliamentary History of England,* the second is the *Tour.* See Geoffrey Holmes and Daniel Szechi, *The Age of Oligarchy: Pre-Industrial Britain 1722–1783* (London, 1993), 410.

6 The Jacobite Rising in the *Tour*

1. From the immense trove of literature on relevant matters, I have relied chiefly on a number of sources: on the Rising itself, Daniel Szechi, *1715: The Great Jacobite Rebellion* (New Haven, 2006); on military matters, extending beyond the one battle, Stuart Reid, *Sheriffmuir, 1715: The Jacobite War in Scotland* (Barnsley, 2013); still useful, P. W. J. Riley, *The Union of England and Scotland: A Study of Anglo-Scottish Politics of the Eighteenth Century* (Manchester, 1978); on Jacobitism more generally, for a concise summary of the wider context, Murray G. H. Pittock, *Jacobitism* (Basingstoke, 1998); and on the Highland clans, Bruce Lenman, *The Jacobite Clans of the Great Glen 1650–1784* (London, 1984).
2. Daniel Szechi, *The Jacobites: Britain and Europe 1688–1788* (Manchester, 2008), 73.
3. Naturally Defoe had mentioned the Rising in earlier sections of the *Tour.* However, he is brief on the main English theatre of the invasion, Northumberland. In contrast to the passages almost amounting to a threnody alluding to the captured Scottish rebels, there is no mention of the fate of Lord Widdrington, Thomas Forster, and especially the Earl of Derwentwater. The trial and execution of Derwentwater were perhaps still recent sores; but Defoe does not avoid his fellow victim, Kenmure (see above, pp. 146–7).
4. Szechi, *The Jacobites*, 72.
5. 'In 1706 he was a government agent, employed specifically to support the union in any way he could' (Riley, *Union*, 240: see 240–45 for a critical assessment of Defoe's writings in this capacity). Twenty years later, Defoe was no longer in government service, but he was anxious to dispel fears among the Whig elite that he could not be trusted.
6. F. Bastian suggested that Defoe may have visited a number of locations including the Orkney and Shetland Islands, Galloway, and south-eastern Scotland between 1690 and 1703: see *Defoe's Early Life* (London, 1981), 150–51, 178–80, 211–14, 284–6. These speculative journeys have not been generally accepted by scholars, though none is impossible.
7. *Letters*, 230.
8. Out of more than eighty subscribers who comprise the fairly small list, twenty appear by name in the *Tour.* Apart from Mar and his kinsman Sir John Erskine, and Polwarth, they make up a solidly Whig and pro-Union phalanx. Another

document revealing the close interest Defoe took in current affairs is the cipher list he sent to Harley in October 1710, which covers a number of the Scottish people and issues mentioned in the *Tour* (British Library, Add. MS. 70314).

9. Macky, 3: 299–311. This is a reissue of the text of the 1723 edition, though repaginated owing to an error in sig. I4. The author had died in exile in 1726.
10. See *Libraries*, passim. As is well known, the catalogue mixes the works owned by Defoe and Farewell. However, the former's obsessive interest in history (especially that of Scotland) and geography appears not to have been shared by the latter to any real extent (see *Libraries*, xviii–xxi). It is not clear why the Anglican vicar of a small parish in Rutland would have needed to consult books such as Sibbald's, or items like an account of the coronation of Charles II at Scone in 1650. Four volumes by George Buchanan were central to Defoe's concerns, hardly at all to Farewell's.
11. When describing the College of Physicians (*TGB* 3:170), Defoe mentions Sibbald's *Auctarium Musaei Balfouriani e Sibbaldino* (Edinburgh, 1697), and he may have known the same author's topographic works on Fife, Stirlingshire and adjacent counties.
12. William L. Payne, *Index to Defoe's Review* (New York, 1948), 54–6.
13. On the Royal Bounty, see Lenman, *Jacobite Clans*, 20–22; and Domhnall Uilleam Stiùbhart, 'The Genesis and Operation of the Royal Bounty Scheme, 1725–30', *Records of the Scottish Church History Society*, 33 (2003): 63–141.
14. There is a contrast between the anxiety Defoe felt at the time (seen for example in *Letters*, 136–53 and *Review*, 17 December 1706) with his later dismissive judgement ('all the little Tumults and Disorders of the Rabble as well at *Edinburgh* as at *Glasgow*, and other Places, being timely suppress' (3: 280).
15. *Letters*, 378.
16. Alistair M. Duckworth, '"Whig" Landscapes in Defoe's *Tour*', *Philological Quarterly*, 61 (1982): 453–65 (458). Nigel Everett's chapter on 'The Whig Idea of Landscape and Its Critics,' in *The Tory View of Landscape* (New Haven, 1994), 38–90, does not discuss Scotland, and has no reference to the dynastic disputes of the age.
17. Defoe wrongly asserted that Aberdour in Fife had come into the control of Tweeddale: it was the family home of the Earl of Morton, and though it was damaged during the Rising the Earl moved into an adjacent property. The observation, 'The House is old, but magnificent, and the Lands about it, as all must do, that come into the managing Hands of the Family of *Tweedale*, have been infinitely improv'd by Planting and Enclosing' (3: 228) thus misses its full propagandist aim.
18. Macky, 3: 315.

19. *Letters*, 229.
20. [Daniel Defoe], *A Trumpet Blown in the North, and Sounded in the Ears of John Eriskine, call'd by the Men of the World, Duke of Mar* (London, 1715), 3.
21. Macky, 3: 184.
22. The most interesting case among family members is that of Sir John Erskine of Alva (1678–1739), although he remained a marginal figure in the conduct of the Rising, as he seems to have been distrusted by the Pretender. Defoe conceals a fact that still compromised Erskine, even though he had been effectively pardoned in 'a frankly corrupt deal' with the minister Lord Townshend (Szechi, *1715*, 224). Macky was les tactful: 'He was in the Rebellion, but sav'd his Estate by discovering to the Government a Silver Mine in his Lands, which produces a great deal of Silver' (Macky, 3: 193).
23. Macky, 3: 158–9.
24. Macky, 3: 11.
25. Macky, 3: 43.
26. Christopher Sinclair-Stevenson, *Inglorious Rebellion: The Jacobite Risings of 1708, 1715 and 1719* (St Albans, 1973), 189.
27. Macky, 3: 127.
28. Macky, 3: 135.
29. Defoe discusses Marischal's father among the peers who were 'Declar'd profest Jacobites' in a letter to Harley in November 1710 (*Letters*, 295).
30. Macky, 3: 103–4.
31. Edward M. Furgol, 'Keith, George, styled tenth Earl Marischal, *ODNB*, https://doi-org.ezproxy.lib.usf.edu/10.1093/ref:odnb/15265 .
32. Macky, 3: 121.
33. Szechi, *1715*, 248.
34. Another case where Defoe suppresses the full truth, which involves the family of the Duke of Atholl, who had been widely expected to join the Pretender but held fast to the government. The *Tour* says a good deal about him, acknowledging that 'His *Grace* was always an Opposer of the Union . . . but he did not carry his Opposition to the Height of Tumult and Rebellion.' However, he does not mention the Duke's son William Murray, Marquess of Tullibardine, even though the seat of this name (later demolished after the rebellion of the Young Pretender) is covered (3: 280–81). Attainted with his two brothers after the battle of Preston, Tullibardine fled to France and took part in the Jacobite attempts of 1719 and 1745–6. McVeagh (3: 338, n. 76) mixes up the Duke and his son.
35. Macky, 3: 200.
36. *Letters*, 230.
37. Macky, 3: 153.

38. *Letters*, 185.
39. Macky, 3: 278–90.
40. Macky, 3: 116.
41. *Letters*, 218, 247.
42. Writing a little earlier, Macky (3: 125) does mention Seaforth's part in the 1719 expedition.
43. Szechi, *1715*, 240.

7 The Impact of the Bubble

1. Maximillian E. Novak, *Daniel Defoe: Master of Fictions* (Oxford, 2001), 575.
2. *Letters*, 345–9.
3. *Letters*, 347.
4. *Atlas Maritimus & Commercialis* (London, 1728), 318. See Chapter 12 below.
5. The political background to South Sea is clearly set out by Ragnhild Hatton, *George I: Elector and King* (London, 1978), esp. Chapters 7–9.
6. *The Anatomy of Exchange-Alley* (London, 1719), 37–8.
7. *Anatomy*, 40–41.
8. *The Case of Mr. Law Truly Stated.* (London, 1720 for 1719), 3, 5–6, 8, 24, 18.
9. P. N. Furbank and W. R. Owens, *A Critical Bibliography of Daniel Defoe* (London, 1998), 256.
10. Novak, *Defoe*, 604.
11. See my essay, '"This Calamitous Year": *A Journal of the Plague Year* and the South Sea Bubble', in *Eighteenth-Century Encounters* (Brighton, 1985), 151–67 (155).
12. *A Journal of the Plague Year*, ed. Louis Landa (Oxford, 1990), 248.
13. 'Aside from the ownership of shares, connections between the Child family and the East India Company weakened after Josiah's death, and Richard appears to have had little involvement in the company.' Quoted from Hannah Armstrong, 'The Lost Landscapes and Interiorscapes of the Eighteenth-Century Estate: Reconstructing Wanstead House and its Grounds', PhD dissertation, Birkbeck College, University of London (2016), 106. Defoe mentions Wanstead as one of the fine houses built by London merchants 'equall to the pallaces of some princes abroad' in *The Compleat English Gentleman*, ed. Karl. D. Bülbring (London, 1890), 263.
14. *CET*, 1.i: 301.
15. Macky, 2: 4–5. The writer had already spent four ages describing Wanstead in the first volume.
16. *CET*, 1.i: 309; *Compleat English Gentleman*, 262, 265.
17. *The History of Parliament: The House of Commons, 1715–1754*, ed. Romney Sedgwick, 2 vols (London, 1970), 2: 171.
18. *House of Commons*, ed. Sedgwick, 2: 172.

19. John Carwell, *The South Sea Bubble* (Stroud, 2001), 178.
20. *CET*, 1.i: 301, 303, 309; *Compleat English Gentleman*, 261.
21. Ann M. Carlos and Larry Neal, 'Women Investors in Early Capital Markets, 1720–1725', *Financial History Review* 11 (2004): 197–224 (198, 205–8).
22. *Daily Post*, 19 December 1722. William Lee, *Daniel Defoe: His Life and Recently fDiscovered Writings*, 3 vols (London, 1869), 3: 80, prints this story from the *Daily Post* as though it was written by Defoe: this is conceivable, but no more.
23. *CET*, 2.i: 95.
24. *Daily Journal*, 3 April 1722. Hodges actually had the lowest holding of anyone in the Bank of England stock ledgers, just £4: see Ann M. Carlos and Larry Neal, 'The Micro-Foundations of the Early London Capital Market: Bank of England Shareholders during and after the South Sea Bubble, 1720–25', *Economic History Review*, 59 (2006): 498–538 (530).
25. *CET*, 1.i: 164.
26. *CET*, 1.i. 37–8; 1.i: 59.
27. *CET*, 2.i: 94; 2.i: 29.
28. *CET*, 2.ii: 7–8.

8 Local Proverbs and Folk Wisdom

1. By far the best discussion of Defoe's attitude to linguistic diversity is to be found in George A. Starr, 'Defoe's Tour through the Dialects and Jargons of Great Britain', *Modern Philology*, 110 (2012), 74–95.
2. She sometimes travelled with her mother, or some other gentlewomen, and propriety may have limited her opportunities for casual exchanges with strangers. She visited relatives scattered around the country, and once was greeted with 'a very civil treate' by the mayor of Chester, 'being an acquaintance of my Brother [in law]' (Fiennes 179). Defoe had scarcely any such family distractions.
3. The formula 'they tell us' occurs around thirty times but it often seems to mean no more than 'I have learnt, I was informed', presumably from books or other virtual sources.
4. Adam Fox, *Oral and Literate Culture in England 1500–1700* (Oxford, 2000), 112–71 (112). Fox's next chapter, on 'Old Wives' Tales and Nursery Lore', could be applied to numerous legends and superstitions mentioned sceptically by Defoe: to give only a single instance, the dismissal as 'Country Tales' of the myths surrounding two pools called 'Hell's Kettles' near Darlington, because ''Tis evident, they are nothing but old Coal Pits filled with Water by the River *Tees*' (3: 115). See text, p. 187.
5. References are supplied as follows: Morris P. Tilley, *A Dictionary of the Proverb in England in the Sixteenth and Seventeenth Centuries* (Ann Arbor,

MI 1966), cited as 'Tilley' with the index number; F. P. Wilson, *The Oxford Dictionary of English Proverbs* (Oxford, 1970), cited as '*ODEP*' with page number; G. L. Apperson, *The Wordsworth Dictionary of Proverbs* (Ware, Hertfordshire, 1993), cited as 'Apperson' with page number.

6. *Robinson Crusoe*, ed. Evan R. Davis (Peterborough, ON, 2010), 57. Proverbs 30: 8 is quoted even earlier in the text (48).
7. *The Farther Adventures of Robinson Crusoe* (London, 1719), 1.
8. See *Moll Flanders*, ed. Pat Rogers (London, 1993), 38, 45, 93, 149, 220.
9. See *Roxana: The Fortunate Mistress*, ed. David Blewett (London, 1982), 46, 50, 304–5.
10. *An Essay upon Projects* (London, 1697), 1, 22, 33–4, 301.
11. *The Poor Man's Plea* (London, 1698), 28, 30.
12. *The True-Born Englishman, A Satyr* (London, 1701), 12.
13. Other familiar sayings found in this book are 'Ex quo vis ligno non fit Mercurio' (an Erasmian adage, which was adopted into English: see Tilley M893 and *ODEP* 227); 'Scribendo disces scriber', another expression sometimes Anglicised (*ODEP* 923); and 'birds of a feather flock together' (Tilley B393). In addition, Defoe creates a mock legal maxim, 'Qui sharpat sharpabatur' (*CET*, 2. ii: 133). He refers to the sayings of Solomon at least nine times in the two volumes, not counting oblique references that derive from this source.
14. *The Compleat English Gentleman*, ed. K. D. Bülbring (London, 1890), 42. This is not the only raid in this work to the hoard of proverbs; there are also several allusions once more to the wisdom of Solomon.
15. *Every-body's Business is No-body's Business* (London, 1725), 3. Other proverbs quoted in this pamphlet are 'Never a Barrel the better Herring' (Tilley B94), 24; and 'The Devil take the hindmost' (Tilley D267), 29.
16. Quotations are taken from *The Worthies of England*, ed. John Freeman (London, 1952), cited as 'Fuller.'
17. Fiennes, 114.
18. Fiennes, 16.
19. Jacqueline Simpson and Steve Roud, *A Dictionary of English Folklore* (Oxford, 2000), 55.
20. It also appears in the form, 'Hence it is grown Proverbial among the Inhabitants, for Lemster Bread, Weobly Beer, none can come near', in James Brome, *Travels over England, Scotland and Wales* (London, 2nd ed., 1707), 94. Brome's account is largely derivative, from Camden in particular: it would have proved of little independent value for Defoe, though he may have picked up an occasional detail from this source.
21. Apperson's example comes from the next county and the next century, that is *Lancashire Folk-Lore* (1867), but it conforms to the earlier drift of the expression.

22. Richard Rawlinson, *The History and Antiquities of the Cathedral Church of Salisbury, and the Abbey Church of Bath* (London, 1723), vi.
23. 'Captain Bland', *The Northern Atalantis* (London, 1713), 43.
24. *CET*, 2.i: 211; [Defoe], *The History and Remarkable Life of the Truly Honourable Col. Jacque* (London, 1723), 122.
25. This is despite the fact that he acknowledges the kind reception he received in some places, for example the 'many extraordinary Civilities' bestowed by the gentlemen of Galloway (3: 194).
26. Naturally, the *Tour* draws on more straightforward proverbial lore, without any local reference, as when Defoe writes of Saltash, 'We saw many Houses as it were falling down, and I doubt not but the Mice and Rats have abandoned many more, *as they say they will, when they are likely to fall*' (1: 232) This ancient saying (Tilley M1243) is signalised typographically by the use of italics. Similarly, the statement that the Cumbrian fells are 'all barren and wild, of no use or advantage either to Man or Beast' (3: 136) draws on a saying about the east wind, recorded by John Ray and Fuller among others (Tilley W442).

9 The Uses of Topography

1. J. H. Andrews, 'Defoe and the Sources of his "Tour"', *Geographic Journal*, 168 (1960): 268–77. Cited in the text as 'Sources'.
2. Christopher Parkes, '"A True Survey of the Ground": Defoe's *Tour* and the Rise of Thematic Cartography', *Philological Quarterly*, 74 (1995): 395–415; Jesse Edwards, 'Defoe the Geographer: Redefining the "Wonderful" in *A Tour thro' the Whole Island of Great Britain*', in *Travel Narratives, the New Science, and Literary Discourse, 1569–1750*, ed. Judy A. Hayden (Farnham, 2012), 179–94; and 'Geographic Literacy and Defoe's Complete Englishmen: Mere Bookcases v. Walking Maps', *Journal for Eighteenth-Century Studies*, 35 (2012): 325–41. For useful discussion of sources, see also John McVeagh's Introduction in *Tour* 1: 20–28.
3. See *Libraries*, 14. Defoe first cited the 1695 version in his *Essay upon Projects* (1697), 71. Unless otherwise indicated, I cite the 1722 text here, as it is more accessible and easier to use by bringing the additional material into closer contact with Camden's original.
4. 'Sources', 273. See also J. H. Andrews, 'A Case of Plagiarism in Defoe's "Tour"', *Notes & Queries*, 204 (1959): 399. Monuchdenny is the name given by John Speed to the highest point in the Brecon Beacons, and in the whole of southern Wales (2,906 feet); now known as Pen y fan. Defoe perhaps found it in Morden's map in *Britannia*, or perhaps in Bowen, 163. Defoe refers to Speed elsewhere (2: 146, 148).
5. See my article, 'Defoe's Use of Maps of Wales', *English Language Notes*, 42 (2004): 30–35.

6. It is this state of the map that appears in *Magna Britannia, antiqua & nova* (London, 1738), vi. [opp. 1].
7. Defoe also mentions '*Wharton* from *Wharton Hall*' among ancient families in the locality. McVeagh (3: 322) suggests this refers to the descendants of George Wharton of Kirkby Kendal, but as is made clear by Gibson (*Britannia*, 2: 988), it certainly means the baronial line settled at Wharton Hall, at the foot of the Mallerstang valley, currently represented by the mercurial Philip, Duke of Wharton.
8. The lines are quoted in *The Oxford Dictionary of English Proverbs*, 3rd ed. (1970), 740, but without explanation that the two succeeding names refer to Helvellyn (3,117 feet or 950 metres) and its outrider Catstye Cam (2,920 feet or 890 metres). As is well known, all three peaks are lower than Scafell Pike.
9. Surprisingly Moll omits Skiddaw in *A New Description*, facing 320, although he does include Hard Knott Hill, and the accompanying text in its slavish reproduction of *Britannia* copies out the passage on Skiddaw verbatim (324). Such instances disprove the suggestion by G. D. H. Cole that Defoe 'undoubtedly used Moll's work, and may have collaborated with him to some extent' (see Cole's edition of the *Tour* (London, 1927), 1: xxvii). *A New Description* adds very little to *Britannia* that could augment Defoe's coverage, especially in the remote areas where he was at his weakest.
10. Despite these opprobrious references, Senex made wholesale reuse of the *Tour* in many sections of his *Atlas Maritimus & Commercialis* (1728). Indeed, it is probable that Defoe was responsible for editing his own text for this project, which Senex had initiated with William Taylor in the same year that Taylor published *Robinson Crusoe* (1719): see Chapter 12.
11. For this journey, see *Letters*, 108–18.
12. Jerom (sic) Merch, *A History of the Presbyterian and General Baptist Churches in the West of England* (London, 1835), 268–70.
13. *CET*, 2.i: 57, 2.ii: 133; *A Brief Deduction of the Original, Progress, and Immense Greatness of the British Woollen Manufacture* (London, 1727), 12; *Plan* (London, 1728), 84–5. See also *Tour*, 1: 109.
14. The regulations concerning the mines as set out at the Barmote Court in 1665 would be reprinted in *The Compleat Mineral Laws of Derbyshire* (London, 1734), 80–122, but I have not found a version readily accessible in 1726.
15. Some parallels can be found in the *Tour* with *A New Description of England and Wales* (1724), with maps by Moll, but in each case the common source is *Britannia*.

16. Robert Thoroton, *The Antiquities of Nottinghamshire* (London, 1677), 220–28. The ancestral information here was provided by the great naturalist Francis Willughby (1635–72), shortly before his death.
17. The *Tour* (2: 203) cites Dugdale's *Antiquities of Warwickshire* (1661) on the county town and on the Beauchamp family.
18. One source on antiquities that appeared just too late to be used in Letters 9 to 13 was Alexander Gordon, *Itinerarium septentrionale: or, A Journey thro' most of the Counties of Scotland, and those in the North of England.* This was published a few weeks before Defoe's third volume on 7 May 1726, by a group of booksellers headed by George Strahan, whose name also appears first in the imprint of the *Tour*.
19. Rosemary Sweet, *The Writing of Urban Histories in Eighteenth-Century England* (Oxford, 1997), 80–82.
20. The dedication in Midgley is signed 'William Bently', who has been identified as parish clerk at St John the Baptist church, Halifax.
21. Defoe refers to this occurrence in *CET*, 1: 91.
22. Macky, 2: 130.
23. Macky, 1: 133; 2: 169. In the fourth edition (1724), 1:130, Macky alters the tense of his remark about Jansson's estate, but he does not explain why.
24. Macky, 2: 153.
25. The source is not identified by McVeagh or previous commentators.
26. Macky, 1: 113–31.
27. For example, it is no longer safe to accept an attribution to Defoe such as *The Bristol Riot* (1714), which Andrews took as an indication that Defoe visited the city in that year. More has come to light on his early experiences as a trader, and the likely nature of his travels in that capacity. New editions of many works, including the *Review*, supplement observations by Andrews. Finally, the writer pointed out in 1960 that, except for an edition of the London segments in 1929, 'which has notes on mainly architectural topics, no part of the book has appeared with modern notes, index or other editorial apparatus' ('Sources', 275, n. 1). This no longer holds true in the light of the edition by McVeagh.

10 Road-testing the First Turnpikes

1. William Albert, 'The Turnpike Trusts,' in Derek H. Aldcroft and Michael J. Freeman (eds), *Transport in the Industrial Revolution* (Manchester, 1983), 211.
2. The careers of both Webbs, Sidney (1859–1947) and Beatrice (1858–1943), social reformers, Fabians and scholars, are fully documented. William Thomas Jackman (1871–1951) is less well remembered. He taught at the University of

Toronto from 1915 to 1941 and wrote several later books, most notably *Economics of Transportation* (1926).

3. Some important articles, each of which exhibits the emphases in theme and period mentioned, include Dan Bogart, 'Turnpike Trusts and the Transportation Revolution in 18th Century England', *Explorations in Economic History*, 42 (2005): 479–508; 'Turnpike Trusts, Infrastructure Investment, and the Road Transportation Revolution in Eighteenth-Century England', *Journal of Economic History*, 65 (2005): 540–43; and 'Did Turnpike Trusts Increase Transportation Investment in Eighteenth-Century England?', *Journal of Economic History*, 65 (2005): 439–68; Dorian Gerhold, 'Productivity Change in Road Transport before and after Turnpiking', *Economic History Review*, 49 (1996): 491–515; and 'The Development of Stage Coaching and the Impact of Turnpike Roads, 1653–1840', *Economic History Review*, 67 (2014): 818–45. The book by Theo Barker and Dorian Gerhold, *The Rise and Rise of Road Transport, 1700–1990* (London, 1993), is predominantly weighted in the direction of events after 1830, but it does contain a single citation from the *Tour*.
4. Godfrey Davies, 'Daniel Defoe's *A Tour thro' the Whole Island of Great Britain*,' *Modern Philology*, 48 (1950): 21–36. Davies states (33, n. 35) that the abridgment was dropped after 1738, but this is wrong: it appeared in the third edition of 1742.
5. See William Albert, *The Turnpike Road System in England 1663–1840* (Cambridge, 1972); and Eric Pawson, *Transport and Economy: The Turnpike Roads of Eighteenth Century Britain* (London, 1977). The wider focus on the national economy in Pawson's book enables him to cite a more diverse range of Defoe's views from the *Tour*.
6. G. D. H. Cole, *Persons and Periods* (Harmondsworth, 1945), 21, 31–2, 79.
7. G. M. Trevelyan, *Illustrated English Social History, vol. III: The Eighteenth Century* (Harmondsworth, 1964), 18, 53–4. See also Defoe's observations on muddy roads in the Weald of Sussex, quoted by Trevelyan, 105.
8. Paul Langford, *A Polite and Commercial People: England 1727–1783* (Oxford, 1989), 396. See also comments by Peter Borsay in *The Eighteenth Century 1688–1715*, ed. Paul Langford (Oxford, 2002): in his *Tour* Defoe 'delivered an extended and effusive paean to the wonders of turnpiking'. As Borsay goes on to say, 'Significantly this account preceded by some decades the great bulk of turnpike legislation' (187).
9. This interest is clear from a passage in the *Tour* describing in considerable detail the flight of one 'Nicks' after he had committed a robbery near Gravesend (1: 144–5). The course of this journey to York resembles that later assigned to the highwayman Dick Turpin, whose legend grew posthumously. See the account of the episode in Defoe: 'that wonderful source for eighteenth-century economic and social history', in James Sharpe, *Dick Turpin: The Myth of the English Highwayman* (London, 2005), 74.

10. On Defoe's novels in relation to criminal biography generally, see Lincoln B. Faller, *Crime and Defoe: A New Kind of Writing* (Cambridge, 1993), It should be noted that he had written a good deal on the subject in his journalism, for example articles in *Applebee's Journal* on the capture and execution of the French bandit Cartouche (Louis-Dominique Garthausen) in 1721.
11. Backscheider, 465.
12. Albert, *Turnpike Road System*, 44.
13. César de Saussure, *A Foreign View of England in the Reigns of George I. & George II.*, tr. Madame Van Muyden (London, 1902), 146–7.
14. Defoe has Moll Flanders and her highwayman husband carry out some of their tricky exploits on this section of the Chester Road.
15. Albert, *Turnpike Road System*, 31–3.
16. In a novel published at the start of 1722, his famous character Moll Flanders takes a thieving tour of the region, stopping at Sturbridge Fair outside Cambridge, Newmarket and Bury St Edmunds, then moving on to Ipswich, Harwich and Colchester. Defoe claims to have known Ipswich as long ago as 1668 (1: 86).
17. This count is based on the tables in Albert, *Turnpike Road System*, 202–5, checked against Pawson, *Transport and Economy*, 341–4.
18. John Latimer, *Annals of Bristol in the Eighteenth Century* (Bristol, 1893), 155–7.
19. See R. W. Malcolmson, '"A Set of Ungovernable People": The Kingswood Colliers in the Eighteenth Century', in *An Ungovernable People: The English and Their Law in the Seventeenth and Eighteenth Centuries*, eds. John Brewer and John Styles (London, 1980), 85–127; and William Albert, 'Popular Opposition to Turnpike Trusts in Early Eighteenth-Century England,' *Journal of Transport History*, 5 (1979): 1–17.
20. Sidney Webb and Beatrice Webb, *English Local Government: The Story of the King's Highway* (London, 1913), 75. See also W. T. Jackman, *The Development of Transportation in Modern England* [1916], 3rd ed. (London, 1966), 68–9.
21. *Essay upon Several Projects* (London, 1702), 95, 104, 86.
22. *Essay upon Projects*, 110–11; compare *Tour*, 1: 187; 2: 243.
23. *Essay upon Projects*, 75–6, 109.
24. Peter Borsay observes that 'The *Tour* is not so much a travelogue as an anatomy (even a vision) of the nation ... [It] traverses not only a topographical landscape but also the social and economic contours of the country.' See 'Urban Development in the Age of Defoe,' in *Britain in the First Age of Party*, ed. Clyve Jones (London, 1987), 195–219 (195).
25. *Plan* (London, 1728), 86. In *CET*, 2.ii: 27–33, there is a substantial discussion of the way in which carriage costs increase the price of heavy goods. Defoe's

repeated stress on the importance of carriers marks him off from many commentators on turnpikes.

26. *The Great Law of Subordination Consider'd* (London, 1724), 47–51. Leicestershire and Lincolnshire were two Midland counties described by Defoe as 'a vast Magazine of Wool for the rest of the Nation' (2: 206).
27. Macky, 2: 11.
28. John Gay, *Poems on Several Occasions* (London, 1729), 1: 281.
29. Pawson, *Transport and Economy*, 18, noted that 'Defoe was one of the first observers to describe the centrality of London in the national *system* of internal trade. Indeed, it was one of his key themes in the Tour' (italics mine).
30. W. G. Hoskins, 'Foreword', *Crisis and Order in English Towns 1500–1700: Essays in Urban History*, eds. Peter Clark and Paul Slack (London, 1972), vii.

11 Defoe on Bristol

1. See two abridgments, the first edited by Pat Rogers (Harmondsworth, 1971), with one note on the entry (705), and the second by P. N. Furbank and W. R. Owens (New Haven, 1991), with none. The full edition is that of John McVeagh, notes 119 and 120 at 2: 291.
2. The passage here draws chiefly on David Cordingly, *Spanish Gold: Captain Woodes Rogers and the True Story of the Pirates of the Caribbean* (London, 2011). Bryan Little, *Crusoe's Captain: Being the Life of Woodes Rogers, Seaman, Trader, Colonial Governor* (London, 1960) remains useful.
3. The most thorough investigation remains A. W. Secord, *Studies in the Narrative Method of Defoe* (Urbana, IL, 1924; reprinted New York, 1961).
4. Thomas Wright, *The Life of Daniel Defoe* (London, 1894), xvi, 171–2.
5. There is a passing reference to 'one Mr. Rogers, a Merchant there [Bristol]' in *The Farther Adventures of Robinson Crusoe* (London, 1719), 36, but this could easily proceed from second-hand familiarity with the name of Francis Rogers, which figures in the introductory sections of *A Cruising Voyage* (1712), iii, 19, and in Edward Cooke's *Voyage to the South Sea* (London, 1712), sig. b3^r, b5^v. The author of *Atlas Maritimus* (1728), probably Defoe, had read both Rogers and Cooke, but gives no sign of personal acquaintance. Information in this paragraph is taken from numerous sources, notably Tim Beattie, *British Privateering Voyages of the Early Eighteenth Century* (Woodbridge, 2015); and two works by W. E. Minchinton, *The Trade of Bristol in the Eighteenth Century* (Bristol, 1957), and *Politics and the Port of Bristol* (Bristol, 1963). Like all students of the period, I am indebted to John Latimer, *Annals of Bristol in the Eighteenth Century* (Bristol, 1893). There is useful background in Madge Dresser, *Slavery Obscured: The Social History of the Slave Trade in an English Provincial Port* (London, 2016).

6. On all topographic matters, I rely on M. D. Lobel and E. M. Carus-Wilson, 'Bristol', in *The Atlas of Historic Towns*, vol. II, ed. M. D. Lobel (Baltimore, 1975), a valuable summary garnished with excellent maps by W. H. Johns.
7. His acquaintance with the area may have gone back as far as 1685, since he was involved in the Monmouth rebellion, and may have seen action with the Duke's army at Keynsham and Norton St Philip.
8. *Letters*, 110–11.
9. *Letters*, 115.
10. On the Quaker community, see *Minute Book of the Men's Meeting of the Society of Friends in Bristol 1686–1704*, ed. Russell Mortimer (Bristol, 1977). Defoe refers to 'our Battery works erected at *Bristol*' in *CET*, 2.ii: 70.
11. On Darby, see Arthur Raistrick, *Dynasty of Iron Founders: The Darbys and Coalbrookdale*, 2nd ed. (Coalbrookdale, 1989). On the Goldneys, see P. K. Stembridge, *The Goldney Family: A Bristol Merchant Dynasty* (Bristol, 1998).
12. Bristol Record Office, 20122/12.
13. Copies of relevant Wade family wills are found in Gloucestershire Archives, D1332/F1.
14. For confirmation, see David Hussey, *Coastal and River Trade in Pre-Industrial England: Bristol and its Region, 1680–1730* (Exeter, 2001), which documents the way in which an extensive coastal and river network centred on Bristol provided links at this period with the South-west, the West Midlands, the Border Counties and South Wales.
15. He even has Robinson Crusoe start out his career as a Guinea trader, a term then embracing more or less the whole of West Africa. Even in his last years Defoe was putting forward a scheme to increase British trade to the region: see *A Plan of the English Commerce* (London, 1728), 327–43. The African Company succeeded the Guinea Company, founded in 1618.
16. Macky, 2: 132–4.
17. There are a number of parallels with the observations made by Celia Fiennes in the 1690s. These must be chance, since her diaries were still unpublished: see Fiennes, 237–9.
18. The measure (5 and 6 Wm & Mary, c.10) levied two duties of sixpence and fourpence per chaldron: some of the proceeds went towards the building of St Paul's cathedral and the Queen Anne churches. The weight of a London chaldron was approximately 3,140 lb, that of a Newcastle chaldron 5,940 lb. Prices quoted by Defoe seem remarkably cheap, as the rate to consumers in London ran at twice as much; this may be the price paid by the coal masters to the producers.

12 Atlas Maritimus

1. P. N. Furbank and W. R. Owens, *Defoe De-Attributions: A Critique of J. R. Moore's Checklist* (London, 1994).
2. Ashley Marshall, 'Beyond Furbank and Owens: A New Consideration of the Evidence for the "Defoe" Canon', *Studies in Bibliography*, 59 (2015), 131–90. The main thrust of this article is in effect to recommend an even more cautious approach towards attribution than that of Furbank and Owens, a conclusion that I wholly accept.
3. The involvement of these figures in the book trade, along with Halley and others, is one of the issues considered in my article, 'The Making of *Atlas Maritimus* (1728): A Shift towards Commercial Geography', forthcoming in a journal of historical geography.
4. For Halley as surveyor, cartographer, sea captain and engineer, see Alan Cook, *Edmond Halley: Charting the Heavens and the Seas*, (Oxford, 1998), esp. 315–18.
5. This emphasis distinguished the work from rival productions such as *The Compleat Geographer* (4th ed., 1723), with a full array of maps by Herman Moll, which provides a broad conspectus of the territorial extent of the earth. There is no substantial discussion of trade.
6. J. R. Moore, 'The Canon of Defoe's Writings,' *The Library*, 5th ser., 11 (1956): 155–69 (167–8); *A Checklist of the Writings of Daniel Defoe*, 2nd ed. (Hamden, CT, 1971), 215.
7. P. N. Furbank and W. R. Owens, *A Critical Bibliography of Daniel Defoe* (London, 1998), 276–9. It has passed unobserved that among the sources named here, the relevant works by Joseph Pitton de Tournefort, Walter Ralegh and Gabriel Dellon (author of *Nouvelle Relation d'un Voyage Fait aux Indes Orientales*) were all listed in Defoe's library. Many unacknowledged borrowings in *AMC* can be detected from authors such as Woodes Rogers and Alexandre Exquemelin.
8. Marshall, 'Beyond Furbank and Owens', 183.
9. Jess Edwards, 'Daniel Defoe and *Atlas Maritimus & Commercialis*', in *Topographies of the Imagination: New Approaches to Daniel Defoe*, ed. Katherine Ellison et al., (New York, 2014): 141–66, finds the evidence for Defoe 'highly persuasive' (144), but ultimately sits on the fence by treating *AMC* as characteristic of Defoe's ideas, whether or not he was the author.
10. Jeffrey Hopes, 'L'Atlas Maritimus et Commercialis de 1728', *XVII–XVIII. Bulletin de la société d'études anglo-américaines des XVIIe et XVIIIe siècles*, 38 (1994): 113–23 (117–19).
11. Backscheider, 471–3 (471).
12. Maximillian E. Novak, *Daniel Defoe Master of Fictions: His Life and Ideas* (Oxford, 2001), 387–8, 687–8. One extensive case we could cite to show the

relation between the two texts is the similarity of the chapter in *Plan*, 312–17, on a proposal for 'rooting out' the Barbary pirates, to the section in *AMC* (241–3) on the west coast of Africa (cf. also p. 266). It would require an exorbitant amount of space to provide all similar examples. One indicative comparison might be made between *Plan* (331) and *AMC* (118–19) on the cultivation of coffee at Mocha on the Red Sea and at Batavia. Equally striking is the close equivalence in content and phrasing between the discussion of Flemish cambrics and lace in *Plan* (209) and *AMC* (139). The two books were published only three months apart: there would not have been time for the compiler to raid *Plan* to extract material of this kind as he does throughout his text.

13. Defoe gives 'sixteen Chapels of Ease' in *Plan*, 87. As one more instance, speaking of the export of wool from Leeds, Halifax and adjoining towns, *Tour* (3: 76) singles out Hamburg, Nuremberg, Frankfurt, Leipzig and Augsburg among German cities involved in the trade, under which aspect *AMC* (109) follows the same roster of names. For the same list, plus Ulm, see *A Plan of the English Commerce*, 162; with similar information in *CET*, 2.ii: 67.
14. Accepted as a 'highly probable' ascription in *Critical Bibliography*, 139.
15. Defoe refers to the craze for diving engines while charting the Cornish coast (*Tour* 1: 274). He refers to his own involvement in one scheme in 1691 during discussion of risky ventures as early as *An Essay upon Projects* (1697), and reverts to the topic much later in *The Director* in 1720. For the background, see Peter Earle, *Treasure Hunt: Shipwrecks, Diving, and the Quest for Treasure in an Age of Heroes* (New York, 2007), esp. Chapters 4 and 5.
16. J. H. Andrews, 'Defoe and the Sources of His "Tour",' *Geographical Journal*, 126 (1960): 268–77 (270–71).
17. Distribution agents included members of the leading mercantile families in Bristol, Bridgwater, Lowestoft, Chester and Gainsborough. Defoe's coadjutors, the Norwich linen draper John Fransham and the Newcastle bookseller Joseph Button, could have enhanced his knowledge of local trade. All these men were dissenters.
18. *Libraries*, 28. As an example, compare James Wallace, *An Account of the Islands of Orkney* (London, 1700), 7–8, with *AMC* 50.
19. Minor additions are made on topics such as offensive smells from fish at Yarmouth (2), with an update at a few places such as Dover (11), and infilling at the Thames-side district around Abingdon (19), omitted in the *Tour*. The entry for Dover illustrates a tendency slightly to soften the asperity with which he writes about the governor of the castle (compare *Tour* 1: 160 with *AMC* 11).
20. Defoe's extensive sojourn in lowland Scotland predictably colours passages dealing with Edinburgh and the borders. Here and there we can pick up a glimpse of the underlying occasion: on the upper Firth of Forth, near Alloa,

AMC 6 copies *Tour* 3: 209, but the original observation was made years earlier. See Defoe to Robert Harley, 5 September 1710, in *Letters*, 284–5.

21. *Robinson Crusoe*, ed. Evan R. Davis (Peterborough, ON, 2010), 53–7.
22. A significant moment occurs when the hero catches a glimpse of 'the *Pico* of *Teneriffe*, being the high top of the Mountain *Teneriffe* in the *Canaries*' (*Crusoe*, 68). Compare *Tour* 3: 219, on the top of the Cheviot Hills, which 'at a Distance, looks like the *Pico-Teneriffe* at the *Canaries*'; and *AMC* 244, on the extreme height of the '*Pico Teneriffe* [which] is seen a very great way at Sea'.
23. *Brief Observations on Trade and Manufacture* (London, 1721), 110; see also *CET*, 2.ii: 70, and *Plan*, 337. A nice example of rewriting without (quite) repeating the exact phraseology occurs in the description of the Cobb at Weymouth (*AMC* 12; *Tour* 1: 246).
24. In the *Tour* (3: 240) Defoe had described the retreat of the Pretender's fleet off the Firth of Forth in 1708. *AMC* (6) follows his account closely, but adds the name of the British admiral, Sir George Byng – who happened to be a subscriber to the volume under his title of Viscount Torrington.
25. The account of a flood in Chester (*AMC* 16–17) comes like most of this entry from *Tour* (2: 190), but Defoe's own source was probably Applebee's *Weekly Journal*, 31 December 1720 (an organ with which he was connected). The newspaper does not use the word 'Inundation,' as the *Tour* and *AMC* do. Defoe returns to the event in more emotional terms in *CET*, 1: 75.
26. *A General History of Discoveries and Improvements* (London, 1725–6). See also comments by P. N. Furbank in his edition of the work (London, 2001), 1–2.
27. Defoe's admiration for the Phoenicians is made clear as early as the *General History of Trade*, July 1713, 13–14.
28. Later the count is '40 to 60000 Barrels' (*AMC* 104). Some fuzziness also appears in the number of barrels cured in Scotland: compare *AMC* 104: 'The *Scots* alone are said to cure on the East and West-sides of *Britain* every Year, near 5000 Lasts of Herring, which is 50000 Barrel' (104), with *Plan*: 'The *Scots* are said to cure sixty Thousand Barrels of Herrings for Exportation, one Year with another' (236).
29. *The Storm*, ed. Richard Hamblyn (London, 2003), 51, 148. *AMC* 2 also refers to the loss of a man of war, the *Reserve*, not mentioned in the *Tour*, but covered in detail by *The Storm*, 140.
30. J. Paul Hunter, 'Defoe, Journalism, and the Early English Novel', in *Prose Fiction in English from the Origins of Print to 1750*, ed. Thomas Keymer (Oxford, 2017), 515–29 (521–22). Defoe's model gentleman was likewise enjoined to collect and study maps and charts (*Compleat English Gentleman*, 227–8).
31. *Robinson Crusoe*, 100. According to Woodes Rogers, Alexander Selkirk had also retained during his island sojourn 'his Mathematical Instruments and Books' (cited in *Crusoe*, ed. Davis, 326).

Select Bibliography

The list is confined to books and articles in two categories: (1) items bearing directly on the content of the *Tour*, or on its place in Defoe's career; (2) items relating to early modern Britain that deal with issues that figure centrally in the *Tour*. It does not attempt to provide a full bibliography of works about Defoe or about the period.

Editions

A Tour thro' the Whole Island of Great Britain, Divided into Circuits or Journies . . . By a Gentleman. 3 vols. (1724–7, for 1728).

A Tour thro' the Whole Island of Great Britain. 2 vols, with introduction by G. D. H. Cole (London, 1928).

A Tour thro' London about the Year 1725, edited with introduction and notes by Sir Mayson M. Beeton and E. Beresford Chancellor (London, 1929; reprinted New York, 1969). Contains Letter 5 and opening of Letter 6.

A Tour thro' the Whole Island of Great Britain, 2 vols, with introductions by G. D. H. Cole and D. C. Browning (London, 1962). This edition was originally published in 1927 without the Scottish sections as *A Tour through England and Wales*.

A Tour thro' the Whole Island of Great Britain, abridged and edited by Pat Rogers with introduction and notes (Harmondsworth, 1971).

A Tour thro' the Whole Island of Great Britain, 3 vols, with introduction by Pat Rogers (London, 1983).

A Tour thro' the Whole Island of Great Britain, abridged and edited by Pat Rogers with introduction, and photographs by Simon McBride (Exeter, 1989).

A Tour thro' the Whole Island of Great Britain, abridged and edited with introduction and notes by P. N. Furbank and W. R. Owens (New Haven, 1991; reissued London, 2007).

A Tour thro' the Whole Island of Great Britain, 3 vols, edited with introduction and notes by John McVeagh. In *Writings on Travel, Discovery and History by Daniel Defoe*, 4 vols. (London, 2001).

Reference

Furbank, P. N. and W. R. Owens. *A Critical Bibliography of Daniel Defoe* (London, 1998). The most dependable listing of the works, in which many dubious attributions are discarded.

The Letters of Daniel Defoe, edited by G. H. Healey (Oxford, 1955). Still standard.

The Libraries of Daniel Defoe and Phillips Farewell, edited with introduction by Helmut Heidenreich. (Berlin, 1970). Contains excellent introduction and full indexes.

Biography

Backscheider, Paula R. *Daniel Defoe: His Life* (Baltimore, 1989). The most detailed account of the writer's career.

Bastian, F. *Defoe's Early Life* (Basingstoke, 1981). Contains much solid fact among more speculative suggestions.

Novak, Maximillian E. *Daniel Defoe: Master of Fictions* (Oxford, 2001). The fullest reading of the canon by the pre-eminent Defoe scholar of our time.

Richetti, John. *The Life of Daniel Defoe: A Critical Biography* (Chichester, 2005), Lively and intelligent within a comparatively short space.

Early Modern Britain

Colley, Linda. *Britons: Forging the Nation 1707–1837* (New Haven, 2nd ed., 2005). Central to an understanding of the forces that made the nation both unified and disparate at the time the *Tour* was written.

Holmes, Geoffrey and Daniel Szechi, *The Age of Oligarchy: Pre-Industrial Britain 1722–1783* (London, 1993). Describes in convincing detail the world that was just beginning to open up as the *Tour* appeared.

Hoppit, Julian. *A Land of Liberty? England 1689–1727* (Oxford, 2000). The best broad survey of a period that coincided almost exactly with the span of Defoe's writing career.

Langford, Paul. *Eighteenth-Century Britain: A Very Short Introduction* (Oxford, 2000). A masterly feat of compression.

ed. *The Eighteenth Century 1688–1815* (Oxford, 2002). Seven essays by experts that repeatedly touch on the concerns prominent in the *Tour.*

A Polite and Commercial People: England 1727–1783 (Oxford, 1989). Indispensable guide to the country as Defoe saw (and foresaw) its evolution.

Speck, W. A. *Stability and Strife: England 1714–1760* (London, 1977). Especially good on the transition from Stuart to Hanoverian regimes.

Social Issues

Fox, Adam. *Oral and Literate Culture in England 1500–1700* (Oxford, 2000). A brilliant evocation of a range of practices still important to Defoe.

Hay, Douglas and Nicholas Rogers. *Eighteenth-Century English Society: Shuttles and Swords* (Oxford, 1997). Concentrates largely on the labouring poor.

Mingay, G. E. *English Landed Society in the Eighteenth Century* (London, 1963). A balanced survey of the structure and functions of the landed classes, and well-chosen references to illustrate country living, with several citations from the *Tour*.

Porter, Roy. *English Society in the Eighteenth Century* (London, rev. ed., 1990). Fizzes with ideas, as always with this author.

London

Bucholz, Robert O. and Joseph P. Ward, *London: A Social and Cultural History 1550–1750* (Cambridge, 2012). Broad and informative.

Earle, Peter. *A City Full of People: Men and Women of London 1650–1750* (London, 1994). Strong on the class of people from whom Defoe emerged.

Gatrell, Vic. *The First Bohemians: Life and Art in London's Golden Age* (London, 2013). A brilliant portrayal of Covent Garden, Drury Lane and the Strand, a district Defoe and his fictional characters such as Moll Flanders knew well, and where several of his publishers operated.

Rudé, George. *Hanoverian London 1714–1808* (London, 1971). Starts from a tour in Defoe's footsteps.

Spence, Craig. *London in the 1690s: A Social Atlas* (London, 2000). Walks a reader round the changing city that Defoe surveyed, with the aid of modern charts and statistical techniques he would have admired and envied.

Waller, Maureen. *1700: Scenes from London Life* (London, 2000). Enjoyable and well organised 'cradle-to-grave' portrait for the general reader. It is based on original sources, among which the voice most frequently heard is that of Defoe.

White, Jerry. *A Great and Monstrous Thing: London in the Eighteenth Century* (London, 2012). Enormous in conception and execution.

Town and Country

Borsay, Peter. *The English Urban Renaissance: Culture and Society in the Provincial Town, 1660–1770* (Oxford, 1989). A book that might almost have been written as a background to large sections of the *Tour*.

and Lindsay Proudfoot, eds, *Provincial Towns in Early Modern England and Ireland: Change, Convergence and Divergence* (Oxford, 2002). Contains several relevant essays.

Clark, Peter, ed., *The Cambridge Urban History of Britain*, vol. II: *1540–1840* (Cambridge, 2000). Authoritative contributions which regularly bump into Defoe's account of the nation.

Corfield, P. J. *The Impact of English Towns 1700–1800* (Oxford, 1982). Informative, readable and reliable.

Ellis, Joyce. *The Georgian Town 1680–1840* (Basingstoke, 2001). Clear and compact survey of the kinds of places with which Defoe was intimately familiar.

Thirsk, Joan, ed. *The Agrarian History of England and Wales*, vol. V: *1640–1750: Agrarian Change* (Cambridge, 1984). Contributors to this major series regularly cite the *Tour* on rural landscape and agricultural practices.

ed. *Rural England: An Illustrated History of the Landscape* (Oxford, 2000). A broad sweep of differing landscape forms, almost all of which figure in Defoe's narrative, including downs, wolds, parks, river valleys, meadows, heaths, forests, marshes, fens, moors, dales and common land. Several contributors cite the *Tour*.

The Economy

Ashton, T. S. *Economic Fluctuations in England 1700–1800* (Oxford, 1959). Good account of the patterns of change that explain some of the things that Defoe observed.

Carswell, John. *The South Sea Bubble* (rev. ed., Stroud, 2001). Still the most accessible and coherent narrative of the events underlying Defoe's treatment of recent financial history.

Dickson, P. G. M. *The Financial Revolution in England: A Study in the Development of Public Credit, 1688–1756* (London, 1967). An influential work, which once more covers the crucial years in Defoe's career, with its midpoint in 1727.

Mathias, Peter. *The Transformation of England: Essays in the Social and Economic History of England in the Eighteenth Century* (London, 1979). Studies bearing on several aspects of economic activity touched on in the *Tour*.

Travel and Transport

Albert, William. *The Turnpike Road System in England 1663–1840* (Cambridge, 1972). A standard work on one of Defoe's special subjects.

Fiennes, Celia. *Journeys*, edited by Christopher Morris (London, 1949). Provides an illuminating contrast with Defoe.

Macky, John. *A Journey though England [Scotland] in Familiar Letters*, 3 vols (1714–23). Possibly the spur for the *Tour*, and certainly its principal contemporary rival.

Moir, Esther. *The Discovery of Britain: The English Tourists 1540 to 1840* (London, 1964). Sympathetic treatment of Defoe in the context of Leland, Fiennes. Stukeley, Young, Cobbett and others.

Pawson, Eric. *Transport and Economy: The Turnpike Roads of Eighteenth Century Britain* (London, 1977). Particularly valuable for its treatment of the wider transport system and of carriers, both topics germane to the coverage in the *Tour.*

Tinniswood, Adrian. *The Polite Tourist: Four Centuries of Country House Visiting* (New York, 1999). Helps to set Defoe's sometimes impolite tourism in context.

Topography and Antiquities

Andrews, J. H. 'Defoe and the Sources of his *Tour*', *Geographical Journal*, 126 (1960): 268–77.

'Defoe's *Tour* and Macky's *Journey*', *Notes & Queries*, ns. 7 (1960): 290–92. Pioneering articles by a major historian of cartography.

Bowen, Emanuel. *Britannia Depicta: or Ogilby Improved*, introduction by J. B. Harley (1720, reprinted Newcastle upon Tyne, 1970). Representative of the roadbooks which Defoe certainly knew.

Camden, William. *Britannia*, edited by Edmund Gibson (1695, reprinted Newton Abbot, 1971). Defoe's most important single source.

Harley, J. B. *The New Nature of Maps: Essays in the History of Cartography* (Baltimore, 2001). Influential and in places illuminating on Defoe's sense of the world.

Haycock, David Boyd. *William Stukeley: Science, Religion and Archaeology in Eighteenth-Century England* (Woodbridge, 2002). Stukeley's *Itinerarium* was made across England in the same period as the *Tour*, but with a different intent. This scholarly account helps to illuminate the ways in which the landscape could be interpreted.

Sweet, Rosemary. *Antiquaries: The Discovery of the Past in Eighteenth-Century Britain* (London, 2004). Excellent study of a group of writers whom Defoe claimed to disdain but regularly consulted.

Demography

Houston, R. A. *The Population History of Britain and Ireland 1550–1750* (Cambridge, 1995). Briskly supplies basic facts that illuminate Defoe's world.

Wrigley, E. A. *People, Cities and Wealth: The Transformation of Traditional Society* (Oxford, 1987). Contains classic essays by a noted historical demographer, some with obvious links to the materials of the *Tour.*

and R. S. Schofield, *The Population History of England 1541–1871: A Reconstruction* (Cambridge, 1989). The bible of this subject.

Jacobitism

Allan, David. *Scotland in the Eighteenth Century: Union and Enlightenment* (Abingdon, 2013). Solid all-round survey.

Pittock, Murray G. H. *Jacobitism* (Basingstoke, 1998). A fine introduction by a leading scholar in this area.

Riley, P. W. J. *The Union of England and Scotland: A Study of Anglo-Scottish Politics of the Eighteenth Century* (Manchester, 1978). Remains unsupplanted.

Szechi, Daniel. *1715: The Great Jacobite Rebellion* (New Haven, 2006). Authoritative account of an episode hovering behind the *Tour*.

General

Blanning, Tim. *The Pursuit of Glory: The Five Revolutions That Made Modern Europe 1648–1815* (London, 2007). A superb conspectus of cultural history across the entire continent. Provides essential background to Defoe's treatment of Britain, covering topics such as communications, demographics, trade and manufacture, social change, religion, leisure, the rural world, architecture and gardening and much more.

Cole, G. D. H. *Persons and Periods* (1938; reprinted Harmondsworth, 1945). Although mildly dated in places, these 'studies' (including essays on Defoe's England; town life; London; roads, rivers and canals; and Cobbett) preserve Cole's apposite commentary on matters relevant to the *Tour*.

Earle, Peter. *The World of Defoe* (London, 1976). A shrewd assessment of the writer and his work in relation to national and international concerns of the day, by an authority whose research interests coincided with many of Defoe's own preoccupations.

Rogers, Pat. *The Text of Great Britain: Theme and Design in Defoe's* Tour (Newark, DE, 1998). Discusses the making of the *Tour*, its rhetorical workings, and its historical context.

Shorter Studies

Bastian, F. 'Defoe's *Tour* and the Historian', *History Today*, 17 (1967): 845–51.

Borsay, Peter. 'Urban Development in the Age of Defoe', in *Britain in the First Age of Party*, ed. Clyve Jones (London, 1987), 195–219.

Bowers, Terence N. 'Great Britain Imagined: Nation, Citizen and Class in Defoe's *Tour thro' the Whole Island of Great Britain*'. *Prose Studies*, 16 (1993): 148–77.

Duckworth, Alistair M., 'Whig Landscapes in Defoe's *Tour*', *Philological Quarterly*, 61 (1982): 453–65.

Hill, Gerald. 'Circling Defoe', *Arion*, 21 (1990): 69–84.

Parkes, Christopher. '"A True Survey of the Ground": Defoe's *Tour* and the Rise of Thematic Cartography', *Philological Quarterly*, 74 (1995): 395–415.

Rogers, Pat. 'Daniel Defoe's Knowledge of Essex: The Evidence of *A Tour thro' the Whole Island of Great Britain*', *Essex Society for Archaeology and History Transactions*, 4th series, vol. 9 (2020 for 2018): 127–41.
Schellenberg, Betty A. 'Imagining the Nation in Defoe's *A Tour Thro' the Whole Island of Great Britain*', *ELH*, 62 (1995): 295–311.
Speller, Trevor. 'Violence, Reason, and Enclosure in Defoe's *Tour*', *Studies in English Literature, 1500–1900*, 51 (2011): 585–604.

General Index

Main entries are in bold type.

Index of Places

Printed by Printforce, United Kingdom